RETHINKING THE
DSM

RETHINKING THE

DSM

A Psychological Perspective

**EDITED BY LARRY E. BEUTLER
AND MARY L. MALIK**

AMERICAN PSYCHOLOGICAL ASSOCIATION
WASHINGTON, DC

First printing February 2002
Second printing January 2004

Published by
American Psychological Association
750 First Street, NE
Washington, DC 20002
www.apa.org

To order
APA Order Department
P.O. Box 92984
Washington, DC 20090-2984

Tel: (800) 374-2721, Direct: (202) 336-5510
Fax: (202) 336-5502, TDD/TTY: (202) 336-6123
Online: www.apa.org/books/
Email: order@apa.org

In the U.K., Europe, Africa, and the Middle East, copies may be ordered from
American Psychological Association
3 Henrietta Street
Covent Garden, London
WC2E 8LU England

Typeset in Goudy by EPS Group Inc., Easton, MD

Printer: United Book Press, Baltimore, MD
Cover designer: NiDesign, Baltimore, MD
Technical/Production Editor: Jennifer Powers

Library of Congress Cataloging-in-Publication Data
Rethinking the DSM : a psychological perspective / edited by Larry E. Beutler and Mary
L. Malik.
    p. cm—(Decade of behavior)
    Includes bibliograpical references and index.
    ISBN 1-55798-841-2 (alk. paper)
    1. Diagnostic and statistical manual of mental disorders.
I. Beutler, Larry E.   II. Malik, Mary L.   III. Series.

2002016481

British Library Cataloguing-in-Publication Data
A CIP record is available from the British Library.

Printed in the United States of America

CONTENTS

III. REPRESENTATIONAL ALTERNATIVES

CONTRIBUTORS

Lynne Angus, Department of Psychology, York University, Toronto, Ontario, Canada

Larry E. Beutler, Department of Education, Counseling/Clinical/School Psychology Program, University of California, Santa Barbara

Roger K. Blashfield, Department of Psychology, Auburn University, Auburn, AL

Peter Buchheim, Department of Psychology, University of Muenchen, Germany

Laura Campbell, Department of Psychology, Boston University, Boston, MA

Manfred Cierpka, Department of Psychology, University of Heidelberg, Germany

Rainer W. Dahlbender, Department of Psychology, University of Ulm, Germany

Ann Doucette, Center for Mental Health Policy, Vanderbilt University, Nashville, TN

Elizabeth H. Flanagan, Department of Psychology, Auburn University, Auburn, AL

Harald J. Freyberger, Department of Psychology, University of Greifswald, Germany

Tilmann Grande, Department of Psychology, University of Heidelberg, Germany

Óscar F. Gonçalves, Department of Psychology, University of Minho, Braga, Portugal

Gereon Heuft, Department of Psychology, University of Münster, Germany

Amy Kegley Heim, Department of Psychology, Boston University, Boston, MA

Sven O. Hoffmann, Department of Psychology, University of Mainz, Germany

Arthur C. Houts, Department of Psychology, University of Memphis, Memphis, TN

Paul L. Janssen, Department of Psychology, University of Bochum, Germany

Thomas E. Joiner, Jr., Department of Psychology, Florida State University, Tallahassee

John F. Kihlstrom, Department of Psychology, University of California, Berkeley, and Institute for the Study of Healthcare Organization and Transactions, Richmond, CA

Yifaht Korman, Department of Psychology, York University, Toronto, Ontario, Canada

Joachim Küchenhoff, Department of Psychology, University of Basel, Switzerland

Paulo P. P. Machado, Department of Psychology, University of Minho, Portugal

Mary L. Malik, Department of Education, Counseling/Clinical/School Psychology Program, University of California, Santa Barbara

Gregory J. Meyer, Department of Psychology, University of Alaska–Anchorage

Kate Morrison, Department of Psychology, Boston University, Boston, MA

Aribert Muhs, Karlsruhe, Germany

Marcus Patterson, Department of Psychology, Boston University, Boston, MA

Gerd Rudolf, Department of Psychology, University of Heidelberg, Germany

Ulrich Rüger, Department of Psychology, University of Göttingen, Germany

Norman B. Schmidt, Department of Psychology, Ohio State University, Columbus

Wolfgang Schneider, Faculty of Medicine, University of Rostock, Germany

Gerhard Schüssler, Department of Psychology, University of Innsbruck, Germany

Drew Westen, Center for Anxiety and Related Disorders, Boston University, Boston, MA

PREFACE

Throughout recorded history, people have engaged in a process of classifying the phenomena around them. Beyond the fact that knowledge advances by classification and measurement, the pervasiveness of classification systems suggests that we appear to have a deep-seated need to find a way to simplify and conceptualize objects in our world by identifying some common parameters. This drive to classify has been extended to the arena of behavioral deviations for well over 1,000 years. Accordingly, people in various eras have developed methods for describing and categorizing other people's mental and emotional problems (Blashfield, 1984). These efforts have not always been as purely heuristic as they might appear on the surface. Often embedded in these classification schemes are subtle and not-so-subtle value systems and cultural beliefs. Usually in ways that are quite invisible to those who share the cultural system, an analysis of each classification method unveils to an outsider a particular set of culturally endorsed values.

For example, compare our contemporary Western classifications of animals (e.g., mammals, insects, birds) to those of the ancient Chinese (Borges, 1960), whose functional perspective defined some classes by their implied use or status within the cultural mythology (e.g., embalmed, owned by the emperor, trained, sucklings, sirens and mermaids, fabulous, abandoned). Other groupings were based on the animal's appearance (e.g., those that are drawn with an exquisite and fine paintbrush with hair of a camel, those that from afar look like flies), whereas still others were classified by the assumption of an implied inner process (e.g., those who are as excited as lunatics, those that have just broken a porcelain vase).

Several points can be drawn from the contrast between these two ways of grouping animals. The first is that the same (or very similar) phenomena can be categorized in strikingly different ways across different cul-

ix

tures and periods of time, illustrating that there are always alternatives available (although we may have difficulties in seeing them). The second point is that all classification schemes, however seemingly objective the criteria, are developed and agreed upon by humans to meet particular human needs: Whereas it is useful for animal breeders or horticulturists to have an understanding of the evolutionary relationships between species, it is also clearly important under other circumstances to know whether or not a particular animal is considered to belong to the emperor. Finally, all classification systems can be seen to be associated with at least an implicit assumption of who is to do the classifying (biologists trained in systematics in the case of a phylogenetically based system, but most likely the emperor in the case of the animals that are seen as belonging or as not belonging to him). Thus, the extent to which the system "works" is due as much to its ability to meet our current needs as it is to the agreement of the system with some underlying reality, making it reasonable to suppose that even quite different approaches to classification may be useful depending on the particular needs at hand.

During the past 50 years, the primary system used for classifying mental disorders in the United States has been developed around the American Psychiatric Association's *Diagnostic and Statistical Manual of Mental Disorders* (DSM). Influenced by the work of Emil Kraepelin in the late 19th and early 20th centuries, the first edition of the DSM (DSM–I), published in 1952, divided patients into categories on the basis of lists of potential symptoms. Although increasing amounts of research and effort have been expended in clarifying inclusion criteria and in improving diagnostic reliability (cf. Widiger et al., 1994, 1996, 1997), the current DSM (DSM–IV; American Psychiatric Association, 1994) continues in the Kraepelian tradition of assigning people to diagnostic categories on the basis of symptom presentation. Although most people agree that the reliability and validity of diagnostics have improved since 1952, the modifications have all occurred within a very specific framework and have come with a number of implications about how psychopathology is to be identified and treated. Specifically, the problems in mood and living generally classified as *psychopathology* have increasingly been seen as diseases or illnesses that are most appropriately treated by pharmacological interventions. Although there are situations in which such an approach clearly is useful, the increasing prevalence of this model across the enormous range of interpersonal, emotional, and behavioral problems considered "mental health" issues raises questions about such widespread application of what is universally acknowledged to be an as-yet imperfect approach to diagnostics. To illustrate a potential shortcoming of such an approach, we consider an analogy based on a disagreement between R. A. Fisher and Sewall Wright, two of the major founders of the field of population genetics.

In debating the issue of whether or not most species are at their optimal levels of evolutionary fitness, Fisher (see Provine, 1986) argued that they are—a situation we can picture by imagining the species at the top of a mountain peak that represents the highest possible levels of survival and reproduction for that species, with the valleys all around representing areas of lower fitness (i.e., lower survival or reproduction). In contrast, Wright (cited in Provine, 1986) argued that Fisher's claim is true only when a species consists of a very large interbreeding population, such that the best possible combination of genes is passed on in every generation. Wright saw this as an unlikely scenario for most species, and he pointed out that if the number of interbreeding individuals is relatively small, chance events can play a role, and optimal levels of fitness may not be obtained. Under this scenario, argued Wright, Fisher's single adaptive peak is more realistically represented by an adaptive landscape: a series of fitness peaks of varying heights, each surrounded by a valley of lower fitness. In this case, natural selection still acts at all times to increase fitness, such that a species can be pictured as gradually ascending the nearest mountain. However, because the peaks are all separated by valleys of lower fitness, a species may end up at a local optimum (i.e., at the top of the nearest peak) but still be far from the greatest possible level of fitness represented by the highest peak on the landscape. Moreover, when a species arrives at the top of a peak, whatever its height, natural selection is no longer able to work; in the absence of chance events, the species is now stuck at a less-than-optimal level of fitness.

Adopting this analogy to describe the development of classification systems, we see the work on refining the *DSM* as moving the classification of psychopathology closer to the local optimum represented by the top of the nearest mountain: The diagnostic criteria are more clear than in 1952, diagnoses are more reliable, and efforts have been made to increase validity. Clearly, we have made some gains. However, what we do not know is the relative height of the peak we are currently ascending as compared to other potential peaks on the landscape of the classification of mental disorders. If research monies and resources were unlimited (analogous to Fisher's very large populations), we could at least be fairly certain that we were at least headed up a relatively high peak. Unfortunately, in a world of limited time and funding (more analogous to the situation proposed by Wright), we have no such assurance. Thus, the most prudent course of action under the circumstances would appear to be to use our vantage point to take a look around us or, better yet, to send scouting parties out to explore the surrounding terrain before committing all of our energy to the climb.

As editors of this volume, we believe that it is time to make an active effort to weigh the pros and cons of the current system and to consider potential alternatives. We also believe that psychology has significant insights to offer and that it is important for psychologists and other behaviorally minded mental health professionals to continue to actively contribute to the diagnostic process. We had originally intended to offer with this book an extensive list of different models and taxonomies of diagnosis, and we began talking to friends and colleagues accordingly. We discovered during this process that despite the many promising ideas on ways to better our diagnostic system, most have not yet been fostered to the point that they can serve as a practical alternative to the DSM. Thus, to a large extent, this book represents a brainstorming session, with the intent of providing a vehicle for the further development of ideas about classification. We view these treatises, then, as providing the beginnings of a dialogue about some general ideas and the rationales behind them, as well as offering some promising and reasonably articulated approaches that are worthy of further exploration and development. In accordance with this objective, we have solicited chapters from authors who have a wide range of perspectives on the strengths and limitations of the DSM diagnostic system. All of them have suggestions on ways in which the current system falls short, and many of them propose novel approaches to the diagnosis and treatment of mental disorders.

As the editors of this book on classification, we have succumbed ourselves to what appears to be a pervasive human need to classify, dividing the book into three main sections based on our impressions of the differing foci of each author. The first section contains an introduction that provides background information on the history of diagnostics and summarizes the remaining chapters (Malik & Beutler), followed by a chapter critiquing existing practices of classification (Houts). The second section consists of three chapters representing a methodological critique of current diagnostic practices (Meyer; Joiner & Schmidt; Flanagan & Blashfield). Finally, the third section consists of six chapters outlining representative (but not exhaustive) diagnostic schemes that illustrate potential alternatives or supplements to a DSM-type diagnostic system (Gonçalves et al.; Schneider et al.; Doucette; Westen et al.; Beutler & Malik; Kihlstrom).

We hope that by moving beyond a critique of the DSM to the beginnings of the expression of specific modifications and alternatives, we are able more easily to determine whether our future course should involve improvements and refinements within the basic DSM framework, or whether alternative diagnostic systems would better serve those in need of mental health services. Consequently, we see this collection of essays as an initial step in what we hope will be a serious effort to ferret out the details of new ideas and to compare the strengths and weaknesses of current diagnostic practices with these and other possible alternatives. We hope that this work helps motivate those within the professions of psychology and within the American Psychological Association (APA) to urge the development of a psychologically minded classification system.

We appreciate and thank the contributors to this volume. They have shared some very creative thoughts and ideas. We hope that these ideas serve as seeds to further challenge the narrow confines of the medical and illness models by which we in Western societies are frequently bound. We also appreciate the willingness of the APA to publish this volume.

Finally, we thank our colleagues in the University of California Psychotherapy Research Program for their ideas and support. Work on this book has been partially supported by National Association of Drug Abuse Grant RO1-DA09394 to develop new conceptualizations of treatment. A natural outgrowth of this process has been the development of dissatisfaction with the way patients are currently classified and diagnosed. We hope and believe that a better classification system will assist the development of better systems of treatment.

REFERENCES

American Psychiatric Association. (1952). *Diagnostic and statistical manual of mental disorders*. Washington, DC: Author.

American Psychiatric Association. (1994). *Diagnostic and statistical manual of mental disorders* (4th ed.). Washington, DC: Author.

Blashfield, R. K. (1984). *The classifiation of psychopathology: Neo-Kraepelinian and quantitative approaches*. New York: Plenum Press.

Borges, J. L. (1960). *El idioma analitico de John Wikins, Otras inquisiciones*. Editores: Buenos Aires.

Provine, W. B. (1986). *Sewall Wright and evolutionary biology*. Chicago: University of Illinois Press.

Widiger, T. A., Frances, A. J., Pincus, H. A., Ross, R., First, M. B., & Wakefield Davis, W. (Eds.). (1994). *DSM–IV sourcebook* (Vol. 1). Washington, DC: American Psychiatric Association.

Widiger, T. A., Frances, A. J., Pincus, H. A., Ross, R., First, M. B., & Wakefield Davis, W. (Eds.). (1996). *DSM–IV sourcebook* (Vol. 2). Washington, DC: American Psychiatric Association.

Widiger, T. A., Frances, A. J., Pincus, H. A., Ross, R., First, M. B., & Wakefield Davis, W. (Eds.). (1997). *DSM–IV sourcebook* (Vol. 3). Washington, DC: American Psychiatric Association.

I

INTRODUCTION AND BACKGROUND

1

THE EMERGENCE OF DISSATISFACTION WITH THE *DSM*

MARY L. MALIK AND LARRY E. BEUTLER

Emil Kraepelin, a German psychiatrist, is generally considered to have laid the foundations for our current system of classification. In 1883 Kraepelin, who had studied with Bernhard von Gudden and Wilhelm Wundt, published a small textbook on psychiatric classification titled *Compendium of Psychiatry*. This textbook, which Kraepelin later called *Short Textbook of Psychiatry*, underwent eight revisions before his death in 1927. Kraepelin did not set out to design a novel system for the classification of psychiatric disorders (although he did introduce the then-revolutionary categories of *manic–depressive insanity* and *dementia praecox*, now known as *manic–depressive disorder* and *schizophrenia*, respectively). Rather, Kraepelin arranged the sections of his book in a way that he felt best expressed the then-current thinking about major types of psychopathology, and he initially attracted readers primarily because of his frequent use of interesting clinical examples and by the clarity of his writing (Blashfield, 1984).

Although Kraepelin's work was widely read and many of his major categories of psychopathology are similar to those in use today, his *Textbook* did not immediately lead to a generally accepted or standardized system of classification. Indeed, the first classification of psychiatric disorders, in the

United States, was developed and used by the U.S. Census Bureau in 1840 (American Psychiatric Association, 1994). This system simply differentiated between "idiocy" and "insanity." A nonresponse identified individuals as "normal." This trifarcated system became more complex, as such systems are wont to become, and in 1880 this simple categorical system was expanded to seven different disorders.

DEVELOPMENT OF THE *DSM*

The diagnosis of psychopathology remained idiosyncratic for some time, and it was conducted in a different way in each hospital and institution. It was not until 1933 that the American Psychiatric Association developed its own comprehensive system of psychiatric nomenclature. This system focused predominantly on the problems commonly observed in inpatients and others with severe neurological disorders. Following World War II, this system was seen to be inadequate in light of the mental health needs of returning war veterans, most of whose problems were acute rather than chronic and rarely involved psychosis (Nathan, 1998).

As a result of these new pressures, the American Psychiatric Association began work on the development of the first *Diagnostic and Statistical Manual*, now referred to as *DSM–I*. Published in 1952, *DSM–I* and the second edition of the *Diagnostic and Statistical Manual*, *DSM–II* (1968), were both relatively short volumes that provided a listing of psychiatric disorders with a brief description of each. The two volumes represented an attempt to apply uniform diagnostic standards for psychological problems, but the first two editions of the *DSM* were critiqued both for low reliability and for low validity. That is, the descriptions provided for each disorder did not contain enough details to result in high levels of agreement between clinicians from different theoretical backgrounds when diagnosing the same client. Moreover, the ecological validity and acceptability of the diagnostic system were low, probably because the descriptions themselves were developed by a small number of senior academic psychiatrists rather than being either empirically based (Kirk & Kutchins, 1992) or being particularly friendly to the range of clinicians who did not share the loose, psychoanalytic viewpoint embodied in these categories.

Because of problems such as these, the development of the third edition of the *Diagnostic and Statistical Manual* (*DSM–III*; American Psychiatric Association, 1980) marked the beginning of a concerted effort by the association to increase the reliability and validity of the *DSM* through a more clearly described approach to assigning diagnoses and by linking diagnoses to research findings rather than simply the consensus of members or experts. The approach ultimately used was similar to that proposed in an influential paper by Feighner et al. (1972). Feighner et al.'s criteria were translated into an interview format (Endicott & Spitzer, 1978) and proposed as a means for enhancing the reliability of research-defined samples. The Schedule for Affective Disorders and Schizophrenia (SADS) provided the framework for the later *DSM–III*, according to which patients were assigned a particular diagnosis if and only if they met a certain number of preset criteria. Most of these criteria were based on symptoms, but some included other factors such as family history and prior morbidity. In addition, *DSM–III* marked the first use of a multiaxial system where patients were diagnosed along axes measuring physical conditions (Axis III) and stressors (Axis IV) that were seen as potential contributors to the psychopathology assessed by Axes I and II, as well as along a global measurement of adaptive functioning (Axis V).

To increase the reliability of the diagnostic system, the very long and difficult SADS interview procedure was revised, simplified, and introduced along with the *DSM–III* and the third revised edition, *DSM–III–R* (American Psychiatric Association, 1987). This revised interview was pilot tested as the Structured Clinical Interview for *DSM–III* (SCID; Spitzer, 1983) with the expectation that it would increase reliability of diagnosis by providing standardized ways of collecting information about symptoms.

CRITICISM OF THE *DSM*

Despite these improvements, *DSM–III* and *DSM–III–R* were criticized on several grounds. For example, many of the *DSM–III* diagnoses included hierarchical exclusionary rules such that certain diagnoses could not be assigned if the symptoms occurred during the course of another disorder that occupied a higher level in the hierarchy. These exclusion rules were seen as problematic because this arrangement was not empirically based and because it made the study of lower ranking diagnoses very difficult, and most were dropped in *DSM–III–R* (Clark, Watson, & Reynolds, 1995). Such criticisms have largely been addressed by extending the options of multiple diagnoses and working to make the criteria more specific and sensitive. However, other criticisms of the *DSM* system have persisted and, as one can note from their appearance throughout this volume, they have not been resolved to the satisfaction of many.

For example, although *DSM–III* and *DSM–III–R* did draw on the results of research, many have continued to argue that the great increase in the number of diagnoses observed between *DSM–III* and earlier versions of the *DSM* was much larger than could be accounted for by any real increase in knowledge (e.g., Rutter & Schaffer, 1980). This concern has been accompanied by the observation that the designers of *DSM–III* and *DSM–III–R* (and to a lesser extent the fourth edition [*DSM–IV*; American Psychiatric Association, 1994] and the text revision [*DSM–IV–TR*; American Psychiatric Association, 2000]) were still predominantly senior White male psychiatrists who embedded the documents with their biases.

Criticisms of *DSM–III* and *DSM–III–R* that continue to be evoked by later versions are manifold. For example, the explicitly atheoretical organization of *DSM–III* and its derivatives has been criticized as masking an implicitly medical model of psychopathology, which places the diagnosis and treatment of psychopathology firmly in the field of the psychiatric profession to the exclusion of psychologists, social workers, and other mental health professionals (e.g., Schacht, 1985). *DSM–III* and *DSM–III–R* have also been criticized for their reliance on a categorical approach to diagnosis by which people are determined to either have or to not have a particular disorder. This criticism continues to dominate many critics' views of later editions of the *DSM*; critics of the categorical approach propose the adoption of dimensional models where maladies or disorders can be conceptualized as falling somewhere along a continuum ranging from normal to pathological (e.g., Cantor, Smith, French, & Mezzich, 1980). In addition, it has been argued that the polythetic approach to diagnosis adopted widely in *DSM–III–R* and its later renditions, although avoiding the overly restrictive monothetic inclusion criteria of many *DSM–III* diagnoses, may result in considerable within-group heterogeneity as individuals who exhibit different symptoms may be assigned the same diagnosis.

Finally, whereas some critics of the *DSM* system (e.g., Nathan, 1998) have agreed that reliability did indeed increase with the development of *DSM–III* over the first two editions, others (e.g., Kirk & Kutchins, 1992) have maintained that the real improvements in reliability have been much less and more limited than generally acknowledged (see also Blashfield, 1984, for a critical discussion of the reliability debate surrounding *DSM–III*).

The authors of *DSM–IV* tried explicitly to address many of the concerns raised with respect to *DSM–III* and *DSM–III–R*. For example, to circumvent the criticism that *DSM–III–R* only added to the already great difficulty of communicating with professionals outside of the United States, who relied on a different diagnostic system, the developers of the *DSM–IV* attempted to ensure that the new system corresponded closely to the mental disorders section of the 10th edition of the *International Classification of Diseases and Related Health Problems* (*ICD–10*) published by the World Health Organization (1992).

Likewise, in response to the charges of "diagnosis by committee" leveled at earlier editions, the *DSM–IV* Task Force took several steps to allay these concerns. First, in response to the concern that earlier editions of the *DSM* reflected the views of only a small group of privileged, White, male, academic psychiatrists, the development of *DSM–IV* involved several hundred mental health professionals, including the 27-member task force that coordinated the process, the 13 work groups responsible for each of the major diagnostic categories, and the many individuals who served as consultants to the task force or work groups. Efforts were made to include women and racial and ethnic minorities in this process, as well as to include nonpsychiatric mental health professionals such as psychologists and social workers (Nathan, 1998).

In addition, the creators of DSM–IV sought to adhere to an empirically more rigorous approach to evaluating and modifying diagnostic criteria than they had in DSM–III and DSM–III–R. This procedure involved a three-stage process:

1. Each of the 13 work groups began by conducting an extensive literature review to uncover gaps in existing research literature with respect to specific diagnoses or diagnostic questions.
2. In cases where gaps were determined to exist, the work group considered the option of using existing data sets to resolve the difficulty.
3. If existing data were deemed to be insufficient, the work group was encouraged to design and carry out a field trial to address the problem, the costs of which were supported by the MacArthur Foundation, the National Institute of Mental Health, the National Institute on Drug Abuse, or the National Institute on Alcohol Abuse and Alcoholism (Nathan, 1998).

Results of this development process and of the literature reviews have been published in a series of *Sourcebooks* (Widiger et al., 1994, 1996, 1997), and the results of many of the field trial reports have also been published (e.g., see Foa and Kozak's 1995 report on obsessive–compulsive disorder). However, many authors, including many of those who have made contributions to this volume, have not been persuaded that these extensive efforts provided the needed protection against medical bias. Concerns continue to be expressed about the influence of consensus seeking and political agenda infiltrating the definition of the diagnostic process.

As pointed out by Clark, Watson, and Reynolds (1995), the large amount of data generated and reviewed by the DSM–IV Task Force and work groups have made it very challenging to evaluate the end product as embodied in DSM–IV. Given the family resemblance of DSM–IV to DSM–III–R and the efforts to address specific problem areas such as Axis V, it seems likely that the overall reliability and validity of DSM–IV are at least as good as that of DSM–III–R. In fact, given the work and effort expended in the development of DSM–IV, one can hope that its validity is higher. However, it has been argued (e.g., Clark et al.) that the very success and widespread use of the DSM model of diagnosis may have the unintended side effect of constraining us to work within a less-than-optimal system of diagnosis, a situation analogous to that of expending considerable time and resources in the ascent of a single mountain, while neglecting to explore the possibility that even higher peaks may exist nearby.

To illustrate, one of the criteria used in some of the literature reviews by the *DSM–IV* work groups to evaluate potential diagnoses for inclusion in *DSM–IV* (e.g., "minor depression") was that studies to be included in the reviews must have selected clients based on a formal diagnostic procedure. However, because diagnosis in recent years has increasingly been determined by means of the *DSM*, such a constraint, however reasonable, effectively limits the research used to evaluate the *DSM* to that conducted according to the *DSM*. Thus, even rigorous attention to the literature is almost guaranteed to result in what is essentially a modification (although hopefully an improvement) of current approaches to diagnosis, rather than any real exploration of optimal ways of classifying psychopathology.

Moreover, several criticisms originally made about *DSM–III* and *DSM–III–R* have been raised again about *DSM–IV*, with some chagrin that these issues have not been addressed in this later system. For example, the *DSM*'s continuing focus on descriptive rather than theoretically relevant criteria has been critiqued extensively, both by those who argue that this supposedly atheoretical focus masks an underlying assumption of a medical model of psychopathology and by those who argue that a descriptive approach is not the best way to uncover underlying etiological processes (e.g., Carson, 1991). Many of the other critiques have involved the *DSM*'s use of a categorical method of classification by which people are determined either to have (or not have) a particular mental disorder. For example, as with *DSM–III* and *DSM–III–R*, some critics have focused on *DSM–IV*'s polythetic approach, in which assignment to a particular diagnosis is determined by whether or not a client meets a certain number of equally weighted criteria. This system results in considerable symptom heterogeneity within any given diagnostic category, arguably weakening the likelihood of uncovering links between diagnosis and etiology or treatment response. In addition, the focus on a categorical diagnostic system is problematic for the large numbers of people with a combination of symptoms that does not meet the criteria for a particular diagnosis, resulting in the development of the catch-all modifier *not otherwise specified*, or NOS. Comorbidity has also proven to be a continuing problem for the *DSM* system, as research suggests that most people meet the criteria for more than one *DSM* diagnosis, especially in the domain of personality disorders (Axis II). In a related way, at least some comorbid diagnoses may have a synergistic effect in that the treatment responses of clients with these disorders is not recognized in the *DSM* and is not easily predicted by knowing the component diagnoses (see Clark et al., 1995, for a detailed critique of the problems of a categorical approach).

OVERVIEW OF THIS BOOK

Although even supporters of *DSM–IV* see it as an imperfect work in progress, the general consensus appears to be that we do not yet know enough about diagnosis to propose viable alternatives. However, a reluctance to consider alternatives may well be a self-fulfilling prophecy because the longer diagnosis is determined according to the *DSM*, the fewer opportunities there will be for the exploration of alternatives. Thus, the chapters collected here include both essays critical of existing practices as well as suggestions for alternative diagnostic systems. This book is divided into three main parts: (a) *Introduction and Background*, which includes the current introductory chapter and a chapter by Arthur C. Houts that critiques the *DSM* system; (b) *Methodological Considerations*, which critiques aspects of current approaches to diagnostics; and (c) *Representational Alternatives*, a series of chapters in which authors present some alternative diagnostic systems and concepts.

In chapter 2, "Discovery, Invention, and the Expansion of the Modern *Diagnostic and Statistical Manuals of Mental Disorders*," Houts takes a critical view of the great increase in the number of diagnoses from *DSM–I* to *DSM–IV*, arguing that this increase does not reflect a corresponding increase in our knowledge about psychopathology. He draws on Hempel's 1965 logical empirical argument to contend that an expansion of the number of psychiatric disorders actually indicates a lack of progress, because a true increase in understanding should lead to a reduction in the number of categories as regularities underlying psychopathological processes are uncovered. Houts then contrasts the increase in mental disorders seen in the *DSM* with the increase in physical disorders found in the *ICD*, arguing contrary to Wakefield's (1999a, 1999b) assertion that the two increases are not truly comparable. Houts contends that the increase in *DSM* disorders can be more accurately seen as a reflection of current social values and goals rather than as representing a true increase in our understanding of mental problems.

The *Methodological Considerations* part of the book opens with chapter 3 by Gregory J. Meyer, "Implications of Information-Gathering Methods for a Refined Taxonomy of Psychopathology." Meyers points out that diagnosing psychological disorders requires not only an organizational framework, but also a method of gathering information about a patient or client. He reviews the literature on diagnosis and demonstrates that, although structured or semistructured interviews increase interrater reliability, reliance on a single source (whether patient, clinician, or other) often results in diagnoses that are unstable and inaccurate. Consequently, he recommends gathering information from multiple sources, no matter what diagnostic system is used.

In chapter 4, "Taxometrics Can 'Do Diagnostics Right' (And Isn't

Quite as Hard as You Think)," Thomas E. Joiner, Jr., and Norman B. Schmidt argue against the rote assumption that all problems in psychopathology are best expressed as categories rather than dimensions. They express the need for an approach that allows us to distinguish empirically between syndromes best described as categories and those better described as dimensions. They argue that Paul Meehl's work on taxometrics provides such an approach but that presentations to date have been so complex as to make the subject effectively unapproachable for many researchers. They then devote the bulk of the chapter in providing a clear explanation of the concepts behind taxometric analysis, and they walk the reader through an application of these concepts to clinical data.

In chapter 5, Elizabeth H. Flanagan and Roger K. Blashfield ("Psychiatric Classification Through the Lens of Ethnobiology") argue that *DSM–IV*, which lacks a theoretical basis for its conception of psychopathology, may be viewed as a folk taxonomy. They describe folk taxonomies in detail, distinguishing between superordinate categories (which tend to be more influenced by culture) and subordinate categories (which tend to be conceptualized in similar ways across cultures). They then outline the ways in which they see the *DSM–IV* as fitting the characteristics of a folk taxonomy, and they argue that this conceptualization of the *DSM* may be helpful to psychologists interested in learning the extent to which *DSM* categories are "real." They conclude that an essentialist viewpoint is most likely to be relevant at the lower category level (e.g., autism, antisocial personality disorder) but that this viewpoint is likely to be less helpful in a discussion of higher category levels (e.g., psychosis, psychopathology).

Part III, *Representational Alternatives*, begins with chapter 6 by Óscar F. Gonçalves, Paulo P. P. Machado, Yifaht Korman, and Lynne Angus, "Assessing Psychopathology: A Narrative Approach." In this essay, Gonçalves et al. open with a discussion of the Rosenhan study (1973), for which volunteers were able to gain admittance to psychiatric hospitals by feigning a single symptom while otherwise behaving normally. Gonçalves et al. note that although the deception of the pseudopatients was not detected by the medical staff, it was guessed by some of their fellow patients. They use this example to illustrate their view of psychopathology as a system of meanings that expresses itself through individuals' organization of language or narratives. They state that a patient's discourse is typically viewed as a second-order variable, seen primarily as a vehicle for accessing the client's inner world. The authors argue that narrative structure is of great interest in and of itself as an organizer of client experience. From this point of view, understanding psychopathology becomes a process of meaning making between clinician and client, and aspects of the narrative itself (e.g., incoherence, complexity) can provide information on client problems. The authors describe a coding system where a narrative prototype is constructed to help clinicians in categorizing their clients' narratives. They describe data from their research group in which they were able to extract prototypical narratives for a number of diagnostic groups, and they argue that diagnosis should involve a process of examining narrative in the search for appropriate treatment.

In chapter 7, "Operationalized Psychodynamic Diagnostics: A New Diagnostic Approach in Psychodynamic Psychotherapy," Wolfe Schneider and his colleagues describe a novel diagnostic system that they have been developing in Europe. Drawing on other psychodynamically oriented research, Schneider et al. have developed the system "operationalized psychodynamic diagnostics," through which they intended to address the need for a broad and theoretically consistent view of diagnosis. They propose five domains ("axes") that are not to be confused with the axes of the DSM. These five axes or domains each reflect an aspect of patient functioning that is necessary to understanding patient functioning within complex environments. Axis I, "Experience of Illness and Prerequisites of Treatment," evaluates the patient's suitability for treatment by exploring factors such as the patient's experience of illness, motivation for treatment, cognitive and affective resources, and environmental variables such as the availability of social support. Axis II evaluates the client with respect to relational issues, whereas Axis III summarizes information on the nature of conflicts that produce psychopathology and distress. The authors introduce the view that relationships exist among both conscious and unconscious processes and describe both passive and active roles that patients may take to resolve these. Axis IV presents an outline of the structure of psychopathology, which emphasizes how mental, interpersonal, and intrapersonal behaviors are organized in a person with a disorder. The clinician attempts to identify the interrelationships that exist among self- and object perceptions, self-regulation, defenses, attachment patterns, and interpersonal communication. Only Axis V is devoted to the concepts that are inherent in conventional systems of diagnostic classification. This axis focuses on symptoms and indices of severity that interrelate to the behaviors in the other domains.

In "Child and Adolescent Diagnosis: The Need for a Model-Based Approach" (chapter 8), Ann Doucette critiques the DSM system from the perspective of a child and adolescent psychologist, observing several ways in which the current system falls short, such as the relative lack of attention to ways in which symptoms of a particular problem (such as depression) may manifest differently in children and adults, as well as the relative lack of emphasis on environmental factors that tend to be very important in determining treatment approaches for children. She concludes the chapter with two main suggestions. She first recommends that an expansion of the environmentally oriented Axis IV and the V-codes used to indicate relationship problems could improve the functionality of the current diagnostic system with respect to child and adolescent psychopathology. She also suggests developing a new diagnostic system using a model based measurement approach. She visualizes such a system as using statistical techniques such as confirmatory factor analysis and item response theory to develop a system of empirically grounded divisions such as is illustrated by the contrast between internalizing versus externalizing disorders. She maintains that such an approach may lead to a parsimonious, empirically based system and provide us with the tools to detect and explore any potentially important differences across groups of interest such as gender, ethnicity, or rater.

Drew Westen, Amy Kegley Heim, Kate Morrison, Marcus Patterson, and Laura Campbell have contributed chapter 9, "Simplifying Diagnosis Using a Prototype-Matching Approach: Implications for the Next Edition of the DSM." The aim of this chapter is to suggest ways of improving the empirical grounding of the diagnostic system while developing a system that is easy for clinicians to use. In this chapter, Westen et al. distinguish between the problem of developing a classification system and the problem of identifying patients with particular problems after a system has been developed. Citing problems with the current diagnostic system including the high frequency of comorbidity and subclinical diagnoses, they propose the development of a prototype-matching system. Drawing on recent research by Westen in the study of personality disorders, they suggest that a valid and easily applied diagnostic system might be developed by using statistical aggregation techniques with sets of plausible items to uncover empirically based criteria. To diagnose a client, then, clinicians would rate the extent to which a client meets a prototypic description of a particular problem such as narcissistic personality disorder. Such a system could include both dimensional and categorical elements by combining a rating of the degree of fit with the inclusion of thresholds and cutoffs. Westen et al. argue that this diagnostic system would be both empirically based and easy for clinicians to apply because it asks for a gestalt impression that is closer to the way clinicians diagnose in practice. They comment that this system also avoids the problem of subthreshold symptoms and catch-all categories such as NOS.

In chapter 10, "Diagnosis and Treatment Guidelines: The Example of Depression," we develop several lines of evidence to argue that depression is more accurately seen as a general indicator of distress than as a specific disease. We then describe the treatment approach "systematic treatment selection," which draws on the research literature to suggest ways of matching treatment interventions to client characteristics in a way that optimizes outcome. We advocate using depressive symptoms as an outcome measure rather than as information that determines assignment to a diagnostic category, and we argue that this matching approach is likely to be more useful for many clients with depressive symptoms than the assignment of a diagnosis.

In chapter 11, "To Honor Kraepelin . . .: From Symptoms to Pathology in the Diagnosis of Mental Illness," John F. Kihlstrom argues that the medical model of psychopathology is often mistakenly criticized for assuming that psychological disorders are biological in origin, when the primary basis of the medical model is the view that psychopathology is the result of natural causes and so can be studied by empirical methods. He describes Kraepelin, the father of our current diagnostic system, as having intended to base his classification system on differential courses and outcomes, resorting to symptoms by default because of the lack of information about causes. Kihlstrom points out that medical diagnostics for physical problems have moved beyond a focus on symptoms to the use of laboratory tests that indicate the underlying problems. He emphasizes the increase in knowledge we have experienced with respect to mental disorders since Kraepelin's original work in diagnostics, and he suggests that we are now positioned to shift the focus from symptoms to underlying deficits for mental disorders. He suggests that cognitive neuropsychology provides a model for this sort of work and argues that we could begin to develop a new diagnostic system centered around systematically measured deficits in cognitive, emotional, and motivational functioning with respect to experience, thought, and action.

As can be seen, the chapters included in this book represent a variety of ideas and viewpoints and suggest actions ranging from relatively minor modifications of existing approaches to strikingly different conceptualizations of assessment and diagnosis. As the editors of this volume, we hope that this collection of chapters will stimulate continued dialogue and discussion about potential alternatives to the current diagnostic system. Our ultimate hope is that the ideas presented here, some of which are in the process of empirical evaluation, will lead to continued research into the development of more effective approaches to diagnostics.

REFERENCES

American Psychiatric Association. (1952). *Diagnostic and statistical manual of mental disorders*. Washington, DC: Author.

American Psychiatric Association. (1968). *Diagnostic and statistical manual of mental disorders* (2nd ed.). Washington, DC: Author.

American Psychiatric Association. (1980). *Diagnostic and statistical manual of mental disorders* (3rd ed.). Washington, DC: Author.

American Psychiatric Association. (1987). *Diagnostic and statistical manual of mental disorders* (3rd ed., rev.). Washington, DC: Author.

American Psychiatric Association. (1994). *Diagnostic and statistical manual of mental disorders* (4th ed.). Washington, DC: Author.

American Psychiatric Association. (2000). *Diagnostic and statistical manual of mental disorders* (4th ed., text revision). Washington, DC: Author.

Blashfield, R. K. (1984). *The classification of psychopathology: Neo-Kraepelinian and quantitative approaches.* New York: Plenum.

Cantor, N., Smith, E. E., French, R. S., & Mezzich, J. (1980). Psychiatric diagnosis as prototype categorization. *Journal of Abnormal Psychology, 89,* 181–192.

Carson, R. C. (1991). Dilemmas in the pathway of the DSM–IV. *Journal of Abnormal Psychology, 100,* 302–307.

Clark, L. A., Watson, D., & Reynolds, S. (1995). Diagnosis and classification of psychopathology: Challenges to the future system and future directions. *Annual Review of Psychology, 46,* 121–153.

Endicott, J., & Spitzer, R. L. (1978). A diagnostic interview. *Archives of General Psychiatry, 35,* 837–844.

Feighner, J. P., Robins, E., Guze, S. B., Woodruff, R. A., Winokur, G., & Munoz, R. (1972). Diagnostic criteria for use in psychiatric research. *Archives of General Psychiatry, 26,* 57–63.

Foa, E. B., & Kozak, M. J. (1995). DSM–IV field trial: Obsessive–compulsive disorder. *American Journal of Psychiatry, 151,* 90–96.

Kirk, S. A., & Kutchins, H. (1992). *The selling of the DSM: The rhetoric of science in psychiatry.* New York: Aldine de Gruyter.

Kraepelin, E. (1883). *Compendium der Psychiatrie: Zum Gebrauche fur Studirende und Aerzte* (1st ed.). Leipzig: Verlag von Ambr-Abel.

Nathan, P. E. (1998). The DSM–IV and its antecedents: Enhancing syndromal diagnosis. In J. W. Barron (Eds.), *Making diagnosis meaningful: Enhancing evaluation and treatment of psychological disorders* (pp. 3–27). Washington, DC: American Psychological Association.

Rosenhan, D. (1973). On being sane in insane places. *Science, 179,* 250–258.

Rutter, M., & Schaffer, D. (1980). DSM–III: A step forward or back in terms of the classification of childhood psychiatric disorders? *Journal of the American Academy of Child Psychiatry, 19,* 371–394.

Schacht, T. E. (1985). DSM–III and the politics of truth. *American Psychologist, 40,* 513–526.

Spitzer, R. L. (1983). Psychiatric diagnosis: Are clinicians still necessary? *Comprehensive Psychiatry, 24,* 399–411.

Wakefield, J. C. (1999a). The concept of disorder as a foundation for the DSM's theory-neutral nosology: Response to Follette and Houts, Part 2. *Behaviour Research and Therapy, 37,* 1001–1027.

Wakefield, J. C. (1999b). Philosophy of science and the progressiveness of the DSM's theory-neutral nosology: Response to Follette and Houts, Part 1. *Behaviour Research and Therapy, 37,* 963–999.

Widiger, T. A., Frances, A. J., Pincus, H. A., Ross, R., First, M. B., & Wakefield Davis, W. (Eds.). (1994). *DSM–IV sourcebook* (Vol. 1). Washington, DC: American Psychiatric Association.

Widiger, T. A., Frances, A. J., Pincus, H. A., Ross, R., First, M. B., & Wakefield

Davis, W. (Eds.). (1996). DSM–IV *sourcebook* (Vol. 2). Washington, DC: American Psychiatric Association.

Widiger, T. A., Frances, A. J., Pincus, H. A., Ross, R., First, M. B., & Wakefield Davis, W. (Eds.). (1997). DSM–IV *sourcebook* (Vol. 3). Washington, DC: American Psychiatric Association.

World Health Organization. (1992). *International classification of diseases and related health problems* Vol. 1 (10th ed.). Geneva, Switzerland: Author.

2

DISCOVERY, INVENTION, AND THE EXPANSION OF THE MODERN *DIAGNOSTIC AND STATISTICAL MANUALS OF MENTAL DISORDERS*

ARTHUR C. HOUTS

This chapter is biased and unbalanced. I admit it from the outset, and I do not pretend to rise above my historical circumstances of having become a chief opponent of the modern *Diagnostic and Statistical Manuals of Mental Disorders* (DSM). After 25 years of following changes in the various editions of the DSMs, I have concluded that there is far more pseudoscience than real science in the modern DSMs. To be sure, some solid advances have been made in the scientific basis for making some distinctions between mental disorders, and many sources of commentary correctly laud such achievements (Fink, 1988; A. J. Frances, 1994; Glass & Vergare, 1994; Guze, 1995; Nathan, 1998; Wakefield, 1996, 1998a, 1999b; Weissman, 1987). In my opinion, however, those commentaries also often overemphasize the successes of the modern DSMs and get carried away with praise for the limited scientific advances that have been made. I take a

Support for this work was provided by a Centers of Excellence Grant from the State of Tennessee to the Department of Psychology of the University of Memphis.

different view of all of this, a view that is far more skeptical and far more critical (some might even say cynical). Here I do not emphasize or devote much attention to the small yet genuine scientific advances of the modern *DSMs*. Instead, I counterbalance what I regard as the overstatement of scientific progress by various proponents of the modern *DSMs*. The fundamental theme of this chapter is that we should be very skeptical about any sweeping assessment of the modern *DSMs* that claims that the expansion of the domain of mental disorders witnessed over the past four decades is consonant with and a sign of scientific advance.

The stance I take is the stance of the skeptic, the spoiler of the party, and the thorn in the flesh of the mental health professions. I have been reinforced for thinking critically and for questioning current orthodoxy, and in the end, I am a thoroughgoing Protestant in the reformed tradition, a tradition at least some have viewed as a major source of values for our modern scientific outlook (Merton, 1970). I take a critical stance toward the modern *DSMs* also because someone needs to do so from within the mental health professions. The professions and the people they serve benefit if the professions eschew complacency in their knowledge and remain uncomfortable with their latest achievements. Having critics around is good for everyone.

This chapter is organized into two major sections that represent two different approaches to the overarching question: What sense can we make of the fact that we have witnessed a 300% increase in the number of diagnoses for mental disorders in the past four decades? I have referred to the first approach to addressing this question as the *discovery model* or *discovery approach* to the mental health field. My chief aim in reviewing the various versions of discovery, or standard scientific progress approaches, is to show that the developments of the modern *DSMs* do not square with such approaches. To put it bluntly, I cannot even see the emperor, let alone whether or not he is clothed. The second major section of this chapter takes up another entirely different way of looking at the development of the modern *DSMs*, and I have called this approach a *social invention model of diagnosis* in the mental health field. This social invention approach to understanding diagnosis in the mental health field makes some sense of the expansion of the modern *DSMs* and raises some questions about the entire process by which diagnoses come and go in the modern *DSMs*.

I do not have an alternative to the modern *DSMs*. I hope however, that this volume provides some satisfaction to those who are seeking more specific alternatives to the modern *DSMs*. Obviously, I do not accept the argument that one should not criticize a current system of diagnosis until one has something to replace it. Criticism of the current system of diagnosis is good for the mental health professions whether or not there is something to replace it. Criticism can sharpen the problem areas and expose the empty rhetoric so that we can see what can be reasonably expected from this or any other approach to classification in the mental health field. Criticism of the modern *DSMs* does not make them go away, but it can curtail their misuse and lessen the chance that their contents are misinterpreted as being more soundly scientific than they actually are.

Criticism can clear space to think differently. One of the great dangers of the modern *DSMs* is that they have been taken for granted as scientifically established by so many people that alternative ways of thinking are rarely considered. Criticism of the modern *DSMs* can serve the function of questioning the whole edifice and encourage alternative ways of thinking about mental health problems. For example, one of the most successful and better validated interventions in the mental health field, Gordon Paul's Social-Learning Program (SLP), was developed without regard to a *DSM* diagnosis. Paul (2000) noted that "A significant majority of treated clients has carried a diagnosis of 'schizophrenia,' but traditional *DSM* diagnoses have little predictive power for response to SLPs" (p. 7). Paul's work has been based on an alternative way of thinking, one that values construct validity and careful behavioral measurement over the kind of thinking that supports classification according to clusters of signs and symptoms (Paul, Mariotto, Redfield, Licht, & Power, 1986). Paul's assessment system presents one very clear alternative to the *DSM* approach to assessment, and Paul's strategy could and should be replicated in outpatient settings with different populations and problem areas.

EXPANSION OF THE MODERN *DSMS*

When you look at the current edition of the *Diagnostic and Statistical Manual of Mental Disorders* (*DSM–IV*; American Psychiatric Association, 1994), you may not be immediately impressed by the fact that it is more than 850 pages long. The *DSM–IV–TR* (American Psychiatric Association, 2000) is a minor text revision of the *DSM–IV* and is about 50 pages longer. You might think that *DSM–IV* is about what you would expect from a graduate-level textbook, which is one of its major uses. Without the historical context of seeing previous editions of the *DSM*, you can be easily unimpressed. This would be a mistake.

What is stunning about changes in the successive editions of the *DSM* from 1952 to the present is the massive expansion of the manual in both physical size and the number of diagnostic labels included. Seeing the series of editions from *DSM–I* to *DSM–IV–TR* on a bookshelf makes an instant impression. The expansion is also evident in Figure 2.1 and Figure 2.2, which show, respectively, the expansion of the *DSM* in the number of diagnoses and the number of pages from 1952 to the present. *DSM–I* (American Psychiatric Association, 1952) and *DSM–II* (American Psychiatric Association, 1968) were small-page, spiral-bound booklets. *DSM–*

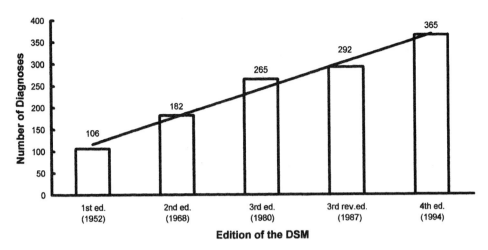

Figure 2.1. Number of Diagnoses in the *Diagnostic and Statistical Manual of Mental Disorders* (*DSM*) Across Editions (1952–1994)

I and *DSM–II* each weighed several ounces. The current book size format was adopted with the third edition, *DSM–III* (American Psychiatric Association, 1980) and continued through the present. *DSM–IV–TR* now weighs 5 pounds. In fact, *DSM–I* was not even called *DSM–I* but simply the *DSM*. This apparently reflected the idea that there might be revisions, but none so radical as to require radical revamping of the basic nomenclature. In contrast to the current direction started with *DSM–III*, *DSM–I* reflected the emerging orientation of American psychiatrists as they turned away from biological models of mental disorders and toward social reaction and psychoanalytic models of psychopathology (Grob, 1991; Houts, 2000).

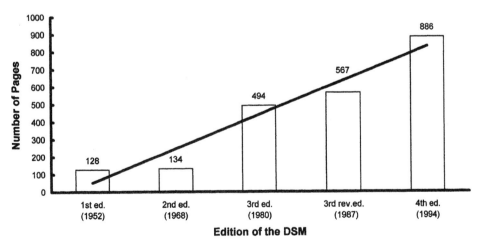

Figure 2.2. Number of Pages in the *Diagnostic and Statistical Manual of Mental Disorders* (*DSM*) Across Editions (1952–1994)

DSM–I was small, and over the intervening 16 years, *DSM–II* did not grow much larger.

As Figures 2.1 and 2.2 clearly show, a major expansion took place in the 12-year period (1968–1980) between *DSM–II* and *DSM–III*, and *DSM–III* marks the beginning of the modern DSMs. With the third revised edition (*DSM–III–R*; American Psychiatric Association, 1987) and *DSM–IV*, the expansion of the manual has continued. If one looks back over the 42-year period from *DSM–I* to *DSM–IV* (1952–1994), the number of specific diagnoses has increased by more than 300% in a little over four decades. This is remarkable. What are we to make of this fact? Does this mean that mental illness has tripled in only four decades? Could it mean that the sciences of medicine and psychology have made such rapid advances over the past 42 years that we now can identify mental illnesses that were there all along but went unrecognized because our knowledge of physiology and human behavior was so primitive in the early 1950s? Alternatively, are we witnessing the expansion of mental health professions, which label as mental disorders human behaviors that only four decades ago we considered either medical disorders or routine difficulties of ordinary life? After all, the number of mental health professionals has also grown, and the economic system under which they have practiced since the 1980s requires a diagnosis to justify payment for mental health services.

How did we get a 300% increase in diagnostic labels in the past four decades? As with most interesting questions, this one has no single or simple answer. We cannot point to one factor and say with any certainty that it caused the expansion of the *DSM* system. What we can say is that investigators have made some guesses and offered some hypotheses about what could account for the expansion of psychiatric diagnoses that we have been witnessing. The purpose of this chapter is to critique some of those hypotheses in hopes that the reader looks at *DSM–IV* and *DSM–IV–TR* (and the inevitable *DSM–V* and so on) with a critical perspective. Such a critical perspective neither rejects the entire concept of nosology for mental health problems, as did an earlier antipsychiatry (as represented by Szasz (1960), Laing (1960), Scheff (1966), and others who argued against labeling on various grounds), nor does it accept the current version of the *DSM* as if it were handed down from on high. As Andreasen, Flaum, and Arndt (1992) noted,

> The DSM–III or DSM–III–R are not the Ark of the Covenant, the Ten Commandments, the Talmud, or the Holy Bible. While they serve a useful purpose, they should not be accorded excessive reverence, and excessive faith should not be placed on them. (p. 616).

Criticism is not the mere mongering of negative opinion; rather, it is a careful weighing of alternative views where one is always left open to the possibility that some new perspective will come to light and force one to change one's current opinion. In this sense, criticism is the heart of rational scientific analysis and the lifeblood of a pluralistic and free society such as ours (Albert, 1985; Popper, 1962). This chapter fosters a critical perspective on the *DSM* so that students and professionals treat the current edition and future editions of the manual with both the respect and the skepticism they deserve.

Mental health professionals, whatever their level of training or primary discipline, are now using *DSM–IV–TR* on a daily basis. In fact, within five years of its appearance in 1980, *DSM–III* had become a predominant mode of instruction for students of the mental health professions (Klerman, 1986). It is vital for mental health professionals to have some appreciation of the strengths and weakness of the modern *DSM*s and to appreciate as well that there are many perspectives from which to understand what has been happening with the expansion of the *DSM*s. Only then is it possible to consider alternatives to the *DSM* approach when that approach does not measure up. This chapter approaches the phenomenon of the expansion of the *DSM*s from two broad interpretive frameworks: scientific discovery and social invention.

In what follows, I present the discovery model or discovery narrative first. This includes two major criticisms of the claim that the *DSM* expansion is properly interpreted as scientific progress related to discovery. The first criticism proceeds by explicating one model of scientific progress, a logical empiricist model exemplified in the work of Carl Hempel (1965). The strategy of this critique is to compare the facts of the *DSM* expansion with the ideals of such a model of progress. The second critique of the discovery narrative addresses several attempts to draw an analogy between the expansion of the modern *DSM*s and the recent history of physical medicine. Here I consider the claims of Wakefield (1999a; 1999b) regarding parallel expansion of diseases in the *DSM*s and in the *International Classification of Diseases* (ICDs; World Health Organization [WHO], 1967, 1992), as well as the problems of claiming parallels between the basic definitions of mental disorders and medical disorders. I also introduce the concept of Scadding's (1988) ladder to illustrate how the expansion of the modern *DSM*s differs from the history of physical medicine.

SCIENTIFIC DISCOVERY AS AN INTERPRETATION OF DSM EXPANSION

Investigators in the interdisciplinary field of science and technology have pointed to the importance of rhetoric in scientific disciplines. Sociologists and philosophers of science have identified forms of expression for scientific claims and how those forms of expression influence scientists as well as the general public to accept knowledge claims as "truth" (Curtis,

1994; Fuller, 1988, 1989, 1993, 1997; Gilbert & Mulkay, 1984; Latour, 1987, 1999; Latour & Woolgar, 1986; Pickering, 1984, 1992; Shapin, 1994; Smith, 1988; Weimer, 1979). Recent interest in rhetorical analysis of scientific disciplines coincides with a general philosophical claim that certain grand narratives are the social glue that makes it possible for us to converse at all (Rorty, 1989). The "crisis of modernity" and "postmodernism" have become familiar intellectual slogans. Much of the talk about postmodernism consists of questioning what has been labeled as the grand narrative of scientific progress and discovery (e.g., Kolakowski, 1990; Lyotard, 1984). According to these analyses, scientific disciplines, like organized religions, have certain grand narratives that hold the discipline together and that influence the public at large. Recent struggles between creationists and evolutionists provide one example of clashes between grand narratives about human origins. Clearly, some degree of cultural authority accrues to knowledge claims that are said to have originated from scientific progress. Presenting knowledge claims under the rhetorical mantle of scientific progress and discovery is one of several powerful ways to influence members of a culture to accept the claims as trustworthy.

Since its inception at the end of the 19th century, the field of modern psychopathology has garnered authority and legitimacy, both professional and civic, by casting its knowledge claims within a master narrative of scientific discovery and progress (Foucault, 1965; Scull, 1989). According to this discovery model, the field of psychopathology is retrospectively said to be the result of increasing scientific objectivity that has produced more and more refined knowledge of the types and causes of deviant behavior (e.g., Alexander & Selesnick, 1968). From contemporary standard textbooks, students learn a canonical version of the history of the mental health field. According to these textbooks on abnormal psychology, better research methods and more extensive research programs produced more precise and objective categories of deviant behavior and more enlightened and humane forms of treatment (Micale & Porter, 1994). True to the spirit of discovery, students learn, for example, that demonic possession was eventually explained as some type of nervous system disorder and that burning at the stake was replaced by tilling the garden, singing hymns, and eating three square meals a day. According to the standard story, further progress "revealed" that the nervous system disorder in question was actually seizure activity, and 19th-century moral treatment was eventually replaced by 20th-century anti-seizure medication. When it can be made to work, the discovery narrative reassures us by convincing us that our current formulations of mental disorders are the result of painstakingly careful scientific investigations that belong to a grand picture of human triumph over ignorance and cruelty. Believing in and reciting the discovery narrative makes us feel good.

The crux of the discovery narrative is that there is an objective truth to be discovered by the use of particular scientific rules and procedures. The *DSM* approach to mental health problems borrows directly from medical science not only its methodology and the scientific trappings of physical medicine, but also the discovery narrative. The discovery narrative is also dominant in histories of physical medicine, and in many respects this is what makes the analogy between mental medicine and physical medicine so attractive to those proponents of the modern *DSM*s who claim that they are following in the footsteps of their medical forebears.

Mental health professionals have been steeped in the discovery narrative. It continues to authorize and legitimize their research and clinical work. It protects them from charges that their personal values and biases determine how they view psychopathology. Within the discovery narrative, all professional activity is recast as dispassionate discovery of the true state of nature. The discovery model of psychopathology is so much a part of professional education and everyday life in the culture that it is taken for granted. This story is assumed to be "the truth" to such an extent that the discovery narrative is a way of life (Wittgenstein, 1953), rather than just one among several narratives or models used to make sense of the mental health field. The discovery narrative has pervasive effects on the scientific activities it helps organize and justify.

Critical Perspectives on the Discovery Narrative in Psychopathology

To criticize the fundamental assumptions of one outlook in terms of the assumptions of another is difficult but necessary to attain a critical perspective. This is difficult because fundamental assumptions are taken for granted and therefore are hardly recognized. Whether or not the discovery narrative appeals to a scientist is a reflection of assumptions about nature and science that are built into the narrative itself. One has to "get outside" the narrative even to see it as a narrative. The purpose of the discovery narrative is to legitimize and explain current activity and the history of science in terms of a priori assumptions and especially to explain that the truth of our claims can be judged by how well they correspond with or depict "the state of nature." As an ideal, the discovery narrative is generally not tested. It simply describes the assumed processes of scientific development from particular points of view. When one embraces its fundamental assumptions, the discovery narrative is a logically consistent story about science.

Two approaches to criticism of the discovery narrative are possible. First, it can be noted that, as an ideal, the discovery narrative is a story of science only from a certain vantage point, and most working scientists take it for granted that this is "the right" vantage point. It is possible to identify other stories from different, alternative vantage points. One such alternative story is social invention, and most working scientists regard this as silly if not downright deranged. I consider such a social invention perspective later in this chapter, but now I explore a second two-part critique.

With this second strategy, one can accept the fundamental assumptions of the discovery narrative and embrace it as an ideal. Given such acceptance, the specific case of the expansion of the *DSM* can be examined to see how well it fits this ideal. In other words, the truth of the narrative is assumed, and the "facts" are then examined to see how well they fit.

It is possible to consider two ways of addressing the relative fit between the mental health field and ideals of the discovery approach. One approach is theoretical: Does the expansion of the modern *DSM*s fit with discovery ideals for scientific progress as those ideals have been articulated in traditional philosophies of science, such as logical empiricism? A second approach is more descriptive and empirical: Does the expansion of the modern *DSM*s fit with the pattern of development of a clinical science like physical medicine? This second approach raises another question: Is the mental health field as embodied in the modern *DSM*s comparable to the physical health field as embodied in the various editions of the *ICD*s (WHO, 1967, 1992)?

Once again, we return to the overarching question: How did we get a 300% increase in diagnostic labels in the past four decades? A common answer is that we have been on the path of scientific discovery, and the increase represents scientific progress. If for the moment we accept this at face value, we can then ask, According to what model of scientific progress does the *DSM* expansion constitute scientific progress?

Logical Empiricist Models of Scientific Progress and the Modern DSMs

As the interval between successive *DSM* editions has become shorter and the scope of human behavior that can be diagnosed has become wider with each new edition, commentators have become more and more skeptical about claims that the successive *DSM*s represent growth of scientific knowledge. Critical commentary has ranged from the charge that the American Psychiatric Association has found the goose that lays golden eggs in the form of publication profits with each new edition (Caplan, 1995; Kendell, 1991; Kirk & Kutchins, 1992; Kutchins & Kirk, 1997; Wylie, 1995; Zimmerman, 1990) to more subtle criticisms based on philosophical and historical notions about how taxonomies should look when science is progressing in some domain of inquiry. In this section, the focus is on the question of whether the steady expansion of the *DSM* is consistent with a philosophical model of scientific progress articulated in traditional philosophical and historical studies of science, namely, the logical empiricist model of progress.

An important philosophical analysis of the role of taxonomy in the progress of science was offered by the logical empiricist philosopher of science, Carl Hempel (1965), in an invited address that he delivered in 1959 to the group of psychopathology researchers organized by Joseph Zubin in New York. Members of this research group have played major roles in the *DSM* revisions (see Blashfield, 1984, for a genealogy of the research group). Hempel's essay has been widely cited in discussions of various editions of the *DSM* (e.g., Follette & Houts, 1996; Houts, 1989; Sadler, Wiggins, & Schwartz, 1994). In the paragraphs that follow, I use the following phrases as synonyms: *logical empiricist model of progress, Hempel's model of scientific progress, the Hempelian model,* and *traditional philosophical model of scientific progress.*

Hempel's model of scientific progress declared that progress in knowledge occurs when more and more phenomena are brought under more and more general covering laws. Scientific explanations are viewed as logical deductions from a theory that takes the form of a statement of initial conditions along with some law of nature from which the observed phenomenon could then be logically deduced. For example, the observation that a wall painted white subsequently turned black could be explained by noting that the paint contained lead carbonate and that the gas heater in the room emitted sulfur. These two initial conditions, along with the general law that sulfur and lead carbonate combine to form lead sulfide, permit the logical deduction that the wall turned black by forming a patina of lead sulfide (Kim, 1967). The grander concept of scientific progress in Hempel's logical empiricism was the parallel concept of theory reduction, which should not be confused with physiological reductionism (see Weinberg, 1995, on the distinction between grand reductionism and petty reductionism). Progress is said to have occurred when the concepts and terms of one level of explanation could in turn be explained by the concepts and terms of a broader level of explanation. For example, one could talk about the formation of lead sulfide at the level of physical chemistry and describe regularities with which certain elements combined, but when the laws of atomic theory were articulated, then one could deduce the regularities of physical chemistry using initial conditions of atomic weights and laws of physics. The laws of physics "cover" the laws of physical chemistry.

In the Hempelian model, scientific progress occurs when more and more general covering laws could explain the observed phenomena. Specifically with regard to taxonomy, Hempel (1965) noted that progress occurred when classification systems were reduced by the innovation of a theory to account for the variety of observations. For example, primitive biological knowledge was organized in terms of description and categorization based on surface features of organisms. Before Darwin, complex taxonomies emerged, and the number of categories needed to account for living things proliferated. With the rise of evolutionary theory in the 20th century, classification in terms of surface features was replaced by classification based on phylogenetic and later, genetic concepts. The role of taxonomy changed from one of storing and retrieving information to one of providing evidence for a theory of origins (Mayr, 1982). Taxonomies no longer did the job of explaining but instead became the thing to be explained. According to this model, scientific progress occurs when there is a reduction by theory of the number of taxonomic categories; the mere proliferation of categories is a sure sign that progress has not, in fact, occurred.

From the perspective of logical empiricism, the recent expansions of the modern DSMs to include more and more diagnostic labels does not represent scientific progress. This is contrary to what proponents of the modern DSMs have proclaimed (e.g., Fink, 1988; Glass & Vergare, 1994; Nathan, 1998; Weissman, 1987). Kendell (1991) recognized this basic point when he commented that

> Other branches of medicine and other fields of learning did not progress by a dogged pursuit of better and better classifications of their subject matter. They did so by acquiring new technologies, by developing radically new concepts, and by elucidating fundamental mechanisms. (p. 301)

The proliferation of diagnostic categories observed over succeeding editions of the DSM is not consistent with a traditional model of scientific progress, yet its proponents have routinely claimed that expansions of the DSM are a sign of scientific progress.

If the outcomes of the DSM revisions have not been consistent with what would be expected from philosophical and historical analysis of scientific progress, what about the methods used to make revisions in the modern DSMs? Once again, a close examination of the procedures has shown rather drastic inconsistencies with Hempelian ideals. Margolis (1994) has noted that the aim of taxonomy within a covering law model of scientific knowledge is to collect taxonomic categories that have some constancy precisely because they denote natural kinds of phenomena that can be explained by laws of nature. According to this ideal, the taxonomic categories are not mere prototypes induced from repeated observations and common consensual usage; rather, they are instances of lawlike generalities. What makes the categories stable is not mere social convention but certain empirical regularities that can be subsumed under lawlike generalizations (see Meehl, 1995). This notion is familiar to students of psychometric theory as the concept of construct validation (Cronbach & Meehl, 1955). As Margolis has noted, the problem with the modern DSM approach to taxonomy is that it explicitly aims to base taxonomy on social consensus and deliberately eschews any appeal to theoretical constructs. Hence, procedures for introducing new diagnostic labels and for revising old ones guarantee slippage of the categories rather than stability. What is worse, the slippage goes unnoticed, as Margolis (1994) has noted:

The very use of the *Manual* creates the false, altogether misleading, completely artifactual, impression of the strict constancy of the *Manual*'s diagnostic categories. In a word, the perceived constancy of the taxonomy cannot but be an artifact of historically changing professional perception. Its apparent constancy cannot be justifiably anticipated to remain hospitable to the progressive discovery of pertinent lawlike regularities. (p. 110)

Paul (2000) also made a similar observation about the *DSM* revision process when he noted that literature reviews and summaries were used not as principled means of amassing scientific evidence; such reviews instead served the function of misrepresenting as scientific evidence what were in fact consensus subjective judgments by committees. In effect, while adopting the accouterments of logical empiricism such as *operational definition* and *scientific progress*, the *DSM* has also abandoned the substance of that philosophy of science.

If one accepts a discovery narrative and then compares the methods used and the outcomes attained within the modern *DSMs* to ideals of that narrative with taxonomy, the modern *DSM* expansion does not measure up to those ideals. In fact, according to those ideals of taxonomy, the modern *DSM* expansions represent either stagnation or decay, but certainly not progress. Why does this matter? Why should we care if the changes of the modern *DSMs* do not square with this philosophical and rather abstract model of scientific progress? We should care precisely because such an analysis challenges the claims of those who champion the expansion of the modern *DSMs* as scientific progress. Logical empiricism offers a model of scientific progress and provides a clear standard for judging whether a field has progressed when measured against such an explicit standard. Comparing the *DSM* changes to a logical empiricist standard of scientific progress brings rhetoric about progress out into the open where the claims for progress can be evaluated against some clearly explicated standard. Defenders of the proliferation of diagnoses in the modern *DSMs* in fact do care about how the pattern of expansion fits with logical empiricist ideals (see Wakefield, 1999b), and many clinical scientists within the mental health field hold views about science that are broadly consistent with logical empiricist philosophy of science (Houts & Krasner, 1998; Krasner & Houts, 1984).

Responses to the logical empiricist critique of the *DSM* expansion have varied from accepting the critique to arguing that it is not appropriate for applied clinical science fields. Wakefield (1999b) has noted that certain areas of medicine that almost everyone would agree have been scientifically progressive contradict the logical empiricist model because they have shown an increase in disease classifications rather than a decrease. Wakefield may well be correct that the logical empiricist model of progress is descriptive of biology and physical chemistry, but such a model may not transfer to medicine and other applied areas. This remains to be seen by further application of such a model to fields such as toxicology, dentistry, or veterinary medicine. Certainly, the idea that different domains of science require different domain-specific models to account for their historical trajectory is consistent with the past 30 years of science studies, where the various unity of science theories such as logical empiricism have been rejected in favor of discipline-specific approaches.

Medical Analogy Arguments

Defenders of the DSMs have relied on a more empirically based claim for their rhetoric of progress. This is a familiar claim: The DSMs are alleged to be merely following in the footsteps of physical medicine, and just as no one denies that physical medicine is scientifically progressive, so no one should deny that the modern DSMs are scientifically progressive.

The several versions of this argument are based on a putative analogy between physical medicine and mental health medicine. In what follows, I consider three versions of this analogical argument. The first version concerns a claim made by Wakefield (1999a; 1999b) that the DSM expansion is consistent with what he viewed as ICD expansion in a comparable period. The second version is a broader claim that the history of medical disorders in some way parallels the history of mental disorders, and in evaluating this claim, I draw on what I refer to as Scadding's (1988) ladder of knowledge development for medical disorders. The third version of the mental disorder being analogous to medical disorder concerns issues of basic definition of mental and medical disorders, and in considering the validity of such claims, I analyze Wakefield's (1992a; 1992b) harmful dysfunction approach to mental disorders.

A Comparison of Changes in the ICDs and the Modern DSMs

What about the empirical comparison between physical medicine and mental health diagnoses? Some defenders of the modern DSMs have rejected the applicability of philosophical models of progress to clinical sciences as opposed to physical sciences. They have argued that logical empiricist philosophical models of scientific progress must be incorrect because an examination of the ICDs shows that diagnoses of physical diseases have expanded and not contracted (Wakefield, 1999a, 1999b). Coupled with the observation that not even the most skeptical among us denies the scientific progress of modern medicine, the observation that medical diagnoses have expanded rather than contracted has been taken as a refutation of such philosophical ideals of scientific progress in clinical sciences. What has happened in physical medicine diagnosis, and how does that compare with what has happened in mental disorder diagnosis?

There are two answers to these questions; one is quantitative, and the other is qualitative. The quantitative answer addresses the issue of new diagnoses in the ICDs as compared to new diagnoses in the DSMs. The qualitative answer addresses what is really new in the ICDs and the DSMs by way of example, using ischemic heart disease and sleep disorders, respectively.

A *Quantitative Comparison of* ICD *Change and* DSM *Expansion.* Wakefield has asserted that when one compares increases in diagnoses for mental disorders from *DSM–II* through *DSM–IV* to increases in diagnostic categories for circulatory and digestive diseases in the 8th edition of the ICD (ICD–8; WHO, 1967) through the 10th edition (ICD–10; WHO, 1992), the increase in mental disorder diagnoses is comparable to an increase in physical disorder diagnoses. Wakefield (1998a) stated,

> Thus, during this time period, which covers the claimed expansive period from the advent of the third edition of the DSM (DSM–III; American Psychiatric Association, 1980) through the DSM–IV, the rate of growth in the DSM categories was comparable with or lower than the rates of growth in the other two specialties [circulatory and digestive diseases]. (p. 848)

Wakefield credited Spitzer, a chief architect of the modern DSMs, for pointing out this similarity to him. Does the evidence support Wakefield's claim that changes in the DSMs and in the ICDs during the period 1967 to 1994 are of the same magnitude and type?

Figure 2.3 shows the number of unique disease codes for the circulatory and digestive system sections respectively for ICD–8 and ICD–10.

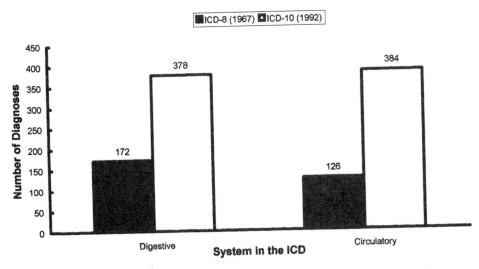

Figure 2.3. Number of Physical Disease Diagnoses for the Digestive and Circulatory System Sections in the 8th and 10th Editions of the *International Classification of Diseases* (*ICD*)

ARTHUR C. HOUTS

Without attending to details, Wakefield repeatedly stated that diseases of the circulatory system increased by 200% and that those of the digestive system increased by 123% from ICD–8 to ICD–10 (Wakefield, 1998a, 1999b). Figure 2.3 clarifies the nature of the so-called increase in diagnoses of physical disorders. Wakefield apparently obtained the 200% increase in circulatory system diagnoses by subtracting the number (126) of diagnostic numerical codes in ICD–8 from the number (384) of diagnostic numerical codes for these diseases in ICD–10 and dividing the resultant number (258) by the number (126) of diagnostic numerical codes in ICD–8. Wakefield similarly obtained a so-called increase in diagnostic labels for digestive system diseases within the ICDs.

This procedure of merely counting code numbers without looking at the labels and the resultant percentage increases are misleading for two reasons. First, as Figure 2.4 shows, most of the changes between ICD–8 and ICD–10 comprised the assignment of new code numbers in ICD–10 for diagnoses that were already listed and named in ICD–8, but these previously listed and named diagnoses did not have a separate code number. In other words, there was no substantial increase in new conditions being named, only a renumbering of already existing diagnoses. Second, when one compares in detail this type of change to the type of change that occurred in the expansion of the modern DSM diagnoses, there is just no comparability. Specifically, when you look at DSM–II, you do not find very many instances where a DSM–IV diagnosis is exactly stated in DSM–II but not given a numerical code there. Changes within the DSMs involved naming new conditions rather than merely adding number codes to con-

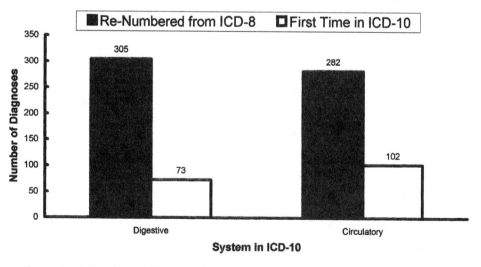

Figure 2.4. Number of Physical Disease Diagnoses for the Digestive and Circulatory System Sections of International Classification of Diseases (ICD) That Were Renumbered From the 8th Edition (ICD–8) and That Appear for the First Time in the 10th Edition (ICD–10)

ditions previously named. From a purely descriptive standpoint, there is just no analogy between the changes in the ICDs and the diagnostic label proliferation of the DSMs. Changes in the two diagnostic systems are qualitatively very different and therefore not at all analogous.

Consider changes in the circulatory system sections of ICD–8 and ICD–10. Only 27% of the named diagnoses in the ICD–10 did not appear previously in ICD–8 as named diagnoses. The new diagnoses that did appear were often ones related to advances in medical treatment and technology. For example, a number of new diagnoses were introduced to describe events following myocardial infarction. This was probably related to the increase in survival rates among heart attack patients in 1992 compared to 1967; moreover, patients in 1992 probably underwent more sensitive testing than did patients in 1967, which resulted in locating specific weaknesses in their hearts. Advances in medical treatment and in diagnostic instrumentation and resolution produced the conditions for new physical maladies to be observed and to be named. Similarly, new diagnoses appeared in the section on cerebral infarction, no doubt related to technological advances in imaging the location of cerebral vascular accidents. Interestingly, in the circulatory system sections of ICD–8 and ICD–10, 73% of the new diagnostic codes comprised conditions already recognized and specifically named as diseases in ICD–8, and these were merely given unique numerical codes in ICD–10. I present below a detailed example to illustrate qualitatively what happened for more than 70% of the differences between ICD–8 and ICD–10. Clearly, the majority of so-called "new" diagnostic codes in the circulatory system section of the ICDs to which Wakefield has referred are not new at all. Although it would reflect changes in the DSMs, Wakefield's (1998a, 1999b) procedure for enumerating and evaluating changes in ICD classification of circulatory system diseases leads to serious error, and the better method I have illustrated above can be applied to the ICD sections on the digestive system.

Using the aforementioned better method for analyzing ICD changes, a comparable pattern was found for changes in diseases of the digestive system between ICD–8 and ICD–10. Only 19% of the ICD–10 codes in this section represented new diseases that had not been previously named and listed in ICD–8. In most cases, the introductions of new diagnoses for digestive disorders were attributable to new etiologies being discovered, new treatments being developed, and new diagnostic technologies being introduced. For example, Crohn's disease and diverticular disease, both of which were listed in ICD–8, were expanded to provide specific numerical codes for different parts of the digestive tract. Enhanced diagnostic procedures resulted in greater specification of a known disease. Alcohol-induced chronic pancreatitis was added to diseases of the pancreas in ICD–10. However, just as was the case with diseases of the circulatory system, fully 81% of the so-called "new" diagnoses of the digestive system were not new at all and had been named and listed as separate diseases under larger aggregate numerical codes in ICD–8.

During the period 1967 to 1992, changes in the ICDs were due primarily to the renumbering of old diagnostic labels rather than to the introduction of entirely new diseases and conditions. When truly new labels and disease conditions were introduced, they were mostly attributable to technological advances in medical assessment and treatment and occasionally to the discovery of new conditions and diseases defined by etiology. The nature of this change in the ICDs should be contrasted with the changes that have occurred from DSM–II to DSM–IV over a comparable period. The best way to illustrate and highlight such drastic differences between them is to consider in detail the qualitative differences that can be discerned by examining two concrete examples of label change, one from the ICDs and one from the modern DSMs.

A *Qualitative Comparison of* ICD *Change and* DSM *Expansion.* Many of the disorders that appeared to be separately coded in ICD–10 had been listed under a single code in ICD–8. Table 2.1 shows a typical example for a section that describes diagnoses for ischemic heart disease. ICD–10 provided for nine numerical codes in this section, whereas ICD–8 provided for only one code. All nine of the ICD–10 codes had appeared by exact name or equivalent in the ICD–8. Of these nine, not a single new disease label was produced, even though a single numerical code in ICD–8 was transformed into nine separate numerical codes in ICD–10. Following the logic of Wakefield's (1998a, 1999b) procedure for enumerating and evaluating the changes of diagnoses in the ICDs, one would calculate that for this specific case, there would have been an 800% increase in the diagnostic labels for ischemic heart disease during the period 1967 to 1992. Such a conclusion would be patently false. Seven of the nine diagnoses in ICD–10 appeared verbatim in the same section in ICD–8 (section 412), and the other two had previously appeared in the ICD–8 under different sections (sections 410 and 414). No new disease conditions were identified, and no new diagnostic labels were introduced in this instance from 1967 to 1992.

This relative stability of a diagnostic system should be contrasted with what happened in the DSMs from 1968 to 1994. The changes in medical diagnosis displayed in Table 2.1 should be contrasted with the changes in psychiatric diagnosis displayed in Table 2.2, which shows the listing of mental disorders in DSM–II and DSM–IV for sleep disorders. The point of choosing sleep disorders is to show in stark contrast the difference between merely giving separate numbers to previously named conditions, as in the ICDs, and adding entirely new conditions as new mental disorders, as in the DSMs. In DSM–II, there was only one listing for sleep problems (306.4 Disorder of Sleep), and this occurred in Section VII, which was devoted to Special Symptoms. In DSM–II, sleep problems were not mental

TABLE 2.1
Changes in Chronic Ischemic Heart Disease Category
From *ICD–8* to *ICD–10*

ICD–8 (1967)	*ICD–10* (1992)
412 Chronic ischemic heart disease	I25 Chronic ischemic heart disease excludes cardiovascular disease NOS (I51.6)
Aneurysm of heart	
Arteriosclerotic heart (disease)	I25.0 Atherosclerotic cardiovascular disease, so described

Cardiovascular
  arteriosclerosis
  degeneration
  disease
  sclerosis
	I25.1 Atherosclerotic heart disease
	  coronary (artery)
	  atheroma
	  atherosclerosis
	  disease
	  sclerosis

Coronary artery
  arteriosclerosis
  atheroma
  disease
  sclerosis
  stricture
	I25.2 Old myocardial infarction
	  healed myocardial infarction
	Past myocardial infarction diagnosed by ECG or other special investigation, but currently presenting no symptoms

Healed myocardial infarct	I25.3 Aneurysm of heart
	  aneurysm:
	    mural
	    ventricular

Ischemic
  degeneraton
    heart
    myocardium
  heart disease
	I25.4 Coronary artery aneurysm (listed under 410 in ICD–8)
	  coronary ateriouvenous fistula, acquired
	  excludes congenital coronary (artery) aneurysm (Q24.5)

Post-myocardial infarct syndrome	I25.5 Ischemic cardiomyopathy
Any condition in 410 (Acute myocardial infarction) specified as chronic or with a stable duration of over 8 weeks	I25.6 Silent myocardial ischemia (listed under 414 in ICD–8) I25.8 Other forms of chronic ischemic heart disease Any condition I21–I22 and I24; specified as chronic or with a stated duration of more than 4 weeks (more than 28 days) from onset
	I25.9 Chronic ischemic heart disease, unspecified Ischemic heart disease (chronic) NOS

Note. Diagnoses italicized in *ICD–10* column are those given a new and separate numerical code in *ICD–10* even though they appear in *ICD–8* under the single numerical code of 412. NOS = not otherwise specified. References are to the 8th and 10th editions of the *International Classification of Diseases* (*ICD–8* and *ICD–10*; respectively).

TABLE 2.2

Changes in Sleep Disorders Category From *DSM–II* to *DSM–IV*

DSM–II (1968)	*DSM–IV* (1994)

306 Special symptoms not elsewhere classified
306.3 Disorder of sleep
	Primary Sleep Disorders
	Dyssomnias
	307.42 Primary Insomnia
	307.44 Primary Hypersomnia
	347 Narcolepsy
	780.59 Breathing-Related Sleep Disorder
	307.45 Circadian Rhythm Sleep Disorder
	    Delayed Sleep Phase Type, Jet Lag Type,
	    Shift Work Type, Unspecified Type
	307.47 Dyssomnia NOS
	Parasomnias
	307.47 Nightmare Disorder
	307.46 Sleep Terror Disorder
	307.46 Sleepwalking Disorder
	Sleep Disorders Related to Another Mental
	    Disorder
	307.42 Insomnia Related to . . . Indicate Axis
	    I or II disorder
	307.44 Hypersomnia Related to . . . Indicate
	    Axis I or II disorder
	Other Sleep Disorders
	780.xx Sleep Disorder Due to . . . Indicate the
	    General Medical Condition
	  .52 Insomnia Type, .54 Hypersomnia Type
	  .59 Parasomnia Type, .59 Mixed Type
	  —:—Substance-Induced Sleep Disorder refer
	    to Substance-Related Disorders for sub-
	    stance-specific codes
	Specify type: Insomnia Type, Hypersomnia
	    Type, Parasomnia Type, Mixed Type
	Specify if: With Onset During Intoxication,
	    With Onset During Withdrawal

Note. References are to the 2nd and 4th editions of the *Diagnostic and Statistical Manual of Mental Disorders* (*DSM–II* and *DSM–IV*, respectively).

disorders in and of themselves, except on very rare occasions. The whole idea of sleep disorders being mental disorders was generally rejected in the *DSM–II*. Instead, sleep problems were conceptualized as manifestations of physical conditions such as medical illness, or occasionally they were secondary side effects of mental disorders. This conceptualization of sleep problems reduced the number of sleep problems that could be considered mental disorders. In fact and in retrospect, the adherence of the first two editions of the *DSM* to psychoanalytic theory actually constrained the number of mental disorders that could be separately listed (Houts, 2000). Contrast that older conceptualization of sleep problems with the proliferation of mental disorder diagnoses devoted to sleep problems in *DSM–IV*, the far right column of Table 2.2.

DSM–IV continued the expansion of DSM–III–R, where sleep disorders were first introduced as a new major category of mental disorders to be coded on Axis I. Note that DSM–III did not contain a separate section devoted specifically to sleep disorders. The former DSM–II Disorder of Sleep diagnosis went away. DSM–III listed only Sleepwalking Disorder and Sleep Terror Disorder within the section on childhood disorders. Moreover, DSM–III (American Psychiatric Association, 1980) contained the following explanatory note regarding the listing of only two sleep disorders:

> Of the many disorders of sleep, DSM–III includes only these two because of their marked behavioral manifestations, because of the frequency with which they come to the attention of a mental health professional, and because by tradition, they are thought of as mental disorders. (A new classification of Sleep and Arousal Disorders appears in Appendix E.) (p. 383)

The authors of DSM–III made an explicit statement that whereas there were other kinds of sleep problems, in DSM–III as in DSM–II, these other sleep problems were not considered mental disorders. In fact, the authors of DSM–III reproduced as an appendix the 1979 version of the classification of sleep disorders previously published by the Sleep Disorders Classification Committee of the Association of Sleep Disorder Centers (ASDC; ASDC & the Association for the Psychophysiological Study of Sleep, 1979). I have been told that the ASDC nomenclature was published as an appendix in DSM–III because the manual had already gone to press and that it was therefore too late to include the ASDC taxonomy in the body of the text (P. J. Hauri, personal communication, March 29, 2000). Similar to the infighting between American psychiatry and the WHO regarding the DSMs and the ICDs, the background stories of the political and territorial disputes between sleep medicine specialists and organized psychiatry have yet to be told. In any case, the DSM–III approach to sleep problems was very similar to that seen in DSM–II by minimizing the sleep problems that should be regarded as mental disorders, and this approach can be contrasted with the approach of DSM–IV.

If one considers all the permutations of the 14 types of sleep disorder listed in DSM–IV and displayed in Table 2.2, the codeable number of distinct mental disorder diagnoses for sleep problems increased into the hundreds. None of these appeared in DSM–II. This marked proliferation of mental disorders from DSM–II to DSM–IV is altogether different from the mere number changes that occurred within the ICDs. What could account for this increase of mental disorders under the heading of sleep disorders?

Manufacture of Mental Disorders and the Case of Sleep Disorders

As might be expected from the influence of the grand narrative of discovery and progress, the current state of affairs is very often reconstructed to appear to be the inevitable outcome of a prior history. In this way, history is actually distorted to serve the purpose of a story of progress. Just such distortion of the historical record can be illustrated in the case of Wakefield's (1999b) claims about the relationship between sleep disorders in the *DSM–II* and *DSM–IV*. Wakefield has asserted that the increase in mental disorders seen over sequential editions of the modern *DSMs* has been the same phenomenon as the so-called increase in medical diagnoses observed over sequential editions of the *ICDs*. He stated,

> In fact, a cursory examination of the changes from the DSM–II to the DSM–IV reveals that a widening of the scope of disorder *cannot* be a major cause of the increase in categories. Mostly, the increase is due —exactly as in the physical medicine specialties—to making finer distinctions among conditions already considered disorders. . . . The DSM–II's one category for "disorders of sleep" is replaced by 15 [sic] DSM–IV categories, from primary insomnia to breathing-related sleep difficulties, all of which would have been diagnosed as DSM–II disorders of sleep. (p. 980)

Wakefield's general point has been that expansion of the modern *DSMs* is qualitatively the same as the changes in the *ICDs*, and he attempted to illustrate this claim by looking backward from *DSM–IV* and reading into *DSM–II* those disorders found only in *DSM–IV*. The claim was quite explicit, even though no references were cited to back up the general claim or the specific cases mentioned, such as sleep disorders. As Wakefield (1999b) stated,

> Unlike the ICD categories noted by Houts and Follette (1998), most of the new DSM categories were not explicitly mentioned as uncoded variations in the DSM–II, although some were passingly referred to in the text (e.g., four new DSM–IV categories of dissociative disorder were mentioned in DSM–II's description of its category of hysterical neurosis, dissociative type). However, this is a matter of style, not substance. In the vast majority of cases, either the textbooks at the time of DSM–II clearly indicated that the undifferentiated conditions were considered to fall under the coded categories, or we can confidently infer that a condition unrecognized at the time would have been so categorized. The point is that, just as in Follette and Houts's explanation of the changes in ICD, the new DSM categories did not represent an expansion of the domain of disorder but rather a refinement of diagnostic distinctions among disorders. (p. 981)

I have shown this claim to be false in the case of sleep disorders

(Houts, 2001a). *DSM–III* clearly stated that it did not include most sleep disorders because they were not considered to be mental disorders. The reasons that only two sleep problems (sleep walking and sleep terror) were considered mental disorders in *DSM–III* were threefold: (a) marked behavioral manifestation, (b) their treatment by mental health professionals, and (c) tradition. Did any of these conditions change in the following 6 years to justify inclusion of some new sleep problems as new mental disorders in *DSM–III–R*? This is hardly likely.

I examined textbooks from the period surrounding *DSM–II* in the late 1960s and compared them as they progressed through various editions of the modern *DSMs*. In the period surrounding *DSM–II*, there was little or no mention of sleep disorders, and this was consistent with their relative lack of importance in *DSM–I* and *DSM–II*. In fact, there is not a shred of evidence that sleep problems that are today recognized to be sleep disorders would have been recognized as mental disorders and classified under the *DSM–II* diagnosis of Disorder of Sleep, with the possible exception of sleepwalking and night terrors.

Wakefield's claim that there has been continuity and gradual elaboration of sleep disorders as mental disorders, his analogy to the *ICD* changes for physical disorders, is false. There was little or no continuity, nor was there some gradual detailing and exposition of categories with finer and finer discrimination in the classification of sleep disorders. The real history simply presents a different story. In fact, before *DSM–III–R*, sleep disorders were not generally regarded to be mental disorders at all. The declaration that sleep disorders were mental disorders occurred with *DSM–III–R* and was elaborated in *DSM–IV*. One searches in vain for the breakthrough research that demonstrated that finally after over 40 years, these sleep problems were in fact found to be mental disorders. It is as though sleep problems became mental disorders overnight sometime in 1987. How did we end up with so many new mental disorders suddenly overnight? Was this a bad dream?

One answer is that organized psychiatry in the form of the American Psychiatric Association Work Group to Revise *DSM–III* voted to declare that the sleep disorders that had formerly been presented as an appendix in *DSM–III* were promoted to a new section of mental disorders for Axis I in *DSM–III–R*. Voting, not theory or research, made sleep disorders into mental disorders sometime between 1985 and 1987 (American Psychiatric Association, 1985). This familiar procedure for moving disorders from speculative status into full inclusion without any clear standards has been noted by critics of the modern *DSMs* (Blashfield, Sprock, & Fuller, 1990). *DSM–IV* has classified as separate mental disorders those sleep problems related to medical conditions, those related to other psychiatric conditions, and those related to substance use. This is analogous to claiming that fever caused by measles is a separate disorder from fever caused by typhoid. Fever is a symptom of both diseases and not itself a separate disease.

The case of sleep disorders has illustrated very clearly the considerable discontinuity in the classification of mental disorders from *DSM–I* to *DSM–IV*. Moreover, this kind of discontinuity is not found in the *ICD*s over the equivalent period. What has happened in the classification of mental disorders is very different from what has happened in the case of medical disorders.

Physical Medicine, Mental Medicine, and Hempel's Ideals Revisited

What in fact has gone on in physical medicine? Are the modest additions of disease labels observed in the *ICD*s and exemplified in the aforementioned discussion and analysis clear counterexamples of a Hempelian model of scientific progress? What do we mean when we say that medicine has progressed scientifically, and by what means has that progress been achieved?

What has happened in the history of physical medicine is rather complicated and subject to different levels of analysis than is revealed by a mere inspection of *ICD* labels from *ICD–8* to *ICD–10*. In physical medicine, one can see a technologically driven process where new refinements of existing disease conditions were added because of greater acuity in the instrumentation used to conduct physiological and functional examination. A parallel process very rarely occurred in the modern *DSM*s; on the contrary, the modern *DSM*s added numerous new mental disorders without any input from some refinement in diagnostic technical acuity (e.g., Frotteurism, Identity Problem, Intermittent Explosive Disorder, Kleptomania, Mathematics Disorder, Nightmare Disorder, Pathological Gambling, Sexual Disorder NOS, Voyeurism, and Unspecified Mental Disorder [nonpsychotic]). As the previous analytic comparison between the *ICD* sections on chronic ischemic heart disease and the *DSM* sections on sleep disorder showed, the quantity and quality of diagnostic label change in physical medicine is very different from the expansion of the *DSM*s.

If we take into account the long history of physical medicine preceding the *ICD*s, there is a sense in which modern disease nomenclature reflected in the *ICD*s has in fact produced a theoretical reduction of disease labels. For example, the discovery of infectious microbes and viruses greatly reduced the domain of illnesses classified by symptom topography alone. The clinical science of medicine progressed from a classification of physical symptoms to a classification of etiologies because of advances in basic research in microbiology. Research in basic sciences such as endocrinology, immunology, and molecular genetics extended the concept of disease as deviation from physiological norms and accounted for numerous diseases that were classified as failures of normal physiological functioning. Although the etiology of many of these latter conditions remains unclear, objective physiological reference points define such conditions as hypertension. Now, numerous types of cancer are classified according to cell type, for example. However, we can anticipate that such classification will recede into the background in terms of importance when the more specific genetic mechanism abnormalities that produce each type of cell are discovered. Eventually and perhaps in the not-too-distant future, cancers will be classified by etiological process rather than physical topographical appearance. That is the kind of theoretical reduction predicted under a Hempelian model of scientific progress in taxonomy. Physical medicine has shown signs of reduction in disease labels that are consistent with a Hempelian model of progress in taxonomy, but these signs have been distinctly more subtle than can be detected directly by examination of changes within the limited window from *ICD–8* to *ICD–10*.

The contrast between physical disorders and mental disorders can be further illustrated by considering the work of Scadding and what I refer to as Scadding's ladder of scientific development in clinical taxonomy.

Scadding's Ladder of Taxonomic Knowledge in Medicine

Scadding (1988, 1990, 1996) recognized that a hierarchy existed in the development of disease concepts in medicine and that changes in the naming of diseases often reflected this hierarchy. Scadding's ladder is illustrated in Figures 2.5 and 2.6. According to this view of the history of medicine, disorders were first specified in terms of signs and symptoms. Scadding regarded this elementary clinical syndrome level of analysis to be a mere starting point. Specifically, he regarded most psychiatric disorders as remaining at this primitive stage of development. A second level of development in the accumulation of knowledge about disorders and the naming of them was evident when mere syndromal description was

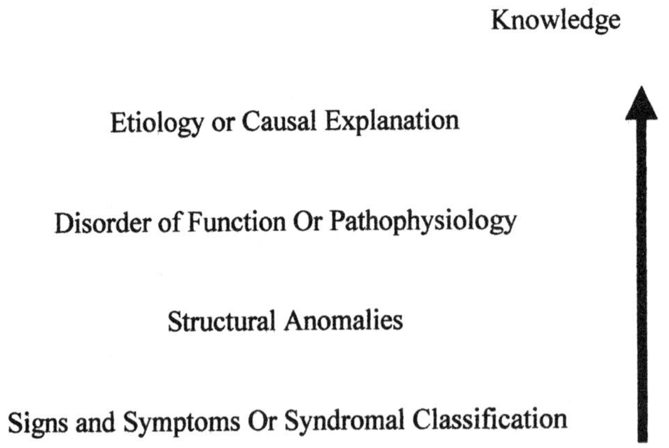

Knowledge

Etiology or Causal Explanation

Disorder of Function Or Pathophysiology

Structural Anomalies

Signs and Symptoms Or Syndromal Classification

Figure 2.5. Scadding's Ladder of Medical Disorder Diagnostic Knowledge

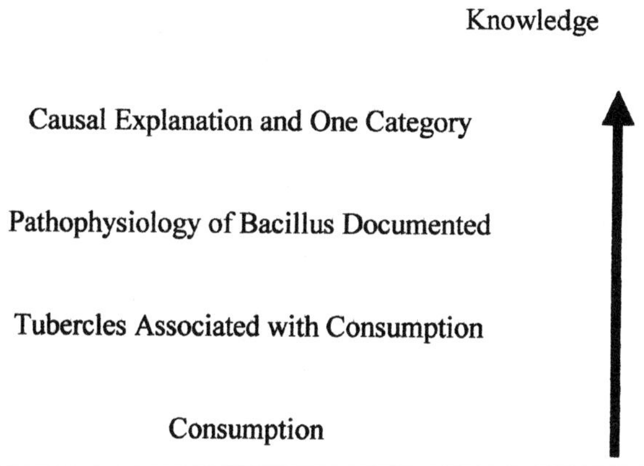

Knowledge

Causal Explanation and One Category

Pathophysiology of Bacillus Documented

Tubercles Associated with Consumption

Consumption

Figure 2.6. Tuberculosis on Scadding's Ladder

replaced by associated structural anomalies, as when the knowledge of tubercles was associated with the syndromally defined early description of tuberculosis (or consumption). A third level in the hierarchy of knowledge about diseases was discovery of disorder of function or of pathophysiology. Finally, according to Scadding, what medical nosology aimed for was etiology, to identify what caused the deformation or morbid structure and to demonstrate what led to failed functions, as when the tubercle bacillus was isolated. In the case of tuberculosis, Scadding noted that the identification of the cause of the syndromally defined disorder and of the morbid structure defined disorder led to a reduction in disease labels: "This led to the unification of a number of diseases previously defined syndromally or morbid-anatomically into a single aetiologically defined category" (1988, p. 124).

This broad historical description of the development of medical diagnosis stands in sharp contrast to the expansion of labels for mental disorders in successive editions of the modern *DSMs*. Furthermore, if the Scadding type of developmental analysis is correct regarding medical disorders, and I think that it generally squares with the historical evidence, then various appeals to medical analogies to defend the label proliferation of the modern *DSMs* are misguided. According to Scadding's developmental analysis of progress in medicine, progress would occur, not when syndromally defined disorders proliferate as in the modern *DSMs*, but when syndromally defined disorders are reduced by etiological explanation. Here again, we see a rather marked difference between the history of physical disorder classification and the recent history of mental disorder classification exemplified in the modern *DSMs*.

Scadding's developmental analysis of knowledge and the naming of disorders within medicine also clarifies Wakefield's recent attempts to rescue current psychiatric disorders from the charge that they are not objective. Viewed within Scadding's framework, what Wakefield has attempted to do in harmful dysfunction analysis is to move the concept of mental disorder from the elementary and beginning conceptualization of a syndrome to the next level of analysis wherein disorders are defined by the presence of a dysfunction (Wakefield, 1992a, 1992b). In the actual history of physical medicine, this transition from a focus on syndrome to a focus on broken function took place not by verbal decree but by amassing evidence for broken functions. In the course of defending and improving the modern DSMs, what Wakefield has proposed is a mere edict that disorders in the modern DSMs are there because they have associated dysfunctions (Wakefield, 1999a, 1999b). Such a rhetorical move is certainly understandable in light of Scadding's analysis because making such a move does in fact take us one step closer to a more objective definition for mental disorders. The difference between what has happened with harmful dysfunction analysis and the modern DSMs and what has happened in physical medicine is striking. Physical medicine made such a transition when the knowledge of pathological function was amassed for a given syndromally defined disorder. In contrast, harmful dysfunction analysis has made the transition, but it has done so without the requisite scientific evidence. This amounts to science by some other means rather than science by normal evidentiary toil and investigation.

To summarize: We can say that the mental medicine and physical medicine analogy does not hold empirically when you compare ICD changes to the DSM expansion. Moreover, in a broader framework of historical development, the expansion of the DSMs is not parallel to the hierarchical development of knowledge observed in the history of physical medicine as exemplified by Scadding's ladder. Finally, we have to consider the claim that mental disorders and medical disorders are defined basically identically or in parallel fashion. This claim has been advanced most consistently by Wakefield in elaborating his harmful dysfunction approach to defining mental disorders. The question is this: Does the harmful dysfunction approach to defining mental disorders render mental disorders somehow analogous or parallel to medical disorders? Recall that in the overall scheme of the discovery narrative, this matters because the framers of the modern DSMs and their proponents want to claim the mantle of scientific progress associated with physical medicine, and one way to do this is to say that mental disorders are medical disorders.

Problems of Harmful Dysfunction Analysis

Physical medicine has followed a different path of development than has official mental health diagnosis. The modern DSMs have introduced labels for mental disorders on the basis of committee voting rather than on the basis of known etiology or objectively defined failures of functioning. Wakefield (1999b) has argued that the modern *DSMs* have been scientifically progressive because they have approached the issue of mental disorders as objectively defined behavioral signs that may be attributed to some plausible dysfunction. Wakefield's concept of "plausible dysfunction" is altogether inadequate because his procedures for inferring dysfunction are not epistemologically sound, and the dysfunctions he manufactures are not ontologically grounded.

Epistemological Problems of Harmful Dysfunction Analysis

The epistemological problem is one of abductive inference. The line of reasoning Wakefield has proposed for inferring that some set of syndromally defined behaviors constitute a mental disorder is as follows.

> The surprising set of behaviors, C (disorder), is observed;
> But if A were broken (dysfunction), C would be the expected result,
> Hence, there is reason to suspect that A is broken.

The key issue is this: What is the basis for claiming that when A is broken, the result is C, the observed set of behaviors? For this type of argument to be valid, we would need independent evidence that the hypothetical statement "if A were broken, C would be the expected result" was in fact true. We would need to know that when you break A, this causes C, and breaking A reliably produces the outcome C. For most of the mental disorders listed in the modern *DSMs*, we have no such evidence. (Certain organic brain syndromes and substance use problems may be the only exceptions.) The fact is, without such independent evidence for a causal relationship between the broken hypothetical mechanism and the observed behavior, this line of reasoning is tautological, entirely circular (Houts, 2001a; Houts & Follette, 1998). Not only is the procedure for making inferences to dysfunctions flawed within harmful dysfunction analysis, the kinds of dysfunctions that are permitted often lack any material objectivity that is analogous to the kinds of broken functions that are used to define disorders within physical medicine.

Ontological Problems of Harmful Dysfunction Analysis

The ontological problems of harmful dysfunction analysis are evident when one examines the kind of mechanisms Wakefield has considered to be plausible. For example, he has claimed that agraphia is caused by broken "mechanisms that enable children to learn to write" (Wakefield, 1996, p. 649). Depression is supposedly caused by broken "loss–response mechanisms" (Wakefield, 1998b), and pica is caused by broken mechanisms designed to constrain "food choices." Such ad hoc appeals to freely invented mechanisms illustrate the serious problems with harmful dysfunction analysis related to the lack of constraints on the plausibility clause of so-called plausible dysfunctions. Without physiological and material constraints, one is free to invent all manner of so-called broken mechanisms to justify calling correlated behaviors mental disorders.

On the whole, then, serious doubts can be raised about the extent to which the recent history of the modern *DSMs* can be accurately fitted to a grand narrative of scientific discovery. To be sure, there have been some substantial gains in scientific knowledge within certain domains covered by the modern *DSMs*. However, if one takes a broad look throughout *DSM–IV* and measures the 368 diagnoses listed against a strict criterion of verified broken causal functions, not many of the disorders listed measure up. The expansion of the modern *DSMs* is not consistent with the model of scientific progress espoused in logical empiricism, and the comparison of the *DSM* expansion to changes in physical disorder diagnoses in medicine shows that the *DSM* expansion is quite different from the history of physical medicine. Another way of looking at the *DSM* expansion is worth exploring, and I have given this the provocative label *social invention narrative*.

SOCIAL INVENTION AND THE MODERN *DSMS*

What if we take a different strategy and examine the modern *DSM* expansion from the standpoint of another narrative, a social invention narrative? Here the task requires laying out an alternative story as a tool of interpretation. We can then ask, How does the expansion of the *DSM* fit or fail to fit with this alternative approach? Once again, the task is to try to make sense out of the fact that we have a 300% increase in the number of diagnoses for mental health problems in the past four decades alone.

A Social Invention Narrative

Steeped in positivistic philosophies of science, most mental health professionals have assumed that scientific knowledge is achieved primarily through accumulation of observations about deviant behavior. The free play of imagination and the wild speculation of the poet or novelist may be useful for manufacturing aesthetically pleasing forms of entertainment, but not for producing trustworthy scientific knowledge. Whereas invention may be the modus operandi of artistic creation, discovery is the modus operandi of scientific progress. This distinction, canonized in C. P. Snow's (1959) two cultures (the literary and the scientific), has been widely accepted in our academic institutions and in popular culture.

Prompted by recent postmodernist critiques of scientific ideals, scholars in the interdisciplinary field of science and technology have begun to raise serious questions about the wisdom of this once strict demarcation between discovery and invention. Now in retrospect, even eminent scientists such as Einstein had reservations about such a distinction. In a letter (dated January 6, 1948) to his friend Michele Besso, Albert Einstein offered the following observation about invention and discovery in commenting on the positivistic philosophy of Ernst Mach:

> Mach's weakness, as I see it, lies in the fact that he believed more or less strongly, that science consists merely of putting experimental results in order; that is, he did not recognize the free constructive element in the creation of a concept. He thought that somehow theories arise by means of *discovery* [durch Entdeckung] and not by means of *invention* [nicht durch Erfindung]. (quoted in A. I. Miller, 1984, p. 4; emphasis in original)

Einstein was speaking of the role of the individual scientist and the relative importance of discovery and invention in the context of the solitary theoretician. What is important for understanding the *DSM* expansion according to some narrative other than a traditional discovery narrative is that invention is part of a social process. We are interested in social invention rather than individual cognitive invention.

Some Philosophical Assumptions of a Social Invention Narrative

Important foci of this view of scientific activity are the contexts in which that activity happens: the scientist's history, social context, philosophy, purpose, and so on. From the standpoint of a social invention narrative, there can be no one true, correct, or right model of psychopathology. The truth of a scientific position is not to be found in its correspondence to an objective world, alone and cut off from the scientist. Instead, the truth of some scientific claim is found in the coherence or workability of the claim. What is true is what people find useful, and finding it useful makes it true. The concept of "objective truth" as the correspondence between our claims and "the real world" is replaced by a concept of pragmatic truth where claims are judged on their utility and evaluated against specified aims, values, and goals.

To a traditional scientist and especially to a traditional philosopher of science, this is a very bizarre point of view. In its more extreme forms, a social invention narrative is likely to be dismissed as being "crackpot" insofar as it is interpreted as denying such obvious facts as that there is a world apart from our interactions with it and that science has been a form of progressive knowledge. Critiques of various social invention perspectives have been offered by scientists and other thinkers (Gross & Levitt, 1994; Hacking, 1999; Weinberg, 1992; Wolpert, 1992). The present brief exposition is not an endorsement of either extreme view but is merely an exercise in critical perspective taking on the question of how we might make sense of the expansion of the *DSM* over the past 40 years.

Science as Social Behavior

Recent sociological and ethnomethodological analyses of scientific activity have developed the notion that science itself is human action influenced by the situation in which scientific behavior occurs. From these viewpoints, science is profoundly social, or to put it more extremely, science is social all the way down because there is no bedrock of nature apart from our social consensus on the matter. Scientific knowledge is understood as the product of the practices of research communities. Nature is as solid as our practices make it out to be. The solidity of nature is a reflection of social solidarity among those who make pronouncements about nature. Scientific knowledge is said to be literally manufactured (Knorr-Cetina, 1981; Latour & Woolgar, 1986; Pickering, 1984, 1992). From this standpoint, theories of knowledge are forms of social organization (Fuller, 1988), and claims to knowledge mobilize material and social resources (Fuller, 1997; Latour, 1987; Rouse, 1987). What knowledge claims come to be taken as verified depend not so much on their correspondence to so-called "facts of the matter," but on the social judgments of the scientific community at a particular time and place and for a particular purpose. For example, Fuller (1995) has commented as follows regarding the significance of consensus in a scientific community:

> The temptation to treat science's "uniformity" as bearing the mark of "nature" or "truth" often reflects a failure to appreciate science's underlying social complexity. For example, does the absence of explicit disagreement over a theory or result warrant the conclusion that some deep "consensus" of belief obtains among members of the scientific community? Would it not make more empirical sense to examine institutional mechanisms that discourage scientists from contesting claims beyond a certain point, and then ask why these mechanisms seem to work so effectively? Here an account of the differences in how scientists and other academics are trained would explain a lot. How do scientists become predisposed to find certain displays of epistemic authority persuasive and others not? How do scientists master a common writing style that enables them to translate the idiosyncrasies of their work situations into moments in a narrative common to other workers in their field? Is there anything more to the "uniformity" of science than these factors taken together, as continually reinforced by various gatekeeping practices? (p. 311)

This new look at the activities of scientists is useful for understanding the expansion of the *DSM* as belonging to a narrative of invention rather than to a narrative of discovery. The truth criteria of such approaches are pragmatic. Because there is no assumption of a "true" world of parts, the validity of categorical concepts is measured not in terms of correspondence or fit but in terms of how well the concepts facilitate work toward certain goals.

Pragmatic Effects of Diagnoses

To apply a social invention perspective to the expansion of the DSMs, it is useful to treat diagnosis as a practice. A first step is to ask, At a pragmatic level, what does diagnosis, the activity, do? Notice that this is asking about diagnosis as a verb or a practice rather than a noun or a thing. The answer regarding diagnosis as an activity is that diagnosis does many things to and for many people. At a minimum, there are three parties involved in the practice of diagnosis. First, there is a specific patient to whom the diagnosis is applied. Second, there is the mental health professional who applies the diagnosis. Finally, there is a third party called the *society*, or others (e.g., relatives of the patient, hospital staffs, insurance companies, pharmaceutical manufacturers, the media, courts) for whom the practice of diagnosis has consequences. The focus is on the functions of diagnosing and diagnoses, especially those social consequences that may be reinforcing and that may increase the likelihood for new diagnoses to be invented and applied. The current focus is on diagnosis as a behavior that produces consequences. The question is as follows: What consequences could account for the observation that the practice of diagnosis is growing rather than diminishing? What is needed is a rudimentary operational analysis (Houts, 1994).

Diagnosis as a Solution to Social Problems

Applying a diagnosis solves several social problems. Often, an individual comes to the attention of mental health professionals because he or she has created a social disturbance. The disturbance may be as large as scaring an entire community or as small as irritating a spouse or other family member. The application of a diagnosis to the offending individual may then function to justify intervention by mental health professionals. As far as those who were disturbed are concerned, their social problem is solved when the disturbing person is either removed or changed. In this way, the act of diagnosis has positive consequences for those who have been disturbed by the distressing behavior of the patient. The more diagnoses we have at our disposal, the more options we have to bring relief to those who benefit from including disturbing behavior under the authority and sanction of mental health practitioners.

Leaving aside whether diagnosis with the DSM leads to improved treatment (and in some instances it certainly does), the application of a diagnosis may also accomplish some things for the person who gets diagnosed. For example, receiving a diagnosis often entitles the person to get social services that might otherwise not be available or that might not be paid for by a third party. Receiving a diagnosis may be personally comforting to the extent that it provides an individual with a kind of "explanation" for behaviors or feelings that are upsetting even to oneself. The popularity of the phrase *chemical imbalance* attests to the comfort providing function of diagnosis (Valenstein, 1998). It is now commonplace to see public advertisements like the following one that was jointly sponsored by patient advocacy groups and mental health providers during Mental Illness Awareness Week in Memphis, Tennessee in 1989: "Obsessive–compulsive disorder and other mental illnesses are biologically-rooted diseases, and are no more shameful than other medical illnesses, such as high blood pressure, diabetes, or heart disease" (West Tennessee Psychiatric Association & the Mental Health Society of Memphis and Shelby County, 1989). This illustrates an attempt to make obsessive–compulsive behaviors less a matter of shameful personal responsibility or failing in character and more of a medical condition for which the individual should assume less personal responsibility. By medicalizing the behaviors, the person is entitled to the sick role, a positive feature of which is to remove personal blame (Conrad & Schneider, 1985). Receiving a diagnosis may also excuse a person from acts for which they might otherwise be held responsible or even punished. The growth of diagnostic systems suggests that social benefits outweigh social costs, at least from the vantage point of some of the involved parties. To be sure, there are legitimate concerns about the negative social effects of diagnosis such as stigma for the diagnosed person, but a fair analysis of the practice of diagnosis must include the positive consequences of the act even for the diagnosed person.

Diagnosis as a Palliative for Professional Discomfort

What about the social consequences of applying psychiatric diagnoses for the mental health professional as practitioner and researcher? Applying a diagnosis can bring relief to the practitioner who is otherwise confused by the behavior of the patient. Thus, applying the diagnosis relieves distress in the mental health professional. Millon (1986) noted that "the success of categorical taxa may be traced to the ease with which clinicians can use them in making rapid diagnoses with numerous briefly seen patients" (p. 26). In some cases, applying the diagnosis may also dictate a prescribed course of action that the practitioner can follow. Insurance companies typically make payment for services contingent on providing a diagnosis, thus enabling practitioners to be paid. The more diagnoses we have available for use, the more we have access to these positive social functions of providing diagnoses.

Diagnosis as Organizer and Provider of Professional Identity

The practice of diagnosis can also make research easier to conduct and support, even if the quality of the research might be challenged. Persons (1986) has called attention to the ubiquity of what she has termed *diagnostic category designs* (p. 1253) in research literature. Diagnostic category designs simply compare samples of patients from one diagnostic category with samples from another category (including controls). The benefit of diagnostic category designs is that researchers may readily identify populations of patients for study and compare them to other presumably different populations. Such approaches to research fit rather neatly into common habits of testing average group differences against a null hypothesis, and they often generate statistically significant and therefore publishable results. For example, searching for differences between a group of people who have sought mental health treatment and met criteria for some diagnosis as contrasted to a group of people who have not sought treatment and do not meet criteria for the diagnosis in question can be especially misleading. This type of research design to compare a diagnostic category group with a "normal" control group is virtually guaranteed to find some difference between the two groups if for no other reason than the fact that individuals who seek services are likely to have multiple problems that distinguish them from those who do not seek services. The differences between two such groups may be due to a statistical artifact or sampling bias known as *Berkson's bias* or *Berkson's fallacy* (Berkson, 1946). The point is, the research results may be of doubtful reliability and validity, but publishable results are virtually guaranteed with such designs. Again, publishing is the coin of the realm in research communities, and promoting this type of highly publishable research also promotes the practice of diagnosis.

As Persons (1986) has pointed out, diagnostic category designs typically lead researchers away from studying specific problem behaviors or "symptoms" that in the first place led them to place an individual in one or another diagnostic category. For example, instead of examining different types of thought disorder and their controlling variables, researchers are led to study "schizophrenia." Expanding the available number of diagnoses extends the practice of diagnosis to include more and more human behaviors, thereby extending the scope of research that is acceptable, publishable, and fundable.

Another way that the practice of diagnosis makes research easier to conduct concerns public acceptance and funding of research work. Having diagnostic labels for sets of behaviors facilitates funding agencies' calls for research proposals. Funding for mental health research has been organized around diagnoses at the National Institute of Mental Health and the National Institutes of Health. Various study sections may be organized around diagnostic categories. Researchers and research groups now frequently identify themselves with a particular diagnostic label. Having more diagnostic labels also provides researchers with professional identities and areas of expertise that may justify their receiving grants. This research-facilitating role of expanding diagnostic labels was clearly stated in the controversial Appendix A of *DSM–III–R*, where Late Luteal Phase Dysphoric Disorder (Pre-Menstrual Syndrome), Sadistic Personality Disorder, and Self-defeating Personality Disorder were introduced "to facilitate further systematic clinical study and research" (American Psychiatric Association, 1987, p. 367).

Diagnosis as a Marketing Tool

Diagnosis has become a marketing strategy for the pharmaceutical manufacturers. As advertisements for prescription medications have moved increasingly into direct marketing to consumers rather than the previous practice of marketing to the professionals who write the prescriptions, manufacturers of psychotropic medications have learned to endorse diagnoses to market their products. Having new diagnoses or new names for old diagnoses makes this marketing effort more successful. The makers of various serotonin re-uptake inhibitors have been particularly adept at this. Eli Lilly, the maker of Prozac, has consistently supported a national depression screening day. Medical doctors' offices frequently contain promotional materials in the form of questionnaires for emotional problems that encourage medical patients to ask their doctor about such problems if they answer a certain number of questions in the correct direction. Such advertising rarely mentions the drug being promoted, but the condition or diagnosis for which the drug is a problem is clearly promoted. The following story appeared in the *Wall Street Journal* and describes the marketing of obsessive–compulsive disorder as a means to market the drug Luvox.

- In the coming months, OCD (obsessive–compulsive disorder) will be talked about everywhere. Brochures about it will sprout in doctor's offices. A prominent Washington scholar will release a study declaring that OCD costs the US economy $8 billion a year. Doctors who specialize in it will start appearing on talk shows and giving newspaper interviews.
- OCD's sudden burst into public awareness will result from a careful strategy by two giant drug companies, Upjohn Co. of Kalamazoo, Mich., and the Belgian firm Solvay SA.
- The drug companies typically leave few fingerprints, running their disease campaigns through PR firms, patient groups, "institutes" and other third parties. They may discretely identify a corporate sponsor, but seldom a specific drug.
- Solvay and Upjohn designed a campaign to emphasize OCD's severity and biological basis—both, not coincidentally, per-

suasive reasons to treat it with drugs. (M. W. Miller, 1994, p. A1)

The diagnosis is marketed, and so, too, is a particular view about the nature of mental disorders.

Diagnosis can be thought of as a social practice, with a broad range of impacts. Given the funding structures of the mental health industry and the growing numbers of mental health professionals, diagnosis on the basis of form or structure is not likely to decrease, and the invention of new diagnostic labels justified by formal distinctions is likely to continue as we look toward *DSM–V* to *DSM–X*.

Diagnosis as a Generator of Profits for the American Psychiatric Association

As noted before, some commentators have alleged that the production of new revisions of the *DSM* may have become a profitable enterprise in its own right (Caplan, 1995; Kendell, 1991; Kirk & Kutchins, 1992; Kutchins & Kirk, 1997; Wylie, 1995; Zimmerman, 1990). Each addition of a new diagnostic label to the *DSM* expands the practice of diagnosis, and each new edition of the manual guarantees a new round of sales of the *DSM* book. Wylie (1995) noted that

> If success is measured in dollars, as it so often is in America, *DSM–IV* promises to be a very respectable cash cow. In the first 10 months of publication, about 458,000 copies were sold to the tune of roughly $18 million. (p. 25)

In addition to the actual sales of the *DSM* book, there has arisen a small industry of DSM-related materials. With each new edition of the *DSM* come various workshops and continuing education seminars for professionals to teach them how to use the latest version of the manual and to master the latest changes. Various books get revised and updated so that the economic spillover extends well beyond the mere publication of the *DSM* and the profits that accrue to the American Psychiatric Press. Indeed, this very chapter is an example of the expanding influence of the *DSM*, and I hope that I get a chance to revise this chapter and reap some benefits when the next major revision to the *DSM* is published.

It would be a serious mistake to assert that these social effects are the only reasons for expanding the *DSM* and issuing new editions of it. However, according to a social invention perspective on the matter, they are some of the reasons the expansion may have occurred. A social invention perspective can also be applied to the following two questions: (a) How do new diagnostic labels enter new editions of the *DSM*? and (b) How does the *DSM* revision process eliminate old labels for mental disorders?

New Diagnostic Labels in the DSM

New diagnostic labels enter new editions of the DSM by receiving the approval of the current Task Force appointed by the American Psychiatric Association to revise the DSM. The process has typically involved the issuing of a draft version of the proposed changes, and this draft version is circulated among mental health professionals for their comments and suggestions. For example, the draft version of DSM–IV (American Psychiatric Association, 1991) proposed some new diagnostic categories: (a) Telephone Scatalogia (p. L:8), (b) Minor Depressive Disorder (p. G:9), (c) Recurrent Brief Depressive Disorder (p. G:10), and (d) Binge Eating Disorder (p. N:3). From this sample of proposed new labels for mental disorders, only Telephone Scatalogia was eliminated. Rather than gaining full status as declared disorders in DSM–IV, the others were retained in the Appendix B (Criteria Sets and Axes Provided for Further Study). The practice of placing controversial new diagnoses in an appendix and designating them as in need of further study began with DSM–III–R and has continued in much expanded form with DSM–IV. In general, it is more likely for these new and not quite complete disorders to be promoted to full disorder status with later editions of the DSM than it is for them to be eliminated.

Mere voting is not all there is to this matter, but without the approval of the Task Force, new diagnoses do not appear. In the case of DSM–IV, some of the considerations and deliberations of the Task Force were recorded in the DSM–IV Guidebook authored by the framers of DSM–IV (A. Frances, First, & Pincus, 1995). One does not have to look far or wide to find that judgments about what constitutes a new mental disorder in DSM–IV were based on social factors. For example, A. Frances et al. noted that

> The ever-increasing number of new categories meant to describe the less impaired outpatient population raises the question of where psychopathology ends and the wear and tear of everyday life begin. DSM–IV answers this question somewhat tautologically by emphasizing the requirement that the condition cause clinically significant impairment or distress, but it does not clearly operationalize the term *clinical significance*. The evaluation of clinical significance is likely to vary in different cultures and to depend on the availability and interests of clinicians. (p. 15)

Here, then, is an open and quite frank recognition that some new diagnostic categories were decided on according to a criterion that is culturally relative to the changing judgments of mental health professionals. This type of procedure is not what is customarily meant by science-based decision making, and some commentators have specifically noted the problems with the clinical significance criterion (Spitzer & Wakefield, 1999).

The point of citing Frances et al. is not to disparage the efforts of the *DSM–IV* Task Force. For previous editions of the *DSM*, the task force's decisions about including new diagnoses were made primarily on the basis of "expert opinion" (Spitzer, 1991). Had they been made on the basis of empirical support from the research literature, Spitzer, the head of the task force for *DSM–III*, estimated that more than 200 diagnoses would not have been included (Spitzer, 1991). That reduction would have meant that *DSM–III* would have had fewer diagnoses than did *DSM–II*. As compared to previous *DSM* Task Forces, the *DSM–IV* Task Force went to considerable lengths to review research literature relevant to proposed new additions to the *DSM*.

Not only were decisions about specific new disorders based on socially variable criteria, the very phrase *mental disorder* was itself decided on in the context of social factors having to do with various professional rivalries. As A. Frances et al. (1995) noted,

> The use of the term *mental disorder* in the title of *DSM–IV* (*The Diagnostic and Statistical Manual of Mental Disorders*) is an anachronistic preservation of the Cartesian view. This term appears increasingly silly as we learn more and more about the physical correlates of thought, emotion, and psychopathology. The term most frequently suggested as an alternative to replace mental disorders has been *brain disorders*, but this is equally unfortunate and reductionist in the opposite extreme. Preferable terms for the universe of conditions defined in *DSM–IV* would be *psychiatric disorders* or *psychological disorders*, but neither of these is feasible because of the possible professional conflicts they might incite among psychiatrists, psychologists, and other mental health professionals. (p. 16)

In fact, an interesting history of conflict has developed between organized psychiatry and organized psychology on the issue of what to call mental disorders, and this controversy goes back to the early drafts of *DSM–III* in the late 1970s (Houts, 2001b).

What is important to see here is that throughout the manufacture of the *DSM*, people are making decisions and judgments in a social context. Whether or not a set of behaviors warrants a diagnostic label depends on culturally varying judgments about what is clinically significant. Even something as basic as what to call the very subject matter of the *DSM* depends on professional rivalries among mental health professionals. On close examination, those decisions and those judgments may not fit ordinary notions of scientific ideals where what is being sought is "truth" as opposed to mere consensus.

Once again and much to their credit for being so frank, A. Frances et al. (1995) have recognized the role of the task force in making "truth" by consensus:

One often asked question is how much of *DSM-IV* really is based on empirical evidence versus its being the result of the same kind of expert consensus that informed *DSM-III*, *DSM-III-R*, and *ICD-10*. For many issues this is a false dichotomy. Very rarely in any science, and almost never in the clinical science of psychiatry, do empirical data stand up and say "this is the only way I can be understood!" All scientific judgments require some combination of evidence and interpretation that results in the formulation of new hypotheses that are then subject to the collection of more evidence and interpretation, and so on. Although based on empirical data, *DSM-IV* decisions were the result of expert consensus on how best to interpret the data. (p. 34)

Each new edition of the *DSM* is always the product of the actions and opinions of the members of the task force in charge of making revisions. They in turn depend on various work groups that are appointed to review the literature, to solicit opinions from professionals in the field, to conduct field trials of various proposals, and to arrive at some consensus opinion that is forwarded to the task force.

As compared to previous revisions, where the social basis of the consensus of the task force was more obvious, *DSM-IV* attempted to be considerably more research based. For example, the authors of *DSM-III-R* openly acknowledged that their revisions of *DSM-III* were often based solely on clinical judgment rather than empirical studies as follows:

In attempting to evaluate proposals for revisions in the classification and criteria, or for adding new categories, the greatest weight was given to the presence of empirical support from well-conducted research studies, *though, for most proposals, data from empirical studies were lacking.* Therefore, primary importance was usually given to some other consideration, such as: clinical experience . . . . (American Psychiatric Association, 1987, p. xxi; emphasis added)

Elsewhere in the introduction to *DSM-III-R* it was noted that

Most advisory committee decisions were the result of a consensus that emerged among committee members. However, several controversies, particularly in the areas of childhood, psychotic, anxiety, and sleep disorders, could be resolved only by actually polling committee members. (American Psychiatric Association, 1987, p. xx)

From these statements one certainly gets the impression that for at least some portion of the decisions made in *DSM-III-R*, the type of data appealed to was testimony from experts, and when that testimony conflicted, balloting resolved the conflict.

Partly in response to these problems with *DSM-III* and *DSM-III-R*, the group that released *DSM-IV* highlighted its inclusion of data to assist in making their revisions to *DSM-III-R*. The authors of *DSM-IV* proclaimed, "More than any other nomenclature of mental disorders,

DSM–IV is grounded in empirical evidence" (American Psychiatric Association, 1994, p. xvi). In fact, the American Psychiatric Press, the publisher of the DSMs since 1980, has published a five-volume DSM–IV Sourcebook. These five volumes contained the 150 literature reviews, 40 data reanalyses, and 12 new field trials that were used to justify changes in DSM–IV. It is noteworthy that DSM–IV was released prior to releasing the evidence on which it was based. Presumably, that evidence is indeed far better and more extensive than the evidence supporting DSM–III–R.

Despite their concerted efforts to improve the DSM revision process, many of the latest changes in DSM–IV as compared to DSM–III–R cannot be explained without understanding the social factors and professional rivalries that impinge on the change process. For example, whole new axes, as well as new diagnoses, were introduced in Appendix B (Criteria Sets and Axes Provided for Further Study) of DSM–IV. The Defensive Functioning Scale has been proposed as a new axis. It consists of 31 defense mechanisms from which the clinician may note up to 7 at the time of evaluation. What is most interesting about this proposed new axis is that it introduces traditional psychoanalytic concepts and terms of defense mechanisms (e.g., repression, reaction formation, denial) that were explicitly rejected in DSM–III. As Klerman (1986) had foreseen, this was a political concession to the small but vocal minority of psychoanalysts who are members of the American Psychiatric Association and who have lobbied for such a scale since the late 1970s. Another new proposed scale in DSM–IV, the Global Assessment of Relational Functioning (GARF), appears to have been due to a similar effort to include family therapists. In this instance, A. Frances et al. were explicit about the reasons this new axis was proposed for further study:

> Practitioners with a primary interest in the family/systems approach to diagnosis and therapy have felt relatively disenfranchised by the DSM approach. The DSM system is by definition a classification of mental disorders as these present in individual patients. In contrast, family/ systems therapists often view the relational system (rather than any one individual involved in it) as the target of diagnosis and intervention. Therefore, they have been frustrated by the lack of utility of the DSM system for describing families seen in their practices. (p. 81)

When you consider the return of psychoanalytic defense mechanisms and the reason behind the introduction of the GARF, one of the rationales for adding new features to expand the scope of the DSM becomes clear: Make the DSM appeal to as many mental health professionals as possible. To put it another way: Make the DSM so all-inclusive that mental health professionals of all persuasions will join in and support rather than oppose the DSM.

Elimination of Old Labels for Mental Disorders

One problem with the DSM system that can be appreciated only if one looks historically at the various editions of the manual is that some diagnoses that entered the system by clinical judgment and even balloting have remained. New diagnoses may be based on empirical studies of such matters as incidence, course, and response to treatment rather than mere expert consensus judgment, but the diagnoses that entered the DSM system by way of collective judgment rarely disappear. The authors of DSM–IV have acknowledged that historical precedent was a factor in decisions to change DSM–III–R.

> An attempt was made to strike an optimal balance in DSM–IV with respect to historical tradition (as embodied in DSM–III and DSM–III–R), compatibility with ICD–10, evidence from reviews of the literature, analyses of unpublished data sets, results of field trials, and consensus of the field. (American Psychiatric Association, 1994, p. xx)

A problem with allowing historical precedent to determine whether to expunge a particular diagnosis is obvious when one remembers that the overall trend in subsequent revisions of the DSM is to expand the number of diagnoses. In anticipating DSM–IV, Carson (1991) noted the problems with accepting existing literature as the basis for making decisions about existing categories:

> The plan for DSM–IV involves more or less systematic reviews of research data and literature pertaining to patients already allocated to the established diagnostic groupings. This procedure has the character of self-fulfilling prophecy insofar as the major putative taxa are concerned. (p. 303)

Whereas it is certainly true that as compared to its predecessors DSM–IV is more soundly based on research evidence, it also contains a number of diagnostic labels that are based on expert consensus rather than on empirical studies of the reliability and validity of the diagnoses. Much of the so-called empirical evidence used to bolster DSM–IV has been amassed under the conditions of accepting diagnostic criteria that have not been tested against other criteria but that have made their way into the research literature by way of expert consensus and tradition.

Bayer and Spitzer (1985) described a similar process regarding DSM–III when a decision was made to drop the term *neurosis* from the DSM.

> The entire process of achieving a settlement seemed more appropriate to the encounter of political rivals than to the orderly pursuit of scientific knowledge. On each side of the controversy, it was held that

important scientific truths were at stake, and yet the situation had demanded, of those who found themselves in opposition, the adoption of strategic postures and the employment of the techniques of politics. ... Scientific politics is not a mere replica of more ordinary politics, but it is politics nevertheless. (p. 195)

The embrace of social agreement and negotiation as a means for identifying truth could not be clearer.

DSM–IV has made some advances with respect to questions of validity. Among the most important issues is discriminant validity. Do the DSM criteria for certain diagnoses, if followed, allow one to distinguish reliably between individuals in terms of their response to different treatments? This, after all, is the primary reason for having diagnoses in the first place. The answer to this question is sometimes yes and sometimes no, depending on which diagnoses one examines.

These observations do not show whether such approaches to mental health will eventually be successful. To date, however, the DSM system reflects more of the problems these approaches encounter than the successes. In DSM–III and DSM–III–R we find rather explicit rejection of theoretically derived processes as a means for organizing knowledge about mental disorders. Instead, form and structure, signs and symptoms, and social agreement about clinical judgments are the primary focus. The fit between this history of developments in official psychiatric nosologies and a grand narrative of scientific discovery and progress is poor. Perhaps the view that the process of adding and deleting diagnoses to and from the DSM is one more characteristic of social invention rather than scientific discovery is at least partly applicable even if it is not without its own problems.

Problems With a Social Invention Narrative

A social invention narrative is not without liabilities. First, if scientists admit that scientific behavior is not directed by objective truths, but rather by social forces that operate on and between scientists, then they may lose authority, status, and influence in the eyes of the public. A visit to the public information sector of the National Institute of Mental Health Web site points out the problem. There you will find a section on anxiety disorders, and the title is "Anxiety Disorders: Real Illnesses" (http://www.nimh.nih.gov/anxiety/realillness.cfm). The very idea that it is even necessary to emphasize the concept that social phobia, for example, is a real illness belies some concern about the scientific basis of diagnosis. Can you imagine a comparable site at the National Institutes of Health with a title like "Cardiovascular Disorders: Real Illnesses"? To openly acknowledge the social basis of knowledge claims in the mental health field makes scientific behavior much less special in society, a fact that may adversely affect funding for practitioners and researchers.

Second, it is somewhat disconcerting for scientists to ponder the possibility that what directs their scientific behavior is not too different from what directs the brand of cornflakes they purchase. One might suppose that many scientists are acculturated to the belief that there is Truth to be discovered and that thinking otherwise may seem nihilistic or solipsistic. Children learn "the scientific method" in junior high school, and it is recapitulated to them throughout most of their subsequent academic training. In that tradition, pure results lead the scientist, and not some less-pure set of social factors. Thus, the social acceptability of the invention narrative within the scientific community is a serious problem. Such a view may be no less palatable to society that expects its scientists to be above the vicissitudes that may bog down their personal lives. Mental health scientists and practitioners are expected to have real answers to difficult questions, not just any old answers.

One common objection to a social invention account of scientific developments is to raise the specter of relativism. This objection plays on a type of reduction to absurdity argument: A story that says what scientists do is not dictated by "facts" invites a scientific free-for-all. If utility is the criterion against which science is judged, then each scientist is free to say "it works for me." This type of rhetorical ploy can be countered. First, the charge of relativism only makes sense against some backdrop of nonrelativism or "objectivity." However, to assume an "objective realm" is to beg the question (Smith, 1988). Second, the charge of relativism is often conflated with a charge of indeterminism. But a major point of a social invention model is that concepts, methods, and claims to knowledge are in fact determined by the multiple variables that determine scientists' behaviors at a given time and place.

The problems with a social invention narrative or social invention model of the mental health field are more value-laden problems than empirical ones. As a matter of description of the field, the social invention model does fairly well in describing what has happened over the past four decades of expansion in official diagnosis. The major problem with a social invention model is that such a model tends to deflate the status of the field and to call into question the various rhetorical appeals to science and objectivity.

CONCLUSION

I have challenged some of the received views about how to think about the expansion of the modern DSMs as signifying scientific progress. I have proposed an alternative way of looking at the changes that have occurred and gave it the deliberately provocative title *social invention*. Lest the reader conclude that I do not regard mental disorders to be real, let me put that to rest. Mental disorders are real in the sense that they are real problems for people, and they are real challenges for professional practitioners and researchers. What concerns me is not the reality of mental disorders, but the scientific integrity of the mental health professions. I am a mental health professional, and I strongly believe that the mental health professions must base their practices on sound scientific foundations, at least the best science achievable.

The recent history of the modern *DSMs* does not represent the best that we can do, and the expansion of diagnoses for mental disorders raises serious questions about the extent to which we are engaged in self-promotion at the expense of reliable knowledge. Call me a moralist. Marginalize me as a crackpot social constructivist. The fact is, I believe our field, the mental health field, is in danger of being discredited because we entertain and promote the expansion of mental health diagnoses well beyond what might be warranted from a scientific knowledge base.

The idea of taking a social invention perspective seriously is not only meant to be provocative in the tradition of the Socratic gadfly, but it is also a call to come to grips with what may be happening in the mental health field. If we can understand the ways in which mental health diagnoses have proliferated, we may also understand how to intervene to correct the process. Blithely telling ourselves that we are merely engaged in scientific progress and that we are merely following in the footsteps of traditional physical medicine is not helpful because doing so furthers the status quo. What is needed instead is a means to distance ourselves from the process, to be scientific about our own behavior as well as the behavior of people we are called on to assist.

REFERENCES

Albert, H. (1985). *Treatise on critical reason.* Princeton, NJ: Princeton University Press.

Alexander, F., & Selesnick, S. T. (1968). *The history of psychiatry.* New York: New American Library.

American Psychiatric Association. (1952). *Diagnostic and statistical manual of mental disorders.* Washington, DC: Author.

American Psychiatric Association. (1968). *Diagnostic and statistical manual of mental disorders* (2nd ed.). Washington, DC: Author.

American Psychiatric Association. (1980). *Diagnostic and statistical manual of mental disorders* (3rd ed.). Washington, DC: Author.

American Psychiatric Association. (1985). *DSM–III–R in development.* Washington, DC: Author.

American Psychiatric Association. (1987). *Diagnostic and statistical manual of mental disorders* (3rd ed., rev.). Washington, DC: Author.

American Psychiatric Association, Task Force on DSM–IV. (1991). *DSM–IV options book: Work in progress (9/1/91)*. Washington, DC: Author.

American Psychiatric Association. (1994). *Diagnostic and statistical manual of mental disorders* (4th ed.). Washington, DC: Author.

American Psychiatric Association. (2000). *Diagnostic and statistical manual of mental disorders* (4th ed. text revision). Washington, DC: Author.

Andreasen, N. C., Flaum, M., & Arndt, S. (1992). The comprehensive assessment of symptoms and history (CASH): An instrument for assessing diagnosis and psychopathology. *Archives of General Psychiatry, 49*, 615–623.

Association of Sleep Disorders Centers and the Association for the Psychophysiological Study of Sleep. (1979). Diagnostic classification of sleep and arousal disorders (1st ed.). *Sleep, 2*, 1–154.

Bayer, R., & Spitzer, R. L. (1985). Neurosis, psychodynamics, and *DSM–III*: A history of the controversy. *Archives of General Psychiatry, 42*, 187–196.

Berkson, J. (1946). Limitations of the application of fourfold table analysis to hospital data. *Biometrics Bulletin, 2*, 47–53.

Blashfield, R. K. (1984). *The classification of psychopathology: Neo-Kraepelinian and quantitative approaches*. New York: Plenum Press.

Blashfield, R. K., Sprock, J., & Fuller, A. K. (1990). Suggested guidelines for including or excluding categories in the *DSM–IV*. *Comprehensive Psychiatry, 31*, 15–19.

Caplan, P. J. (1995). *They say you're crazy: How the world's most powerful psychiatrists decide who's normal*. Reading, MA: Addison-Wesley.

Carson, R. C. (1991). Dilemmas in the pathway of the *DSM–IV*. *Journal of Abnormal Psychology, 100*, 302–307.

Conrad, P., & Schneider, J. W. (1985). *Deviance and medicalization: From badness to sickness*. Columbus, OH: Merrill.

Cronbach, L. J., & Meehl, P. E. (1955). Construct validity in psychological tests. *Psychological Bulletin, 52*, 281–302.

Curtis, R. (1994). Narrative form and normative force: Baconian story-telling in popular science. *Social Studies of Science, 24*, 419–461.

Fink, P. J. (1988, July 1). Viewpoint [Editorial]. *Psychiatric News*, p. 3.

Follette, W. C., & Houts, A. C. (1996). Models of scientific progress and the role of theory in taxonomy development: A case study of the DSM. *Journal of Consulting and Clinical Psychology, 64*, 1120–1132.

Foucault, M. (1965). *Madness and civilization*. New York: Random House.

Frances, A., First, M. B., & Pincus, H. A. (1995). *DSM–IV guidebook*. Washington, DC: American Psychiatric Press.

Frances, A. J. (1994). Foreword. In J. Z. Sadler, O. P. Wiggins, & M. A. Schwartz (Eds.), *Philosophical perspectives on psychiatric diagnostic classification* (pp. vii–ix). Baltimore: Johns Hopkins University Press.

Fuller, S. (1988). *Social epistemology*. Bloomington: Indiana University Press.

Fuller, S. (1989). *Philosophy of science and its discontents*. New York: Westview.

Fuller, S. (1993). *Philosophy, rhetoric, and the end of knowledge: The coming of science and technology studies*. Madison: University of Wisconsin Press.

Fuller, S. (1995). From pox to pax?: Response to Labinger. *Social Studies of Science, 25*, 309–314.

Fuller, S. (1997). *Science*. Minneapolis: University of Minnesota Press.

Gilbert, G. N., & Mulkay, M. (1984). *Opening Pandora's box: A sociological analysis of scientists' discourse*. New York: Cambridge University Press.

Glass, R. M., & Vergare, M. J. (1994). Diagnosis and treatment of psychiatric disorders: A history of progress. *Journal of the American Medical Association, 272*, 1792.

Grob, G. N. (1991). Origins of DSM–I: A study in appearance and reality. *American Journal of Psychiatry, 148*, 421–431.

Gross, P. R., & Levitt, N. (1994). *Higher superstition: The academic left and its quarrel with science*. Baltimore: Johns Hopkins University Press.

Guze, S. B. (1995). Review of the book *Diagnostic and statistical manual of mental disorders, 4th ed. (DSM–IV)*. *American Journal of Psychiatry, 152*, 1228.

Hacking, I. (1999). *The social construction of what?* Cambridge, MA: Harvard University Press.

Hempel, C. G. (1965). Fundamentals of taxonomy. In C. G. Hempel (Ed.), *Aspects of scientific explanation* (pp. 137–154). New York: Free Press.

Houts, A. C. (1989, November). *Behavior therapy and the new medical model*. Paper presented at the 23rd Annual Convention of the Association for the Advancement of Behavior Therapy, Washington, DC.

Houts, A. C. (1994). Operational analysis, behavior analysis, and epistemology in science and technology studies. *Mexican Journal of Behavior Analysis, 20*, 101–143.

Houts, A. C. (2000). Fifty years of psychiatric nomenclature: Reflections on the 1943 War Department Technical Bulletin, Medical 203. *Journal of Clinical Psychology, 56*, 935–967.

Houts, A. C. (2001a). The diagnostic and statistical manual's new white coat and circularity of plausible dysfunctions: Response to Wakefield, Part 1. *Behaviour Research and Therapy, 39*, 315–345.

Houts, A. C. (2001b). Harmful dysfunction and the search for value neutrality in the definition of mental disorder: Response to Wakefield, Part 2. *Behaviour Research and Therapy, 39*, 1099–1132.

Houts, A. C., & Follette, W. C. (1998). Mentalism, mechanisms, and medical analogues: Reply to Wakefield (1998). *Journal of Consulting and Clinical Psychology, 66*, 853–855.

Houts, A. C., & Krasner, L. (1998). Philosophical and theoretical foundations of behavior therapy. In J. J. Plaud & G. Eifert (Eds.), *From behavior theory to behavior therapy* (pp. 15–37). Boston: Allyn & Bacon.

Kendell, R. E. (1991). Relationship between *DSM–IV* and *ICD–10*. *Journal of Abnormal Psychology, 100,* 297–301.

Kim, J. (1967). Explanation in science. In P. Edwards (Ed.), *The encyclopedia of philosophy* (Vol. 3, pp. 159–163). New York: Macmillan.

Kirk, S. A., & Kutchins, H. (1992). *The selling of DSM: The rhetoric of science in psychiatry.* New York: Aldine DeGruyter.

Klerman, G. L. (1986). Historical perspectives on contemporary schools of psychopathology. In T. Millon & G. L. Klerman (Eds.), *Contemporary directions in psychopathology: Toward the DSM–IV* (pp. 3–28). New York: Guilford Press.

Knorr-Cetina, K. D. (1981). *The manufacture of knowledge: An essay on the constructivist and contextual nature of science.* Oxford, England: Pergamon.

Kolakowski, L. (1990). *Modernity on endless trial.* Chicago: University of Chicago Press.

Krasner, L., & Houts, A. C. (1984). A study of the "value" systems of behavioral scientists. *American Psychologist, 49,* 840–850.

Kutchins, H., & Kirk, S. A. (1997). *Making us crazy: DSM: The psychiatric bible and the creation of mental disorders.* New York: Free Press.

Laing, R. D. (1960). *The divided self: A study of sanity and madness.* Chicago: Quadrangle Books.

Latour, B. (1987). *Science in action.* Cambridge, MA: Harvard University Press.

Latour, B. (1999). *Pandora's hope: Essays on the reality of science studies.* Cambridge, MA: Harvard University Press.

Latour, B., & Woolgar, S. (1986). *Laboratory life: The construction of scientific facts.* Princeton, NJ: Princeton University Press.

Lyotard, J. F. (1984). *The postmodern condition: A report on knowledge.* Minneapolis: University of Minnesota Press.

Margolis, J. (1994). Taxonomic puzzles. In J. Z. Sadler, O. P. Wiggins, & M. A. Schwartz (Eds.), *Philosophical perspectives on psychiatric diagnostic classification* (pp. 104–128). Baltimore: Johns Hopkins University Press.

Mayr, E. (1982). *The growth of biological thought.* Cambridge, MA: Harvard University Press.

Meehl, P. E. (1995). Bootstrap taxometrics: Solving the classification problem in psychopathology. *American Psychologist, 50,* 266–275.

Merton, R. K. (1970). *Science, technology and society in seventeenth-century England.* New York: Harper and Row.

Micale, M. S., & Porter, R. (Eds.). (1994). *Discovering the history of psychiatry.* New York: Oxford University Press.

Miller, A. I. (1984). *Imagery in scientific thought: Creating 20th-century physics.* Boston: Birkhaeuser.

Miller, M. W. (1994, April 25). Creating a buzz: With remedy in hand, drug firms get ready to popularize an illness. *The Wall Street Journal,* pp. A1–A6.

Millon, T. (1986). On the past and future of the *DSM–III*: Personal recollections and projections. In T. Millon & G. L. Klerman (Eds.), *Contemporary directions in psychopathology: Toward the* DSM–IV (pp. 29–70). New York: Guilford Press.

Nathan, P. E. (1998). The *DSM–IV* and its antecedents: Enhancing syndromal diagnosis. In J. W. Barron (Ed.), *Making diagnosis meaningful: Enhancing evaluation and treatment of psychological disorders* (pp. 3–27). Washington, DC: American Psychological Association.

Paul, G. L. (2000). Evidence-based practices in inpatient and residential facilities. *The Clinical Psychologist, 53,* 3–11.

Paul, G. L., Mariotto, M. J., Redfield, J. P., Licht, M. H., & Power, C. T. (1986). *Assessment in residential treatment settings: Principles and methods to support cost-effective quality operations.* Champaign, IL: Research Press.

Persons, J. B. (1986). The advantages of studying psychological phenomena rather than psychiatric diagnoses. *American Psychologist, 41,* 1252–1260.

Pickering, A. (1984). *Constructing quarks: A sociological history of particle physics.* Chicago: University of Chicago Press.

Pickering, A. (Ed.). (1992). *Science as practice and culture.* Chicago: University of Chicago Press.

Popper, K. R. (1962). *The open society and its enemies.* Princeton, NJ: Princeton University Press.

Rorty, R. (1989). *Contingency, irony, and solidarity.* New York: Cambridge University Press.

Rouse, J. (1987). *Knowledge and power: Toward a political philosophy of science.* Ithaca, NY: Cornell University Press.

Sadler, J. Z., Wiggins, O. P., & Schwartz, M. A. (Eds.). (1994). *Philosophical perspectives on psychiatric diagnostic classification.* Baltimore: Johns Hopkins University Press.

Scadding, J. G. (1988). Health and disease: What can medicine do for philosophy? *Journal of Medical Ethics, 14,* 118–124.

Scadding, J. G. (1990). The semantic problems of psychiatry. *Psychological Medicine, 20,* 243–248.

Scadding, J. G. (1996). Essentialism and nominalism in medicine: logic of diagnosis in disease terminology. *Lancet, 348,* 594–596.

Scheff, T. J. (1966). *Being mentally ill: A sociological theory.* Chicago: Aldine.

Scull, A. (1989). *Social order/mental disorder: Anglo–American psychiatry in historical perspective.* Berkeley: University of California Press.

Shapin, S. (1994). *A social history of truth: Civility and science in seventeenth century England.* Chicago: University of Chicago Press.

Smith, B. H. (1988). *Contingencies of value: Alternative perspectives for critical theory.* Cambridge, MA: Harvard University Press.

Snow, C. P. (1959). *The two cultures and the scientific revolution.* Cambridge, England: Cambridge University Press.

Spitzer, R. L. (1991). An outsider–insider's views about revising the DSMs. *Journal of Abnormal Psychology, 100,* 294–296.

Spitzer, R. L., & Wakefield, J. C. (1999). DSM–IV criterion for clinical significance: Does it help solve the false positives problem? *American Journal of Psychiatry, 156,* 1856–1864.

Szasz, T. S. (1960). The myth of mental illness. *American Psychologist, 15,* 113–118.

Valenstein, E. S. (1998). *Blaming the brain: The truth about drugs and mental health.* New York: Free Press.

Wakefield, J. C. (1992a). The concept of mental disorder: On the boundary between biological facts and social values. *American Psychologist, 47,* 373–388.

Wakefield, J. C. (1992b). Disorder as harmful dysfunction: A conceptual critique of DSM–III–R's definition of mental disorder. *Psychological Review, 99,* 232–247.

Wakefield, J. C. (1996). DSM–IV: Are we making diagnostic progress? *Contemporary Psychology, 41,* 646–652.

Wakefield, J. C. (1998a). DSM's theory-neutral nosology is scientifically progressive: A comment on Follette and Houts (1996). *Journal of Consulting and Clinical Psychology, 66,* 846–852.

Wakefield, J. C. (1998b). Meaning and melancholia: Why the DSM–IV cannot (entirely) ignore the patient's intentional system. In J. W. Barron (Ed.), *Making diagnosis meaningful: Enhancing evaluation and treatment of psychological disorders* (pp. 29–72). Washington, DC: American Psychological Association.

Wakefield, J. C. (1999a). The concept of disorder as a foundation for the DSM's theory-neutral nosology: Response to Follette and Houts, Part 2. *Behaviour Research and Therapy, 37,* 1001–1027.

Wakefield, J. C. (1999b). Philosophy of science and the progressiveness of the DSM's theory-neutral nosology: Response to Follette and Houts, Part 1. *Behaviour Research and Therapy, 37,* 963–999.

Weimer, W. B. (1979). *Notes on the methodology of scientific research.* Hillsdale, NJ: Erlbaum.

Weinberg, S. (1992). *Dreams of a final theory: The search for the fundamental laws of nature.* New York: Pantheon.

Weinberg, S. (1995). Reductionism redux [Review of the book *Nature's imagination: The frontiers of scientific vision*]. *The New York Review of Books,* 39–42.

Weissman, M. M. (1987). Psychiatric diagnoses [Letter to the editor]. *Science, 235,* 522.

West Tennessee Psychiatric Association and the Mental Health Society of Memphis and Shelby County. (1989, October 7). Obsessive compulsive disorder [Advertisement]. *The Commercial Appeal,* pp. 10.

Wittgenstein, L. (1953). *Philosophical investigations.* New York: Macmillan.

Wolpert, L. (1992). *The unnatural nature of science: Why science does (not) make common sense.* London: Faber & Faber.

World Health Organization. (1967). *Manual of the international statistical classification of diseases, injuries, and causes of death, eighth revision* (Vol. 1). Geneva: Author.

World Health Organization. (1992). *International statistical classification of diseases and related health problems, 10th ed.* (Vol. 1). Geneva: Author.

Wylie, M. S. (1995, May/June). Diagnosing for dollars? *The Family Therapy Networker*, pp. 22–69.

Zimmerman, M. (1990). Is DSM–IV needed at all? *Archives of General Psychiatry, 47*, 974–976.

II

METHODOLOGICAL
CONSIDERATIONS

3

IMPLICATIONS OF INFORMATION-GATHERING METHODS FOR A REFINED TAXONOMY OF PSYCHOPATHOLOGY

GREGORY J. MEYER

Two things are required before clinicians can assess psychopathology or diagnose psychological disorders. First, one must have a framework to organize the relevant constructs that indicate pathology or disorder. These constructs may be clusters of subjectively experienced symptoms, behavioral acts, dichotomous taxonomies, continuous dimensions derived from factor analyses, or one of many other possible templates for classifying human functioning. Regardless of the framework, the constructs of the classification scheme provide a road map to the phenomena that a clinician should examine to identify health and illness.

A large portion of this book is devoted to identifying limitations with the dichotomous classifications that are applied to symptomatology in the current *Diagnostic and Statistical Manual of Mental Disorders* (4th ed.; *DSM–IV*; American Psychiatric Association, 1994). Another large portion of this book is devoted to explicating alternative, empirically defined, and empirically defensible frameworks that could replace or supplement the *DSM*.

This chapter does neither; I do not advance or address any particular framework of pathology. Instead, I focus on the second element that is required for a classification scheme, namely, the mechanisms or methods that allow one to gather relevant information about a patient (e.g., scales, interviews, performance tasks) to determine whether he or she has the characteristics that fall within a given framework of psychopathology. Thus, I focus on how one classifies or designates patients as having certain characteristics, not on what characteristics get classified or designated.

To ground the issues, I first draw from a large body of evidence that addresses the distinctions among sources of information gathering and the incompleteness of any single source. Next, additional data are used to exemplify how sources of information gathering have a profound impact on traditional *DSM* diagnoses. These data serve three purposes. First, from a psychometric perspective, they demonstrate how reliability and validity coefficients are on a single continuum that measures what can be considered "source overlap" or "criterion contamination." Second, the data demonstrate how the methodological factors associated with individual studies cause the research literature to generate wildly different estimates concerning the validity of the diagnostic information obtained from a given source. Third, and most important, the same data clearly demonstrate that diagnostic decisions can be highly source dependent and thus unstable and less than optimally valid representations of reality.

Finally, regardless of the specific content that defines pathology within any system developed to replace or supplement the *DSM*, I conclude that an empirically guided alternative should formally and systematically require clinicians who use the system to consider multiple, maximally independent sources of information prior to making diagnostic determinations. I review several strategies for doing so and in the process highlight the emerging evidence that indicates that these strategies improve the quality of information used in clinical decision making.

THE IMPORTANCE OF "HOW" RATHER THAN "WHAT"

One may wonder why the manner of assessing psychopathology is important. After all, most clinical training in psychology, psychiatry, and other mental health professions is oriented toward teaching the content to be considered for diagnostic or treatment purposes. As long as the content is clearly specified, shouldn't it be an easy matter to interview a patient and determine whether that particular phenomenological quality is present or absent? Psychologists, more than other mental health professionals, should recognize that the answer to this question is negative. It is not easy to obtain clear or definitive answers about psychological characteristics, and it never has been. The historical and contemporary evidence unambiguously indicates that it is virtually impossible to assess any psychological characteristic in a clear or definitive way.

As a discipline, we were first alerted to this conundrum more than 40 years ago (Campbell & Fiske, 1959). Since that time, important works have appeared with some regularity to remind us of the problem (e.g., Achenbach, McConaughy, & Howell, 1987; Cook & Campbell, 1979; Kagan, 1988; Michell, 1997; Mischel, 1968/1996; Nisbett & Wilson, 1977). Although these articles and books address many distinct points, they share a common thread, namely, that psychological content cannot be separated from the mechanisms or methods used to assess that content. With virtually all psychological phenomena, when the "same" construct or characteristic is assessed by distinct methods, different conclusions are obtained. For instance, to know the extent of depression in a girl seeking treatment, one would arrive at different conclusions depending on whether the source of information about her depression came from the child herself, her mother, her father, her teacher, her peers, or her prior therapist (see Achenbach et al., 1987).

For some reason, research and applied practice have been slow to embrace these findings, particularly with adults, where it is standard to obtain information from just the patient. Perhaps this is because the results are humbling. It would be comforting to think that conducting a skilled interview with a reasonably open patient would allow us to learn all that is necessary to reach a firm understanding and draw sensible conclusions about the patient. However, the data indicate that this is not so. Although impressions from interviews are certainly valuable, like every source of information, they are inherently limited and incomplete.

It is unlikely that anyone would strongly dispute the notion that impressions from interviews are limited and incomplete. After all, it would be preposterous to assert that they were perfect sources of information, just as it would be preposterous to assert that any source of information was perfect. What becomes important then is evidence on the extent to which different sources of information are incomplete. We should be very clear about the degree of association that exists between one source of information and another, particularly when considering the impact that diagnostic determinations in applied practice may have on the life of an individual. Knowing the degree of association between one source of clinical data and another should allow us to reach level-headed conclusions about whether our reliance on imperfect data sources really constitutes a salient problem in applied clinical practice.

RELIANCE ON PATIENT SELF-REPORT IN CURRENT DIAGNOSTIC PRACTICES

Before considering data pertaining to the relationship between different data sources, it is instructive to briefly review some issues related to diagnostic decision making. DSM diagnoses are fundamentally made by collecting data from clinical interviews with the patient (or, in the case of a child, with the child's caregiver). Thus, even though *DSM–IV* mentions "associated laboratory findings" or "associated physical examination findings" that may help contribute to diagnostic determinations (e.g., memory testing or neuroimaging for dementia disorders, toxicology for substance use disorders, hypnotizability for dissociative disorders, polysomnography for sleep disorders), clinicians are rarely encouraged to obtain diagnostically relevant information from sources other than the patient. There are several exceptions. For instance, when assessing delirium disorders, *DSM–IV* states that patients may be incoherent and that "under these circumstances" (American Psychiatric Association, 1994, p. 125) it may be helpful to obtain information from family members or other informants. Patients with anorexia nervosa are said to frequently lack insight into their eating problems. Consequently, it is "often necessary" (p. 540) to obtain information from third parties to evaluate weight loss and other symptoms. For personality disorders, *DSM–IV* states that it "may be helpful" to obtain "supplementary information from other informants" (p. 630) to overcome the fact that patients with a personality disorder may not consider their personal characteristics to be problematic. Perhaps the strongest instructions for considering additional sources of information besides the patient's self-report come in the section on substance-related disorders. Although it is not formalized in any of the diagnostic criteria for these disorders, clinicians are told that they should consult additional sources of information "whenever possible" (p. 185) while they are obtaining a detailed substance use history. Despite these exceptions, but consistent with the interview schedules that have been developed over the past 20 years, making a diagnosis fundamentally revolves around obtaining information directly from the patient.

Historically, diagnoses were formulated from free-flowing clinical interviews that did not have a proscribed structure or a standard set of probe and follow-up questions. During an interview, clinicians tracked the patient's discourse and intermittently intervened by asking impromptu questions that followed up on hunches, or they solicited examples here and there to help gain a more complete and fleshed-out view of the patient's complaints. Unfortunately, the absence of a general structure to the interviews seemed to contribute to rather poor reliability. Different clinicians would often disagree about the same patient's core problems. For instance, across seven data sets obtained between 1956 and 1978, the average agreement on the *DSM* diagnoses from unstructured joint or separate interviews was $\kappa = .64$ ($N = 1,141$; 3–26 disorders considered; data were combined from Spitzer, Forman, & Nee, 1979; and Spitzer & Fleiss, 1974; although Study 5 was excluded from Spitzer & Fleiss because it compared clinical diagnoses to structured research diagnoses).

To deal with this problem, semistructured and fully structured interviews have been developed. Fully structured interviews provide specific probe and follow-up questions to address almost every contingency that may emerge in the interview. These schedules have gone so far to remove clinical judgment from the diagnostic interview process that they have been fully automated. Thus, in a demonstration of oxymoronic labeling, one can use "computer-administered diagnostic interviews" to make diagnoses. With the most highly structured interviews, different clinicians attending the same interview can produce almost exactly identical diagnoses. For instance, Wittchen (1994) reviewed data on the Composite International Diagnostic Interview (CIDI), a fully structured interview that can be administered by clinicians or by computer. Wittchen demonstrated that two clinicians attending the same interview produced near-identical results across 21 diagnostic categories, with a mean kappa of .92 ($N = 575$).

Semistructured interviews have also produced positive results when clinicians observe the same interview. For instance, across 3–22 Axis I disorders, semistructured joint interviews have produced an average diagnostic reliability of $\kappa = .72$ ($N = 514$; data were combined from Keller et al., 1995; Riskind, Beck, Berchick, Brown, & Steer, 1987; Segal, Hersen, & Van Hasselt, 1994 [using data from Table 1 that were otherwise unavailable]; Skre, Onstad, Torgersen, & Kringlen, 1991; and Steinberg, Rounsaville, & Cicchetti, 1990). Similarly, across 4–12 Axis II disorders, semistructured joint interviews have produced an average diagnostic reliability of $\kappa = .76$ ($N = 1,120$; data were combined from Bernstein et al., 1997; Gómez-Beneyto et al., 1994; Maffei et al., 1997; and Zimmerman, 1994, and the Zimmerman data were supplemented by published results in Loranger et al., 1994).

Although interclinician diagnostic agreement may well have improved with the advent of structured and semistructured interview schedules,[1] this shift brings about other important changes as well. As one moves from unstructured clinical interviews to semistructured interviews to fully

---

[1] The reliability values presented here can raise legitimate questions about whether more highly structured interviews improve reliability. If unstructured interviews produce an average kappa of .64, whereas semistructured interviews produce average values of .72 or .76, the change does not seem very dramatic—particularly when recognizing that all of the semistructured coefficients emerge from joint rather than independent interviews. Indeed, when independent interviews are conducted over short retest intervals, reliability declines for structured and semistructured interviews. For instance, Wittchen's (1994) review of the fully structured CIDI revealed an average kappa of .68 over a 1–3 day period (mean $N = 117$ over 25 disorders). For semistructured interviews, Williams et al. (1992) found an average kappa of .60 for Axis I disorders over a 1–14 day period ($N = 592$; 9–19 disorders) and Zimmerman's (1994; Table 2) review indicated an average kappa of .52 over the same time period for Axis II disorders ($N = 358$; 6–11 disorders). Although these findings paradoxically suggest that unstructured diagnostic interviews may be about as reliable as structured or semistructured interviews, the data reported here are imprecise and incomplete. For instance, a number of the samples that examined unstructured interviews had confounds that would artificially increase reliability values (e.g., cases of disagreement were not always included in Spitzer et al.'s, 1979, analysis), and none of these data emerge from an exhaustive search of the relevant literature. This limited survey is provocative, but a more definitive review is necessary to adequately address the issue.

structured interviews, there is a parallel shift in the emphasis given to the source of information used in the diagnostic process. Progressing along this continuum produces a decreasing reliance on the clinician's inferences and an increasing reliance on the patient's self-report.

Diagnostic determinations that are made from an unstructured clinical interview are certainly informed by the patient's self-report. However, the clinician is in the central role of synthesizing information and making inferences. As such, unstructured clinical interviews rely heavily on the skill and sophistication of the clinician. In contrast, clinical inference is completely absent from fully structured interviews. Here, patients are asked specific questions, and they provide specific answers. Endorsement of the presence or absence of a particular symptom is in the hands of the patient, not the clinician. This should be no surprise. Fully structured interviews were developed to remove clinical skill from the equation (see L. N. Robins, Helzer, Croughan, & Ratcliff, 1981).

As the reliability data presented above attest, fully structured joint interviews maximize interrater reliability. Regardless of the clinician conducting the interview or processing the information, virtually identical diagnoses are derived. This seems like it should be a good thing. Perhaps so. However, it also means that diagnostic determinations are much more source dependent because they rely exclusively on the perspective of the patient. Of course, patient perceptions can be marred by memory problems, confusion, a distorted self-image, the denial of or failure to recognize personal characteristics, and deliberate efforts to present oneself in a slanted and inaccurate manner (e.g., John & Robins, 1994; Malgady, Rogler, & Tryon, 1992; Meyer, 1997; Rogler, Malgady, & Tryon, 1992). Although most clinicians find structured or semistructured interviews to be helpful when evaluating Axis I symptomatology, clinicians almost across the board revert to an unstructured interview format when attempting to understand the broader matrix of the patient's personality (Westen, 1997). In essence, when the increased reliability offered by highly structured interviews is purchased, it is paid for with dependence on the patient as the primary source of diagnostic information. This is not necessarily a sound investment.

DATA ON THE CORRESPONDENCE BETWEEN DIFFERENT SOURCES OF INFORMATION

Meyer et al. (2001) organized a large array of data that examined the extent of association between distinct ways of assessing the same construct. The methods included structured interviews, semistructured interviews, unstructured interviews, self-reports, parent reports, spouse or significant other reports, peer reports, teacher reports, observed behavior, performance tasks, and inferences synthesized from multiple sources of information.

Table 3.1 presents those findings. Although the results do not emerge from an exhaustive search of all the relevant literature, they appear representative and generalizable, because they draw on data from more than 800 samples and more than 185,000 participants. When constructing this table, studies were excluded if they used aggregation strategies to maximize associations (e.g., self-reports correlated with a composite of spouse and peer reports; see Cheek, 1982; Epstein, 1983; Tsujimoto, Hamilton, & Berger, 1990), and moderators of agreement that may have been identified in the literature were ignored. Studies were also excluded if data sources were not reasonably independent. For instance, studies were omitted if patients completed a written self-report instrument that was then correlated with the results from a structured interview that asked the same or comparable questions in an oral format (e.g., Richter, Werner, Heerlein, Kraus, & Sauer, 1998).

A careful review of Table 3.1 indicates that distinct information emerges when distinct sources are consulted about the same psychological characteristic. This is evident from the relatively low to moderate associations that are seen between independent methods of assessing similar constructs. The findings hold for both children and adults, and they hold when various types of knowledgeable informants (e.g., self, clinician, parent, peer) are compared to one another or to observed behaviors and task performance.

For instance, the information obtained from children and adolescents has only moderate correspondence with the same information obtained from parents (table entries 1–4), teachers (table entries 8–10), clinicians (table entries 5 and 6), or other observers (table entry 7). Furthermore, the information obtained from parents, teachers, clinicians, or observers is largely independent; each of these sources has only moderate associations with the other sources (table entries 12–18 and 20–21). For adults, the information obtained from self-reports of personality and mood has only small to moderate associations with the same information when it is obtained from those who are close to the target person (table entries 23–25 and 29–30), from peers (table entries 26–28), from clinicians (table entries 31–34), from performance tasks (table entries 37–43), or from observed behavior (table entries 44–46).

The substantial independence between sources of information is not a phenomenon that is limited to rarified psychological research on personality; the independence pervades all aspects of human functioning and, as such, it clearly extends into the office of every clinician who attempts to treat or understand the psychopathology of his or her patients. Not only do patients, clinicians, parents, and observers have different views about psychotherapeutic progress or functioning in treatment (see table entries

TABLE 3.1

A Sample of Cross-Method Convergent Associations Indicating the
General Accuracy of Single, Independent Sources of Information

Sources of Data and Constructs	r	κ	N
Children and Adolescents			
1. Self vs. parent: Behavioral and Emotional Problems	.29		14,102
2. Self vs. parent: Behavioral and Emotional Problems (Q-Correlations of profile similarity)	.29		1,829
3. Self vs. parent: Symptom Change in treatment	.19		199
4. Self vs. parent: DSM Axis I disorder		.24	1,136
5. Self vs. clinician: Behavioral and Emotional Problems	.14		1,079
6. Self vs. clinician: DSM Axis I disorder		.23	998
7. Self vs. clinical observer: Change in treatment	.28		199
8. Self vs. teacher: Behavioral and Emotional Problems	.21		9,814
9. Self vs. teacher: Behavioral and Emotional Problems (Q-Correlations of profile similarity)	.17		1,222
10. Self vs. teacher: Test Anxiety	.23		3,099
11. Self vs. aggregated peer ratings: Behavioral and Emotional Problems[b]	.26		8,821
12. Parent vs. teacher: Summed Behavioral and Emotional Problems	.29		29,163
13. Parent vs. teacher: Specific Behavioral and Emotional Problems	.16		1,161
14. Parent vs. teacher: Behavioral and Emotional Problems (Q-correlations of profile similarity)	.22		2,274
15. Parent vs. teacher: *DSM* Axis I disorder		.13	1,229
16. Parent vs. clinician: Behavioral and Emotional Problems	.34		1,725
17. Parent vs. clinician: *DSM* Axis I disorder		.39[a]	786
18. Parent vs. direct observer of child behavior: Behavioral and Emotional Problems	.27		279
19. Parent vs. cognitive test: Attention Problems	.03		451
20. Teacher vs. clinician: Behavioral and Emotional Problems	.34		1,325
21. Teacher vs. direct observer of child behavior: Behavioral and Emotional Problems	.42		732
22. Teacher vs. cognitive test: Attention Problems	.10		483
Adults			
23. Self vs. spouse–partner: Personality and Mood	.29		2,011
24. Self vs. spouse–partner: "Big Five" Personality Traits (Domains and Facets)	.44		1,774
25. Self vs. parent: Personality Characteristics (including the "Big Five")	.33		828
26. Self vs. peer: Personality and Mood	.27		2,119
27. Self vs. peer: "Big Five" Personality Traits (domains and facets)	.31		1,967
28. Self vs. peer: Job Performance	.19		6,359
29. Self vs. significant other: Attention Problems and Impulsivity	.22		202
30. Self vs. significant other: *DSM* Axis II personality disorder diagnosis		.12	768

Table Continues

TABLE 3.1
(Continued)

Sources of Data and Constructs	r	κ	N
31. Self vs. clinician: Treatment Related Functioning, Symptomatology, and Outcome	.29		7,903
32. Self vs. clinician: *DSM* Axis II personality disorder characteristics	.33[a]		2,778
33. Self vs. clinician: *DSM* Axis II personality disorder diagnosis		.18[a]	2,859
34. Self vs. clinician: *DSM* Axis I disorders		.34[a]	5,990
35. Self vs. clinician: "Big Five" Personality Traits (domains only)	.32		132
36. Self vs. supervisor: Job Performance	.22		10,359
37. Self vs. subordinate: Job Performance	.14		5,925
38. Self vs. cognitive test or grades: General Intelligence	.24		904
39. Self vs. cognitive test or grades: Scholastic Ability[c]	.38		8,745
40. Self vs. cognitive test: Memory Problems	.13		5,717
41. Self vs. cognitive test: Attention Problems	.06		522
42. Self vs. Thematic Apperception Test: Achievement Motivation[c]	.09		2,785
43. Self vs. Thematic Apperception Test: Problem Solving	.13		199
44. Self vs. Rorschach: Emotional Distress, Psychosis, and Interpersonal Wariness	.04		689
45. Self vs. observed behavior: Personality Characteristics	.16		274
46. Self vs. observed behavior: Attitudes	.32		15,624
47. Peers vs. observed behavior: Personality Characteristics	.15		264
48. Clinician vs. consensus best estimate: *DSM* Axis II Personality Disorder Diagnosis		.28	218
49. Significant other vs. significant other: Target Patient's *DSM* Personality Disorder Diagnosis		.32	386
50. Significant other vs. clinician: Target Patient's Depressive Signs and Symptoms		.13	141
51. Judgments from one source of test data vs. another: Personality, Needs, and IQ[d]	.12		158
52. Supervisor vs. peers: Job Performance	.34		7,101
53. Supervisor vs. subordinate: Job Performance	.22		4,815
54. Peers vs. subordinate: Job Performance	.22		3,938
55. Objective criteria vs. managerial ratings: Job Success	.32		8,341

Note: Citations and specific notes for each entry are provided in Meyer et al. (2001). r = Pearson correlation; κ = kappa coefficient; N = number of participants; *DSM* = *Diagnostic and Statistical Manual of Mental Disorders*; IQ = intelligence quotient. From "Psychological Testing and Psychological Assessment: A Review of Evidence and Issues," by G. J. Meyer, S. E. Finn, L. D. Eyde, G. G. Kay, K. L. Moreland, R. R. Dies, E. J. Eisman, T. W. Kubiszyn, and G. M. Reed, 2001, *American Psychologist, 56*, pp. 146–149. Copyright 2001 by the American Psychological Association.
[a] These coefficients are inflated by criterion contamination. For instance, in an effort to maximize cross-observer correspondence, one study went so far as to exclude the inferences that clinicians developed from their direct observations of the patient as a way to increase diagnostic agreement between patients and clinicians. [b] Because much of these data reflect the correlation between aggregated peer ratings and self-ratings, the coefficient is larger than would be obtained between self-ratings and the ratings of a single peer. [c] Result combines some data from children and adolescents with adults. [d] These studies were from the late 1950s and early 1960s. It is unclear whether the data may be different using more contemporary scoring and interpretive practices.

3, 7, and 31), but diagnoses have only moderate associations when they are derived from self-reported information or the information reported by parents, significant others, and clinicians (see table entries 4, 6, 15, 17, 30, 33, 34, 47, and 48). For instance, personality disorder diagnoses derived from self-report bear little resemblance to those derived from clinicians (κ = .18, N = 2,859; table entries 33) or to those based on semistructured interviews with significant others in the patient's life (κ = .12, N = 768; table entry 30).

DATA ON THE RELIABILITY–VALIDITY CONTINUUM AND THE POTENTIALLY EPHEMERAL NATURE OF DIAGNOSES

Given the purpose of this book, the findings on diagnostic (dis)-agreement across distinct sources of information deserve closer scrutiny. In this section, I review existing research on the accuracy or validity of diagnostic decisions derived from patients as the sole source of information. These data illustrate three points. First, although not central to the goals of this chapter, the data demonstrate a psychometric principle: Reliability and validity coefficients are on a single continuum that measures what can be considered "source overlap" or "criterion contamination." Second, the data show how the methodological decisions that are made when designing individual studies force the research literature to produce wildly different estimates concerning the accuracy of diagnoses obtained from a given source of information. Third, and most important, the data show how final diagnostic decisions can be incredibly source dependent. As a result of this source dependence, clinical diagnoses are often unstable and inaccurate representations of reality.

My main thesis here is that different sources of information provide distinct clinical data that are relevant to the diagnostic process. A hypothesis that flows from this is that as methods of information gathering become more distinct, the extent of association between different data sources will decline. Stated differently, to the extent that sources of information overlap or become confounded with each other, cross-source diagnostic agreement will become elevated. This can lead to an illusion of accuracy whereby a given source of diagnostic information is viewed as more accurate or trustworthy than is warranted.

To examine this illusion of accuracy in a diagnostic context, evidence about the accuracy of fully structured interviews is reviewed. Over the past 20 years, a fairly extensive literature has developed to determine the accuracy or validity of these measures. The two most prominent tools are the CIDI, which was mentioned earlier, and its direct predecessor, the Diagnostic Interview Schedule (DIS; L. N. Robins et al., 1981). The sole purpose of both instruments is to make diagnoses according to the *DSM* or the *International Classification of Diseases* (ICD). Because both instruments are fully structured, they are ultimately self-report scales (as evidenced by their ability to be administered by either an interviewer or a computer).

According to the hypothesis outlined above, one should expect that the DIS or CIDI produces higher validity coefficients with other methods of making a diagnosis when the alternative methods largely draw on the same source of information as the DIS and CIDI. Thus, when both the CIDI or DIS diagnoses and the external criterion diagnoses are largely derived from the patient's self-reported information, the CIDI or DIS diagnoses should display the highest levels of agreement with the external criterion diagnoses. This should occur, for example, when the clinician who makes the external diagnosis has also administered the CIDI or DIS and has not considered much information beyond that obtained during the CIDI or DIS interview. In contrast, CIDI or DIS diagnoses should display the lowest levels of agreement with external criterion diagnoses when the latter are derived from the most independent sources of data. This should occur, for instance, when criterion diagnoses are assigned by the consensus of clinicians who have observed hospitalized patients over time, interviewed them on multiple occasions (particularly with both structured and unstructured interviews), and solicited information from additional people who know the patient well (e.g., family members, therapists, friends).

The two research designs mentioned above fall at opposite ends of a methodological continuum of validity. This continuum indicates the extent to which criterion diagnostic decisions are confounded with the predictor diagnostic determinations obtained from the CIDI or DIS. In the language of psychometrics, this continuum addresses *criterion contamination*, which is present to the extent that a criterion is influenced or determined by the very information that is also used to predict it.

Most often, criterion contamination is identified when the results from a traditional test scale inform the criterion judgments that are used to validate the scale. For instance, if intelligence test scores are used to predict teacher ratings of intelligence, but the teacher ratings are completed after the teachers are exposed to the results of the intelligence test, the study would have criterion contamination and would produce artificially high evidence of validity for the intelligence test.

However, this is just one phenotypic manifestation of the underlying problem; criterion contamination emerges in other ways, too. What I focus on here is how artificially inflated estimates of validity or diagnostic accuracy can emerge as a function of the source of information that informs both the predictor and the criterion. This can be considered a source overlap problem. In terms of diagnoses, when criterion diagnoses are derived from the same source of information that generates the predictor diagnoses, the predictor and criterion information is confounded and should produce artificially high estimates of the predictor's validity or accuracy.

For instance, when the CIDI is administered to a patient by a lay interviewer and then shortly thereafter it is administered by a psychologist or psychiatrist, the predictor (i.e., diagnoses from the CIDI by the lay interviewer) and the criterion (i.e., diagnoses from the CIDI by the professional interviewer) are quite confounded because both sets of diagnoses draw on the same source of information for making diagnostic decisions (i.e., the patient's self-report). To the extent that both the predictor and the criterion drink exclusively from the same well, they are both similarly influenced by whatever was in that water. In the case of the fully structured CIDI, which is completely dependent on the patient's self-report, both the predictor diagnoses and the criterion diagnoses would be entirely determined by the same single source of information.

These ideas lead to expectations for what should be observed as one looks across the research literature. Those studies that are designed in such a way that the predictor and criterion rely most heavily on the same source of information should produce the largest estimates of validity or accuracy. To organize the literature examining CIDI or DIS diagnoses as the predictor relative to criterion diagnoses derived by some additional or alternative method, four categories of research methodology are delineated. These four methods vary in their degree of source overlap or criterion contamination and thus are expected to produce quite different estimates of CIDI or DIS validity.

First, high coefficients of agreement should be found when clinicians make the criterion diagnoses after having just attended or performed the CID or DIS interviews but supplement that information with the results from some additional questions designed to clarify remaining ambiguities related to the diagnostic criteria. If one thinks in terms of Venn diagrams, the criterion diagnoses would be drawn from a universe of information that encompasses and is just slightly larger than the CIDI or DIS universe of information (e.g., the outline of a dime inside the outline of a penny). In terms of relative proportions, the criterion diagnoses are almost completely determined by the same information that generated the CIDI or DIS diagnoses.

Second, moderately high coefficients of diagnostic agreement would be expected when the criterion diagnoses are derived from a highly structured interview that is administered on the same day as the CIDI or DIS but in the context of an independent interview. Using a highly structured interview for the criterion diagnoses ensures that the patient is the key source of information for both the predictor and the criterion. In addition, by administering the CIDI or DIS and the criterion interviews on the same day, the immediate proximity in time ensures that the patient will provide highly similar responses to both sets of diagnostic questions. In terms of a Venn diagram, the degree of criterion contamination from this methodology could be represented as two circles of roughly similar size that almost fully overlap, though one is offset to the right.

Third, moderately low coefficients would be expected when the criterion diagnoses are derived from an independently conducted structured interview that is completed within the same week (but not the same day) as the CIDI or DIS interview. In terms of a Venn diagram, the circles would still largely overlap but now one would be offset further to the right.

Fourth, low coefficients would be expected when criterion diagnoses systematically draw on a wide range of information, including clinical inferences that emerge from observing the patient over time, from unstructured interviews and interactions, from input by significant others in the patient's life, from input by other mental health professionals who have treated the patient, from historical records, and so on. Following the LEAD model (i.e., Longitudinal, Expert evaluation of All Data; Spitzer, 1983), criterion diagnoses may even use CIDI or DIS information. Although this would produce some degree of criterion contamination or source overlap, it should not be very problematic so long as the CIDI or DIS results were just one of many sources of information that influenced the final diagnostic decisions. In terms of Venn imagery, the CIDI or DIS diagnoses relative to the criterion diagnoses would be like a dime inside or partially overlapping a basketball.

The prior paragraph describes the optimal design for producing independent and unconfounded criterion diagnoses. Unfortunately, few studies meet these conditions. Thus, for the current analysis, the final category contained all remaining studies that did not fit within one of the three categories described earlier. As such, it included criterion diagnoses that were derived from formal team consensus, from traditional clinical interviews, from observations over the course of a hospitalization, from chart reviews, and from independently conducted semistructured clinical interviews. For all of these studies, the criterion diagnoses should have less source contamination with the CIDI or DIS diagnoses than found in the other three designs.

To test these expectations for how methodological overlap influences the apparent accuracy of diagnoses from fully structured interviews, one would need a large number of relevant studies. Fortunately, the literature contains many studies that have examined the correspondence between fully structured interviews like the CIDI or DIS and an external diagnostic criterion. Furthermore, a wide variety of designs have been used in the literature.

After conducting a thorough search of MEDLINE and PsycINFO and following up on all the pertinent citations listed in relevant articles, I found 43 adult samples that examined the validity of fully structured diagnostic interviews. The first column of Table 3.2 reports citation information for these 43 samples. The next seven columns report methodological or design

TABLE 3.2
The Validity of Fully Structured Diagnostic Interviews Relative to Clinical Diagnoses: Studies, Potential Moderators, and Average Agreement

Study	False BR	Lifetime Dx	Crit incl pred	Same int	Same day	Same week	Both struc quest	Expt corr	# Dx	N	Mean κ
Anthony et al., 1985	1	0	0	0	0	0	1	1	0	810	.15
Brugha et al., 1999	1	0	0	0	0	0	1	1	15	205	.11
Eaton et al., 2000[a]	1	1	0	0	0	0	0	1	1	349	.26
Erdman et al., 1987	1	0	0	0	0	0	0	1	14	220	.14
Goethe & Ahmadi, 1991[b]	0	0	1	0	0	0	0	1	1	162	.56
Helzer et al., 1985	1	1	0	0	0	0	1	1	11	370	.35
Koenig et al., 1989	1	0	0	0	0	1	0	1	1	69	.38
Mathisen et al., 1987	0	0	0	0	0	1	1	1	5	135	.34
McLeod et al., 1990	0	0	0	0	0	0	1	1	4	347	.21
Murphy et al., 2000	1	1	0	0	0	0	1	1	1	139	.26
North et al., 1997[a]	1	1	0	0	0	0	0	1	5	97	.52
North et al., 1997	1	1	0	0	0	0	0	1	5	33	.37
Peters & Andrews, 1995	0	0	0	0	0	0	0	1	7	98	.36
L. N. Robins et al., 1982[a]	0	0	0	0	0	0	0	1	10	167	.23
Rosenman et al., 1997	0	0	0	0	0	1	0	1	70[c]	126	.10
Thornton, Russell, & Hudson, 1998	1	1	0	0	0	0	1	1	3	44	.60
Anduaga, Forteza, & Lira, 1991	1	1	0	0	0	1	1	2	14	149	.30
Booth, Kirchner, Hamilton, Harrell, & Smith, 1998	1	0	0	0	0	1	1	2	1	54	.53
Compton, Cottler, Dorsey, Spitznagel, & Mager, 1996	1	1	0	0	0	1	1	2	4	123	.57
Cooper, Peters, & Andrews, 1998	1	0	0	0	0	1	1	2	2	73	.13
Cottler et al., 1997; Pull et al., 1997[d]	1	1	0	0	0	1	1	2	12	420	.32
Hesselbrock, Stabenau, Hesselbrock, Mirkin, & Meyer, 1982	1	1	0	0	0	1	1	2	7	42	.80
Hwu, Yeh, & Chang, 1986[a]	0	0	0	0	0	1	1	2	3	100	.69
Ross, Swinson, Larkin, & Doumani, 1994	0	1	0	0	0	1	1	2	12	174	.31
Andrews, Peters, Guzman, & Bird, 1995	0	0	0	0	1	1	1	3	5	101	.40

Burnam, Karno, Hough, Escobar, & Forsythe, 1983	0	1	0	0	1	1	3	21	151	.30
Canino et al., 1987[e]	1	1	0	0	1	1	3	16	189	.56
Canino et al., 1987[e]	1	1	0	0	1	1	3	16	189	.42
Farmer, Katz, McGuffin, & Bobbington, 1987	1	0	0	0	1	1	3	5	30	.55
Hwu et al., 1986	1	0	0	0	1	1	3	11	187	.42
Peters et al., 1996	1	1	0	0	1	1	3	1	91	.46
L. N. Robins et al., 1981	1	1	0	0	1	1	3	18	204	.68
Ross et al., 1994[a,f]	0	1	1	1	0	1	3	11	80	.51
Wittchen et al., 1985	1	1	0	0	1	1	3	12	262	.62
Canino et al., 1987	1	1	1	1	1	1	4	16	189	.59
Helzer et al., 1985	1	1	1	1	1	1	4	16	189	.59
Helzer et al., 1985	1	1	1	1	1	1	4	11	370	.79
Janca, Robins, Bucholz, Early, & Shayka, 1992, & Janca, Robins, Cottler, & Early, 1992	0	0	1	1	1	1	4	3	20	.79
Kovess, Sylla, Fournier, & Flavigny, 1992	0	1	1	1	1	1	4	7	139	.66
Robins, Helzer, Ratcliff, & Seyfried, 1982	1	1	1	1	1	1	4	10	204	.65
Wittchen, Kessler, Zhao, & Abelson, 1995	1	1	1	1	1	1	4	1	36	.47
Wittchen, Zhao, Abelson, Abelson, & Kessler, 1996	1	1	1	1	1	1	4	1	40	.32
Wittchen et al., 1996	1	1	1	1	1	1	4	1	37	.54
Wittchen et al., 1996	1	1	1	1	1	1	4	1	34	.79
Correlation of moderator with mean κ	.08	.36	.48	.47	.49	.43	.29	.60	−.29	−.31

Note. BR = base rate; Dx = diagnosis; Crit incl pred = criterion diagnosis included or considered the predictor diagnosis; Int = interview; Both struc quest = both structured set of questions; Expt corr = expected correspondence between predictor and criterion (1 = low, 4 = high); # Dx = number of diagnoses examined. [a] Kappa coefficients were computed or recomputed for this study. [b] Even though Diagnostic Interview Schedule (DIS) diagnoses were available to clinicians when making final diagnoses, this study was classified as having low expected validity because the criterion diagnoses took into account a wide range of additional information. [c] This represents the maximum number of diagnoses that could have been considered. The authors did not indicate how many different diagnoses were assigned by the Composite International Diagnostic Interview (CIDI) or by the clinicians. [d] One of these studies reported correspondence with Diagnostic and Statistical manual of Mental Disorders criterion diagnoses, while the other reported correspondence with International Classification of Diseases criterion diagnoses. For this table, agreement was averaged across diagnostic systems. [e] These entries use the same sample of patients. The first entry compared lay administered DIS diagnoses to criterion diagnoses made by psychiatrists after they independently completed the DIS. The second entry compared the lay DIS diagnoses to the diagnoses made by the psychiatrists after completing the DIS and any additional follow-up questions they felt were necessary for diagnostic clarification. This study was classified as having moderately high expected validity because DIS diagnoses played a large role in final diagnostic decisions. [f] The latter were made from the results of two Structured Clinical Interview for DSM-III-R interviews in conjunction with the DIS findings.

features that were considered potential moderators of validity. These include whether the study used criterion diagnoses that were (a) derived from an artificial base rate (i.e., where diagnostic variance was increased by using diverse targeted patient groups or by mixing nonpatients with targeted patient groups), (b) based on lifetime rather than current symptomatology, (c) made after considering information from the CIDI or DIS interview, (d) made by clinicians who had attended or performed the CIDI or DIS interviews, (e) made on the same day as the CIDI or DIS diagnoses, (f) made during the same week as the CIDI or DIS diagnoses, and (g) derived from a structured set of questions or criteria (like those found on the CIDI and DIS). The ninth column contains the codes for my global expectations regarding source overlap after considering all of the methodological features in each study. In this scheme, 1 indicates the least confounded design, which should generate the lowest validity coefficients, and 4 indicates the most confounded design, which should generate the highest agreement coefficients. The next three columns report the number of diagnoses examined in each sample, the number of participants in the sample, and the average agreement (expressed by the kappa coefficient) between CIDI or DIS diagnoses and criterion diagnoses. Finally, the last row at the bottom of the table reports the correlation between each of the potential moderators and the average agreement rates that are reported in the last column.

Before examining the impact of study design on the magnitude of the final results, it is useful to briefly consider the correlations in the last row of Table 3.2. Contrary to my expectation, an artificial base rate did not have a positive univariate association with the magnitude of agreement. Although I did not have clear expectations for lifetime versus current diagnoses, lifetime diagnoses led to higher rates of diagnostic agreement. The remaining coefficients were statistically significant in the expected direction. Validity coefficients were larger when the criterion judgments took into consideration the predictor results, when criterion diagnoses were made by clinicians who attended or performed the predictor interviews, when both predictor and criterion diagnoses were determined on the same day or in the same week, and when a structured set of items or questions was used to make criterion diagnoses. As expected, the overall ranking of study designs had the largest association with the average study results ($r = .60$).[2] Finally, both the number of diagnoses under consideration and the number of patients in the study had a negative relationship with the overall magnitude of the findings. Thus, researchers who examined just a few di-

---

[2] When considering all potential moderators except for the overall classification scheme, the best predictors of average agreement across studies were the following: (a) criterion diagnoses that were made in the same week as the predictor diagnoses, (b) criterion diagnoses that were made after considering results from the CIDI or DIS predictor, (c) the number of diagnoses that were considered (inversely), and (d) a focus on lifetime rather than current diagnoses. With either a forward stepwise entry model or a backward removal model, the multiple R was .67 for these variables.

agnostic conditions in a specialty setting obtained higher estimates of CIDI or DIS validity, whereas those who conducted comprehensive large-scale studies tended to obtain lower estimates of validity.

Table 3.3 presents summary information concerning the methodological impact of criterion contamination on CIDI or DIS validity. Individual studies were organized according to the four categories of source overlap that were described earlier and listed in column 9 of Table 3.2. Recall that the extent of source overlap should predict the extent of agreement observed in the literature. The table reports the number of studies and participants in each of the four source overlap categories and provides several alternative measures for the average agreement coefficient in the literature. Moving from left to right, the summary coefficients go from the least refined (i.e., the unweighted mean, where every study is given equal weight) to the most refined (i.e., the mean after weighting studies by the number of participants included and the number of diagnoses considered). Considering coefficients in the last column, one can see that methodological artifacts have a very large impact on the apparent extent to which CIDI or DIS diagnoses accurately predict the criterion diagnoses. The studies with the least amount of source overlap and criterion contamination produce the lowest estimates of accuracy (i.e., mean = .19). As predictor diagnoses and criterion diagnoses share more source contamination, the coefficients steadily increase in magnitude (i.e., means = .34 and .51) until they reach their peak, which occurs when clinicians make their criterion diagnoses on the basis of just the CIDI or DIS interview and a limited number of additional, nonscripted follow-up questions (mean = .69). Thus, source overlap plays a mighty role in determining the seeming accuracy of fully structured diagnostic interviews across studies in the research literature.

Next, these data on validity are linked with data on reliability to demonstrate that methodological factors affecting cross-source agreement

TABLE 3.3
Summary of the Accuracy of Fully Structured Diagnostic Interviews as a Function of Predictor–Criterion Overlap

Degree of Source Overlap	K	Total N	Mean κ		
			Unweighted	N weighted	N and # of Dx weighted
Low	16	3,371	.3090	.2510	.1867[a]
Moderately low	8	1,135	.4562	.3898	.3414
Moderately high	10	1,484	.4933	.5067	.5087
High	9	1,069	.6235	.6763	.6903
Across all samples	43	7,059	.4451	.3915	.3689

Note. K = number of studies; Dx = diagnoses. [a]One study considered up to 70 diagnoses, which was an outlier relative to other studies. When the number of diagnoses was limited to a maximum of 30 to make this study more consistent with others, the sample and diagnosis weighted average κ was .2032.

are on a single uniform continuum. The continuum is one that characterizes the independence of information sources. The upper end of this continuum should be anchored by reliability designs that make use of maximally similar information, whereas the lower end should be anchored by validity coefficients that are derived from truly independent sources of information.

More than 40 years ago, Campbell and Fiske (1959) succinctly described this dimension and the terms *reliability* and *validity*. Their classic article contained the section "Convergence of Independent Methods: The Distinction Between Reliability and Validity." In it they said the following:

> Both reliability and validity concepts require that agreement between measures be demonstrated. A common denominator that most validity concepts share in contradistinction to reliability is that this agreement represents the convergence of independent approaches. . . . The importance of independence recurs in most discussions of proof. . . . Independence is, of course, a matter of degree, and in this sense, reliability and validity can be seen as regions on a continuum. . . . Reliability is the agreement between two efforts to measure the same trait through maximally similar methods. Validity is represented in the agreement between two attempts to measure the same trait through maximally different methods. (p. 83)

Campbell and Fisk proceeded to illustrate this continuum by discussing both reliability and validity designs that have greater and lesser degrees of source overlap. Thus, from their perspective, the propensity to think of coefficients in dichotomous terms as indicating either "reliability" or "validity" is quite mistaken. Various types of reliability designs produce a continuum of source independence, as do various types of validity designs. Furthermore, as Campbell and Fiske pointed out, traditional concepts of reliability and validity do not form distinct regions on the source overlap continuum. Some designs that are traditionally considered indicative of validity could be more properly considered indicative of reliability and vice versa.

Previously, I reported CIDI reliability data from Wittchen's (1994) review of the literature. In line with a continuum of source independence, diagnostic decisions derived from a joint interview design should produce the highest reliability coefficients because all information is held constant. Determinations from separate, independently conducted interviews should produce lower reliability coefficients, and coefficients should decline as the delay between interviews becomes longer. Wittchen presented fairly extensive evidence on the reliability of joint interviews. He reported a mean kappa of .92 ($N = 575$) across 21 diagnostic categories for this type of design. These reliability data were added as the fifth point on the continuum of methodological overlap. Consequently, the continuum had now the following range: 1 = low source overlap and low expected agreement coefficients; 2 = moderately-low source overlap and moderately-low expected agreement coefficients; 3 = moderately-high source overlap and moderately-high expected agreement coefficients; 4 = high source overlap and high expected agreement coefficients; and 5 = total source overlap (i.e., joint interview reliability) and highest expected agreement coefficients.

Figure 3.1 displays the average coefficients relative to each of these five categories. There is a near-perfect linear relationship between these five methodological categories and the average degree of cross-source agreement observed in the research literature. Reliability and validity clearly are on a single continuum. This continuum varies as a function of how much

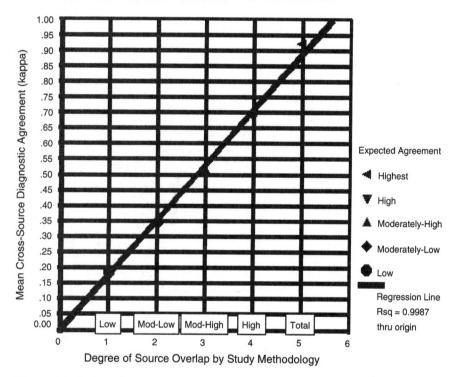

Figure 3.1. Average cross-source agreement for fully structured diagnostic interviews as a function of criterion contamination based on methodologically driven source overlap. The source overlap categories are as follows: Low = predictor diagnoses derived from structured interviews and criterion diagnoses derived from alternative and largely independent sources of information (N = 3,371); Moderately-Low = predictor and criterion diagnoses derived from independently administered structured interviews within the same week (N = 1,135); Moderately-High = predictor and criterion diagnoses derived from independently administered structured interviews on the same day (N = 1,484); High = criterion diagnoses derived from clinicians who considered little information beyond the structured interviews that also determined the predictor diagnoses (N = 1,135); Total = joint interview reliability designs (N = 575). Rsq = R^2.

one source of measurement overlaps or influences the other source of measurement. Thus, the validity or accuracy of a single source of measurement relative to a common criterion is not fixed. Rather, accuracy fluctuates as a function of how much source overlap exists between the predictor and the criterion. In terms of diagnoses, the accuracy of CIDI or DIS diagnoses that are determined by patient self-reports relative to clinician diagnoses is not constant. Indeed, many studies in the research literature produce an illusion of CIDI and DIS accuracy because they use a design that is heavily confounded by source overlap, and this artificially inflates the statistical results.

Although I anticipated a positive relationship as one moved up the validity–reliability continuum, the remarkable linear association in Figure 3.1 was unexpected. After the average coefficients are organized by methodological features in the primary studies, they have virtually no deviation from a perfect linear relationship (a regression line through the origin of Figure 3.1 explains 99.87% of the variance in the aggregated coefficients; i.e., $R^2 = .9987$). However, this result is accidental in the sense that there was no reason to believe that the five gross categories of source overlap on the horizontal axis should have produced essentially equal interval scaling. For instance, if sufficient data from other reliability designs with high source overlap had been available, it is possible that the joint reliability coefficients that are currently in category 5 would have been placed in a category labeled 6 or 7. Doing so would have produced a curvilinear relationship in Figure 3.1.

Similarly, the figure could have plotted results from a reliability design that is relatively free of source overlap problems (e.g., the stability of lifetime disorders over 1 year with baseline and retest interviews conducted by independent clinicians). If one were thinking in terms of traditional reliability versus validity categories rather than in terms of source overlap, the results from these relatively unconfounded reliability studies could have been (erroneously) assigned to a category greater than 4. Doing so would have again produced a different looking graph than that presented in Figure 3.1.

Despite these issues, the linear relationship displayed in Figure 3.1 provides strong support for the overall hypothesis. The figure could also provide a tentative template for examining the results of alternative methodological designs. For instance, if a sample of studies examining the 1-year retest stability of independently conducted CIDI or DIS interviews produced an average agreement coefficient of .40, Figure 3.1 would suggest that these studies have a source overlap "score" of approximately 2.25. In turn, this would indicate that this reliability design has less contamination from source overlap than two of the validity designs commonly reported in the literature.

The data presented in Table 3.3 and Figure 3.1 have been discussed in terms of the accuracy of CIDI or DIS diagnoses as predictor variables. However, these same data speak to the accuracy of the criterion diagnoses. Every study in Table 3.2 used what the authors believed would be reasonable or optimal clinical diagnoses to validate the CIDI or DIS. If criterion clinical diagnoses were genuine clinical realities, they would remain fixed or constant across studies, and the findings from different samples would converge on the same statistical parameter regarding the accuracy of CIDI or DIS diagnoses. As such, the only factor that would influence the observed estimates of accuracy from one study to the next would be sampling error (e.g., Hunter & Schmidt, 1990). However, because the average agreement coefficients vary widely, the data clearly indicate that the literature is not estimating a single statistical parameter for CIDI and DIS accuracy or for the accuracy of the criterion diagnoses.

Instead, criterion diagnoses are shaped by and conform to the sources of information that are considered in the diagnostic process. When a clinician has only the patient's self-report on a given occasion as a source of information, diagnostic decisions conform to the limitations imposed by that source. As the clinician considers more and more independent sources of information, diagnostic decisions increasingly diverge from the decisions that would be suggested by that self-reported information.

The upshot of this is important. In the absence of conflicting or contradictory data from independent sources, a clinician who consults a single source of information makes decisions that conform to the data provided by that source. The clinician is likely to feel confident about those decisions (after all, there would be no data to suggest otherwise), but as Table 3.3 and Figure 3.1 indicate, these decisions are most likely to be unstable, ephemeral, and ultimately inaccurate.

STRATEGIES FOR SYNTHESIZING INFORMATION AND DATA INDICATING THE VALUE OF DOING SO

The findings presented so far indicate a primary challenge that faces any system developed to replace or supplement the current *DSM*. Regardless of the specific content that is used to define pathology, an empirically guided alternative system should formally require clinicians who use the system to systematically consider multiple, maximally independent sources of information prior to making diagnostic determinations.

If the extensive body of data reviewed in Table 3.1 is taken to heart, it is clear that any single source of information is incomplete and limited. Sophisticated clinicians and researchers should expect associations of about .20–.30 between alternative data sources, and this should fuel the motivation to systematically gather data from multiple independent sources whenever an accurate understanding of the patient is required.

These principles really should not come as a surprise to psychologists. They have been embedded in the classic literature on psychometrics (e.g., Campbell & Fiske, 1959) and experimental design (e.g., Cook & Campbell, 1979). For instance, Cook and Campbell illuminated how the construct validity of nomothetic research can be seriously compromised by mono-method and mono-operation bias. As such, optimal nomothetic research maximizes construct validity by obtaining data from multiple methods of assessment, multiple sources of information, and multiple operational definitions of the target construct. Meyer et al. (1998; Meyer et al., 2001) pointed out how these nomothetic research principles also provide an optimal guide for idiographic clinical practice. Just as optimal research recognizes that any given source of information is incomplete, optimal clinical practice should recognize that identical limitations are in place when conceptualizing the complex life of a single patient. As such, clinicians should seek to minimize mono-method and mono-operation bias in their clinical work by synthesizing information gathered from multiple sources.

Several strategies can be used for synthesizing multisource information. These include simple procedures of mathematical aggregation, the integration of data by a single clinician, and the integration of data by two or more clinicians. In the process of describing the strengths and limitations of these approaches, I also highlight the emerging evidence that indicates these strategies improve the quality of information used in clinical decision making.

Simple Mathematical Aggregation

A long psychometric history speaks to the value of an aggregated mean or sum as a procedure for improving the reliability and validity of information. Indeed, when the principle of aggregation is applied to the number of items in a scale (akin to the number of criteria required for a diagnosis), it forms the basis of the well-known Spearman-Brown Prophecy Formula for estimating the reliability of a composite. (For overviews and recent extensions, see Li, Rosenthal, and Rubin, 1996, and Drewes, 2000.) More important, classics in the research literature have demonstrated how aggregating information over occasions (i.e., longitudinally), over stimuli (e.g., one diagnostic interview format and another), over methods of measurement (e.g., highly structured and unstructured), and over sources of information (e.g., self-report and spouse report) can drastically increase the validity of the aggregated information (see Epstein, 1980, 1983; Rushton, Brainerd, & Pressley, 1983).

Tsujimoto et al. (1990) presented a formula for estimating the validity of a score or judgment that should emerge when aggregating across sources of information. Although Tsujimoto et al.'s formula was devised for use with different kinds of raters, it could also incorporate different occasions, stimuli, or methods as sources of data. The expected validity of a composite (subject to sampling error) is a function of three things: the degree of validity typically found with a single source of information, the number of sources that contribute data to the aggregated ratings, and the average pairwise agreement between the different sources. Considering this information, Tsujimoto et al. demonstrate how the validity of the aggregated score or judgment hinges on the average agreement between information sources. Although superficially counterintuitive, validity increases when cross-source agreement decreases. Thus, validity is maximized when sources of information provide independent and nonredundant data about the same phenomenon.

How practical is this approach to integrating information? Consider an example related to diagnoses. Consistent with Table 3.1, assume that a diagnostic construct obtained from the patient's self-report correlates with the same construct assessed by an external judge at a magnitude of .30. Further assume that other sources of information (e.g., parent, spouse, friend, coworker, therapist) also agree with each other at a magnitude of .30. Theoretically, according to Tsujimoto et al.'s (1990) formula, if a final diagnostic determination was based on the average rating from three of these sources (e.g., the patient, a peer, and his or her therapist), the expected validity of the diagnostic construct would be .41 rather than .30. This is a salient positive change. Note, however, that this example draws on three independent sources of information with low levels of agreement between them. If the sources were largely redundant, the expected validity would not improve much. For instance, consider a patient's self-reports of diagnostic symptomatology and the diagnostic ratings provided by two clinicians who attended the same highly structured interview with the patient. If we assume that the true validity of the patient's rating remains fixed at .30 and assume that the two clinicians produce ratings that correlate with each other at .80, the validity of the three-rater composite only increases from .30 to .32.

The main advantage of using mathematical aggregation to maximize validity is that it is simple. Sophisticated clinical judgment is not required to synthesize the multisource information. Instead, every data source is treated as equally valid and equally error prone. Thus, all that is required is some mechanism for computing an average or combined score across the different sources. The chief disadvantage of this approach is identical to its main advantage. Because every data source is treated as equally error prone and because clinical judgment is not used to synthesize the information, meaningful and important cross-method discrepancies are likely to be overlooked.

For instance, with this approach, one would not be able to identify the propensity of narcissistic individuals to present themselves in an overly favorable and biased light relative to the view held by external observers (e.g., Colvin, Block, & Funder, 1995; Gosling, John, Craik, & Robins, 1998; R. W. Robins & John, 1997). Indeed, whereas research has clearly demonstrated that aggregated information provides enhanced validity for assessing the moods and personality traits of nonpatients (e.g., Cheek, 1982; Kolar, Funder, & Colvin, 1996; Moskowitz & Schwarz, 1982; Watson & Clark, 1991), the findings have been mixed in the area of clinical diagnoses (e.g., Bird, Gould, & Staghezza, 1992; Ezpeleta, de la Osa, Doménech, Navarro, & Losilla, 1997; Jensen et al., 1995; Offord et al., 1996; Piacentini, Cohen, & Cohen, 1992; Rubio-Stipec et al., 1994; Schwab-Stone et al., 1996).

For instance, Offord et al. (1996) examined several methods for combining diagnostic information about a large sample of children using data from parents and teachers ($N = 1,134$). They found that composite information was not decisively more valid than information derived from a single source. In fact, efforts to combine data across sources appeared to mask the distinctive and unique information that could be obtained from each individual source. As a result, Offord et al. concluded that childhood diagnoses should be considered source specific entities. Diagnoses derived from parents are inherently different than diagnoses derived from teachers, and both should be treated as distinct and unique data rather than combined.

Integration of Multisource Information by a Clinician

A clear advantage of having a clinician integrate multisource information is that the clinician can attend to meaningful cross-source discrepancies on the basis of the patient's idiographic characteristics. Thus, unlike the simple mathematical rules described above, a clinician can consider forms of bias that may affect different sources (e.g., the patient's denial mechanisms or excessive criticisms, the observer's inability to access the patient's internal states) or genuine variations in the way problems may be expressed across settings (e.g., that which is seen by a spouse but not a peer or vice versa) in order to identify how the data fit a meaningful pattern or when one source of information should be given more credence than another. When done properly, this would allow the clinician to synthesize all the available multisource information to generate a cohesive and individualized picture of the patient and his or her presenting problems.

The disadvantage of this approach lies in its complexity and the absence of clear models that specify how to weigh opposing information from distinct sources. To meaningfully integrate discrepant sources of data requires sophisticated clinical judgment, a theory about how people are put together, and a capacity to diligently and faithfully think through all of the observed discrepancies. This can be accomplished by clinicians working alone, although it is often a challenge because clinical reasoning is itself subject to various lapses in judgment (see, e.g., Arkes, 1981; Borum, Otto, & Golding, 1993; Garb, 1998).

Integration by Two or More Clinicians

The final option for integrating multisource data is to have two or more clinicians synthesize information from various sources. This approach allows for an idiographic understanding of meaningful cross-method disparities while simultaneously minimizing the errors that can creep into the reasoning of a single clinician working alone. This process can be implemented formally through team discussions or informally through consultation. Much of the relevant research literature has examined the more formal mechanism of team discussion, although this may be too expensive or unrealistic to implement in many settings. As such, informal consultation with another professional can provide a practical alternative. This often can be accomplished most readily by referring patients for a multimethod psychological or neuropsychological evaluation (see Meyer et al., 1998; Meyer et al., 2001).

Probably the most frequently researched procedure for synthesizing multisource information emerges from what Spitzer (1983) briefly described as the longitudinal expert evaluation of all data (LEAD) model for generating gold standard judgments. In this approach, expert clinicians evaluate a patient over time and independently use all available sources of information to formulate a diagnosis or make a description of the patient's personality. Subsequently, the experts jointly review the determinations they had made independently, identify points of disagreement, and resolve any discrepancies to arrive at final decisions. Although time intensive and demanding, the LEAD method has been successfully applied in numerous investigations (e.g., Fennig, Craig, Tanenberg-Karant, & Bromet, 1994; Klein, Ouimette, Kelly, Ferro, & Riso, 1994; Leckman, Sholomskas, Thompson, Belanger, & Weissman, 1982; Mazaide et al., 1992; Pilkonis, Heape, Ruddy, & Serrao, 1991). When properly implemented, the LEAD procedure provides clinical data that come about as close to optimal as possible.

A number of studies have examined the interrater reliability of these best-estimate, multisource diagnoses and have found them to be reproducible despite the absence of explicit guidelines for how clinicians should go about integrating the discrepant information (e.g., Fennig et al., 1994; Leckman et al., 1982; Maziade et al., 1992). However, because the same sources of information are used by all the clinicians making determinations (i.e., interview transcripts, medical records), the design is similar to the joint interview reliability study, in which there is extensive source overlap (e.g., Figure 3.1).

More impressive evidence regarding the value of multisource determinations would emerge from studies that fall further along on the validity end of the continuum. Although I am not aware of studies comparing the relative validity of single-source and multisource diagnostic assessments against a truly external criterion measure (e.g., independently measured etiological factors), studies have examined the stability of diagnoses that should remain constant over time. These include personality disorders and diagnoses that are assigned for the lifetime history of a disorder. If multisource assessments are necessary to accurately capture clinical phenomena, then lifetime disorders and personality disorders should show higher levels of stability when they are diagnosed using multisource procedures rather than single sources of information.

The most compelling evidence on this topic comes from the research of Daniel Klein and his colleagues (1994). These investigators devised a set of seven guidelines to integrate the information provided by patients, relatives, and treatment records in the context of deliberations made by a team of clinicians. They reported retest stability coefficients (kappa) for multisource determinations that were made twice over a period of approximately 2.5 years. Diagnostic determinations were made for 12 personality disorder classifications and for 7 Axis I lifetime diagnoses. Their results are presented in Tables 3.4 and 3.5, along with relevant comparison data.

Table 3.4 deals with the stability of Axis II personality disorders. This table also contains multisource results from a study by Pilkonis et al. (1991). The two multisource assessment studies are presented on the left, and the results from seven single-source assessment studies are on the right. The multisource findings from Klein et al. (1994) in the second column can be compared in a fairly direct manner with the single-source findings that are reported in the fourth column. Both sets of results were generated from the same ongoing project, but the latter coefficients were obtained from the Personality Disorder Examination (PDE), which is a semistructured interview that relies on the patient as the sole source of information (see Ferro, Klein, Schwartz, Kasch, & Leader, 1998). The Pilkonis et al. (1991) study provides a direct comparison for multisource assessments (3rd column) and single-source assessments made with the PDE (8th column). The remaining studies in Table 3.4 provide single-source stability coefficients across time periods that ranged from 2 years to less than 2 weeks.

Overall, Table 3.4 reveals that multisource assessments produce substantially larger stability coefficients than single-source assessments. In fact, all of the 2.5-year stability coefficients from Klein et al.'s study of synthesized judgments exceed the stability coefficients reported in each of the single-source studies, including the very short 1- to 14-day retest coefficients that were obtained by First et al. (1995). Similarly, the multisource determinations from Pilkonis et al. are more stable over 6 months than the relevant comparison data drawn from equivalent or shorter retest in-

TABLE 3.4

The Stability of Personality Disorder Diagnoses Derived From Multiple vs. Single Sources of Information as Measured by the Kappa Coefficient

Disorder	Multisource		Single Source						
	Klein[a] (2.5 y, N = 92)	Pilkonis[b] (6 m, N = 31)	Klein[c] (2.5 y, N = 92)	Cacciola[d] (2 y, N = 219)	Mattanah[e] (2 y, N = 65)	Weiss[f] (1 y, N = 31)	Pilkonis[g] (6 m, N = 31)	Zimmerman[h] (5 m, N = 66–457)	First[i] (1–14 d, N = 284)
Any personality disorder	.93	.84	.22	.51	.18		.54	.58	.49
Any Cluster A disorder	.78		.60	.12	.14	.47			.45
Any Cluster C disorder	.91		.34	.47	.20	.27			.56
Any Cluster B disorder	.75		.28	.25	.19	.42			.44
Schizoid	.88		.42[j]	.09					
Antisocial	.94		.16[j]	.45		.41		.48	.71
Borderline	.84		.40	.30	−.01	.02		.61	.48
Histrionic	.86		.48	−.06		.59		.43	.62
Narcissistic	.93		−.02[j]	.35		.59		.25	.42
Avoidant	.82		.33[j]	.23		−.15		.47	.54
Obsessive–compulsive	.73		.10[j]	−.04		.26		.35	.24
Passive–aggressive	.90		.16[j]	.21	.16	.63		.09	.41
Mean	.86	.84	.29	.24	.14	.35	.54	.41	.49

Note. y = years; m = months; d = days. [a]Klein et al., 1994. [b]Pilkonis et al., 1994. [c]Ferro et al., 1998 (this sample was drawn from the same overall project as Klein et al., 1994). [d]Cacciola, Rutherford, Alterman, McKay, & Mulvaney, 1998. [e]Mattanah, Becker, Levy, Edel, & McGlashan, 1995 (this study used adolescents, which may have contributed to lower stability; it also used a quasi-longitudinal expert evaluation of all data procedure at baseline, although the follow-up data were drawn solely from a structured interview with the patient). [f]Weiss, Najavits, Muenz, & Hufford, 1995 (coefficients were computed from raw data). [g]This study uses the same sample as that used in the Pilkonis et al., 1991, multisource diagnoses. [h]Zimmerman, 1994 (standardized interview data were obtained from the review presented in Table 3 and were supplemented with Loranger et al.'s [1994] more detailed results. The specific sample sizes were as follows: any personality disorder, 391; antisocial, 363; borderline, 457; histrionic, 423; narcissistic, 144; avoidant, 421; obsessive–compulsive, 101; and passive–aggressive, 66). [i]First et al., 1995 (when it was not possible to obtain exact coefficients across all participants from their tables, the weighted average coefficient was computed from the patient and nonpatient samples). [j]Coefficients were generated from the reported data, but they were not calculated by the authors because the disorders had a base rate less than .05 at either baseline or retest. Only narcissistic personality disorder had a base rate less than .05 on both occasions.

TABLE 3.5
The Stability of Lifetime Axis I Diagnoses Derived From Multiple vs. Single Sources of Information as Measured by the Kappa Coefficient

Disorder	Klein[a] (2.5 y, N = 92)	Rice[b] (6 y, N = 1,629)	Prusoff[c] (24.7 y, N = 413)	Fendrich[d] (2 y, N = 69)	Bromet[e] (1.5 y, N = 391)	Keller[f] (6 m, N = 84–95)	Andreasen[g] (6 m, N = 50)	Helzer[h] (6 w, N = 394)	Williams[i] (1–14 days, N = 592)
Major depression	.90	.61	.80	.54	.41	.36	.75	.50	.62
Recurrent major depression	.77						.21		
Dysthymia	.75					.53			.44
Alcoholism	.86	.70	.41	.66			.72	.68	.74
Drug abuse	1.00	.56	.56	.66				.52	.85
Phobia	1.00	.34	.32	.33				.36[j]	.50[j]
Any anxiety disorder	.94	.30[k]	.55[k]	.41			.15[k]		.56[k]
Mean	.89	.50	.53	.52	.41	.45	.46	.52	.62

Note. All studies were single source except Klein, which was multisource. [a] Klein et al. (1994). [b] Rice, Rochberg, Endicott, Lavori, and Miller (1992). [c] Prusoff, Merikangas, and Weissman (1988). [d] Fendrich, Weissman, Warner, and Mufson (1990). Coefficients are from participants aged 18 years or older at the baseline evaluation. The coefficient for any substance abuse is reported in both the alcoholism and drug abuse row. [e] Bromet, Dunn, Connell, Dew, and Schulberg (1986). [f] Keller et al. (1995). [g] Andreasen et al. (1981). The follow-up diagnoses in this sample were obtained from the consensus of two independent interviewers. [h] Helzer et al. (1985). [i] Williams et al. (1992). [j] Coefficient reflects the average value for social phobia and simple phobia. [k] Coefficient is for generalized anxiety disorder.

tervals. These findings clearly illustrate the importance of conducting a multisource assessment to maximize the validity of clinical determinations.

Similar findings are evident for the lifetime Axis I disorders presented in Table 3.5. The 2.5-year stability coefficients from Klein et al.'s (1994) multisource, synthesized clinical judgments are presented on the left, and single-source comparison data drawn from various retest intervals are presented on the right. Note that two of the comparison studies used a substantially longer re-evaluation interval than Klein et al. (4.7 and 6 years vs. 2.5 years), so they should be expected to produce lower stability coefficients (e.g., Roberts & DelVecchio, 2000). Moreover, none of the comparison studies draw on the same sample of patients as Klein et al., and the coefficients fluctuate substantially from one sample to another (e.g., the stability of a major depressive disorder is about .60 in the two largest studies, even though the retest interval is just 1–14 days in one study and it is 6 years in the other). Because differences in samples and study designs undoubtedly contribute to the fluctuating stability coefficients, it is more difficult to isolate the impact of a multisource assessment method. Nevertheless, the results appear clear-cut. Determinations about Axis I lifetime disorders that are made on the basis of multiple, independent sources of information appear to be much more valid than the same determinations made from interviews with the patient as the sole source of information.

CONCLUSION

This chapter has a very simple take-home message. If we wish to accurately describe or classify patients, we must synthesize information from multiple independent methods and multiple independent sources. This is not just a good idea. Rather, it is a necessity if we wish to have a refined, empirically grounded taxonomy of psychological health and illness. The data presented here have been collected over many years, across a diverse range of patients, and over a broad domain of psychological attributes. They amply illustrate how any classification system applied to human functioning and pathology remains ephemeral and elusive unless clinical determinations are grounded in carefully synthesized judgments that incorporate data drawn from diverse sources of information, assessment methods, and points in time.

REFERENCES

Achenbach, T. M., McConaughy, S. H., & Howell, C. T. (1987). Child/adolescent behavioral and emotional problems: Implications of cross-informant correlations for situational specificity. *Psychological Bulletin, 101,* 213–232.

American Psychiatric Association. (1994). *Diagnostic and statistical manual of mental disorders, 4th ed. (DSM–IV)*. Washington, DC: Author.

Andreasen, N. C., Grove, W. M., Shapiro, R. W., Keller, M. B., Hirschfeld, R. M. A., & McDonald-Scott, P. (1981). Reliability of lifetime diagnosis: A multicenter collaborative perspective. *Archives of General Psychiatry, 38*, 400–405

Andrews, G., Peters, L., Guzman, A. M., & Bird, K. (1995). A comparison of two structured diagnostic interviews: CIDI and SCAN. *Australian and New Zealand Journal of Psychiatry, 29*, 124–132.

Anduaga, J. C., Forteza, C. G., & Lira, L. R. (1991). Concurrent validity of the DIS: Experience with psychiatric patients in Mexico City. *Hispanic Journal of Behavioral Sciences, 13*, 63–77.

Anthony, J. C., Folstein, M., Romanoski, A. J., Von Korff, M. R., Nestadt, G. R., Chahal, R., Merchant, A., Brown, C. H., Shapiro, S., Kramer, M., & Gruenberg, E. M. (1985). Comparison of the lay Diagnostic Interview Schedule and a standardized psychiatric diagnosis: Experience in Eastern Baltimore. *Archives of General Psychiatry, 42*, 667–675.

Arkes, H. R. (1981). Impediments to accurate clinical judgment and possible ways to minimize their impact. *Journal of Consulting and Clinical Psychology, 49*, 323–330.

Bernstein, D. P., Kasapis, C., Bergman, A., Weld, E., Mitropoulou, V., Horvath, T., Klar, H., Silverman, J., & Siever, L. J. (1997). Assessing Axis II disorders by informant interview. *Journal of Personality Disorders, 11*, 158–167.

Bird, H. R., Gould, M. S., & Staghezza, B. (1992). Aggregating data from multiple informants in child psychiatry epidemiological research. *Journal of the American Academy of Child and Adolescent Psychiatry, 31*, 78–85.

Booth, B. M., Kirchner, J. E., Hamilton, G., Harrell, R., & Smith, G. R. (1998). Diagnosing depression in the medically ill: Validity of a lay-administered structured diagnostic interview. *Journal of Psychiatric Research, 32*, 353–360.

Borum, R., Otto, R., & Golding, S. (1993). Improving clinical judgment and decision making in forensic evaluation. *Journal of Psychiatry & Law, 21*, 35–76.

Bromet, E. J., Dunn, L. O., Connell, M. M., Dew, M. A., & Schulberg, H. C. (1986). Long-term reliability of diagnosing lifetime major depression in a community sample. *Archives of General Psychiatry, 43*, 435–440.

Brugha, T. S., Bebbington, P. E., Jenkins, R., Meltzer, H., Taub, N. A., Jana, M., & Vernon, J. (1999). Cross validation of a general population survey diagnostic interview: A comparison of CIS–R with SCAN ICD–10 diagnostic categories. *Psychological Medicine, 29*, 1029–1042.

Burnam, M. A., Karno, M., Hough, R. L., Escobar, J. I., & Forsythe, A. B. (1983). The Spanish Diagnostic Interview Schedule: Reliability and comparison with clinical diagnoses. *Archives of General Psychiatry, 40*, 1189–1196.

Cacciola, J. S., Rutherford, M. J., Alterman, A. I., McKay, J. R., & Mulvaney, F. D. (1998). Long-term test–retest reliability of personality disorder diagnoses in opiate dependent patients. *Journal of Personality Disorders, 12*, 332–337.

Campbell, D. T., & Fiske, D. W. (1959). Convergent and discriminant validation by the multitrait–multimethod matrix. *Psychological Bulletin, 56*, 81–105.

Canino, G. J., Bird, H. R., Shrout, P. E., Rubio-Stipec, M., Bravo, M., Martinez, R., Sesman, M., Guzman, A., Guevara, L. M., & Costas, H. (1987). The Spanish Diagnostic Interview Schedule: Reliability and concordance with clinical diagnoses in Puerto Rico. *Archives of General Psychiatry, 44*, 720–726.

Cheek, J. M. (1982). Aggregation, moderator variables, and the validity of personality tests: A peer-rating study. *Journal of Personality and Social Psychology, 43*, 1254–1269.

Colvin, C. R., Block, J., & Funder, D. C. (1995). Overly positive self-evaluations and personality: Negative implications for mental health. *Journal of Personality and Social Psychology, 68*, 1152–1162.

Compton, W. M., Cottler, L. B., Dorsey, K. B., Spitznagel, E. L., & Mager, D. E. (1996). Comparing assessments of *DSM–IV* substance dependence disorders using CIDI–SAM and SCAN. *Drug and Alcohol Dependence, 41*, 179–187.

Cook, T. D., & Campbell, D. T. (1979). *Quasi-experimentation: Design & analysis issues for field settings.* Boston: Houghton Mifflin.

Cooper, L., Peters, L., & Andrews, G. (1998). Validity of the Composite International Diagnostic Interview (CIDI) psychosis module in a psychiatric setting. *Journal of Psychiatric Research, 32*, 361–368.

Cottler, L. B., Grant, B. F., Blaine, J., Mavreas, V., Pull, C., Hasin, D., Compton, W. M., Rubio-Stipec, M., & Mager, D. (1997). Concordance of *DSM–IV* alcohol and drug use disorder criteria and diagnoses as measured by AUDADIS–ADR, CIDI, and SCAN. *Drug and Alcohol Dependence, 47*, 195–205.

Drewes, D. W. (2000). Beyond Spearman-Brown: A structural approach to maximal reliability. *Psychological Methods, 5*, 214–227.

Eaton, W. W., Neufeld, K., Chen, L.-S., & Cai, G. (2000). A comparison of self-report and clinical diagnostic interviews for depression: Diagnostic Interview Schedule and Schedules for Clinical Assessment in Neuropsychiatry in the Baltimore Epidemiologic Catchment Area follow-up. *Archives of General Psychiatry, 57*, 217–222.

Epstein, S. (1980). The stability of behavior: II. Implications for psychological research. *American Psychologist, 35*, 790–806.

Epstein, S. (1983). Aggregation and beyond: Some basic issues on the prediction of behavior. *Journal of Personality, 51*, 360–392.

Erdman, H. P., Klein, M. H., Greist, J. H., Bass, S. M., Bires, J. K., & Machtinger, P. E. (1987). A comparison of the Diagnostic Interview Schedule and clinical diagnosis. *American Journal of Psychiatry, 144*, 1477–1480.

Ezpeleta, L., de la Osa, N., Doménech, J. M., Navarro, J. B., & Losilla, J. M. (1997). Diagnostic agreement between clinicians and the Diagnostic Interview for Children and Adolescents (DICA–R) in an outpatient sample. *Journal of Child Psychology and Psychiatry, 38*, 431–440.

Farmer, A. E., Katz, R., McGuffin, P., & Bobbington, P. (1987). A comparison between the Present State Examination and the Composite International Diagnostic Interview. *Archives of General Psychiatry, 44,* 1064–1068.

Fendrich, M., Weissman, M. M., Warner, V., & Mufson, L. (1990). Two-year recall of lifetime diagnoses in offspring at high and low risk for major depression: The stability of offspring reports. *Archives of General Psychiatry, 47,* 1121–1127.

Fennig, S., Craig, T. J., Tanenberg-Karant, M., & Bromet, E. J. (1994). Comparison of facility and research diagnoses in first-admission psychotic patients. *American Journal of Psychiatry, 151,* 1423–1429.

Ferro, T., Klein, D. N., Schwartz, J. E., Kasch, K. L., & Leader, J. B. (1998). 30-month stability of personality disorder diagnoses in depressed outpatients. *American Journal of Psychiatry, 155,* 653–659.

First, M. B., Spitzer, R. L., Gibbon, M., Williams, J. B. W., Davies, M., Borus, J., Howes, M. J., Kane, J., Pope, H. G., Jr., & Rounsaville, B. (1995). The Structured Clinical Interview for *DSM–III–R* Personality Disorders (SCID–II). Part II: Multi-site test-retest reliability study. *Journal of Personality Disorders, 9,* 92–104.

Garb, H. N. (1998). *Studying the clinician: Judgment research and psychological assessment.* Washington, DC: American Psychological Association.

Goethe, J. W., & Ahmadi, K. S. (1991). Comparison of Diagnostic Interview Schedule to psychiatrist diagnoses of alcohol use disorder in psychiatric inpatients. *American Journal of Drug and Alcohol Abuse, 17,* 61–69.

Gómez-Beneyto, M., Villar, M., Renovell, M., Pérez, F., Hernandez, M., Leal, C., Cuquerella, M., Slok, C., & Asencio, A. (1994). The diagnosis of personality disorder with a modified version of the SCID–II in a Spanish clinical sample. *Journal of Personality Disorders, 8,* 104–110.

Gosling, S. D., John, O. P., Craik, K. H., & Robins, R. W. (1998). Do people know how they behave? Self-reported act frequencies compared with on-line coding of observers. *Journal of Personality and Social Psychology, 74,* 1337–1349.

Helzer, J. E., Robins, L. N., McEvoy, L. T., Spitznagel, E. L., Stoltzman, R. K., Farmer, A., & Brockington, I. F. (1985). A comparison of clinical and Diagnostic Interview Schedule diagnoses: Physician reexamination of lay-interviewed cases in the general population. *Archives of General Psychiatry, 42,* 657–666.

Hesselbrock, V., Stabenau, J., Hesselbrock, M., Mirkin, P., & Meyer, R. (1982). A comparison of two interview schedules: The Schedule for Affective Disorders and Schizophrenia-Lifetime and the National Institute for Mental Health Diagnostic Interview Schedule. *Archives of General Psychiatry, 39,* 674–677.

Hunter, J. E., & Schmidt, F. L. (1990). *Methods of meta-analysis: Correcting error and bias in research findings.* Newbury Park, CA: Sage.

Hwu, H. G., Yeh, E. K., & Chang, L. Y. (1986). Chinese Diagnostic Interview Schedule: I. Agreement with psychiatrist's diagnosis. *Acta Psychiatrica Scandinavica, 73,* 225–233.

Janca, A., Robins, L. N., Bucholz, K. K., Early, T. S., & Shayka, J. J. (1992). Comparison of Composite International Diagnostic Interview and clinical *DSM–III–R* criteria checklist diagnoses. *Acta Psychiatrica Scandinavica, 85,* 440–443.

Janca, A., Robins, L. N., Cottler, L. B., & Early, T. S. (1992). Clinical observation of assessment using the Composite International Diagnostic Interview (CIDI): An analysis of the CIDI Field Trials–Wave II at the St Louis site. *British Journal of Psychiatry, 160,* 815–818.

Jensen, P., Roper, M., Fisher, P., Piacentini, J., Canino, G., Richters, J., Rubio-Stipec, M., Dulcan, M., Goodman, S., Davies, M., Rae, D., Shaffer, D., Bird, H., Lahey, B., & Schwab-Stone, M. (1995). Test–retest reliability of the Diagnostic Interview Schedule for Children (DISC 2.1). *Archives of General Psychiatry, 52,* 61–71.

John, O. P., & Robins, R. W. (1994). Accuracy and bias in self-perception: Individual differences in self-enhancement and the role of narcissism. *Journal of Personality and Social Psychology, 66,* 206–219.

Kagan, J. (1988). The meaning of personality predicates. *American Psychologist, 43,* 614–620.

Keller, M. B., Klein, D. N., Hirschfeld, R. M. A., Kocsis, J. H., McCullough, J. P., Miller, I., First, M. B., Holzer, C. P., III, Keitner, G. I., Marin, D. B., & Shea, T. (1995). Results of the *DSM–IV* mood disorders field trial. *American Journal of Psychiatry, 152,* 843–849.

Klein, D. N., Ouimette, P. C., Kelly, H. S., Ferro, T., & Riso, L. P. (1994). Test–retest reliability of team consensus best-estimate diagnoses of Axis I and II disorders in a family study. *American Journal of Psychiatry, 151,* 1043–1047.

Koenig, H. G., Goli, V., Shelp, F., Cohen, H. J., Meador, K. G., & Blazer, D. G. (1989). Major depression and the NIMH Diagnostic Interview Schedule: Validation in medically ill hospitalized patients. *International Journal of Psychiatry and Medicine, 19,* 123–132.

Kolar, D. W., Funder, D. C., & Colvin, C. R. (1996). Comparing the accuracy of personality judgments by the self and knowledgeable others. *Journal of Personality, 64,* 311–337.

Kovess, V., Sylla, O., Fournier, L., & Flavigny, V. (1992). Why discrepancies exist between structured diagnostic interviews and clinicians' diagnoses. *Social Psychiatry and Psychiatric Epidemiology, 27,* 185–191.

Leckman, J. F., Sholomskas, D., Thompson, W. D., Belanger, A., & Weissman, M. M. (1982). Best estimate of lifetime psychiatric diagnosis. *Archives of General Psychiatry, 39,* 879–883.

Li, H., Rosenthal, R., & Rubin, D. B. (1996). Reliability of measurement in psychology: From Spearman-Brown to maximal reliability. *Psychological Methods, 1,* 98–107.

Loranger, A. W., Sartorius, N., Andreoli, A., Berger, P., Buchheim, P., Channabasavanna, S. M., Coid, B., Dahl, A., Diekstra, R. F. W., Ferguson, B., Jacobsberg, L. B., Mombour, W., Pull, C., Ono, Y., & Regier, D. A. (1994).

The International Personality Disorder Examination: The World Health Organization/Alcohol, Drug Abuse, and Mental Health Administration international pilot study of personality disorders. *Archives of General Psychiatry, 51,* 215–224.

Maffei, C., Fossati, A., Agostoni, I., Barraco, A., Bagnato, M., Deborah, D., Namia, C., Novella, L., & Petrachi, M. (1997). Interrater reliability and internal consistency of the Structured Clinical Interview for *DSM–IV* Axis II Personality Disorders (SCID–II), Version 2.0. *Journal of Personality Disorders, 11,* 279–284.

Malgady, R. G., Rogler, L. H., & Tryon, W. W. (1992). Issues of validity in the Diagnostic Interview Schedule. *Journal of Psychiatric Research, 26,* 59–67.

Mathisen, K. S., Evans, F. J., & Meyers, K. (1987). Evaluation of a computerized version of the Diagnostic Interview Schedule. *Hospital and Community Psychiatry, 38,* 1311–1315.

Mattanah, J. J. F., Becker, D. F., Levy, K. N., Edel, W. S., & McGlashan, T. H. (1995). Diagnostic stability in adolescents followed up 2 years after hospitalization. *American Journal of Psychiatry, 152,* 889–894.

Maziade, M., Roy, M.-A., Fournier, J.-P., Cliche, D., Mérette, C., Caron, C., Garneau, Y., Montgrain, N., Shriqui, C., Dion, C., Nicole, L., Potvin, A., Lavallée, J.-C., Pirès, A., & Raymond, V. (1992). Reliability of best-estimate diagnosis in genetic linkage studies of major psychoses: Results from the Quebec Pedigree Studies. *American Journal of Psychiatry, 149,* 1674–1686.

McLeod, J. D., Turnbull, J. E., Kessler, R. C., & Abelson, J. M. (1990). Sources of discrepancy in the comparison of a lay-administered diagnostic instrument with clinical diagnoses. *Psychiatric Research, 31,* 145–159.

Meyer, G. J. (1997). On the integration of personality assessment methods: The Rorschach and MMPI-2. *Journal of Personality Assessment, 68,* 297–330.

Meyer, G. J., Finn, S. E., Eyde, L. D., Kay, G. G., Kubiszyn, T. W., Moreland, K. L., Eisman, E. J., & Dies, R. R. (1998). *Benefits and costs of psychological assessment in healthcare delivery: Report of the Board of Professional Affairs Psychological Assessment Work Group, Part I.* Washington, DC: American Psychological Association.

Meyer, G. J., Finn, S. E., Eyde, L. D., Kay, G. G., Moreland, K. L., Dies, R. R., Eisman, E. J., Kubiszyn, T. W., & Reed, G. M. (2001). Psychological testing and psychological assessment: A review of evidence and issues. *American Psychologist, 56,* 128–165.

Michell, J. (1997). Quantitative science and the definition of *measurement* in psychology. *British Journal of Psychology, 88,* 355–383.

Mischel, W. (1996). *Personality and assessment.* Mahwah, NJ: Erlbaum. (Original work published 1968)

Moskowitz, D. S., & Schwarz, J. C. (1982). Validity comparison of behavior counts and ratings by knowledgeable informants. *Journal of Personality and Social Psychology, 42,* 518–528.

Murphy, J. M., Monson, R. R., Laird, N. M., Sobol, A. M., & Leighton, A. H.

(2000). A comparison of diagnostic interviews for depression in the Stirling County study: Challenges for psychiatric epidemiology. *Archives of General Psychiatry, 57,* 230–236.

Nisbett, R. E., & Wilson, T. D. (1977). Telling more than we can know: Verbal reports on mental processes. *Psychological Review, 84,* 231–259.

North, C. S., Pollio, D. E., Thompson, S. J., Ricci, D. A., Smith, E. M., & Spitznagel, E. L. (1997). A comparison of clinical and structured interview diagnoses in a homeless mental health clinic. *Community Mental Health Journal, 33,* 531–543.

Offord, D. R., Boyle, M. H., Racine, Y., Szatmari, P., Fleming, J. E., Sanford, M., & Lipman, E. L. (1996). Integrating data from multiple informants. *Journal of the American Academy of Child and Adolescent Psychiatry, 35,* 1078–1085.

Peters, L., & Andrews, G. (1995). Procedural validity of the computerized version of the Composite International Diagnostic Interview (CIDI–Auto) in the anxiety disorders. *Psychological Medicine, 25,* 1269–1280.

Peters, L., Andrews, G., Cottler, L. B., Chatterji, S., Janca, A., & Smeets, R. M. W. (1996). The Composite International Diagnostic Interview posttraumatic stress disorder module: Preliminary data. *International Journal of Methods in Psychiatric Research, 6,* 167–174.

Piacentini, J. C., Cohen, P., & Cohen, J. (1992). Combining discrepant diagnostic information from multiple sources: Are complex algorithms better than simple ones? *Journal of Abnormal Child Psychology, 20,* 51–63.

Pilkonis, P. A., Heape, C. L., Ruddy, J., & Serrao, P. (1991). Validity in the diagnosis of personality disorders: The use of the LEAD standard. *Psychological Assessment, 3,* 46–54.

Prusoff, B. A., Merikangas, K. R., & Weissman, M. M. (1988). Lifetime prevalence and age of onset of psychiatric disorders: Recall 4 years later. *Journal of Psychiatric Research, 22,* 107–117.

Pull, C. B., Saunders, J. B., Mavreas, V., Cottler, L. B., Grant, B. F., Hasin, D. S., Blaine, J., Mager, D., & Üstün, B. T. (1997). Concordance between *ICD–10* alcohol and drug use disorder criteria and diagnoses as measured by the AUDADIS–ADR, CIDI and SCAN: Results of a cross-national study. *Drug and Alcohol Dependence, 47,* 207–216.

Rice, J. P., Rochberg, N., Endicott, J., Lavori, P. W., & Miller, C. (1992). Stability of psychiatric diagnoses: An application to the affective disorders. *Archives of General Psychiatry, 49,* 824–830.

Richter, P., Werner, J., Heerlein, A., Kraus, A., & Sauer, H. (1998). On the validity of the Beck Depression Inventory. A review. *Psychopathology, 31,* 160–168.

Riskind, J. H., Beck, A. T., Berchick, R. J., Brown, G., & Steer, R. A. (1987). Reliability of *DSM–III* diagnoses for major depression and generalized anxiety disorder using the Structured Clinical Interview for *DSM–III. Archives of General Psychiatry, 44,* 817–820.

Roberts, B. W., & DelVecchio, W. F. (2000). The rank-order consistency of personality traits from childhood to old age: A quantitative review of longitudinal studies. *Psychological Bulletin, 126,* 3–25.

Robins, L. N., Helzer, J. E., Croughan, J., & Ratcliff, K. S. (1981). National Institute of Mental Health Diagnostic Interview Schedule: Its history, characteristics, and validity. *Archives of General Psychiatry, 38,* 381–389.

Robins, L. N., Helzer, J. E., Ratcliff, K. S., & Seyfried, W. (1982). Validity of the Diagnostic Interview Schedule, Version II: *DSM–III* diagnoses. *Psychological Medicine, 12,* 855–870.

Robins, R. W., & John, O. P. (1997). Effects of visual perspective and narcissism on self-perception: Is seeing believing? *Psychological Science, 8,* 37–42.

Rogler, L. H., Malgady, R. G., & Tryon, W. W. (1992). Evaluation of mental health: Issues of memory in the Diagnostic Interview Schedule. *Journal of Nervous and Mental Disease, 180,* 215–222.

Rosenman, S. J., Korten, A. E., & Levings, C. T. (1997). Computerized diagnosis in acute psychiatry: Validity of CIDI–Auto against routine clinical diagnosis. *Journal of Psychiatric Research, 31,* 581–592.

Ross, H. E., Swinson, R., Larkin, E. J., & Doumani, S. (1994). Diagnosing comorbidity in substance abusers: Computer assessment and clinical validation. *Journal of Nervous and Mental Disease, 182,* 556–563.

Rubio-Stipec, M., Canino, G. J., Shrout, P., Dulcan, M., Freeman, D., & Bravo, M. (1994). Psychometric properties of parents and children as informants in child psychiatry epidemiology with the Spanish Diagnostic Interview Schedule for Children (DISC.2). *Journal of Abnormal Child Psychology, 22,* 703–720.

Rushton, J. P., Brainerd, C. J., & Pressley, M. (1983). Behavioral development and construct validity: The principle of aggregation. *Psychological Bulletin, 94,* 18–38.

Schwab-Stone, M. E., Shaffer, D., Dulcan, M. K., Jensen, P. S., Fisher, P., Bird, H. R., Goodman, S. H., Lahey, B. B., Lichtman, J. H., Canino, G., Rubio-Stipec, M., & Rae, D. S. (1996). Criterion validity of the NIMH Diagnostic Interview Schedule for Children Version 2.3 (DISC–2.3). *Journal of the American Academy of Child and Adolescent Psychiatry, 35,* 878–888.

Segal, D. L., Hersen, M., & Van Hasselt, V. B. (1994). Reliability of the Structured Clinical Interview for *DSM–III–R*: An evaluative review. *Comprehensive Psychiatry, 35,* 316–327.

Skre, I., Onstad, S., Torgersen, S., & Kringlen, E. (1991). High interrater reliability for the Structured Clinical Interview for *DSM–III–R* Axis I (SCID–I). *Acta Psychiatrica Scandinavica, 84,* 167–173.

Spitzer, R. L. (1983). Psychiatric diagnosis: Are clinicians still necessary? *Comprehensive Psychiatry, 24,* 399–411.

Spitzer, R. L., & Fleiss, J. L. (1974). A re-analysis of the reliability of psychiatric diagnosis. *British Journal of Psychiatry, 125,* 341–347.

Spitzer, R. L., Forman, J. B. W., & Nee, J. (1979). *DSM–III* field trials: I. Initial interrater diagnostic reliability. *American Journal of Psychiatry, 136,* 815–817.

Steinberg, M., Rounsaville, B., & Cicchetti, D. V. (1990). The Structured Clinical Interview for *DSM–III–R* Dissociative Disorders: Preliminary report on a new diagnostic instrument. *American Journal of Psychiatry, 147,* 76–82.

Thornton, C., Russell, J., & Hudson, J. (1998). Does the Composite International Diagnostic Interview underdiagnose the eating disorders? *International Journal of Eating Disorders, 23,* 341–345.

Tsujimoto, R. N., Hamilton, M., & Berger, D. E. (1990). Averaging multiple judges to improve validity: Aid to planning cost-effective clinical research. *Psychological Assessment, 2,* 432–437.

Watson, D., & Clark, L. A. (1991). Self- versus peer ratings of specific emotional traits: Evidence of convergent and discriminant validity. *Journal of Personality and Social Psychology, 60,* 927–940.

Weiss, R. D., Najavits, L. M., Muenz, L. R., & Hufford, C. (1995). Twelve-month test–retest reliability of the structured clinical interview for *DSM–III–R* personality disorders in cocaine dependent patients. *Comprehensive Psychiatry, 36,* 384–389.

Westen, D. (1997). Divergences between clinical and research methods for assessing personality disorders: Implications for research and the evolution of Axis II. *American Journal of Psychiatry, 154,* 895–903.

Williams, J. B. W., Gibbon, M., First, M. B., Spitzer, R. L., Davies, M., Borus, J., Howes, M. J., Kane, J., Pope, H. G., Jr., Rounsaville, B., & Wittchen, H.-U. (1992). The Structured Clinical Interview for *DSM–III–R* (SCID): II. Multisite test–retest reliability. *Archives of General Psychiatry, 49,* 630–636.

Wittchen, H.-U. (1994). Reliability and validity studies of the WHO–Composite International Diagnostic Interview (CIDI): A critical review. *Journal of Psychiatric Research, 28,* 57–84.

Wittchen, H.-U., Kessler, R. C., Zhao, S., & Abelson, J. (1995). Reliability and clinical validity of UM–CIDI *DSM–III–R* generalized anxiety disorder. *Journal of Psychiatric Research, 29,* 95–110.

Wittchen, H.-U., Semler, G., & von Zerssen, D. (1985). A comparison of two diagnostic methods: Clinical *ICD* diagnoses vs *DSM–III* and Research Diagnostic Criteria using the Diagnostic Interview Schedule (version 2). *Archives of General Psychiatry, 42,* 677–684.

Wittchen, H.-U., Zhao, S., Abelson, J. M., Abelson, J. L., & Kessler, R. C. (1996). Reliability and procedural validity of UM–CIDI *DSM–III–R* phobic disorders. *Psychological Medicine, 26,* 1169–1177.

Zimmerman, M. (1994). Diagnosing personality disorders: A review of issues and research methods. *Archives of General Psychiatry, 51,* 225–245.

4

TAXOMETRICS CAN "DO DIAGNOSTICS RIGHT" (AND ISN'T QUITE AS HARD AS YOU THINK)

THOMAS E. JOINER, JR., AND NORMAN B. SCHMIDT

Objective nature does exist, but we can converse with her only through the structure of our taxonomic systems. (Gould, 1996, p. 39)

In 1980, the *Diagnostic and Statistical Manual of Mental Disorders* (3rd ed.; *DSM–III*; American Psychiatric Association, 1980) changed the way that mental health professionals and experimental psychopathologists conduct their business. It is perhaps only a slight overstatement to say that one cannot get paid—either by insurance or granting agencies—unless *DSM* diagnoses are assigned.

The *DSM–III* revolution, carried on by the third revised edition (*DSM–III–R*; American Psychiatric Association, 1987), the fourth edition (*DSM–IV*; American Psychiatric Association, 1994), and beyond, has exerted a salutary effect in numerous ways. The *DSM* provides a shorthand with which professionals can efficiently communicate; has greatly enhanced the reliability of diagnoses; and has focused research efforts, such that various researchers can be sure that they are studying the same thing.

However, *DSM* has gone as far as it can go, a point that is demonstrated by at least two sources of discontent with *DSM*. The first is that the *DSM* categories and their particulars—the "same things" that scientists are studying—may not be "things" at all. That is, the categories and indicators are decided more by committee than by science. Although the *DSM* committees pay careful attention to available psychopathology science, it is also true that the basic methodology of the *DSM* for inclusion and delineation of disorders is committee consensus, the pitfalls and gross errors of which can be substantial.

The second area of discontent with the *DSM* is its rote assumption that areas of psychopathology comprise categories, not dimensions. That is, according to the *DSM*, a person either has or does not have a disorder; people's maladies differ by kind, not by degree. This assumption in itself is not illogical, and it actually may be accurate for many disorders. The problem lies in the broad-band and empirically untested assumption that all areas of psychopathology represent classes or categories and not dimensions or continua. Moreover, whether the syndrome is a category or not, a related area of confusion involves just what diagnostic criteria of a given syndrome should be included and why.

Heated controversy exists about this fundamental question: Do psychopathological syndromes represent "all-or-none," "either-you-have-it-or-you don't" categories, or rather, are they graded, dimensional continua, along which everybody can be placed, ranging from those with absent or minimal symptoms, on up to those with very severe symptoms? The particulars of a post-*DSM* diagnostic manual hinge on the answer to this question.

Yet with regard to the vast majority of mental disorders, we do not know the answer. Take depression, as just one example. Articles in *Psychological Bulletin* have capably and persuasively defended both positions (Coyne, 1994; Vredenburg, Flett, & Krames, 1993). It is interesting that psychologists tend to reflexively assume continua, whereas psychiatrists tend to reflexively assume categories, yet neither have definitive empirical evidence for their assumptions. Regarding psychologists' rote dimensional assumptions, Meehl (1999) stated, "There is a dogmatism among many American psychologists that no taxa exist, or could *possibly* exist, in the realm of the mind. Are they unaware of the more than 150 Mendelizing mental deficiencies, to mention one obvious example?" (p. 165). Those who assume by rote a categorical approach fare similarly in Meehl's estimation:

> My main criticism of the DSM is the proliferation of taxa when the great majority of clients or patients do not belong to any taxon but are simply deviates in a hyperspace of biological, psychological and social dimensions, arousing clinical concern because their deviant pattern causes trouble. Further, for that minority of DSM rubrics that do denote real taxonic entities, the procedure for identifying them and the criteria for applying them lack an adequate scientific basis. (p. 166)

It is worth highlighting that Meehl, whose name is rightly associated with a taxonic approach to classification, has gone on record (e.g., Meehl, 1997) that a minority of psychopathology syndromes probably represent categorical phenomena, with the rest representing dimensional continua.

What is needed, then, is an applied data-analytic tool that discriminates categories from continua, and furthermore, one that establishes the true indicators of presumed categories. Moreover, this tool should be widely applicable to various psychopathological syndromes. In our view, only this will allow the field to go much beyond the *DSM*. Fortunately, we believe there is a highly promising solution, represented by the work of Paul Meehl and colleagues on taxometrics.

One of us (Thomas E. Joiner, Jr.) vividly remembers reading an article on taxometrics for the first time. It was on a plane returning from the 1995 Association for the Advancement of Behavior Therapy (AABT) meeting in Washington, DC. Reading Meehl's (1995) Distinguished Professional Contributions Award article, Joiner had two simultaneous and unsettling thoughts: (a) "As a psychopathology researcher, I should learn this," and (b) "This is so hard to understand that I'll never learn this." It turned out that the first thought was right and the second one was not.

Our goal in this chapter is to dispel fear of taxometrics by presenting some of its basics in an accessible fashion that any researcher can grasp. In doing this, we have distilled complex and obscure material, available elsewhere (see especially Meehl, 1992, 1995, 1997; Meehl & Yonce, 1996; Waller & Meehl, 1998), into an abstracted and accessible digest. A larger goal is to encourage researchers to apply it to their own area of research, and thereby contribute to "doing *DSM* right."

CONCEPTUAL PRIMER: WHAT IS—AND WHAT IS NOT—A TAXON?

The principle is that of division into species according to natural formation, where the joint is, not breaking any part as a bad carver might. (Plato's *Phaedrus*)

Waller and Meehl (1998) defined a *taxon* as "a non-arbitrary class, a natural kind" (p. 4). The meaning of the term is also captured by *category* and *type*. Perhaps a better way of understanding the concept is by example. Consider Meehl's comment (cited by Waller & Meehl) that "there are gophers, there are chipmunks, but there are no gophmunks" (p. 11). When it comes to gophers and chipmunks, there is no dimensional continuum the midpoint of which is "gophmunk." Rather, there are two distinct classes, kinds, types, or taxa (*taxa* being the plural for *taxon*)—"chipmunks" and "gophers," and if we chanced upon a "gophmunk," we likely would view it not as a midpoint on the chipmunk–gopher continuum, but as a third category (perhaps created in a genetics laboratory). Similarly, Meehl

(1999) noted, "When we empty the dishwasher, we sort utensils into knives, forks, and spoons, and we do not consider the possibility of coming across sporks" (p. 165). These utensils form distinct categories, and if we chance upon a "spork" (which we well may at a fast-food restaurant), it is better to see it as a distinct category (or, as with the "gophmunk," the grafting of one category onto another) rather than as a point along a graded, dimensional continuum.

In his novel *Love in the Time of Cholera*, Gabriel García Márquez (1989) provides a colorful example of taxonic thinking:

> Florentino Ariza remembered a phrase from his childhood, something that the family doctor, his godfather, had said regarding his chronic constipation: "The world is divided into those who can shit and those who cannot." On the basis of this dogma, the Doctor had elaborated an entire theory of character, which he considered more accurate than astrology. But with what he had learned over the years, Florentino Ariza stated it another way: "The world is divided into those who screw and those who do not." He distrusted those who did not. . . . Those who did formed a secret society, whose members recognized each other all over the world. . . . (p. 183)

This passage not only illustrates what a taxon is (e.g., constipated vs. not), but it also shows why it matters; that is, "entire theories" (one hopes more accurate than astrology) may emerge on the basis of clear definitional foundations, such as a taxonic distinction can provide. For example, regarding phenylketonuria (PKU) which, unlike other forms of mental retardation, is prevented by a diet lacking phenylalanine, Mendels (1970) wrote,

> Had we taken 100, or even 1,000, people with mental deficiency and placed them all on the phenylalanine-free diet, the response would have been insignificant and the diet would have been discarded as a treatment. It was first necessary to recognize a subtype of mental deficiency, phenylketonuria, and then subject the value of a phenylalanine-free diet to investigation in this specific population. (p. 35)

In psychopathological research, these theories often are about the causes of a particular syndrome. In fact, Waller and Meehl (1998) designated a "causal origin taxon" (p. 5) as a type or class for which the etiology is both known and defining of it. Notice that a causal origin taxon is simply a general (or, in Waller & Meehl's terms, *common sense*) taxon with the qualifier that the etiology is known and defining. This etiology may—but need not—be genetic or "biological." PKU is a clear taxon of the causal origin type (with both genetic and environmental causes). Either you have PKU or you do not—it is a taxon—and if you have it, it is because of a deficiency in the metabolism of phenylalanine combined with consumption of foods containing phenylalanine. (PKU is a causal origin taxon.) PKU illustrates another important point; as Waller and Meehl stated, "the convenient dichotomy taxonic vs. dimensional should, strictly speaking, read 'taxonic-dimensional vs. dimensional only'" (p. 9). That is, within the PKU taxon, there are dimensional gradations of IQ, of serum accumulation of phenylalanine, and so forth. That there are gradations within the PKU taxon does not gainsay the essential fact that it is a taxon.

Taxa are all around us, and it is a mistake to view them as strictly genetic or biological in origin. As Waller and Meehl (1998) noted, "Some of the strongest, most tightly knit taxa in human behavior are what Cattell (1946) called "environmental mold" types (just as there are environmental mold dimensions)," (p. 5). Occupational taxa are good examples. Others include Trotskyite, bridge player, Fascist, surgeon, hurricane, Gothic cathedral, and sonnet (Meehl, 1992).

What of nontaxa? Assuming a thing is a valid entity in nature, and given that it is not a taxon, by default it is a dimensional continuum (e.g., people's temperature, height, weight; according to Meehl [1997, 1999], a probable majority of psychopathological syndromes represent continua). Regarding dimensional continua, it is important to note that taxometric analysis (to be described next) only applies to distinguishing them from taxa; after something is designated by taxometrics as a nontaxon, the definitional task shifts, from an analytic viewpoint, to approaches more suited to delineating dimensions (e.g., confirmatory factor analysis imbedded within a general construct validity approach).

ANALYTIC PRIMER: HOW DO YOU DO TAXOMETRICS?

Lacking a gold standard criterion, the only rational basis for inferring the existence of a taxonic entity, a real class, a nonarbitrary natural kind, must lie within the pattern displayed by the presumed indicators of the conjectured taxon. (Meehl, 1995, p. 269)

A third definition of taxon offered by Waller and Meehl (1998), in addition to "common sense taxon" and "causal origin taxon," is "formal-numerical taxon" (pp. 4–6), which means the formal and quantitative demonstration that either of the first two types of taxon actually do possess taxonic qualities—the main point of analytic taxometrics. In what follows, we describe the logic and technique behind one of the more prominent of the taxometric analytic techniques, MAXCOV-HITMAX (Meehl & Yonce, 1996). MAXCOV-HITMAX is not the only such procedure but, consistent with our goal of demystifying taxometrics and encouraging more researchers to apply it, we believe that understanding this one technique would serve as an entree into the general field. (Readers interested in the other techniques will find them in Meehl, 1995, 1997; Waller & Meehl, 1998, and citations therein.)

The first step in understanding taxometrics is to understand its general logic. An example is instructive. Consider biological gender which, most would agree, is a true categorical phenomenon (i.e., it is a taxon, not a continuum). More specifically, let us consider male gender and two valid but imperfect indicators of male gender—height and baldness. It is emphasized that height and baldness are not perfect indicators of male gender, but, as we show, the approach works even despite this. If you note the height and baldness of the next 100 people you see, men and women alike, you find that height and baldness are correlated. This is true because the taller people you meet (in whom men are overrepresented) are more likely than the shorter ones (among whom women are overrepresented) to be bald. Why are height and baldness correlated? The answer to this question goes to the key idea of taxometrics. Height and baldness, like the indicators of any true taxon, correlate precisely and only *because* they differentiate men from women.

To see this, consider the correlation of height and baldness among "pure" samples of men or among "pure" samples of women. Within both "pure" samples—that is, within the two taxa—where there is no differentiation to be made between men and women, height and baldness are negligibly correlated. Within a sample of men, how tall one is says little about whether one is bald (the same is true for a sample of women). In a mixed sample of men and women, however, the taller people are a little more likely to be bald than the shorter people.

This is how the indicators (even if imperfect) of true taxa behave—they intercorrelate in samples where taxon members and nonmembers are mixed, and they do not correlate in pure samples of taxon members or in pure samples of taxon nonmembers. This fact about the behavior of taxon indicators is the rational basis for inferring the existence of a taxon on the basis of the pattern of interrelations displayed by the presumed indicators of the conjectured taxon (Meehl, 1995).

And so the strategy is to presume a taxon—say, for example, depression. Next, we conjecture the presumed taxon's indicators—say, sadness, anhedonia, and suicidality. Presume and conjecture on what basis? Clinical experience, intuition, past theory and research . . . it really does not matter. The presuming and conjecturing take place in what Popper (1959) called the "context of discovery" (pp. 31–32), where ideas, theories, and hypotheses are born, from whatever source. The empirical evaluation of these ideas, however, takes place in Popper's "context of justification"; when the question is a taxometric one, the context of justification involves taxometric analysis.

Thus, we first presume a taxon and some indicators, and then we assign scores to a group of individuals on each indicator (e.g., everyone gets a score from 1 to 7 on each of sadness, anhedonia, and suicidality), much as one does with the Beck Depression Inventory (Beck & Steer, 1987) and similar scales. Last, we examine the pairwise intercorrelations of the indicators at all possible values of all other indicators. In the depression example, then, we would examine the correlation of sadness and anhedonia for those who score 1 on suicidality, those who score 2, and so on, up the scale to those who score 7. Similarly, we would examine the correlation of sadness and suicidality for those who score 1 on anhedonia, those who score 2, and so forth, for all possible combinations of indicators.

If depression is a taxon, two indicators (e.g., sadness and anhedonia) will correlate negligibly at the low end of the third indicator (e.g., among those who score 1 on suicidality), where the majority of taxon nonmembers would be. The two indicators will correlate more and more highly as the midrange of the third indicator is approached (where the mixture of taxon members and nonmembers would peak), and will correlate negligibly at the high end of the third indicator (where the majority of taxon members would be). If depression is not a taxon, but rather is a dimensional continuum, the intercorrelation of any two indicators will not systematically vary as a function of a third indicator. In broad brush, this is MAXCOV-HITMAX.

To clarify further, we go back through the depression example, but in more detail. Assume we have whatever reason to conjecture a depression taxon. (Again, the reason does not matter; this is Popper's [1959] context of discovery, not context of justification [yet].) Similarly, assume we have whatever reason to conjecture valid indicators of this presumed taxon (let us stick with sadness, anhedonia, and suicidality).

Assume $N = 10,000$; indicators on 1–7 scales.

Let us single out anhedonia for a moment, and slice up the sample using the anhedonia scores, as follows:

Anhedonia = 1; n = 4,000
Anhedonia = 2; n = 2,000
Anhedonia = 3; n = 1,000
Anhedonia = 4; n = 1,000
Anhedonia = 5; n = 800
Anhedonia = 6; n = 700
Anhedonia = 7; n = 500

Next, compute the covariance between the other two indicators (sadness and suicidality) for each anhedonia interval, as follows:

Anhedonia = 1; n = 4,000—COVsad.suic = ?
Anhedonia = 2; n = 2,000—COVsad.suic = ?
Anhedonia = 3; n = 1,000—COVsad.suic = ?
Anhedonia = 4; n = 1,000—COVsad.suic = ?
Anhedonia = 5; n = 800—COVsad.suic = ?
Anhedonia = 6; n = 700—COVsad.suic = ?
Anhedonia = 7; n = 500—COVsad.suic = ?

Assume the results are as follows:

Anhedonia = 1; n = 4,000—COVsad.suic = .0012
Anhedonia = 2; n = 2,000—COVsad.suic = .0089
Anhedonia = 3; n = 1,000—COVsad.suic = .067
Anhedonia = 4; n = 1,000—COVsad.suic = .098
Anhedonia = 5; n = 800—COVsad.suic = .131
Anhedonia = 6; n = 700—COVsad.suic = .399
Anhedonia = 7; n = 500—COVsad.suic = .0014

Here are the same results, merely rotated and graphed in Figure 4.1. Figure 4.2 depicts similar results and setup but with different axes. With three indicators, three such graphs are possible. With >3 indicators (i), number of possible graphs = i × (i − 1)!/(i − 3)! × 2. (Recall that 0! = 1.)

What to do with these graphs? If the underlying structure is taxonic, graphs of the conditional covariances generated by MAXCOV tend to be peaked (Meehl & Yonce, 1996). A series of peaked graphs thus indicates taxonicity; a series of flat graphs indicates dimensionality. Figure 4.3, for example, has no clear peak and would be inconsistent with the conjecture of a depression taxon.

The determination of whether a graph is peaked or not is done the old-fashioned way—by visual inspection. In response to the concern that visual inspection lacks the clarity that a statistical test would provide, Meehl and Yonce (1996) had five people of varying degrees of statistical

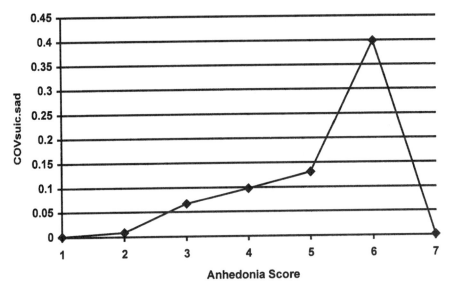

Figure 4.1. Peaked Covariance (COV) Function for the Indicators Suicidality and Sadness (suic.sad) as a Function of a Third Indicator (anhedonia)

Figure 4.2. Peaked Covariance (COV) Function for the Indicators Suicidality and Anhedonia (suic.anhe) as a Function of a Third Indicator (sadness)

sophistication inspect 90 MAXCOV graphs with various properties (e.g., some peaked; others not). Agreement was perfect.

It is important to note that the location of a graph's peak (if there is one) depends on the latent base rate of the taxon (i.e., the proportion of taxon members in the overall sample). A base rate of .50 (i.e., half of

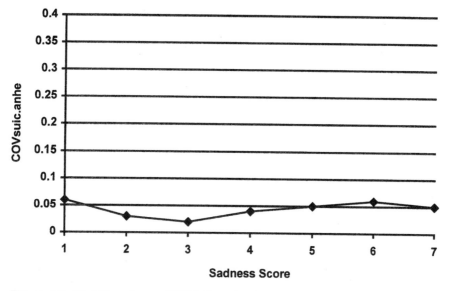

Figure 4.3. Flat Covariance (COV) Function for the Indicators Suicidality and Anhedonia (suic.anhe) as a Function of a Third Indicator (sadness)

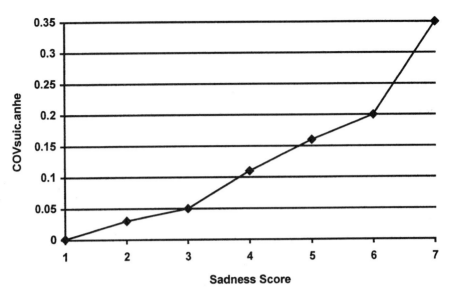

Figure 4.4. Right-Shifted Peaked Covariance (COV) Function for the Indicators Suicidality and Anhedonia (suic.anhe) as a Function of a Third Indicator (sadness)

individuals are taxon members) produces a centered peak; low base rates (common in psychopathology research) produce right-shifted peaks, such as those in the depression example; high base rates produce left-shifted peaks. Peaks can be shifted so much that they appear to be "shifted off" a graph. For example, Figure 4.4 would be interpreted as consistent with the taxonic conjecture (i.e., as peaked), with an extreme right-shifted peak, indicative of a low base-rate of taxon members in the sample.

A potential problem with low-base rate situations is that very few individuals fall in the final interval, making computation of covariance in that interval tenuous. In the depression example, if there are very few people who are in the depression taxon, then very few people will score 7 on sadness. The minimum recommended *n* for an interval is 15, with much higher numbers desirable, as always. The only satisfactory solution to this problem is large samples. A recommended samplewide minimum N is 300; although the technique works with imperfect indicators, the better the indicators, the clearer the findings.

Hitmax and Base Rate

The *hitmax* is that point on the graph's x-axis where the mixture of taxon and nontaxon members is at its maximum (i.e., the graph's peak), and it is used in computation of the taxon's base rate. In computing base rates, a value "K" is used, which equals 4 × the covariance at the peak.

For each interval on the x-axis (e.g., from 1 to 7 in the depression example), we solve for the base rate in that interval, which is

$$p_{interval} = K + \sqrt{(K^2 - [4 \times K \times cov_{interval}])}/2K$$

The term "$cov_{interval}$" denotes the covariance for that particular interval. Note that the square root sign applies only to the elements within the parentheses—it does not extend to the "2K" at the end of the equation. Note also that there is a "plus or minus" sign (i.e., +). For intervals to the right of the hitmax, use plus; for intervals to the left, use minus.

For each interval, we thus have a value for $p_{interval}$ (the proportion of taxon members in that interval). We can then multiply $p_{interval}$ times the number of participants in that interval to determine the number of taxon members in that interval (nontaxon members = total in interval − taxon members in interval). The sum of the taxon members across the intervals, divided by the total N, gives the overall taxon base rate (see Meehl & Yonce, 1996, and Waller & Meehl, 1998, for deeper treatment).

Negative covariances may occur in some intervals; the convention in such cases is to assume $p_{interval} = 0$ in intervals to the left of the hitmax, and $p_{interval} = 1$ in intervals to the right of the hitmax. Furthermore, covariance in an interval can be so high as to result in a negative number in the square root term; the convention is to assume the square root term = 0 in such cases.

Computation of the graphs' base rates provides a type of internal validation check for the visual judgments of graphs' peaks. Specifically, if a series of graphs is judged to be peaked (i.e., taxonic), then the variance of the graphs' base rates should be low (indicating that each graph is returning more or less the same estimate for the base rate, which should be the case if each graph is depicting the same underlying taxon).

Consistency checks are a key part of taxometric thinking. Ideally, before concluding that something is a taxon, each of the following conditions should be met: (a) MAXCOV graphs are clearly and consistently peaked; (b) variance of base rates is low; (c) distribution of individual subjects' taxon membership probabilities (possibly using Bayes's theorem; see Waller & Meehl, 1998) should cluster around 0 and 1; (d) conditions a through c are replicated on a separate sample; and (e) the same conclusions are reached using a separate taxometric procedure (e.g., MAMBAC; MAXSLOPE; see Waller & Meehl, 1998). For something to be deemed a taxon, then, it must clear several hurdles; taxometrics is thus more rigorous (not less) than most analytic approaches.

Indicator Validity

The procedures described so far allow the discernment of taxa from continua—a key decision that is currently made without the adequate scientific basis that taxometrics provides. Taxometric analysis also allows evaluation of which indicators are particularly good markers of a taxon. Regarding psychopathology syndromes, this, too, is key, in that the validity of diagnostic criteria (cf. indicators) can be assessed.

A straightforward approach to indicator validity is to assess the simple difference between taxon members' score on the indicator (e.g., anhedonia in the depression example) versus nontaxon members' score on the indicator. To do this, the indicator's mean among taxon members, and the indicator's mean among nontaxon members, are needed.

Taxon Mean = Sum (midpoint$_{interval}$ $\times$ n (taxon) in interval)/overall N in taxon

Nontaxon Mean

= Sum (midpoint$_{interval}$ $\times$ n (nontaxon) in interval)/overall N in nontaxon

In the depression example described earlier, the intervals have just one value (i.e., 1 to 7), which would be used as the midpoint$_{interval}$ per each interval. The various values for n and N derive from the calculation of base rates, described earlier. When the overall taxon mean is subtracted from the overall nontaxon mean, an index of indicator validity is provided; as a rough guideline, differences that exceed two standard deviations or more (indicator's standard deviation taken from the entire sample) demonstrate good indicator validity.

CONCLUSION AND FUTURE DIRECTIONS

Why even bother with taxometrics? Not only is it complex, but what does it matter if a thing is a category or not? In our view, the answers to these questions are many (e.g., scientific realism as a goal in itself; in assessment situations, the difference between assigning an individual to a category versus locating an individual on a dimension; theoretical vistas open when fundamental definitional questions are resolved), but we emphasize one answer especially: Without taxometrics, real progress in nosology is unlikely. Taxometrics, alone among all scientific tools, can distinguish psychopathological categories from continua. If a category is established, taxometrics can identify its true indicators (i.e., its diagnostic criteria). If a continuum is established—it is important to recall that none currently exist in the *DSM* system—another family of techniques related to factor analysis (i.e., structural equation modeling) and general construct validity can be used to establish true indicators.

When this general approach is widely and systematically applied to various psychopathological syndromes, the result is likely to be a thoroughgoing revision of the current diagnostic scheme—some categories become continua, some diagnostic criteria are eliminated, others are introduced, and so on. This is "DSM done right." Our hope is that readers use our chapter as a starting place to understand the potential importance, general logic, and some technical aspects of taxometrics. From this starting place, a next logical step is to read the few current applications of taxometrics to psychopathology (e.g., Gleaves, Lowe, Green, Cororve, & Williams, 2000, and Gleaves, Lowe, Snow, Green, & Murphy-Eberenz, 2000, on eating disorder symptoms; Harris, Rice, & Quinsey, 1994, on psychopathic personality symptoms; Lenzenweger & Korfine, 1992, on schizotypal symptoms; Waller, Putnam, & Carlson, 1996, on dissociative symptoms). To give just one example of how taxometrics can do DSM right, Gleaves et al. (2000) found that bulimia nervosa and the binge–purge subtype of anorexia nervosa—currently construed in the DSM as separate disorders —likely comprise one single diagnostic category. We hope that, with Waller and Meehl's (1998) book as a guide, investigators will apply taxometrics to extant and accruing psychopathology data sets. Researchers who take on this challenge may find that taxometrics is not as hard as they think, and that without it, the DSM will be done wrong.

REFERENCES

American Psychiatric Association. (1980). *Diagnostic and statistical manual of mental disorders* (3rd ed.). Washington, DC: Author.

American Psychiatric Association. (1987). *Diagnostic and statistical manual of mental disorders* (3rd ed., rev.). Washington, DC: Author.

American Psychiatric Association. (1994). *Diagnostic and statistical manual of mental disorders* (4th ed.). Washington, DC: Author.

Beck, A. T., & Steer, R. A. (1987). *Manual for the Beck Depression Inventory*. San Antonio, TX: Psychological Corporation.

Cattell, R. B. (1946). *Description and measurement of personality*. New York: World Book.

Coyne, J. C. (1994). Self-reported distress: Analog or ersatz depression? *Psychological Bulletin, 116,* 29–45.

Gleaves, D., Lowe, M., Green, B., Cororve, M., & Williams, T. (2000). Do anorexia and bulimia nervosa occur on a continuum? A taxometric analysis. *Behavior Therapy, 31,* 195–220.

Gleaves, D., Lowe, M., Snow, A. C., Green, B., & Murphy-Eberenz, K. P. (2000). Continuity and discontinuity models of bulimia nervosa: A taxometric investigation. *Journal of Abnormal Psychology, 109,* 56–68.

Gould, S. J. (1996). *Full house*. New York: Three Rivers Press.

Harris, G. T., Rice, M. E., & Quinsey, V. L. (1994). Psychopathy as a taxon:

Evidence that psychopaths are a discrete class. *Journal of Consulting and Clinical Psychology, 62,* 387–397.

Lenzenweger, M., & Korfine, L. (1992). Confirming the latent structure and base rate of schizotypy: A taxometric analysis. *Journal of Abnormal Psychology, 101,* 567–571.

Márquez, G. G. (1989). *Love in the time of cholera.* New York: Penguin.

Meehl, P. E. (1992). Factors and taxa, traits and types, differences of degree and differences of kind. *Journal of Personality, 60,* 117–174.

Meehl, P. E. (1995). Bootstrap taxometrics. *American Psychologist, 50,* 266–275.

Meehl, P. E. (1997). Credentialed persons, credentialed knowledge. *Clinical Psychology: Science & Practice, 4,* 91–98.

Meehl, P. E. (1999). Clarifications about taxometric method. *Applied & Preventive Psychology, 8,* 165–174.

Meehl, P. E., & Yonce, L. (1996). Taxometric analysis: II. Detecting taxonicity using covariance of two quantitative indicators in successive intervals of a third indicator (MAXCOV procedure). *Psychological Reports, 78,* 1091–1227.

Mendels, J. (1970). *Concepts of depression.* New York: Wiley.

Popper, K. R. (1959). *The logic of scientific discovery.* New York: Basic Books.

Vredenburg, K., Flett, G. L., & Krames, L. (1993). Analogue versus clinical depression: A critical appraisal. *Psychological Bulletin, 113,* 327–344.

Waller, N., & Meehl, P. E. (1998). *Multivariate taxometric procedures.* Thousand Oaks, CA: Sage.

Waller, N., Putnam, F., & Carlson, E. (1996). Types of dissociation and dissociative types: A taxometric analysis of the Dissociative Experiences Scale. *Psychological Methods, 3,* 300–321.

5

PSYCHIATRIC CLASSIFICATION THROUGH THE LENS OF ETHNOBIOLOGY

ELIZABETH H. FLANAGAN AND ROGER K. BLASHFIELD

When I cannot speak clearly, I speak in terms of metaphors.
Oscar Wilde

Classification is a simple process that is basic to all sciences (Hempel, 1965). A classification system contains the nouns from which a science develops its language to understand the events within its realm. Like all simple processes, however, classification becomes quite complex when examined closely. Regarding the classification of psychopathology, many alternative models have been proposed (Cantor, Smith, French, & Mezzich, 1980; Costa & McRae, 1992; Foulds & Bedford, 1975; Lorr, 1966; Millon & Klerman, 1986). Developing a psychiatric classification system has not been an easy problem to solve (Kendell, 1975b).

Slightly over a decade before writing this chapter, Roger K. Blashfield and a friend, John Livesley, wrote an article in which they viewed psychiatric classification as a psychological test (Blashfield & Livesley, 1991). There were many reasons to explore this metapor. First, from our experience, much of the effort spent in revising the recent *Diagnostic and Statistical Manual of Mental Disorders* (DSMs; e.g., 4th edition, DSM–IV; American Psychiatric Association, 1994) was devoted to changing or altering the wording of the diagnostic criteria. In effect, these criteria were like items on a test, and the criteria were organized in the form of scales (disorders) with defined threshold scores. Like a test, most empirical analyses of the DSMs focused on the "reliability" and "validity" of these classifications. Moreover, and like a test, the DSMs had extensive manuals to explain to the professional how to use this system to measure the symptoms of patients. However, other aspects of the test metaphor were almost completely ignored. For instance, researchers interested in the DSMs have not attempted to gather normative data with the goal of seeing which criteria sets represent statistical deviance from the behaviors of the general population. Nor have the researchers attempting to improve the DSMs used the extensive literature in psychology on test item development to inform empirical techniques for revising criteria.

In this chapter, we use a completely different metaphor, one borrowed from studies on ethnobiological classification, to explore the classification of psychopathology. Ethnobiology is the scientific study of how (primarily native) people understand living things that exist in their physical environments. Cultural anthropologists who study these systems generally use the term *folk taxonomies* to refer to these classificatory systems. Relatively recently, cognitive psychologists have also become interested in this topic. This convergence of psychologists and anthropologists has used methods from experimental psychology to study these ethnobiological classifications (Atran, 1998; Medin, Lynch, Coley, & Atran, 1997). Unlike the metaphor of a psychological test, the ethnobiological metaphor has little to say about diagnostic criteria. However, as we show below, the ethnobiological metaphor has many implications for the way in which the hierarchical organization of psychiatric classification might be viewed. In addition, ethnobiological classification may illuminate how psychiatric classification might serve the purpose of being a nomenclature for clinicians (Blashfield & Draguns, 1976) and patients (Gordon, 2000) alike.

FOLK TAXONOMY—AN ALTERNATIVE VIEW

In the past 30 years, folk taxonomies have been a subject of interest to cultural anthropologists studying the classification of living organisms by non-Western peoples. The anthropologists were interested in how non-Western peoples classify living organisms, and to what extent their classifications match the "scientific" classifications accepted by Western culture. One of the important books on the structure of folk taxonomies is *Ethnobiological Classification* by Brent Berlin (1992). Berlin is an anthropologist who studied the classifications of plants and animals as recognized by the Tzeltal, a Mayan people found in the highlands of Peru. His original method was to use Tzeltal informants to ascertain how they named various plants and animals that were extant in their environment. He noticed a number of striking regularities in their classification systems that seemed to parallel regularities that occurred in the writings of other anthropologists and biologists who had worked with non-Western peoples. In his 1992 book, he described the folk classifications that he had studied as well as postulated taxonomic principles to account for the regularities in these systems across cultures.

In the last two decades, "folk taxonomies," or "ethnobiological classification," is no longer the focus of anthropologists exclusively; these taxonomies have been studied by biologists, philosophers, and cognitive psychologists. In 1998, part of an issue of *Behavioral and Brain Sciences* was devoted to an article by anthropologist Scott Atran (1998). This article outlined features of folk taxonomies that have been found universally across cultures and then presented a series of studies that compared the structure and usage of folk taxonomies of Mayan people in Peru and university students in Michigan. It was published with almost 30 commentaries from researchers in different fields (e.g., philosophy, psychology, botany, anthropology) discussing particular aspects of folk taxonomies. In 1999, Medin and Atran published an edited book about folk biology that also included articles by anthropologists, psychologists, philosophers, and biologists. These articles investigated many topics including structures of folk taxonomies (e.g., Berlin, 1999; Diamond & Bishop, 1999), cognitive processes used with folk taxonomies (e.g., Coley, Medin, Proffitt, Lynch, & Atran, 1999; Hunn, 1999), as well as the ontological status of folk taxonomic categories and whether folk taxonomies are basically essentialist (Gelman & Hirschfeld, 1999).

STRUCTURE OF FOLK TAXONOMIES

In his 1992 book, Berlin argued that folk taxonomies have a hierarchical structure similar to the Western biological classification system. The categories on the highest level are the largest and include the most subcategories. The categories on the lowest levels are smaller and are not divided into subcategories. This hierarchical structure often has four to six ranks (levels of categories): kingdom, life form, intermediate, generic, species, and varietal. Berlin (1992) postulated that there are four dimensions along which the ranks can be differentiated. The *linguistic* dimension highlights the different types of names given to the categories in the various ranks. In the highest ranks, such as kingdom, often the categories are not named or the names are very long, whereas the lower ranks often have one syllable or one-word names. The psychological dimension refers to the importance (or psychological salience) of the category to the users of the classification system. Usually the categories that are the most important are also the most obvious to outsiders viewing the classification system. For instance, anthropologists studying folk taxonomies would often encounter generic categories first. This suggests that generic categories have the most psychological salience.

The various ranks can also be differentiated on a *taxonomic* dimension. In this dimension, Berlin referred to the different structures of the ranks. For instance, the higher ranks often include many subcategories, whereas the lower categories are often not divided. The final dimension is *biological*. This dimension refers to the correspondence between the folk biology and Western scientific classifications. Surprisingly, at the generic level, folk biological systems and Western scientific classifications are similar. However, at other levels, these systems can diverge markedly.

Kingdom

The highest order category is what Berlin (1992) has called a KINGDOM. This rank corresponds with the kingdom rank in biological classification. In Berlin's approach to differentiating among ranks, the essential feature of a kingdom is *taxonomic*. A category at this rank is often called a "unique beginner" because it is the category at the highest level of the classification and because it includes all other categories in the classification. An example of kingdom in folk classification is the term *plant*. A kingdom-level category is interesting linguistically because most folk classifications do not have a name or even a simple phrase for such a category. Instead, when anthropologists have attempted to inquire about the most inclusive category in botanical classification, they are greeted with comments such as those things that do not walk, do not move, possess roots and are all planted in the earth (Berlin, 1992). In effect, users of folk classifications have difficulty defining or naming a kingdom-level category. The descriptions they do give for a kingdom often appear to be idiosyncratic and to vary markedly across speakers. For instance, other folk descriptions of the kingdom of plants are "all leaves" or "green things that try to reach the sun." Kingdom distinctions are made at an early age, a fact that has psychological significance. Young children make distinctions between plants and nonliving things and between animals and nonanimals. However, these categories are fuzzy for children, and they have trouble maintaining kingdom-level distinctions with clarity and certainty (Gelman & Wellman, 1991; Hatano & Inagaki, 1994; Hickling & Gelman, 1995; Keil, 1994). This research has also shown that cognitive processes vary in the different kingdom domains: When deciding that an object is a plant or animal, people make assumptions that they do not make when deciding that objects belong to other categories such as person, substance, or artifact.

The "unique beginner" for psychiatric classification is the superordinate category of *mental disorder*. Although this concept has a name, its definition is not clear. Most mental health professionals would have a great deal of difficulty formulating a definition. Recently, the *Journal of Abnormal Psychology* devoted an entire issue (Strauss & Clark, 1999) to articles critiquing Wakefield's (1992, 1993, 1999) definition of *mental disorder* as a "harmful dysfunction, where dysfunctions are failures of internal mechanisms to perform naturally selected functions." Lilienfeld and Marino (1995, 1999) oppose Wakefield's conception, arguing that disorder is better characterized as a Roschian concept that lacks defining features and has fuzzy boundaries. Sadler (1997) and Fulford (1989, 1999) discussed the role of values in determining what is a "disorder." Spitzer and Endicott (1978) defined *mental disorder* as a medical disorder that has psychological (or behavioral) manifestations. A disorder is something that causes distress, disability, or disadvantage. Through this definition, they can separate conditions that are mental disorders (such as schizophrenia) from other conditions that are not (such as homosexuality).

Life Form

The second major rank in folk classifications is what Berlin (1992) called the LIFE-FORM rank. The categories at this level are more abstract and inclusive, and they contain most of the generic categories as subsets. For instance, the Rofaifo people of New Guinea recognize two life-form groups of mammals: larger mammals (*Hefa*) and smaller mammals (*Hunembe*). In our folk American classification, life-form categories are described with terms such as *tree*, *fish*, and *mammal*.

Life-form categories are usually named with primary lexemes (simple words; Berlin, 1992). They can be identified by reference to a few easily perceived characteristics that have a great deal of salience in organizing categories. Because of these well-recognized characteristics, classification by life forms often occurs early in childhood (Dougherty, 1979; Mandler, Bauer, & McDonough, 1991; Stross, 1973). These characteristic similarities often represent general adaptations to broad ecological conditions. In the Rofaifo classification of mammals, the major characteristic to separate the two main types is size (larger vs. smaller). In terms of taxonomic structure, life-form categories are relatively few in number and are *polytypic* (further subdivided). These categories can be thought of as superordinate sets that contain generic and other categories as subsets. Finally, in terms of biological information, life-form categories are relatively diverse and often do not correspond to categories in scientific classifications. They are often unique to a particular culture. Our folk concept of *tree* is a good example. A tree generally means a plant that is taller than a human being. The concept of tree has no correspondence with any higher order category in scientific botanical classification. However, a tree is a cognitively useful concept for organizing a series of disparate botanical entities.

Parallel to life-form categories in psychopathology are the major categorical headings of DSM–IV (American Psychiatric Association, 1994): *Anxiety Disorders; Eating Disorders; Personality Disorders; Disorders Usually First Diagnosed in Childhood, Infancy or Adolescence;* and so on. In general, these categories have simple names that represent the core features of the disorders, although these names are not as simple as some life-form names such as *tree* or *bird.* All of these subdivisions are inherently polytypic. Contemporary clinicians would think of these concepts as heterogeneous and requiring subtypes. However, most of these higher order categories do seem to be associated with a relatively few number of symptoms; for example, anxiety disorders are associated with autonomic nervous system distress; personality disorders with chronic interpersonal problems; and substance-related disorders with the ingestion of mind-altering chemicals. It is interesting that most of these potential life-form categories are not defined using diagnostic criteria in DSM–IV (*personality disorders* is an exception). Finally, life-form distinctions are learned early by clinicians. They know that disorders usually first diagnosed in childhood, infancy, or adolescence have different features from personality disorders.

Intermediate

Between life-form categories and generic categories are the INTERMEDIATE categories (Berlin, 1992). They represent groupings that have greater generality than generic categories but greater specificity than life-form categories. An example of an intermediate category in plant classification is *evergreen* that includes *pine, spruce,* and *fir,* yet itself is included within the higher taxon *tree.* Different folk classifications vary in terms of the number of intermediate categories that exist in these systems. In taxonomic terms, intermediate categories cut across life-form categories to make groups of generic categories (e.g., a group of quails and partridges). In general, a generic category has central or prototypical status in this intermediate category and the other generics in the group are arranged in terms of similarity to the prototype. The name of the intermediate category usually reflects the prototypical generic taxon. In terms of biology, intermediate categories often correspond to portions of biologically recognized families. In terms of psychology, intermediate categories are based on gross, visually recognizable, morphological similarities between organisms.

Psychiatric classification includes a considerable number of intermediate categories. These categories serve to organize groups of similar diagnoses within a life-form heading. Under the life-form category of *sexual and gender identity disorders,* the intermediate categories are *sexual desire disorders, sexual arousal disorders, orgasmic disorders, sexual pain disorders, sexual dysfunction due to a general medical condition, paraphilias,* and *gender identity disorder.* Within each of these intermediate categories there are specific diagnoses.

Some life-form categories contain more than one level of interme-diate category. For instance, the life form of *substance-related disorders* in-cludes the intermediate categories of *alcohol-related disorders, caffeine-related disorders,* and *cocaine-related disorders.* Then, within the category of *alcohol-related disorders* are the intermediate categories of *alcohol use disorders* and *alcohol-induced disorders.* Not all life-form categories have intermediate cat-egories as subsets. The life-form categories of *anxiety disorders* and *dissociative disorders* contain only the individual diagnoses.

Generic

The core of any folk taxonomy is the rank of GENERIC (Berlin, 1992). (Berlin actually named this rank *generic species.* However, we find that name too easily confused with the next lower rank of "specific" so we use the more common name *generic.*) Generic categories are the natural taxa of folk classifications. Most generic categories are included in some life form, but some are not (Atran, 1998). Categories are often not in-cluded in life forms if they have some sort of particular cultural interest such as maize for Mayan people (Berlin, Breedlove, & Raven, 1973) and the cassowary (a large bird related to the emu) for the Karam of New Guinea (Bulmer, 1970).

The names for generic categories are generally simple one-word or even one syllable terms. In our American folk classification of living or-ganisms, examples of the names of generic categories are *cat, dog, pine,* and *oak.* In Aguaruna, which is the language of Central American Mayan peo-ple, examples of these simple names are *numi, ipak,* and *takas* (Berlin, 1992). There are exceptions to these one-word names, however. Some generic categories have more complex names. In some cases, these complex names may constitute a Gestalt that has a different meaning than its con-stituent parts. For example, a *prairie dog* according to Berlin refers to a generic category. *Prairie dog* violates the one-word rule for a general cate-gory, but it refers to a kind of animal that is not a type of dog, so its meaning is different from each of the words in its name. For other generic categories that have more complex names, the binomial illustrates the hi-erarchical relationship between the life form and generic category such as *hummingbird* and *oak tree* (Atran, 1998).

Generic categories are some of the most important categories because they refer to commonly occurring objects in the environment (Berlin, 1992). Stross (1973) found that generic categories are very easy to recog-nize and name. Because of this familiarity, the names of generic categories are recognized by almost all speakers of a language, including children, and the identification of instances of these generic categories is highly reliable across different individuals in the culture. Generic categories are usually the first categories encountered by anthropologists learning the language of a non-Western people.

In terms of taxonomy, generic categories usually are *monotypic* and are not subdivided further (although some generic categories are *polytypic*; Berlin, 1992). Another distinctive feature is that most (but not all) generic categories can be unambiguously assigned to superordinate, life-form categories. This general lack of divisibility and unambiguous placing in the hierarchy contributes to the psychological salience of the categories. Basic categories that fit neatly into organizational structures and are low-level categories are easily remembered.

Another important taxonomic feature about generic categories is that the number of generic categories across cultures in a folk taxonomy is reasonably constant across non-Western cultures (Berlin, 1992). Most non-Western people recognize about 500 generic categories. The DSM–IV has approximately 400 diagnoses. The relative consistency in the number of generic categories seems surprising at first. The number of genera and species within the environments of different cultural groups is not constant. For instance, the tiny country of Costa Rica has more different species of frogs than any other country in the world. Given the ecological diversity that different cultural groups inhabit, why is the number of generic categories that people choose to name more or less the same? Berlin explained this similarity by referring to the principle of cognitive economy. Many native people are largely illiterate. Knowledge is passed verbally. Usually, one or two people in the culture (i.e., "wise men and wise women") emerge as the repository of the information that can be handed down from generation to generation. Five hundred categories is a large number, but it probably approximates an upper limit on how many categories (even hierarchical ones) can be stored in memory.

In biological terms, most generic categories in folk classifications correspond to genus-level (or, sometimes, species-level) categories in scientific classifications. Thus, the category of *cat* in our American folk classification serves as the name for the species with the scientific name of *Felis catus*. In the same way, *dog* refers to the species named *Canis familiarus*. In his ethnobiological study of the Rofaifo people, Dwyer (1976) found that two-thirds of the scientific species of mammals existing in New Guinea corresponded to generic categories in their folk classification.

In psychiatric classification, the generic categories are diagnostic concepts such as *obsessive–compulsive disorder, borderline, antisocial,* and even *anorexia.* These all have one-word names in standard clinical ("folk") language, even though their formal names are more elaborate (*anorexia nervosa, borderline personality disorder,* etc.). These are basic concepts in that almost all mental health professionals would recognize them and clinicians are relatively likely to agree on the meaning of these terms. These categories are taught in virtually every textbook of psychopathology. All of these categories are given formal definitions in *DSM–IV*. Finally, these concepts are generally thought of as being monotypic. Although subtypes of these categories have been proposed (e.g., the "as if" *borderline* vs. the dependent *borderline*), these subtypes do not have universal recognition in the field.

Notice that concepts like *passive–aggressive personality disorder*, *substance-induced psychotic disorder*, or *body dysmorphic disorder* are not generic concepts from this perspective. All have complex names that cannot be reduced to one-word names. Textbooks of psychopathology may or may not cover these concepts, and they are unlikely to be emphasized when teaching novices in the mental health professions. Mental health professionals are unlikely to use these concepts uniformly and with a high degree of reliability. Thus, some diagnoses in the *DSM* are better instances of generic categories than others.

Specific

Categories at the SPECIFIC levels are subsets of generic categories (Berlin, 1992). Usually they occur at the lowest ranks of ethnobiological classifications. In linguistic terms, a specific level category is often given a binomial name that often includes the generic name of which it is a subset. Examples of specific categories in our English language folk classification are *Persian cat*, *Siamese cat*, and *Angora cat*, where one of the two names denotes the generic category (cat). However, folk specific categories that have been prominent in a culture for a long time can be named by primary lexemes such as *calico* (a kind of cat) and *winesap* (a kind of apple tree; Atran, 1998).

In psychological terms, specific level categories are important because they are subsets of generic categories that are particularly salient to the people using the classification system (Berlin, 1992). For instance, Berlin stated that the Rofaifo have three specific level categories (Mi *foi*, Mi *sevi*, and Mi *noi*) that refer to subdivisions of Australian possum, an animal that is important to them. In terms of perceptual characteristics, specific categories are usually separated on the basis of one or a few sets of characteristics. For example, three specific-level categories of possum can be separated in terms of their fur. The type of fur also separates the specific-level categories that are used to subdivide cats (*Angora cat* vs. *Siamese cat*).

In terms of taxonomy, specific level categories are subsets of polytypic generic categories (Berlin, 1992). As noted earlier, most generic categories are monotypic. Berlin found that, across six different folk classifications, only 15% of generic categories are polytypic. However, polytypic generic categories are often the most salient to the culture. For instance, in plant folk classifications, specific categories generally referred to plants that were cultivated or protected by the non-Western peoples. Plants that were considered relatively unimportant were monotypic and had no specific categories as subsets.

In terms of biology, Berlin (1992) has noted that specific categories rarely refer to species or subspecies that are recognized in scientific classification. Specific categories are usually culturally important. Even more remarkable is what Berlin noted parenthetically, that monotypic generic categories (which have no specific category subsets) are more likely to correspond to genus level or higher scientific categories. For instance, for most speakers of the English language, *mold* is a monotypic generic category. Most of us do not typically recognize specific categorical subsets of mold. However, there are actually a large number of scientifically recognized subsets of molds.

Examples of specific categories in the classification of psychopathology are *schizophrenia, paranoid type; panic disorder without agoraphobia;* and *dissociative identity disorder.* The parent generic categories for these categories (*schizophrenia, panic disorder,* and *dissociative disorder*) are important, basic-level concepts in modern psychopathology. Notice that each of these specific categories has a two-word name, even if the actual number of words in the names often exceeds two. Furthermore, the specific categories can be differentiated on the basis of only a few characteristics (e.g., the presence of a prominent descriptive symptom, paranoid delusions, for *schizophrenia, paranoid type*).

Varietal

Some specific categories are further subdivided into VARIETIES (Berlin, 1992). These are rare. The generic categories that are subdivided into specific and varietal categories are usually the most important concepts in the folk culture. Usually, varietal categories are distinguished on the basis of the presence or absence of single characteristics that have important economic meaning to the culture. Varietal categories often have three names that indicate their relationship to the generic and specific categories (e.g., *short-haired tabby*).

The generic categories that are less important are not subdivided into specific and varietal types. Instead, instances are named by stating that they are similar to a named instance (Berlin, 1999). For instance, the Mayas might state that a plant was *kol pahaluk sok* X ("it's similar to X"). Through this practice, a classification system could be more comprehensive by having words to describe more different kinds of plants.

The subdivisions in *DSM–IV* of *major depressive disorder, single episode* and *major depressive episode, recurrent* seem to represent "specific rank" categories because the names of these categories are meaningless if the "generic" category of *major depressive disorder* is removed from this name. These two specific disorders are further subdivided in *DSM–IV* by eight different "specifiers" (e.g., longitudinal course, with or without postpartum onset, with or without catatonia). The resulting, awkwardly named diagnoses, such as *major depressive disorder, recurrent, severe with psychotic features, without full interepisode recovery*, are the most obvious parallels to categories that occur at the rank of *variety*.

However, in practice, clinicians do not always use these varietal types, especially because they are cumbersome and impracticably long. Instead, they often refer to odd instances of the disorder as similar to the known generic category (i.e., schizophreniform disorders). Or, if a patient is exhibiting features that resemble a certain disorder but does not meet full criteria, the patient can be said to have a disorder that is similar to another known disorder (i.e., personality disorder not otherwise specified, anxiety disorder not otherwise specified).

Ambiguously Affiliated Generics

Although most categories in folk classifications can be assigned clearly to one of the six ranks, a small subset of categories cannot be clearly identified as belonging to a particular rank (Berlin, 1992). The most important of difficult-to-classify names in folk classifications fall under the rubric that Berlin described as *ambiguously affiliated generics* (p. 172). An example of such a category in the Rofaifo classification of small mammals, according to Berlin, is the category named *Yabo* (dog). The primary difficulty surrounding this category is whether it occurs at the life-form rank or the generic rank. Like life-form categories, the next highest category above Yabo is the "unique-beginner" of this classification. However, unlike other life-form categories, the category Yabo is monotypic. An analysis of the name of the category does not help because the names of both life-form and generic rank categories are usually primary lexemes—a characteristic that fits the name of *Yabo*.

Some anthropologists have attempted to solve this problem by suggesting that categories like Yabo occur at both the life-form and the generic ranks (e.g., Waddy, 1988). Other anthropologists have maintained that unaffiliated generics are life-form categories (Atran, 1985, 1990; Bulmer, 1974). Berlin (1992) disagreed. He believed that these categories are best viewed as generic categories because they have the same psychological and biological properties of other generic categories. That is, these categories are recognized by almost all speakers of the language, they are learned relatively early by new speakers, and they are relatively discrete categories whose instances can be identified with high reliability. In addition, the "ambiguously affiliated generics" are like other generic rank categories in that they are synonymous with categories from Western scientific classifications.

If a single category in psychiatric classification is analogous to an ambiguously affiliated generic, it is *schizophrenia*. This term can be considered to refer to a broad, family-level category that is one of the 17 primary subdivisions under the unique-beginner category of *mental disorder*. Like both generic and life-form (family) rank categories, its name is a primary lexeme. However, it is similar to a generic category in that it is one of the early concepts taught to neophytes. Cantor et al. (1980) performed an empirical study that suggested that *schizophrenia* is a generic rank category. Like life-form categories and some generic categories, *schizophrenia* is polytypic. However, the categories that form subsidiary categories under *schizophrenia* are probably best viewed as "specific" rank categories. The names of these categories (e.g., *schizophrenia, paranoid type*) would change dramatically in meaning if the name of the superordinate category were removed (i.e., the term *paranoid*, to most mental health professionals, is not equivalent in meaning to *schizophrenia, paranoid type*). Moreover, the category of *schizophrenia* is not inherently polytypic. Stated differently, most clinicians would not be surprised if *schizophrenia* turned out to refer to a collection of subsidiary disorders, but similarly no one would be too surprised if all forms of *schizophrenia* were shown to have the same etiological process.

Summary

The ethnobiological (folk taxonomic) model shows a surprisingly good fit to the existing classification system of psychopathology. Folk taxonomies and psychiatric classification share many similarities:

- both have a hierarchical structure;
- both have 4 to 6 ranks;
- the users of both systems have no names for the ranks;
- defining, even naming, the "unique beginner" in both systems is difficult;
- the core of both systems is a set of "generic" categories with terse common names (obsessive–compulsive disorder, borderline, anorexia, posttraumatic stress disorder) that have widespread recognition among users of the classification;
- there are other categories that appear to be "specific" subsets of the generic categories (e.g., *major depressive disorder, recurrent*) whose generality is probably limited; and
- both have some categories whose rank is uncertain (i.e., "ambiguously affiliated generics"; e.g., *schizophrenia*).

Because of these similarities, psychiatric classification appears similar to a highly developed folk taxonomy.

DO MENTAL DISORDERS HAVE AN UNDERLYING ESSENCE?

One of the most hotly debated topics in psychopathology is whether mental disorders are essential categories in the sense that they have palpable, physical essence or are merely constructs that have no basis in reality (cf. Flanagan & Blashfield, 2000; Lilienfeld & Marino, 1995, 1999; Wakefield, 1993, 1999; Zachar, 2000). A similar debate has also occurred in anthropology. Berlin (1992) has argued that folk biological classification systems represent the organic differences between organisms that are recognizable at first glance, whereas other anthropologists have maintained that folk taxonomies reflect the pragmatic interests of society (e.g., Hunn, 1982). Perhaps the arguments in anthropology can inform the debate in psychology.

The Debate Within Psychopathology

An important debate in the philosophy of science concerns the ontological status of concepts. Mental disorders may have an underlying essence or reality. In contrast, some writers view mental disorders as fictions developed by the users of the system. The two poles of this debate have been termed *essentialism* and *nominalism*. Essentialism is the philosophical view that entities have essences and that categories are based on these underlying realities or essences. The goal of an essentialist is to uncover the true nature of the entity so that it can be understood. On the other hand, nominalism is the position that there is no underlying reality to entities. Entities as well as the categories used to describe them are merely constructions of the mind.

Likewise, in psychology the issue concerns whether psychiatric categories are reflective of essential differences in pathology or are only convenient fictions used by clinicians to understand their world. In particular, essentialists in psychopathology believe that mental disorders are diseases that have essences (usually biological or physiological). Thus, the goal of classifiers is to determine the essence of mental disorders and "carve nature at its joints" (Meehl, 1995, p. 268). This is the view advocated by many biologically oriented psychologists. They believe that advances in genetics and psychophysiology will eventually show that mental disorders are the results of different biological malfunctions. However, there has been difficulty agreeing on the essentialist criteria. Lilienfeld and Marino (1999) have pointed out that, although different essentialist criteria have been proposed for the concept of mental disorder, such as structural abnormality (Kendell, 1986) and reduced fertility or longevity (Kendell, 1975a), none of the criteria has been found to be satisfactory.

From a nominalist view of psychopathology, diagnoses are just constructs that clinicians use to organize information. Diagnostic terms do not have some underlying reality of their own; they are names that exist simply to meet some functional goal. For instance, Sadler (1996) argued that values, not essences, are used to define categories of psychopathology. Others have also pointed to the importance of values in defining psychiatric categories (Fulford, 1999, 2000; Sedgwick, 1982). Sarbin (1997) contended that psychiatric concepts are stories that are used to organize knowledge about patients. Cohen (1981) believed that statistical deviance could define abnormality from normality. According to Lilienfeld and Marino (1999), none of the nominalist views has gained wide acceptance.

Most of the writers who debate the ontological status of the concept of mental disorders have addressed *mental disorder* as an essential category. Wakefield (1992, 1993, 1999) is a major proponent of the belief that mental disorders have an underlying physical reality. His basic argument has been that mental disorders are harmful failures of internal mechanisms in their performance of naturally selected functions. He purported that the harmful dysfunction base of mental disorder is nonevaluative and causal–explanatory (Wakefield, 2000). By *nonevaluative*, he meant that evolutionary disadvantage rather than human values is the sole criterion for determining what is dysfunction. This aspect is important because if values were involved in his definition, Wakefield could not reject nominalism completely. He also claimed that harmful dysfunction offers an explanation of the causal mechanisms that underlie psychiatric disorders. This causal mechanism represents the essence of the disorder. For instance, if schizophrenia were found to be "caused" by a dysfunction of a group of genes, these genes would be considered the "essence" of the disorder.

Megone (1998), too, believed in functional explanations for mental disorders. Unlike Wakefield, however, he did not use evolutionary theory as a basis. Instead, he argued that mental illness should be understood in relation to the Aristotelian concept of human nature. In the *Nichomedian Ethics*, Aristotle argued that determining a thing's purpose or function also determines its "goodness." Because mental illness is considered "bad," it must be the result of a failure of function. Wakefield (2000) argued that this theory has limitations because it does not address why and if human beings have a function and what the purpose of the function might be. Moreover, because failure to function also includes the element of "badness" in Aristotle's theory, this theory is evaluative and thus is not strictly essentialist.

A recent issue of *Philosophy, Psychiatry, and Psychology* published many responses to Megone's (1998) argument. Wakefield (2000) argued that values are associated with judgments of function or dysfunction but that the concepts of *function* and *dysfunction* are not intrinsically value concepts because they are based in evolutionary theory. By insisting that *function* and *dysfunction* do not necessarily connote value judgments, Wakefield preserved mental illness as an essentialist concept. Szasz (2000) advanced a nominalistic view, suggesting that people do not have "functions" and that mental illnesses are deviations from social norms rather than biological norms. Fulford (2000) disputed Wakefield, proposing that evaluation occurs in order to decide what is *function* and *dysfunction*, even within an evolutionary framework, and that a system of mental disorders can never be value free. Thus, many writers believe in some evaluative aspects to defining mental disorders; Wakefield stands alone in arguing that *dysfunction* can be defined without using values.

Most of the theorists previously discussed combined some aspects of essentialism and nominalism in their arguments, thus blurring the dichotomy. Instead, more integrative theories are being offered. Fulford (2000) proposed three ways to define biological functions: naturalism (causes without teleology), neonaturalism (teleology without values), and evaluationism (teleology with values). Zachar (2000) argued that mental disorders are practical kinds rather than natural or arbitrary kinds. Each of these theories has essentialist elements (such as causes) and nominalist elements (the inclusion of value).

Two researchers who adopted a more extreme nominalist view are Lilienfeld and Marino (1999). As mentioned previously, Lilienfeld and Marino argued against Wakefield's notions of harmful dysfunction, suggesting that "disorder" is better conceptualized as a "Roschian" concept (Rosch 1973; Rosch & Mervis, 1975). Roschian concepts are different from classical concepts in that they lack defining features and have fuzzy boundaries. Thus, no essentialist criteria exist that can distinguish all instances of the category from noninstances. Instead, Roschian concepts are organized around an ideal mental prototype based on the central features of the category. Then, judgments regarding whether the entity belongs in that category are based on similarity to the ideal prototype of that category. Subsequently, when a clinician decides whether a patient has a certain disorder, he or she had to compare the person to the "ideal" presentation of the disorder and base his or her judgment on the similarity between the two. Thus, according to Roschian analysis, definitions of concepts are based on consensual judgments and are representations of what people mean by that disorder.

Essentialism as Viewed From Folk Taxonomy

According to Medin and Atran (1999), folk taxonomies are neutral as to the ontological status of their concepts, or whether an essence or physical reality underlies the categories. However, there is debate among individual scientists as to which conceptualization is more valid. In ethnobiology, the essentialist view is called the *intellectualist view* and argues that there is an essence to the categories in that "the structure of kinds in nature is comprised of 'chunks' that more or less impose themselves on minds" (p. 8). Evidence for this position is offered by the findings that folk categories often correspond to scientific species or genera and that there is much cross-cultural agreement in folk taxonomic systems (e.g., Atran, 1990; Berlin, 1992).

The nominalist position is the "utilitarian" view that folk taxonomic systems are culture-dependent constructions that are influenced by goals, theories, and belief systems (Medin & Atran, 1999). For example, Ellen (1993) studied Nuaulu animal categorization and concluded that

> systems of classification are not the inventions of individuals (in which case they would more closely reflect a cognitive process), but arise through historical contingency, linguistic constraints, metaphorical extension, ritual prohibitions and so on. Classifications are parts of belief systems, and as such are the productions of interactions, accretions, elaborations, and condensations. (pp. 149–150)

Another anthropologist, Hunn (1982), made a similar argument that, although some categories are based on "pure" life forms, most categories are motivated by practical considerations.

Initially, scholars studying folk taxonomies debated whether categories were intellectualist or utilitarian. Recently theorists have argued that the two positions are not mutually exclusive (Medin & Atran, 1999). Instead, the use and ontological status of a category could depend on contextual factors. Bulmer (1970) argued that the relative influence of the intellectualist versus the utilitarian views may depend on factors such as rank in the hierarchy. For instance, Bulmer claimed that culture has a stronger effect on the use of categories at the life-form level of scientific taxonomy (such as a tree or bird) than at the generic or species level (such as an oak or robin). Applying this argument to psychiatric classification, cultural context might have a stronger influence when defining and identifying concepts like psychotic disorders or mood disorders. However, cultural context is less likely to have an influence on the definition of mental disorders occurring at the generic level such as "*obsessive–compulsive disorder*," "*posttraumatic stress disorder*," or "*attention-deficit hyperactivity disorder*." A proponent of more extreme utilitarianism is Ellen (1999), who believed that the structure and use of folkbiological knowledge were based on the subsistence needs of the culture, especially at the lower levels of the hierarchy.

In addition to studying the structure of the folk taxonomies, researchers have also investigated the cognitive processes involved in using these classification systems. This research has shown that some phenomena are universal and others are more specific to a culture. Atran (1998) argued that what has been found to be a "basic category" according to Rosch, Mervis, Grey, Johnson, and Boyes-Braem (1976) occurs cross-culturally for both objects and living things.[1] However, researchers have found that other inductive strategies employed by users of folk taxonomic systems are not consistent across cultures (Coley et al., 1999). In a study of the Itzaj Mayan folk biology, Atran (1999) found that human interests affect the relationship between inductive thought and folk taxonomies. Specifically, Atran found that folk biologies are set up so that the power from inductive reasoning is greatest for the categories that are most important to humans. Given the range of cultures that have folk taxonomies (i.e., subsistence cultures to industrialized economies), it is likely that the different needs of these cultures would affect which categories would be important. In reference to psychiatric diagnosis, these findings would suggest that the needs of the clinicians would influence the structure of the folk taxonomy. Logically, then, the psychiatric classification system would not reflect essentialistic categories except at the most basic level.

What Psychologists Can Learn From Folk Biologists

The question of whether categories, and in particular mental disorders, are "real" or merely useful constructions of the mind has received much attention in psychology. The analysis has been dualistic, asking whether the "true" nature of concepts is essentialist or involves some value judgment. Most of these analyses have focused on the concept of *mental disorder* and have not discussed whether categories at the diagnostic level are essentialist constructs.

In studies of folk taxonomies, the essentialist nature of categories has also been important. However, folk taxonomic researchers have been more concerned with defining which ranks or categories are essentialist and which are more affected by culture. In folk taxonomies, the "fit" between classificatory concepts in a folk classification and the "natural" organization of living objects most often occurs with the generic concepts. Thus, ethnobiologists have found that the kingdom concepts are more affected by culture, whereas the generic concepts reflect more essential differences.

Psychologists have much to learn from folk biologists, who have avoided polarizing the debate into essentialism–nonessentialism and have instead discussed which kinds of categories are essentialist. Psychologists would do well by examining the complexities of this argument and understanding that the decision depends on the level of analysis. Specifically,

---

[1]Rosch et al. (1976) investigated whether a taxonomic level is preferred by users of the system. They found a "basic level" category in hierarchies of objects and living things. These "basic level" categories were ones in which (a) the instances of the categories have many common features, (b) people interact with instances of the categories in similar ways, (c) category members have similar enough shapes so that an "average shape" can be defined, and (d) the category name is the first to come to mind in the presence of the object (e.g., *guitar* vs. *musical instrument*).

whether a category is essentialist or not might depend on whether it is a superordinate or a more basic category.

A TENTATIVE FOLK CLASSIFICATION OF MENTAL DISORDERS

In 1999, Frances and First published a self-help version of *DSM–IV* that was intended to explain the classification of mental disorders to the public. They titled their book *Am I Okay? A Layman's Guide to the Psychiatrist's Bible*. One reason for the importance of this book is that Frances was the chairman of the American Psychiatric Association committee that created *DSM–IV*, and First was the editor of *DSM–IV*. Thus, this book reflects how Frances and First might have formed a classification of psychopathology if left to their own devices rather than using the complex committee structure that actually created *DSM–IV*. The final version of *DSM–IV* contained nearly 400 categories (242 categories with diagnostic criteria) that were organized under 16 major headings. Frances and First reduced the number of mental disorders to 74 categories and subdivided these categories into 20 problem areas. Each chapter in this self-help version focuses on one of the 20 problem areas. An introductory chapter contained commentaries about the descriptive characteristics of disorders, treatment options available for the disorders, how the disorders differ from normal experience, and references for the lay reader to other self-help books or to Web sites.

Although this was probably not the authors' intention, the Frances and First book (1999) suggests an interesting but tentative outline of what a folk classification of mental disorders by late 20th century Americans might look like. From the categories used by Frances and First, we have created a provisional folk classification (see Exhibit 5.1). The categories in this system are organized under three not-well-specified "kingdoms" (adult disorders usually leading to referral by another adult, adult disorders usually leading to a self-referral, and disorders of children leading to referral by an adult). Under these loosely specified kingdoms are 16 different "life form" categories (e.g., psychotic disorders, cognitive disorders, personality disorders, learning disorders), most of which do represent historically recognized superordinate categories of mental disorders. Below these life-form categories are 39 proposed "generic" categories as well as a smaller collection of "intermediate" categories (e.g., most of the sleep disorders discussed by Frances and First) and "specific" categories (including most of the *DSM–IV* personality disorders). Notice that the names for the 39 tentative generic categories are either one-word names (e.g., *autism* or *schizophrenia* or *antisocial*) or are pithy abbreviations for longer names (e.g., OCD for *obsessive–compulsive disorder*). Generally, these 39 categories represent mental disorder concepts that are discussed

EXHIBIT 5.1
Tentative Folk Classification of Mental Disorders

I. Disorders in an Adult Leading to Referral by Another Adult
  A. Cognitive Disorders
    1. Delirium
    2. Dementia
      a. Alzheimer's
      b. vascular
      c. AIDS
      d. Parkinson's or Huntington's
      e. alcohol
  B. Amnestic Disorders
    1. Head injury
    2. Metabolic
      a. Korsakoff's
  C. Psychotic Disorders
    1. Substance-induced psychotic disorder
    2. Psychotic disorder related to medical condition
    3. Depression or mania with psychotic features
    4. Brief psychotic disorder
    5. Schizophrenic disorders
      a. schizophrenia
        (i) paranoid schizophrenia
        (ii) undifferentiated schizophrenia (hebephrenia)
        (iii) schizo–affective disorder
    6. Delusional Disorder
      a. paranoia
  D. Euphoric Disorders
      a. bipolar I (manic depressive)
      b. bipolar II
      c. cyclothymia
II. Disorders That an Adult Can Self-Diagnose
  A. Depression
      a. major depression
        (i) with psychotic features
        (ii) with melancholic features
        (iii) with atypical features
        (iv) seasonal depression
        (v) postpartum depression
      b. dysthymia
  B. Anxiety Disorders
      a. panic
      b. phobias
        (i) agoraphobia
        (ii) specific phobia
        (iii) social phobia
      c. generalized anxiety disorder (GAD)
  C. Obsessions and Compulsions
      a. obsessive–compulsive disorder (OCD)
  D. Exposure to Trauma
      a. posttraumatic stress disorder (PTSD)
  E. Substance Use Problems
    1. Dependence
    2. Abuse
      a. alcoholism
      b. drug abuse
    3. Substance induced disorders
  F. Abnormal Eating
      a. anorexia
      b. bulimia

Exhibit Continues

EXHIBIT 5.1
(*Continued*)

G. Personality Disorders
  1. Major
    a. antisocial
    b. borderline
    c. schizotypal
  2. Others
      (i) obsessive compulsive personality disorder
      (ii) dependent personality disorder
      (iii) avoidant personality disorder
      (iv) histrionic personality disorder
      (v) narcissistic personality disorder
      (vi) paranoid personality disorder
      (vii) schizoid personality disorder
H. Unexplained Physical Complaints
  1. Focus on physical symptoms
      (i) somatization disorder
      (ii) conversion disorder
      (iii) pain disorder
  2. Focus on fear of disease
    a. hypochondriasis
      (i) body dysmorphic disorder
I. Dissociative Disorders
  1. Dissociative amnesia
  2. Dissociative identity disorder
    a. multiple personality
  3. Depersonalization disorder
J. Sleep Disorders
  1. Substance-induced sleep disorder
  2. Sleep disorder related to medical condition
  3. Sleep disorder related to another mental disorder
  4. Circadian rhythm sleep disorder
  5. Abnormal sleep patterns
    a. insomnia
    b. hypersomnia
    c. sleep terrors
    d. sleepwalking
III. Disorders in a Child Leading to Referral by Adult
  A. Developmental Delays
    a. mental retardation (MR)
    b. autism ("pervasive developmental" disorder)
  B. Learning Disorders
  C. Childhood Behavior Problems
    a. conduct disorder
    b. oppositional defiant disorder (ODD)
    c. attention deficit/hyperactivity disorder (ADHD)
  D. Other childhood disorders
    a. Tourette's (tic disorder)
    b. encopresis
    c. enuresis

Note. This outline view of a folk classification contains five ranks: kingdom (denoted by Roman numerals), life form (preceded by a capital letter), intermediate (preceded by an Arabic numeral), generic (preceded by a lowercase letter), and specific (preceded by a Roman numeral encased in parentheses). This classification is loosely derived from a self-help view of psychiatric classification proposed by Frances and First (1999). The organizational structure of mental disorders represents our view of these categories and does not match the system proposed by Frances and First.

in both the popular press of the late 20th century as well as in professional journals, books, and other media.

The outline shown in Exhibit 5.1 presents what we consider to be the kingdom, life-form, intermediate, generic, and specific-varietal categories and does not use all the categories, nor does it match the organization of the Frances and First (1999) book. For instance, the proposed three kingdoms of mental disorders in Exhibit 5.1 do not appear in the Frances and First book (cf. Blashfield, 2001). Nor do Frances and First make the distinction between generic level personality disorders and specific level personality disorders that we propose in this exhibit. Thus, the exhibit represents *our* view of how the Frances and First self-help classification could be reorganized to fit a folk classification.

CONCLUSION

In this chapter, we outlined how psychiatric classification can be viewed as a folk taxonomy. Each has four to six ranks, contains almost 500 categories, and has a set of generic categories at its core with a series of more vaguely defined superordinate and subordinate categories. Then, we discussed how arguments from anthropologists studying folk taxonomies can inform the essentialism–nominalism debate in psychology. Our analysis suggested that a theorist such as Wakefield, who has devoted his attention to defining the concept of *mental disorder*, is focusing at the incorrect level. Wakefield attempted to propose an essentialist view of a "kingdom"-level category. From a folk taxonomic perspective, the kingdom categories typically are the most vaguely defined and the most likely to be subject to cultural influence. Instead, the field of psychiatric classification would benefit more from conceptual analyses of generic categories (see, for example, Fulford's, 1989, analysis of *alcoholism*). These are the categories for which an essentialist view is most likely to be relevant, although cultural influences can also affect their definition.

We ended this chapter with a tentative example of a folk classification of mental disorders (at least from the perspective of 20th-century Americans). This classification was loosely patterned after a classification of mental disorders proposed by Frances and First (1999) in their self-help book about psychopathology. To show that the details of this classification do or do not meet all of the principles suggested by Berlin would go beyond the scope of this chapter. Instead, we offered this terse outline as a speculative example of what a folk classification of mental disorders might look like.

Many lenses have been offered for viewing psychiatric classification (e.g., classical set theory, a prototype model, a dimensional model). The strength of viewing psychiatric classification through an ethnobiologic lens is that anthropologists have been using this model for the last 30 years. Recently, anthropologists have teamed up with cognitive psychologists and developed sophisticated methods for empirically testing folk taxonomies. This body of work offers a new set of methods that could be usefully applied to the study of psychiatric classification.

REFERENCES

American Psychiatric Association. (1994). *Diagnostic and statistical manual of mental disorders* (4th ed.). Washington, DC: Author.

Aristotle. (1947). Ethics. In R. McKeon (Ed.), *Introduction to Aristotle* (pp. 308–545). New York: Modern Library.

Atran, S. (1985). The nature of folk-botanical forms. *American Anthropologist, 87,* 298–315.

Atran, S. (1990). *Cognitive foundations of natural history.* Cambridge, England: Cambridge University Press.

Atran, S. (1998). Folk biology and the anthropology of science: Cognitive universals and cultural particulars. *Behavioral and Brain Sciences, 21,* 547–568.

Atran, S. (1999). Itzaj Maya folkbiological taxonomy: Cognitive universals and cultural particulars. In D. L. Medin & S. Atran (Eds.), *Folkbiology* (pp. 119–204). Cambridge, MA: MIT Press.

Berlin, B. (1992). *Ethnobiological classification.* Princeton, NJ: Princeton University Press.

Berlin, B. (1999). How a folkbotanical system can be both natural and comprehensive: One Mayan Indian's view of the plant world. In D. L. Medin & S. Atran (Eds.), *Folkbiology* (pp. 71–90). Cambridge, MA: MIT Press.

Berlin, B., Breedlove, D., & Raven, P. (1973). General principles of classification and nomenclature in folk biology. *American Anthropologist, 74,* 214–242.

Blashfield, R. K. (2001). The vulgate DSM–IV [book review]. *Journal of Nervous and Mental Disease, 189,* 3–7.

Blashfield, R. K., & Draguns, J. G. (1976). Toward a taxonomy of psychopathology: The purposes of classification. *British Journal of Psychiatry, 129,* 574–583.

Blashfield, R. K., & Livesley, W. J. (1991). Metaphorical analysis of psychiatric classification as a psychological test. *Journal of Abnormal Psychology, 100,* 262–270.

Bulmer, R. (1970). Which came first, the chicken or the egg head? In J. Pouillon & P. Maranda (Eds.), *Echanges et communications: Mélanges offerts à Claude Lévi–Strauss.* The Hague: Mouton.

Bulmer, R. (1974). Folk biology in the New Guinea Highlands. *Social Science Information, 13,* 9–28.

Cantor, N., Smith, E. E., French, R. D., & Mezzich, J. (1980). Psychiatric diagnosis as a prototype categorization. *Journal of Abnormal Psychology, 89,* 181–193.

Cohen, H. (1981). The evolution of the concept of disease. In A. L. Caplan, H. T. Engelhardt Jr., & J. J. McCartney (Eds.), *Concepts of health and disease: Interdisciplinary perspectives* (pp. 209–220). Reading, MA: Addison-Wesley.

Coley, J. D., Medin, D. L., Proffitt, J. B., Lynch, E., & Atran, S. (1999). Inductive reasoning in folkbiological thought. In D. L. Medin & S. Atran (Eds.), *Folkbiology* (pp. 205–232). Cambridge, MA: MIT Press.

Costa, P. T., & McCrae, R. R. (1992). The five-factor model of personality and its relevance to personality disorders. *Journal of Personality Disorders, 6,* 343–359.

Diamond, J., & Bishop, K. D. (1999). Ethno-ornithology of the Ketengban people, Indonesian New Guinea. In D. L. Medin & S. Atran (Eds.), *Folkbiology* (pp. 17–46). Cambridge, MA: MIT Press.

Dougherty, J. (1979). Learning names for plants and plants for names. *Anthropological Linguistics, 21,* 298–315.

Dwyer, P. (1976). An analysis of Rofaifo mammal taxonomy. *American Ethnology, 3,* 425–445.

Ellen, R. (1993). *The cultural relations of classification.* Cambridge, England: Cambridge University Press.

Ellen, R. (1999). Models of subsistence and ethnobiological knowledge: Between extraction and cultivation in southeast Asia. In D. L. Medin & S. Atran (Eds.), *Folkbiology* (pp. 91–118). Cambridge, MA: MIT Press.

Flanagan, E. H., & Blashfield, R. K. (2000). Essentialism and a folk-taxonomic approach to the classification of psychopathology. *Philosophy, Psychiatry, and Psychology, 7,* 183–190.

Foulds, G. A., & Bedford, A. (1975). Hierarchy of classes of personal illness. *Psychological Medicine, 5,* 181–192.

Frances, A., & First, M. B. (1999). *Am I okay? A layman's guide to the psychiatrist's bible.* New York: Simon & Schuster.

Fulford, K. W. M. (1989). *Moral theory and medical practice.* Cambridge, England: Cambridge University Press.

Fulford, K. W. M. (1999). Nine variations and a coda on the theme of an evolutionary definition of dysfunction. *Journal of Abnormal Psychology, 108,* 412–420.

Fulford, K. W. M. (2000). Teleology without tears: Naturalism, neo-naturalism, and evaluationism in the analysis of function statements in biology (and a bet on the twenty-first century). *Philosophy, Psychiatry, and Psychology, 7,* 77–94.

Gelman, S. A., & Hirschfeld, L. A. (1999). How biological is essentialism? In D. L. Medin & S. Atran (Eds.), *Folkbiology* (pp. 403–446). Cambridge, MA: MIT Press.

Gelman, S., & Wellman, H. (1991). Insides and essences. *Cognition, 38,* 214–244.

Gordon, E. M. (2000). *Mockingbird years: A life in and out of therapy.* New York: Basic Books.

Hatano, G., & Inagaki, K. (1994). Young children's naïve theory of biology. *Cognition, 50,* 171–188.

Hempel, C. G. (1965). *Aspects of scientific explanation.* New York: Free Press.

Hickling, A., & Gelman, S. (1995). How does your garden grow? Evidence of an early conception of plants as biological kinds. *Child Development, 66,* 856–876.

Hunn, E. (1982). The utilitarian factor in folk biological classification. *American Anthropologist, 84,* 830–847.

Hunn, E. (1999). Size as limiting the recognition of biodiversity in folkbiological classifications: One of four factors governing the cultural recognition of biological taxa. In D. L. Medin & S. Atran (Eds.), *Folkbiology* (pp. 47–70). Cambridge, MA: MIT Press.

Keil, F. (1994). The birth and nurturance of concepts by domains: The origins of concepts of living things. In L. Hirschfeld & S. Gelman (Eds.), *Mapping the mind: Domain specificity in cognition and culture* (pp. 235–254). Cambridge, England: Cambridge University Press.

Kendell, R. E. (1975a). The concept of disease and its implications for psychiatry. *British Journal of Psychiatry, 127,* 305–315.

Kendell, R. E. (1975b). *The role of diagnosis in psychiatry.* Oxford, England: Blackwell.

Kendell, R. E. (1986). What are mental disorders? In A. M. Freedman, R. Brotman, I. Silverman, & D. Hutson (Eds.), *Issues in psychiatric classification: Science, practice, and social policy* (pp. 23–45). New York: Human Science Press.

Lilienfeld, S. O., & Marino, L. (1995). Mental disorder as a Roschian concept: A critique of Wakefield's "harmful dysfunction" analysis. *Journal of Abnormal Psychology, 104,* 411–420.

Lilienfeld, S. O., & Marino, L. (1999). Essentialism revisited: Evolutionary theory and the concept of mental disorder. *Journal of Abnormal Psychology, 108,* 400–411.

Lorr, M. (1966). *Explorations in typing psychotics.* Oxford, England: Pergamon Press.

Mandler, J., Bauer, P., & McDonough, L. (1991). Separating the sheep from the goats: Differentiating global categories. *Cognitive Psychology, 23,* 263–298.

Medin, D. L., & Atran, S. (1999). Introduction. In D. L. Medin & S. Atran (Eds.), *Folkbiology* (pp. 1–16). Cambridge, MA: MIT Press.

Medin, D. L., Lynch, E. B., Coley, J. D., & Atran, S. (1997). Categorization and reasoning among tree experts: Do all roads lead to Rome? *Cognitive Psychology, 32,* 49–96.

Meehl, P. E. (1995). Bootstraps taxometrics: Solving the classification problem in psychopathology. *American Psychologist, 50,* 266–275.

Megone, C. (1998). Aristotle's function argument and the concept of mental illness. *Philosophy, Psychiatry, and Psychology, 7,* 187–202.

Millon, T., & Klerman, G. L. (Eds.). (1986). *Contemporary directions in psychopathology: Towards a DSM–IV.* New York: Guilford Press.

Rosch, E. R. (1973). Natural categories. *Cognitive Psychology, 4,* 328–350.

Rosch, E. R., & Mervis, C. B. (1975). Family resemblances: Studies in the internal structure of categories. *Cognitive Psychology, 7,* 573–605.

Rosch, E. R., Mervis, C., Grey, W., Johnson, D., & Boyes-Braem, P. (1976). Basic objects in natural categories. *Cognitive Psychology, 8,* 382–439.

Sadler, J. Z. (1996). Epistemic value commitments in the debate over categorical versus dimensional personality diagnosis. *Philosophy, Psychiatry, and Psychology, 3,* 203–222.

Sarbin, T. R. (1997). On the futility of psychiatric diagnostic manuals (DSMs) and the return of personal agency. *Applied and Preventive Psychology, 6,* 233–243.

Sedgwick, P. (1982). *Psycho politics.* New York: Harper & Row.

Spitzer, R. L., & Endicott, J. (1978). Medical and mental disorder: Proposed definition and criteria. In R. L. Spitzer & D. F. Klein (Eds.), *Critical issues in psychiatric diagnosis* (pp. 15–39). New York: Raven Press.

Strauss, M. A., & Clark, L. A. (Eds.). (1999). The concept of disorder: Evolutionary analysis and critique [Special Section]. *Journal of Abnormal Psychology, 108*(3).

Stross, B. (1973). Acquisition of botanical terminology by Tzeltal children. In M. Edmonson (Ed.), *Meaning and Mayan languages.* The Hague: Mouton Press.

Szasz, T. (2000). Second commentary on "Aristotle's function argument." *Philosophy, Psychiatry, and Psychology, 7,* 3–16.

Waddy, J. A. (1988). *Classification of plants and animals from a Groote Eylandt Aboriginal point of view.* Darwin: Australian National University.

Wakefield, J. C. (1992). The concept of mental disorder: On the boundary between biological facts and social values. *American Psychologist, 47,* 373–388.

Wakefield, J. C. (1993). Limits of operationalization: A critique of Spitzer and Endicott's (1978) proposed operation criteria for mental disorder. *Journal of Abnormal Psychology, 102,* 160–172.

Wakefield, J. C. (1999). Evolutionary versus prototype analysis of the concept of disorder. *Journal of Abnormal Psychology, 108,* 374–399.

Wakefield, J. C. (2000). Aristotle as sociobiologist: The "function of a human being" argument, black box essentialism, and the concept of mental disorder. *Philosophy, Psychiatry, and Psychology, 7,* 17–44.

Zachar, P. (2000). Psychiatric disorders are not natural kinds. *Philosophy, Psychiatry, and Psychology, 7,* 167–182.

III

REPRESENTATIONAL
ALTERNATIVES

6

ASSESSING PSYCHOPATHOLOGY: A NARRATIVE APPROACH

ÓSCAR F. GONÇALVES, PAULO P. P. MACHADO, YIFAHT KORMAN, AND LYNNE ANGUS

Since the publication of the first version of a psychiatric classification in the United States in 1840, the movement for semiological classifications of mental disorders has become unstoppable. Several classification systems have been published by the World Health Organization (International Classification of Diseases; *ICD* system) and the American Psychiatric Association (*Diagnostic and Statistical Manual of Mental Disorders*; *DSM* system), all of which have claimed to be universal classifications of "mental diseases."

However, in 1952 the American Psychiatric Association published its first version of the *DSM*, in which *mental diseases* and their symptoms were identified by experts' consensus. In this process, a panel of specialists in the area of psychopathology voted on the symptoms that constituted a certain mental illness. The categories with the highest number of votes were retained in the *DSM*. As one might expect, the consensus regarding certain mental illnesses has changed over the years, as the underlying historical, cultural, and sociological contexts have changed. Therefore, it is not surprising that in the 7-year interval between the fourth and the fifth versions of the *DSM* (3rd ed., rev; *DSM–III–R*; American Psychiatric Association, 1987; 4th ed., *DSM–IV*; American Psychiatric Association, 1994), diagnostic criteria for 120 disorders changed, 13 new disorders were added, and 8 disorders were eliminated (Beutler, Bongar, & Shurkin, 1998).

Although the rapid changes in the classification systems may reflect an evolving expertise in psychodiagnostic knowledge and practice, such vast and frequent changes may also reflect conceptual confusion in the domain of psychodiagnosis. This was already recognized by Rosenhan (1984), who concluded that "it is clear that we cannot distinguish the sane from the insane" (p. 140). Rosenhan based this statement on groundbreaking research he conducted during the 1970s. In his most famous study (Rosenhan, 1973), he secretly "planted" eight pseudopatients in several psychiatric hospitals and instructed them to indicate during the clinical interview that they heard "empty," "hollow," and "thud" sounds. Aside from this vague symptomatology, the pseudopatients were asked not to allude to having a psychiatric history and to present real facts of their own lives (without allowing their identification). Immediately after their admission, all of the pseudopatients stopped displaying symptomatic behaviors and interacted with the staff and patients in an everyday, normal manner. Their normal behavior, however, did not prevent seven of them from being diagnosed with schizophrenia, and one with manic-depressive psychosis. All were medicated, and their subsequent hospital stay ranged from 7 to 52 days. These data may not be shocking for clinicians who regularly diagnose mental illness and recognize how easy it can be to generate false positives with the traditional (*DSM* or *ICD*) diagnosis classification systems.

Perhaps even more remarkable were the results from a subsequent study, which was conducted to test and refute Rosenhan's findings (Rosenhan, 1984). In another psychiatric institution, whose staff believed that a study like Rosenhan's could not be replicated in their prestigious institution, a similar study was conducted. During a period of 3 months, researchers claimed that several pseudopatients would be sent to the institution's hospital, and members of the staff were asked to rate their degree of confidence in the truthfulness of each patient. Results showed that 41 out of the 183 patients screened at the hospital were identified as pseudopatients by at least one member of the staff, 23 were identified by at least one psychiatrist, and 14 were identified by at least one psychiatrist and one staff member. This massive misidentification of pseudopatients by the psychiatric staff resulted even though researchers had not introduced any pseudopatients to the psychiatric ward. This time, the psychiatric staff had unwittingly committed a Type II error by identifying genuine psychiatric inpatients as "normal" individuals in the hospital setting.

In summary, these studies highlight the ease in which Type I (false positive) and Type II (false negative) errors can be committed when using our traditional diagnostic systems. Given these limitations of the traditional diagnostic systems, the questions we must face are, Can such an unreliable system be considered scientific? And even more important, How ethical is it to use such a capricious diagnostic system?

A side result of these studies could help us establish possibilities for an alternative system of diagnostic formulation. As it turns out, the pseudopatients in Rosenhan's initial study were in fact a source of suspicion for the other psychiatric patients, not the psychiatric staff. The psychiatric patients' suspicions were not based on findings emerging from the application of diagnostic criteria but rather on their own first-hand or naïve observation of the pseudopatients' note-taking behaviors on the ward. The psychiatric patients were suspicious about the pseudopatients' true condition and thought that they might be journalists, professors, or inspectors. Perhaps the genuine psychiataric patients were operating on an alternative and potentially more efficient diagnostic system than the DSM, one that looked at the language of patients not as a sign of internal psychopathology but only as language. As Harré and Gillet (1994) would put it, the pseudopatients' discourse was not taken as the manifestation of a hidden psychopathological phenomenon but instead as the psychological phenomenon itself.

In this chapter we question the traditional DSM and ICD diagnostic systems as a source of identification of underlying psychopathology and mental diseases. We argue that psychopathology is a meaning system that organizes itself through the patient's linguistic and narrative construction. Thus, understanding psychopathology means understanding the patient's narrative construction and the manner in which he or she organizes it. Language is not viewed here as a mere communication device to arrive at a list of symptoms, and narrative is not viewed as revealing an essential and inner pathology. Quite the contrary; it is the manner in which patients construct their narratives that is seen as indicative of psychopathology. We believe that to diagnose means to look at the narrative construction rather than to look through it (Capps & Ochs, 1995). In particular, we view clients' narrative discourse as valuable in and of itself and assert that clients' narratives can be examined according to their structures, contents, and processes. Finally, we present several instruments, which can be used by clinicians to analyze the structures, processes, and contents of clients' narratives.

QUEST FOR PSYCHOPATHOLOGY'S ESSENCE

Nosological systems used to identify and classify psychopathology appear to be based on a paradoxical set of assumptions. Simply put, whereas the defining criteria used to identify and classify mental disorders are almost exclusively symptomatic, it is also assumed that these symptoms are a sign of the underlying mental illness or disease. With the exception of mental disorders resulting from a general medical condition, it is curious that from the almost 400 definitions of diagnoses proposed by *DSM–IV*, not a single illness, whether biological or psychological (or both), can be identified as underlying any particular symptomatology. This is unique in the context of other medical specialties and disciplines. Current psychiatric nosological systems do not view diagnosis as targeting the identification of the cause of the symptomatic expression (as one might expect), but rather they view diagnosis as targeting the identification of the symptom configuration itself. In contrast to general medicine, where the symptom depends on a disease (and where it is possible to have a disease without a symptom), in mental health the disease itself is the symptom (Beutler et al., 1998). We are, then, facing a curious situation of establishing diagnosis without knowing such things as etiology and course of illness, qualities that diagnoses usually are expected to have. Being so, one should question whether there is such a thing as "mental disease" or whether it is a fictional construct created by mental health professionals (Szasz, 1970).

The dominant systems in psychiatry tend to assume that an illness underlies each symptom category, even though our knowledge about the existence of a "true" nosological entity is still in its infancy and "the concept of mental disorder, like many other concepts in medicine and science, lacks a consistent operational definition that covers all situations" (American Psychiatric Association, 1994, p. xxi). Psychiatry tends to invoke anatomical, physiological, and biochemical changes to justify the symptomatic configuration. Psychology, on the other hand, invokes several mental or intrapsychic concepts, usually around the affective, cognitive, or volitional systems in order to explain the same symptomatic configurations. Although it has been possible, in certain historical moments, to reach an "acceptable" consensus regarding the definition of the disorder and its symptomatic configuration, mental health professionals are far from unanimity regarding the etiology and explanatory concepts of a disorder (either biological or psychological). As Szasz (1997) pointed out, there seems to be a curious pact between psychiatry and psychology where each hides its own heuristic deficiencies with the supposed power of the other's heuristics. That is, psychiatry covers the lack of anatomophysiology explanatory power by relying on psychological theories, whereas psychology moves closer to biological models given the growing frustration with the lack of reliability and validity of different psychological theories. It is as if "a silence treaty" was signed, where each profession covers its own deficiencies with the language of its neighbor's profession, each waiting to see which will unveil the essence of psychopathology first.

The attempt to unveil the essence of psychopathology, we believe, is a difficult task and reveals a status quo that is not new in psychology. The study of the structure and function of intrapsychic, mental phenomena was and still is, to a certain extent, psychology's way of justifying its existence as an independent science. Underlying this agenda is the idea that internal and tacit dimensions define the individual and that these aspects constitute the a priori and superstructural features of knowledge. This perspective gave birth to countless explanatory concepts of what people do and say in their daily realities. This explanatory approach is clearly evidenced in psychoanalytic writings (Arlow & Brenner, 1964), which have in turn been very influential in the conceptualization of psychopathological symptom patterns included in various psychodiagnostic systems. It is interesting that, as society became increasingly more psychologically minded, these concepts became integrated into everyday language, resulting in psychological metaphors earning an ontological status.

Important exceptions to the dominant intrapsychic narrative in the history of psychology as a discipline should be noted. In particular, the behavioral paradigm and recent social constructivist and social constructionist models of human functioning have challenged the core assumptions of the intrapsychic paradigm. Moreover, Carl Rogers (1942), founder of client-centered psychotherapy, was a long-standing critic of psychodiagnostic classification systems and viewed the practice as countertherapeutic.

Psychopathologists, heirs to this alliance between medicine and psychology, have inherited the difficult task of finding the biological essence of the diseases and thus turned to a psychological essentialism, creating a professional code that translated the patients' experience into "internist" professional jargon. The typical clinician's attitude has been well-captured by Gergen (1994):

> [therapists] listen to their clients for hours to ascertain the quality and character of their "inner life"—their thoughts, emotions, unarticulated fears, conflicts, repressions, and most important—"the world as they experience it." It is commonly presumed that the individual's language provides a vehicle for "inner access." (p. 144)

In this context, what the individual says (i.e., his or her language) is always seen as a second order variable, a vehicle to the "true" psychopathological essence of the disorder, which is the first order variable (Gonçalves, 1997). As defended by Harré and Gillet (1994), however, the individual's discourse is not merely a manifestation of an internal psychological phenomenon—it is itself a psychological phenomenon.

In limiting themselves and subscribing to the metaphor of mental health as an "internal" phenomenon, psychologists find themselves facing a difficult question that may challenge the legitimacy of their psychological and psychotherapeutic work. As was recently argued by Szasz (1997), the establishment of mental disease by the official system of *DSM–IV* as a legal fact makes indefensible any attempt to solve a hard-core disease by means of a soft-core talking cure. Szasz gave an interesting illustration: "If we view diabetes as a disease, we rightly consider it a serious error—*prima facie* medical negligence—to treat a diabetic person solely by listening and talking to him" (p. 304). Is it possible that because of the recognition of this risk, psychology has progressively turned itself to neurobiological models and psychologists subsequently have requested prescription privileges?

Gergen (1994) has identified a four-phase model, which addresses the psychomedicalization of psychological terms and diagnostic systems. In the first phase of a cycle, a specialist translates the lay language of the client into a complex professional jargon. In a second phase, this professional jargon is disseminated by culture, through the progressive institutionalization of professionals, services, and schools. In a third phase, because of the efficiency of the institutions, it is the culture that "psychomedicalizes" itself, making the previous professional jargon part of common language. Finally, the cycle continues feeding itself by redefining and expanding the professional jargon. New concepts, new theories, and new pathologies arise. Surprisingly enough, old theories survive while new ones come into being, and both maintain the same status in the definition of the psychopathological essence (Harré & Gillet, 1994).

How can one put a stop to this endless cycle? We are convinced that this cycle can only be broken by replacing the professional jargon with language that is closer to the original dialogue or conversation with the client. A paradigmatic example of the power of close proximity, engaged observation, and curiosity is that psychiatric inpatients, not the psychiatric staff, correctly identified the note-taking pseudopatients in Rosenhan's study as researchers or journalists. Psychiatric staff members were more likely to (mis)interpret the pseudopatients' note-taking and engaged observation of ward activities as further evidence of paranoid apprehension and obsessive symptomatology. Thus, it was the psychiatric inpatients who seemed to understand that the language and actions of the pseudopatients were a psychological element of first-order importance—as an important and informative psychological phenomenon in and of itself.

From this perspective, it is not surprising that some authors have claimed that this vicious cycle can only be broken by adopting a "not-knowing" stance:

> The therapist does not "know" a priori, the intent of any action, but rather must rely on the explanation made by the client. By learning, by curiosity, and by taking the client's story seriously, the therapist joins the client in a mutual exploration of the client's understanding and experience. (Anderson & Goolishian, 1992, pp. 29–30)

Maybe in adopting this "not-knowing" attitude suggested by Anderson and Goolishian, we can get close to a lay approach that explores clients' meanings through their language and examines the way people organize their narrative productions.

PSYCHOPATHOLOGY, MEANING, AND NARRATIVE

Clinicians have always relied on clients' language and narratives to guide their actions. As Russell and Wandrei (1996) observed, "Given the fact that humans use language, and specifically narrative, in the most basic to the most complex meaning-making activities, it comes as no surprise that clinical psychologists use narrative in almost all aspects of assessment and intervention" (p. 317). Nevertheless, we have also seen a tendency to use language and narratives as vehicles to accessing an "essential psychopathology" and as means to exploring the presence of biological and psychological pathologies rather than studying language itself.

Recently, however, we have seen a progressive recognition of the central role of language as a meaning construction process (Bruner, 1990). Some authors have referred to this effort of reclaiming language to be the central process of knowing construction as the *second cognitive revolution* (Harré & Gillet, 1994, p. 18). For decades, language was considered to be the epiphenomenon of more important mental structures and other cognitive processes. In other words, language was seen as a second order phenomenon, and as a result clinicians overlooked that realities are created through language itself. The resurgence of viewing language as a first order phenomenon is the basis for the ever-growing interest modern psychology currently gives to discursive, conversational, and narrative knowing (cf. Harré, 1995; Murray, 1995; Shotter, 1995). However, this new trend does not view language as a mere juxtaposition of words; if that were true, we would probably be facing a new psychological essentialism. Rather, the meaning-creating characteristic of language results from the way words relate to one another in a narrative matrix. It is within this matrix that individuals introduce meaning to their experience.

We believe that what we have come to call "reality" or the "world" is basically a chaotic conglomeration of external and internal stimuli. At each moment we are bombarded by both external information (stimuli that impregnate our sensorial experience) as well as internal information (thoughts, emotions). All of the information we are presented with, be it external (thousands of sounds, a plethora of visual impressions, diverse scents and tastes, and an endless number of tactile and kinesthetic sensations) or internal (continuous flow of thoughts and feelings) is essentially unordered and nonhierarchical. To introduce meaning to this chaotic and plural nature of experience, the person has to impose some structure, and it is here that narrative structure appears to be an effective organizer of experience (Gonçalves, Korman, & Angus, 2000; Seligman & Yellen, 1987).

The introduction of a narrative order is probably the most fundamental aspect of human knowing. People understand, store, and relate separate experiences in their lives by representing them in a narrative form.

The narrative ordering processes impose a specific pattern of temporal coherence in what otherwise would be a random and chaotic experience. This narrative ordering enables individuals to represent seemingly distinct experiences as meaningful wholes (Bruner, 1990).

It is not surprising, then, that narrative emerged as the new metaphor to conceptualize clinical work (Angus, Levitt, & Hardtke, 1999; Gonçalves, 1995a, 1995b, 1998; Gonçalves & Machado, 1999; Hermans & Hermans-Jansen, 1995; McLeod, 1997; Rosen, 1996; Russell & Wandrei, 1996; White & Epston, 1990).

In summary, we have seen that the recent interest in the way human beings construe, organize, and transform knowledge resulted in "meaning-making'" becoming the central object of study in psychology. Furthermore, psychology's focus shifted toward a reliance on narratives as a means to understanding this meaning-making process.

Understanding psychopathology as a science of meaning making rather than a biomedical science comes from a long tradition in phenomenological psychology and psychiatry. According to this perspective, nosological classifications in psychopathology are seen as metaphors, or condensed forms of organized meanings. Thus, talking about agoraphobia, depression, or schizophrenia is the same as talking about prototypical organizations of meaning (Guidano, 1991). Psychopathology is, in this context, a science of meaning and, as such, it is inseparable from narrative discourse. It is assumed that the narrative discourse used for diagnosis is the result of a social co-construction between the prototypical meaning forms of the client and the meaning introduced by the interviewer or the clinician. This implies that psychopathology is not an objective external reality, but a product of the encounter of two meaning systems, that of the client and that of the clinician. Psychopathology is understood as a meaning-organizing discursive production inseparable from the conversational and socio-cultural contexts, and what characterizes psychopathology is its existence and not its essence. According to this perspective, it is not only understandable but to be expected that the definitions of what constitutes psychopathology have changed as cultural and sociological changes took place and as mainstream thinking evolved.

We believe that meaning making is the central aspect of human knowledge and the process of understanding different features of human experience. Moreover, we believe that these meanings express themselves through narrative discourse. Thus, we argue that the inspection of the narrative matrix as it manifests itself through the conversational reality allows the assessment of the idiosyncratic meaning of psychopathology. Of course, one must bear in mind that the patient's meanings exist in the context of a conversational reality that is shared with the discursive meanings of the clinician. There is no psychopathology without an interlocutor or a dialogue, and different discourses indicate different pathologies. This feature does not constitute a limitation; on the contrary, it highlights one's ability to have multiple stories and thus flexibility of meanings, which allow room for clinical intervention.

We now turn to the manner in which individuals organize meaning in the narrative matrix. We believe that there are three core dimensions to the process of narrative meaning making:

1. *narrative structure*, the way in which the different aspects of a narrative or story connect with each other, allowing us to have a coherent sense of authorship;

2. *narrative process*, the degree of richness of the narrative as revealed by quality, style, and complexity of the narrative; and

3. *narrative content*, the level of diversity and multiplicity of the narrative that describes the contents of the experience (Gonçalves et al., 2000).

We also present several methods and instruments that clinicians and researchers have developed to analyze the structures, processes, and contents of narratives.

The structural, processing, and content aspects of the narrative create a sense of narrative coherence, complexity, and multiplicity, respectively. Analyzing these aspects of the narrative sheds light on the meaning-making processes of an individual client in a language that is close to his or her own (thus similar to the original narrative conceptualization of the problem), a language that also resembles the therapeutic interventions (i.e., conversational and narrative strategies).

NARRATIVE STRUCTURE AND THE DIAGNOSIS OF COHERENCE

The meaning-making experience is inevitably associated with the individual's ability to establish connections, both within a narrative episode and across episodes or life narratives. Drawing on the work of Baumeister and Newman (1994), Angus et al. (1999) suggested that it is important to distinguish between microlevel and macrolevel narratives when discussing issues of narrative and self-identity in the context of the evaluation of oral discourse. According to the authors, the term *micronarrative* refers to the specific stories or event descriptions told by individuals that have characteristics similar to those of written narratives (i.e., a clear beginning, middle, and end as well as a protagonist and a plot). In contrast, the term *macronarrative* describes the thematic story lines that weave together many different stories or micronarratives. In essence, each chapter in a person's life story, or macronarrative, can be conceptualized as comprising several micronarratives. Accordingly, Gonçalves et al. (2000) have argued that the ontological quest for narrative coherence applies to both micronarrative and macronarrative productions.

Living and experiencing this "self-in-the-world" implies the construction of a coherent narrative process that allows the individual to act as a co-author of his or her own narrative. Individuals continuously face the challenge of attempting to construe events (through their discursive relationship with others) in a coherent manner and maintain a feeling of authorship. To live requires a sense of authorship regarding life itself. This process is not unlike the novelist who feels a growing sense of authorship as the writing of the novel unfolds. As with the novelist, one's sense of authorship depends on the coherence that develops when processing the narrative. We believe that this sense of authorship, which emerges in the narrative construction, expresses itself through its structural organization. In order for the sense of authorship to develop, one must connect the different elements of the narrative together in a significant and coherent way. Similarly, the individual must create and sustain a sense of connection between different singular narratives, throughout life, so that they all cohere.

The sense of identity and personal authorship is, therefore, accomplished through a double search for structural coherence: (a) micronarrative coherence (or coherence within a specific, delimited narrative) and (b) macronarrative coherence (or coherence across micronarratives). Of central importance here is that the individual does not sacrifice diversity of experience for a sense of coherence, but rather integrates diverse experiences into complex micronarrative and macronarrative frameworks in a meaningful and coherent manner.

In the absence of this coherence, the individual is likely to lose the sense of authorship. Furthermore, the inability to perform these connections results in an attempt to distance oneself from the external world and from oneself (the internal world). Feelings of derealization, dissociation, and depersonalization can be understood as the phenomenological expressions of an inability or a difficulty in structuring a coherent narrative.

According to Mancuso (1986), the narrative coherence has two essential characteristics. First, it develops epigenetically, very early in life when the child acquires the ability to build coherent narratives in an apparently chaotic world. Second, this epigenetic development is guided by a motivational system characterized by the need to make life coherent and avoid the apparent ambiguity, disconnection, and chaos that the world presents to us. In other words, the development of a narrative structure is an essential condition for psychological survival. A sense of psychological well-being is in turn based on the individual's ability to give coherence to the multiplicity of experiences provided by life itself. What we call *subjec-*

tivity is the phenomenology of this narrative structure. We establish our own system of coherence by structuring the narratives that seem to capture our experiences. An inability to establish coherence by imposing structure on the narratives of our experiences results in dissociation from the experience (Hermans & Hermans-Jansen, 1995).

The first modern therapeutic approach recognized the significance of narrative incoherence and dissociation. Freud and Breuer's therapeutic objective (1895) can be easily conceptualized as the uncovering of the dissociated and unconscious elements of experience with the aim of integrating them into a coherent narrative. Following this lead, most of the subsequent therapeutic approaches can be re-interpreted as ways of identifying processes of narrative incoherence and as attempts to increase this coherence. For example, Rogers (1942) emphasized the need to open the individual to his or her organismic experience, and Beck, Rush, Shaw, and Emery (1979, p. 43) proposed the strategy of "reality testing" as a method of cognitive restructuring.

It is precisely the levels of coherence that the clinician (implicitly or explicitly) looks for in the process of establishing a diagnosis. Clinicians commonly observe their patients' unorganized and incoherent accounts of their experiences. Meaningless days, lack of direction in life, depersonalization, derealization, and dissociative symptoms are common signs of lack of coherence in the narrative structure. This inability to construe experiences in a coherent way and difficulty in integrating events into meaningful macronarratives results in life narratives that are distorted and disjointed. Hermans and Hermans-Jansen (1995) have noted that dissociation is a common strategy to avoid experiencing events that do not cohere with the individual's self-narrative. Accordingly, dissociative disorders, such as amnesia, fugue, and dissociate identity disorder, can be understood as resulting from difficulties in micronarrative and macronarrative coherence.

Phobic patients, for example, commonly resist facing new challenging experiences because they are unable to integrate them in a coherent manner. In a paradoxical way, as the patient becomes less open to new experiences, it becomes more difficult for him or her to achieve a flexible (and thus healthy) life narrative. Threatened by past, present, or future narratives, the phobic patient organizes obsessive boundaries as a defense mechanism and uses dissociation as a strategy to resist threatening experiences and thus survive psychologically. Common indicators of discursive incoherence in a phobic organization are tangential and superficial speech; over-inclusiveness or excessive abstraction; circumstantial, disconnected, or disorganized presentation; and amnesia.

Other psychopathologies may also be understood in terms of structural narrative incoherence. According to Agar and Hobbs (1982), the speech of individuals with schizophrenia lacks coherence because of the way they structure their micronarratives. The authors noted that the speech of these individuals displays no temporal or causal relationship between one sentence and the next. Thus, it is difficult for the listener to comprehend the connection between successive statements. Moreover, they may appear to be "going on a never-ending tangent" because there is no apparent overall plan or goal to their stories. In contrast, people who suffer from obsessive–compulsive disorder tend to manifest a debilitating pursuit of connectedness in stretches of their speech. Thus, they overly identify the connections between successive statements.

With schizoidal patients, clinicians are confronted with a narrative discourse that is incoherent within the conversational constraints and demands of the therapy hour. Unable to establish or locate the context of meaning appropriate for the interpretation of the patient's talk, the patient's narrative productions are experienced as incoherent and not understandable. In the absence of a coherent narrative organization, the particular event or experience described by the schizoidal client remains dissociated and disconnected from contextual themes or organized in terms of time sequences.

Rasmussen and Angus (1996, 1997) found that clinicians can distinguish between borderline clients and nonborderline clients by attending to their discourse. In a qualitative comparative analysis of therapy sessions of borderline and nonborderline clients, the authors found that nonborderline clients tended to shift the topic of discussion into a thematically related topic, whereas borderline clients tended to shift the topic of discussion into a thematically unrelated topic. The researchers also found that the therapists reported a sense of thematic coherence when working with neurotic clients, which was absent when interacting with borderline clients. The therapists were distressed and frustrated by the absence of coherence in the borderline therapy sessions.

Several authors have claimed that narrative coherence is intimately connected with the individual's ability to organize a narrative structure. Kintsh (1980), for example, alluded to the existence of a *narrative superstructure*, a kind of specific macrosyntax that allows for the organization of meaning. Mandler (1984) proposed that a coherent narrative should obey *narrative grammar structure*, which includes a sequence of seven elements: setting, initiating event, internal responses, goal (character's objective), actions, outcome, and ending. Intensive studies by story grammar theorists (such as Mandler, 1984) on the structure of written narratives such as myths, children's stories, and folk tales revealed that despite gross differences in the stories' contents, these stories all have the same narrative grammar structure (as outlined above). Because of the perceived persuasiveness of this story structure, researchers have begun to refer to it as the *canonical* story structure (Mandler, 1984).

Extensive research in the area suggests that information that is presented in this canonical narrative structure is better recalled (Stein &

Glenn, 1979), read faster (Mandler & Goodman, 1982), and rated as more acceptable examples of stories (Stein & Policastro, 1984) compared to information that is presented in a mixed-up order. These researchers have thus asserted that people tend to organize information according to this narrative structure because it represents a more efficient and coherent construction of knowledge (cf. van den Broek & Thurlow, 1991). In other words, the more a narrative resembles this canonical structure, the more coherent it is perceived to be.

Different methods can be used to evaluate the structure in patients' narratives (cf. Baerger & McAdams, 1999; Main, 1991; Russell & van den Broek, 1992). Russell and van den Broek (1992) have proposed a three-dimensional model of narrative structure that can be empirically tested. The first dimension is *structural connectedness,* which involves two main classes of structural variables: the *event categories* and the *set of relations.* *Event categories* refer to the same structures identified by story grammar theorists (typically consisting of setting, initiating events, protagonist's responses, attempts, consequences, and reaction; Mandler, 1984; Stein & Glenn, 1979). *Set of relations,* on the other hand, refers to the relation between the event categories. Four types have been identified by the researchers: (a) temporal relations, (b) causal relations, (c) co-referential relations (e.g., that "Jason" and "he" refer to the same person), and (d) propositional relations. (Other authors have also alluded to the importance of causal and temporal connections between the event categories; e.g., Kintsch & van Dijk, 1978; Trabasso & van den Broek, 1985.)

A second dimension, offered by the authors, is the *representation of subjectivity,* which refers to the intentions, motivations, and desires that propel the narrator or the characters in the story to act in a certain way. Russell and van den Broek (1992) provided the following example: "I went home" versus "I eagerly went home." Because the latter sentence conveys the narrator's attitude, the authors argued that it is remembered for a longer period of time compared to the first sentence. Research on written myths and folk tales seems to corroborate these assumptions; the subjective relations between events were found to be almost universally present (see Bruner, 1987). The authors claimed that linguistic markers of subjectivity can be crucial information for clinicians as a way of assessing the manner in which clients can overcome their egocentrism and consider another point of view.

The third dimension of narrative structure is the *linguistic–cognitive complexity* of the narrative, which can be determined by the complexity of the style of the spoken narrative. Russell, van den Broek, Adams, Rosenberg, and Essig (1993) argued that "if clients tell truncated, sparse narratives with little degree of conceptual variation and linguistic complexity, therapists not only might note the client's reluctance to reveal details but also might wonder about the possible poverty of the client's experience and lack of psychological mindedness" (p. 342).

Russell and his colleagues have put this theory to test and examined whether patients with different diagnostic characteristics can be differentiated on the basis of their narrative language. The researchers found that they were able to distinguish between the narratives of opiate addicts and those of cocaine addicts on the basis of the patients' elaboration of subjectivity (second dimension). That is, the opiate addicts, when narrating stories regarding their first experience with their drug of choice, tended to constrict the self as a center of subjectivity. In contrast, the cocaine addicts tended to expand the self as the center of subjectivity when talking about their first experience with the drug. It is interesting that these two patient types could not be distinguished on the basis of traditional tests of sensation seeking or levels of defensiveness (Russell & Wandrei, 1996).

The researchers also performed regression analyses to examine the ability of the narrative measures to predict individuals' levels of symptoms of depression, anxiety, and cognitive mediational difficulties. Results suggested that the narrative measures were able to predict a significant amount of the variance of the three psychopathology indices. They also found that narrative structure (first dimension) was most strongly related to the level of psychopathology and that poor narrative structure was associated with the severity of psychopathology (Russell & Wandrei, 1996).

Korman (1998) intensively analyzed the narratives of one depressed client across 17 sequential sessions of her good-outcome, client-centered therapy relationship. They were surprised to find that only a minority of the spoken micronarratives or stories investigated had a clear beginning, middle, and end, and even fewer stories evidenced the full complement of story grammar structures viewed as comprising narrative form. Nonetheless, a substantial increase in story structure was found in the client's micronarratives as therapy progressed. The authors suggested that these findings may be taken to support the assumption that psychopathology is a function of narrative incoherence whereas psychotherapy introduces coherence to clients' narratives.

In summary, imposing narrative structure on the experiences in our lives gives us a sense of coherence and meaningfulness. The more complete the narrative in terms of its grammar, the more coherent the meaning of the experience becomes. It is precisely through this process of experience organization in terms of narrative structure that human beings achieve a sense of coherence. The experience of this coherence allows the emergence of a sense of authorship. As Crites (1986) observed:

> The first type of unhappiness consists in the failure to appropriate my personal past by making a connected, coherent story of it. Of course I cannot fail to have a past, but I can let it to be forgotten, or I can actively suppress it, or I can be so intent on my future project that I

let my roots in the past grow weak. In either case I lose my identity, having no more of a story than the bare chronicle that appears on my curriculum vitae. (p. 171)

NARRATIVE PROCESS AND THE DIAGNOSIS OF COMPLEXITY

The narrative organization is not differentiated only in terms of structural coherence but also in terms of narrative process. By *narrative process* we mean the strategies used to enhance the complexity, depth, and differentiation of the client's self-narrative. It is these processes, according to Gergen and Gergen (1986), that engender the "dramatic commitment" of the interlocutor. These processes are used by both the client and the therapist in the context of co-constructing the client's narratives.

The process of narrative complexity relies on openness to the diversity of human experience. It is through this openness that the individual becomes aware of his or her multipotentiality. A restricted range of one's own experiential world can be seen in patients with panic disorder as they often describe their experiences as falling within a very narrow band of sensorial experience. Usually panic-disordered patients focus exclusively on kinesthetic sensations and are unable to construe their anxiety in terms of other sensorial dimensions like vision, sound, scent, or taste. Sadly, this limitation turns both their experience and their narrative into the singular experience of fear and racing heartbeat.

Another example is what we usually call *obsessive–compulsive disorder*, where the individual is not fully processing the sensorial, emotional, and cognitive elements of his or her experience. The patient with this disorder may impose limits on his or her emotional experience because it is threatening or because it escapes the usual mechanisms of apprehension. In either case, the result is a constriction of articulated emotional experience, which limits the individual's own capacity to generate complex, differentiated understandings of himself or herself and others. The plurality of experiences is reduced to a limited singularity of knowledge. The resulting narrative lacks the qualities that are necessary to engage the listener's active attention: complexity and emotional intensity.

It is important to note that a narrative may be structurally coherent but have a poor level of complexity in terms of narrative process. The obsessive–compulsive patient may have a highly structured narrative in which the elements of the story are connected to each other in a hypercoherent fashion, but this structural hypercoherence may be achieved at the expense of a reduction of the patient's level of perceptual and emotional processing. That is, the patient may restrict certain sensorial, cognitive, and emotional elements of the story.

Other patients may also present emotional, cognitive, or sensorial constriction. When telling their stories, patients may avoid the emotional or cognitive features of the experience through an excessively circumstantial or abstract discourse, or they may interpret their experience in terms of a singular emotion. For example, depressed patients tend to describe their experience in terms of sadness, and phobia patients have difficulty decentering from the emotional experience of danger. A whole range of differentiated feelings and emotional meanings are reduced to the singularity of one salient emotion.

In contrast, what we might term *narrative existence* (or a "healthy" narrative) implies a complex process of knowledge construction. It implies the construal of complex narratives that include a variety of sensorial and emotional experiences, beliefs, a multiplicity of perspectives, and a plurality of meanings. By doing so, we allow ourselves to actualize the different possibilities that are encountered in our engagement with the world. It is our contention that this differentiated manner of processing ongoing experiences of the world is reflected in how we talk about ourselves to ourselves and to others.

Angus, Hardtke, and Levitt (1996) developed a method that allows the identification of central aspects of the narrative process in psychotherapeutic narratives. The authors have argued that all forms of successful psychotherapy entail the articulation, elaboration, and transformation of the client's self-told life story, which is reflected in the increasing presence of emotion-related and meaning-related narrative modes in the therapy discourse (Angus & Hardtke, 1994). Both client and therapist achieve this goal by collaboratively engaging in three distinct modes of inquiry: (a) *external narrative mode*, which entails the description and elaboration of life events in which the question of "what happened" is addressed; (b) *internal narrative mode*, which entails the description and elaboration of subjective feelings, in particular, "what was felt at the moment the event was occurring" and "what is experienced now in the therapy session"; and finally (c) *reflexive narrative mode*, which entails the reflexive analyses of issues arising from the event (external) and what was felt (internal) in which the question "what does it mean" is addressed.

These narrative processing modes encompass both the cognitive and experiential strategies that both clients and therapists engage in when co-constructing stories about self and others, irrespective of therapeutic modality, and encompass almost all of the dialogue spoken in the context of the psychotherapeutic relationship. In essence, the narrative process modes are viewed as essential components of a distinctive mode of human meaning making, which creates, maintains, and (when needed) helps to engender a more differentiated, multifaceted sense of self (macronarrative) in relation to others.

In terms of the functions of spoken narratives, in the external sequences, the narrator or client attempts to verbally show the therapist, by means of descriptive, specific details, the scene, setting, and actions entailed in an event. The more detailed and specific the description provided by the client, the more opportunity the therapist has to develop an imagistic rendering of the event and to empathically adopt the internal frame of the client. Additionally, a number of investigators (Borkovec, Roemer, & Kinyon, 1995; Bucci, 1995; Salovey & Singer, 1993) have argued that the articulation of a detailed description of a personal, episodic memory may provide the client with an opportunity to more fully access emotions and thoughts experienced in the context of a past event. Vague accounts, which lack specificity and detail, make it difficult for the listener to establish an internalized image which would, in turn, facilitate the establishment of an empathic connection between speaker and listener. Moreover, the generation of new experiential and conceptual meanings in the context of the external narrative sequences emerges from the engagement in both internal and reflexive narrative process sequences.

Internal sequences show or describe to the therapist the emotions and feelings that are re-experienced by the client while telling the event (external). Internal sequences may also entail the description of new emotions or feelings emerging during the therapy session. In the context of dealing with physical and psychological trauma, Harber and Pennebaker (1992) have provided compelling research findings that demonstrate that emotional disclosure, in the context of trauma narratives, is predictive of positive immune system response in survivors.

In a similar vein, Borkovec et al. (1995) have argued that obsessive worrying in distressed clients suppresses the key psychological processes of imagery recall, affect, and emotional processing in the context of the experienced traumatic events. For Borkovec et al., the articulation and processing of distressing emotions is a key therapeutic task when working with chronically anxious clients. A growing number of psychotherapy researchers (Greenberg, Rice, & Elliott, 1993; Greenberg & Safran, 1984; Mahoney, 1991; Pennebaker, 1995) are recognizing the importance of emotional disclosure as a basis for the generation of a more differentiated experience and view of self and others in the world.

In the reflexive sequences, the client attempts to make sense of his or her experiences by exploring personal expectations, needs, motivations, anticipations, and beliefs of both the self and those individuals who play significant roles in the client's life. It is in the context of reflexively processing current and past experiences that the client and therapist begin to co-construct a framework of understanding, or macronarrative theme reformulation, which coherently organizes and provides meaning to the client's current and past experiences in the world.

In terms of within-session patterns, reflexive narrative sequences are found when both the client and therapist engage in a process of shared meaning making in relation to the clients' understanding of self and others in the world. This meaning-making process is typically manifested following an in-depth engagement of either external or internal narrative sequences in the context of therapy sessions. Greenberg and Pascual-Leone (1995) have argued that reflexive elaboration and meaning creation can be an important therapeutic consequence of client emotional expression if the therapist actively facilitates the client's focussing on the creation of new meaning (i.e., reflexive narrative sequence) from the aroused emotional material (i.e., internal narrative sequence).

Reflexive narrative processing that does not emerge from the detailed description of events and emotional expression may be a marker of shallow, automated processing (Borkovec et al., 1995) in which the client appears to be retelling a well-rehearsed script. By asking the client for a specific example of the problem or concern, thus directing the client to describe a specific instance (external narrative sequence), the therapist may help the client to engage in a kind of depth of internal and reflexive narrative processing of deeply painful and at times disturbing feelings and beliefs about the self. This allows the patient to articulate and understand them in ways that engender new meanings and perspectives about the self and others.

With this model it has been argued that all three narrative process sequence types have an important function to fulfil in the co-construction of the client's macronarrative or self-narrative and as such are present, although in varying degrees and patterns, in all therapeutic modalities. In a recent study, Angus et al. (1999) have found an increase in the predominance of internal (emotional states and affective reactions) and reflexive narrative sequences (interpretation meaning and comprehension of the experience) in the therapy discourse of good outcome patients, as compared to poor outcome patients, undergoing brief process-experiential treatment for depression.

Similar results were observed in James Pennebaker's (1993) research program on the therapeutic effects of writing about significant life events. One of the most interesting results was that the clients who benefited the most from this writing process were the ones who evolved (in the process of construing their personal narratives) toward an elaboration of the emotions and meaning aspects of the experience. This research seems to imply that therapeutic change corresponds to a narrative enrichment that allows clients to integrate multiple processes in their understanding of their experiences. This narrative attitude seems to be characterized by a variety of narrative modes and processes that grasp the sensorial, subjective, and meaning features of the experience.

In summary, self-differentiation and narrative complexity seem to emerge from the active engagement in narrative processes that include emotional disclosure and meaning-making attempts. A narrative existence entails the engagement in several narrative processes, which together facilitate the differentiation of sensorial, emotional, cognitive, and meaning components regarding our experiences of self and others in the world.

NARRATIVE CONTENT AND THE DIAGNOSIS OF MULTIPLICITY

Narrative content is related to the thematic dimension of narratives. A poorly diversified content is one that is limited in themes and narrative plot. This thematic limitation causes the interlocutor to experience a sense of narrative monotony. It is as if all the narratives told by the patient seem to continuously fall in the same thematic redundancy. The discursive elaboration of his or her experiences and its content becomes painfully predictable. It is this discursive predictability that generates in the clinicians meaning systems (the nosological categories). The redundant themes of the patient are easily framed in typologies of discursive indifferentiation creating a sense of "dejá entendú," almost as if it was possible to predict what the patient will say next. The patient seems to interpret his or her experiences with a fatalist script that transforms experience into an inflexible plot.

The pathological discourse is characterized by an inability to experience the world in a multifaceted way. The patient seems to structure experiences in terms of existing, rigid prototypical narratives. Organizing experiences in terms of these prototypical narratives results in a narrow understanding of the experience itself. Instead of diversity and flexibility, the individual is likely to be a prisoner of a set of thematic invariants that we call *narrative prototypes*. That is, the individual is connected with a prototypical narrative as a meaning system, and his or her past, present, and future experiences are interpreted within this prototypical unity. The narrative prototype, in this case, is a synonym of inflexible narrative authorship, a closed identity that dissociates from or restricts experiences if these do not match the narrative prototype.

In a similar way, Hermans and Hermans-Jansen (1995) considered that dysfunction can be identified as an individual's difficulty in operating in multiple narrative themes:

> A dysfunction can be described as a self-narrative restricted to a single theme. . . . It is as if the person can only create variations on a single theme irrespective of changes in the life situation. . . . Whereas thematic variations may characterize the normally functioning valuation system, only variations on a single persistent theme can be observed in the person with a dysfunctional valuation system. (p. 164)

Below we detail a method developed by Gonçalves and colleagues (cf. Gonçalves, Alves, Soares, & Duarte, 1996; Gonçalves & Machado, 1999) in order to identify and validate prototype narratives in patients diagnosed with different nosological categories.

The narrative prototypes construction method is based on the assumption that patients have a specific and idiosyncratic meaning making that could be organized in different prototypical narratives. These prototype narratives are a product of the convergent themes of the contents of the patients' core self-narratives. To a certain extent, prototypes are the redundant themes of patients' narrative construction and function like scripts to which the individual has to refer continually in an effort to find coherence and identity in the maze of experience (cf. Leahy, 1991). Moreover, different types of nosological categories can be assumed to be a product of invariant thematic story lines which result in prototypical clusters.

The narrative prototypes construction method is based on grounded theory analysis (cf. Strauss & Corbin, 1990). According to Charmz (1995), "in grounded theory analysis you start with individual cases, incidents or experiences and develop progressively more abstract conceptual categories to synthesize, to explain and to understand your data and to identify patterned relationships within it" (p. 28). The method follows a step-by-step procedure suggested by Rennie, Phillips, and Quartara (1988) and consists of the following stages.

1. Collecting significant life narratives. Patients go through a structured interview in which a guided imagery process is used to elicit memory of significant life narratives from different periods of their lives. In the second part of the interview, patients respond to a set of questions regarding the narrative, in order to obtain more details, regarding the external and internal components of the selected experience. All narratives are taped and are subsequently transcribed.

2. Categorization. The transcripts of each narrative are then sorted into seven different categories (setting, initiating event, internal response, goal, actions, outcome, and ending) suggested by Mandler (1984) as a universal narrative grammar structure.

3. Memoing. The content of the different narratives within each dimension of the grammar structure categories is further analyzed to allow the identification of different meaning categories.

4. Parsimony. The meaning categories identified in the memoing phase are further collapsed into clusters of hierarchical meanings to identify more general and abstract categories.

5. Construction of the narrative. Using the clusters of hierarchical meaning, a prototype narrative for the patient or group of patients is constructed based on the abstract categories of

meaning constructed for each element of the narrative grammar structure.

6. Validation of the prototype narrative. Patients are shown the prototypical narratives and are asked to rate on a 5-point Likert scale the degree to which that narrative could be understood as plausible as their own personal life event.

Figure 6.1 presents the prototype narrative resulting from 18 opioid dependent patients. In this study, after we sorted each transcript into the seven dimensions of the narrative grammar structure, the memoing process produced a total of 196 meaning categories. These meaning categories were subsequently the object of hierarchical categorization, which resulted in the emergence of seven clusters of hierarchical meanings, one for each dimension of the narrative–grammar structure: public place (setting); uncontrolled situation (initiating event); pain–suffering and pleasure–relief (internal response); seeking pleasure and avoiding pain (goal); external control and nonconfrontation (actions); status quo (outcome); social loss and loss of personal power (ending).

We constructed a prototype narrative from the hierarchical categories of meaning. This prototype was constructed by collapsing all the 18 narratives into common meaning themes using the seven clusters of hierarchical meaning suggested by the process of hierarchical categorization. Generally speaking, this prototype narrative can be stated as an episode taking place in a public setting and activated by some uncontrolled situation. The objective of individuals in this situation is to avoid some painful situation and to seek pleasure. Their actions are typically nonconfrontational and externally controlled, with a compound of internal states oscillating between the dialectics of pain–suffering and pleasure–relief. The outcome of the narrative is typically the maintenance of the status quo, with individuals ending up with a sense of social loss and loss of personal power. The prototype narrative is illustrated in Figure 6.1.

Several studies from Gonçalves and colleagues' research program on prototype narratives and psychopathology seem to support the hypothesis for prototypical invariants in psychopathology. It generally was possible to identify prototype narratives illustrating several types of psychopathology, namely depression, agoraphobia, eating disorders, alcoholism, and drug dependence. After collecting significant life narratives from different patients, it was possible to extract prototypical narratives, which characterize each of these diagnostic groups. In other words, aggregating all the narratives that were provided by the members of a given diagnostic group allowed for the generation of a typical narrative for that group. Not surprisingly, when faced with several prototypical narratives, each representing a different diagnostic group, patients could easily identy the prototypical narrative of "their own" diagnostic group. Moreover, it is important to mention that

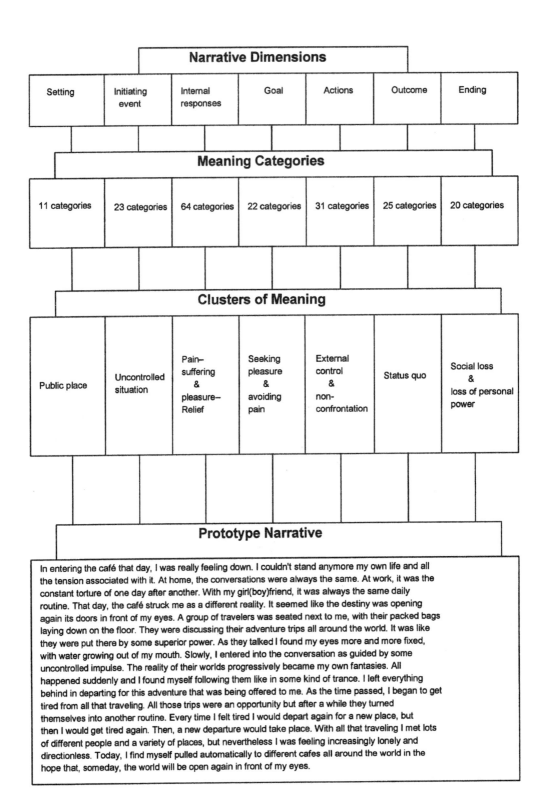

Narrative Dimensions

Setting	Initiating event	Internal responses	Goal	Actions	Outcome	Ending

Meaning Categories

11 categories	23 categories	64 categories	22 categories	31 categories	25 categories	20 categories

Clusters of Meaning

Public place	Uncontrolled situation	Pain–suffering & pleasure–Relief	Seeking pleasure & avoiding pain	External control & non-confrontation	Status quo	Social loss & loss of personal power

Prototype Narrative

In entering the café that day, I was really feeling down. I couldn't stand anymore my own life and all the tension associated with it. At home, the conversations were always the same. At work, it was the constant torture of one day after another. With my girl(boy)friend, it was always the same daily routine. That day, the café struck me as a different reality. It seemed like the destiny was opening again its doors in front of my eyes. A group of travelers was seated next to me, with their packed bags laying down on the floor. They were discussing their adventure trips all around the world. It was like they were put there by some superior power. As they talked I found my eyes more and more fixed, with water growing out of my mouth. Slowly, I entered into the conversation as guided by some uncontrolled impulse. The reality of their worlds progressively became my own fantasies. All happened suddenly and I found myself following them like in some kind of trance. I left everything behind in departing for this adventure that was being offered to me. As the time passed, I began to get tired from all that traveling. All those trips were an opportunity but after a while they turned themselves into another routine. Every time I felt tired I would depart again for a new place, but then I would get tired again. Then, a new departure would take place. With all that traveling I met lots of different people and a variety of places, but nevertheless I was feeling increasingly lonely and directionless. Today, I find myself pulled automatically to different cafes all around the world in the hope that, someday, the world will be open again in front of my eyes.

Figure 6.1. Prototype Narrative of Opioid Dependents

the majority of clinicians were unable to correctly identify which proto-typical narratives belonged to which diagnostic group. Furthermore, some clinicians refused to complete the task, claiming that they did not have adequate training in this form of diagnostics (Gonçalves et al., 1996; Gonçalves & Machado, 1999).

A good example of how an inductive process such as the one outlined above can be helpful in understanding the content dimensions of clients' narratives is presented by Capps and Ochs (1995). They compiled a variety of narratives for their client, Meg, who was diagnosed with panic disorder. By identifying common elements of the different narratives, they were able to construct a well-structured prototype of the panic narrative, in which the following sequence was present:

1. A family member or another close person proposes a future activity involving Meg.
2. Meg has reservations about participating in the proposed activity but does not communicate them.
3. Meg accommodates by participating in the activity.
4. Meg experiences a feeling of panic.
5. Meg directs the other to take her elsewhere, communicating her distress as justification.
6. Meg identifies herself and is identified by the other as ago-raphobic.
7. Meg avoids the location of the panic attack and other locations she deems similarly threatening.
8. When faced with a proposal involving traveling to distant locations, Meg declines, citing her agoraphobia as a warrant. (Capps & Ochs, p. 92).

CONCLUSION

The central idea underlying this chapter is that psychopathology should be understood not as rooted in a psychological or biological essential reality, but quite the contrary as a linguistic narrative construction. To understand the functional and dysfunctional qualities of an individual, the clinician needs to examine the individual's narrative construction. The clinician's attitude that we are defending here is described well by Efran and Cook (2000):

> Our perspective differs from the traditional view that diagnosis is a process that precedes and guides treatment. Instead, we see diagnosis as the primary ingredient of the therapeutic recipe. In other words, what we offer clients is a sharply focused collaborative examination of the language they use in talking to (and about) themselves. (p. 121)

To diagnose is, in this perspective, to examine the patients' narratives. It is the inspection of the narrative matrix, as manifested in the clinical conversation, which allows the assessment of the idiosyncratic meaning of psychopathology. Thus, clinicians need to develop new instruments to look at the content, process, and structure of the narrative matrix, not only as a way of coming to a more naturalistic and ecologically valid understanding of the client but also to create conditions for an alternative and more adaptive prognosis.

REFERENCES

Agar, M., & Hobbs, J. R. (1982). Interpreting discourse: Coherence and the analysis of ethnographic interviews. *Discourse Processes, 5*, 1–32.

American Psychiatric Association. (1952). *Diagnostic and statistical manual of mental disorders*. Washington, DC: Author.

American Psychiatric Association. (1987). *Diagnostic and statistical manual of mental disorders* (3rd ed., rev.). Washington, DC: Author.

American Psychiatric Association. (1994). *Diagnostic and statistical manual of mental disorders* (4th ed.). Washington, DC: Author.

Anderson, H., & Goolishian, H. (1992). The client is the expert: A not-knowing approach to therapy. In S. McNamee & K. Gergen (Eds.), *Therapy as social construction* (pp. 25–39). London: Sage.

Angus, L., & Hardtke, K. (1994). Narrative processes in psychotherapy. *Canadian Psychology, 35*(2), 190–203.

Angus, L., Hardtke, K., & Levitt, H. (1996). *The narrative processing coding system manual: Expanded edition*. Unpublished manuscript, Department of Psychology, York University, Toronto, Canada.

Angus, L., Levitt, H., & Hardtke, K. (1999). Narrative processes and psychotherapeutic change: An integrative approach to psychotherapy research and practice. *Journal of Clinical Psychology, 55*, 1255–1270.

Arlow, J., & Brenner, C. (1964). *Psychoanalytic concepts in the structural theory*. New York: International Universities Press.

Baerger, D. R., & McAdams, D. P. (1999). Life story coherence and its relation to psychological well-being. *Narrative Inquiry, 9*, 69–96.

Baumeister, R. F., & Newman, L. S. (1994). How stories make sense of personal experiences: Motives that shape autobiographical narratives. *Personality and Social Psychology Bulletin, 20*, 676–690.

Beck, A. T., Rush, A. J., Shaw, B. F., & Emery, G. (1979). *Cognitive therapy of depression*. New York: Guilford Press.

Beutler, L. E., Bongar, B., & Shurkin, J. N. (1998). *Am I crazy or is that my shrink?* New York: Oxford University Press.

Borkovec, T., Roemer, L., & Kinyon, T. (1995). Disclosure and worry: Opposite sides of the emotional processing coin. In J. W. Pennebaker (Ed.), *Emotion, disclosure and health* (pp. 47–70). Washington, DC: American Psychological Association.

Bruner, J. (1987). Life as narrative. *Social Research, 54(1)*, 11–32.

Bruner, J. (1990). *Acts of meaning.* Cambridge, MA: Harvard University Press.

Bucci, W. (1995). The power of the narrative: A multiple code account. In J. W. Pennebaker (Ed.), *Emotion, disclosure and health* (pp. 93–124). Washington, DC: American Psychological Association.

Capps, L., & Ochs, E. (1995). *Constructing panic: The discourse of agoraphobia.* Cambridge, MA: Harvard University Press.

Charmz, K. (1995). Grounded theory. In J. A Smith, R. Harré, & L. Van Langenhove (Eds.), *Rethinking methods in psychology* (pp. 27–49). London: Sage.

Crites, S. (1986). Storytime: Recollecting the past and projecting the future. In T. R. Sarbin (Ed.), *Narrative psychology: The storied nature of human conduct* (pp. 152–173). New York: Praeger.

Efran, J. S., & Cook, P. E. (2000). Linguistic ambiguity as a diagnostic tool. In R. A. Neimeyer & J. D. Raskin (Eds.), *Constructions of disorder* (pp. 121–144). Washington, DC: American Psychological Association.

Freud, S., & Breuer, J. (1895). *Studies on hysteria* (Vol. 3). London: Penguin Freud Library.

Gergen, K. J. (1994). *Realities and relationships: Soundings in social construction.* Cambridge, MA: Harvard University Press.

Gergen, K. J., & Gergen, M. M. (1986). Narrative form and the construction of psychological science. In T. R. Sarbin (Ed.), *Narrative psychology: The storied nature of human conduct* (pp. 22–44). New York: Praeger.

Gonçalves, Ó. F. (1995a). Cognitive narrative psychotherapy. In M. J. Mahoney (Eds.), *Cognitive and constructive psychotherapies* (pp. 139–162). New York: Springer.

Gonçalves, Ó. F. (1995b). Hermeneutics of the cognitive behavioral therapies: From the object to the project. In R. A. Neimeyer & M. J. Mahoney (Eds.), *Constructivism in psychotherapy* (pp. 195–230). Washington, DC: American Psychological Association.

Gonçalves, Ó. F. (1997). Postmodern cognitive psychotherapy: From the university to the multiversity. *Journal of Cognitive Psychotherapy, 11*, 105–112.

Gonçalves, Ó. F. (1998). *Psicoterapia cognitiva narrativa: Manual de terapia breve* [Cognitive narrative psychotherapy: A brief therapy manual]. Sao Paulo, Brasil: Editorial Psy.

Gonçalves, Ó. F., Alves, A., Soares, I. C., & Duarte, Z. (1996). Narrativas prototipo y psicopatologia: Un estudio com pacientes alcohólicos, anoréxicos y opiáceo-dependientes [Prototype narratives and psychopathology: A study with opioide, alcoholic and anorexic patients]. *Revista de Psicopatologia y Psicología Clínica (Spain), 1*, 105–114.

Gonçalves, Ó. F., Korman, Y., & Angus, L. (2000). Constructing psychopathology from a cognitive narrative perspective. In R. A. Neimeyer & J. D. Raskin (Eds.), *Constructions of disorder* (pp. 265–284). Washington, DC: American Psychological Association.

Gonçalves, Ó. F., & Machado, P. P. (1999). Cognitive narrative psychotherapy: Research foundations. *Journal of Clinical Psychology, 55,* 1179–1191.

Greenberg, L., & Pascual-Leone, J. (1995). A dialectical constructivist approach to experiential change. In R. Neimeyer & M. Mahoney (Eds.), *Constructivism in psychotherapy* (pp. 169–194). Washington, DC: American Psychological Association.

Greenberg, L., Rice, L., & Elliott, R. (1993). *Facilitating emotional change: The moment-by-moment process.* New York: Guilford Press.

Greenberg, L., & Safran, J. (1984). Integrating affect and cognition. *Cognitive Therapy and Research, 8,* 559–578.

Guidano, V. F. (1991). *Self in process: Toward a postrationalist cognitive therapy.* New York: Guilford Press.

Harber, K. D., & Pennebaker, J. W. (1992). Overcoming traumatic memories. In S. Christianson (Ed.), *The handbook of emotion and memory: Research and theory* (pp. 359–387). Hillsdale, NJ: Erlbaum.

Harré, R. (1995). Discursive psychology. In J. A. Smith, R. Harré, & L. V. Langenhove (Eds.), *Rethinking psychology* (pp. 143–159). London: Sage.

Harré, R., & Gillet, G. (1994). *The discursive mind.* London: Sage.

Hermans, H. J. M., & Hermans-Jansen, E. (1995). *Self-narratives: The construction of meaning in psychotherapy.* New York: Guilford Press.

Kintsch, W. (1980). Learning from text, levels of comprehension, or: Why would anyone read a story anyway. *Poetics, 9,* 87–98.

Kintsch, W., & van Dijk, T. A. (1978). Toward a model of text comprehension and production. *Psychological Review, 85,* 363–394.

Korman, Y. (1998). *Narrative coherence in brief good outcome client-centered psychotherapy.* Unpublished masters thesis, York University, North York, Ontario. Canada.

Leahy, R. L. (1991). Scripts in cognitive therapy: The systemic perspective. *Journal of Cognitive Psychotherapy, 5,* 291–304.

Mahoney, M. J. (1991). *Human change processes: The scientific foundations of psychotherapy.* New York: Basic Books.

Main, M. (1991). Metacognitive knowledge, metacognitive monitoring, and singular (coherent) vs. multiple (incoherent) model of attachment: Findings and future research. In C. M. Parkes, J. Stevenson-Hinde, & P. Marris (Eds.), *Attachment across the life cycle* (pp. 127–159). London: Routledge.

Mancuso, J. C. (1986). The acquisition and use of narrative grammar structure. In T. R. Sarbin (Ed.), *Narrative psychology: The storied nature of human conduct* (pp. 91–110). New York: Praeger.

Mandler, J. M. (1984). *Scripts, stories and scenes: Aspects of schema theory.* Hillsdale, NJ: Erlbaum.

Mandler, J. M., & Goodman, M. S. (1982). On the psychological validity of story structure. *Journal of Verbal Learning and Verbal Behavior, 21*, 507–523.

McLeod, J. (1997). *Narrative and psychotherapy*. London: Sage.

Murray, K. D. (1995). Narratology. In J. A. Smith, R. Harré, & L. V. Langenhove (Eds.), *Rethinking psychology* (pp. 179–195). London: Sage.

Pennebaker, J. (1993). Putting stress in words: Health, linguistic and therapeutic implication. *Behaviour, Research & Therapy, 31*, 539–548.

Pennebaker, J. W. (Ed.). (1995). *Emotion, disclosure and health*. Washington, DC: American Psychological Association.

Rasmussen, B., & Angus, L. (1996). Metaphor in psychodynamic psychotherapy with borderline and non-borderline clients: A qualitative analysis. *Psychotherapy, 33*, 521–530.

Rasmussen, B., & Angus, L. (1997). Modes of interaction in psychodynamic psychotherapy with borderline and non-borderline clients: A qualitative analysis. *Journal of Analytic Social Work, 4(4)*, 53–63.

Rennie, D., Phillips, J. R., & Quartaro, G. K. (1988). Grounded theory: A promising approach to conceptualization in psychology? *Canadian Psychology, 29*, 139–150.

Rogers, C. (1942). *Counseling and psychotherapy: Newer concepts in practice*. Boston: Houghton Mifflin.

Rosen, H. (1996). Meaning-making narratives: Foundations for constructivist and social constructionist psychotherapies. In H. Rosen & K. Kuehlwein (Eds.), *Constructing realities: Meaning making perspectives for psychotherapists* (pp. 3–54). San Francisco: Jossey-Bass.

Rosenhan, D. (1973). On being sane in insane places. *Science, 179*, 250–258.

Rosenhan, D. (1984). On being sane in insane places. In P. Watzlawick (Ed.), *The invented reality: How do we know what we believe we know* (pp. 117–144). New York: Norton.

Russell, R. L., & van den Broek, P. (1992). Changing narrative schemas in psychotherapy. *Psychotherapy, 29*, 344–353.

Russell, R. L., van den Broek, P., Adams, S., Rosenberg, K., & Essig, T. (1993). Analyzing narratives in psychotherapy: A formal framework and empirical analyses. *Journal of Narrative and Life History, 3*, 337–360.

Russell, R. L., & Wandrei, M. L. (1996). Narrative and the process of psychotherapy: Theoretical foundations and empirical support. In H. Rosen & K. Kuehlwein (Eds.), *Constructing realities: Meaning making perspectives for psychotherapists* (pp. 307–336). San Francisco: Jossey-Bass.

Salovey, J. A., & Singer, P. (1993). *The remembered self: Emotion and memory in personality*. New York: Macmillan Press.

Seligman, M., & Yellen, A. (1987). What is a dream? *Behaviour Research & Therapy, 25*, 1–24.

Shotter, J. (1995). Biological psychology. In J. A. Smith, R. Harré, & L. V. Langenhove (Eds.), *Rethinking psychology* (pp. 160–178). London: Sage.

Stein, N. L., & Glenn, C. G. (1979). An analysis of story comprehension in elementary school children. In R. O. Freedle (Ed.), *New directions in discourse processing* (Vol. 2, pp. 53–120). Norwood, NJ: Ablex.

Stein, N. L., & Policastro, M. (1984). The concept of story: A comparison between children's and teacher's viewpoints. In H. Mandl, N. L. Stein, & T. Trabasso (Eds.), *Learning and comprehension of text* (pp. 113–155). Hillsdale, NJ: Erlbaum.

Strauss, A. L., & Corbin, J. A. (1990). *Basics of qualitative research: Grounded theory procedures and techniques.* Newbury Park, CA: Sage.

Szasz, T. (1970). *The manufacture of madness.* New York: Harper & Row.

Szasz, T. (1997). The healing word: In past, present and future. In J. K. Zeig (Ed.), *The evolution of psychotherapy: The third conference* (pp. 299–306). Bristol, PA: Brunner/Mazel.

Trabasso, T., & van den Broek, P. (1985). Causal thinking and the representation of narrative events. *Journal of Memory and Language, 24,* 612–630.

van den Broek, P., & Thurlow, R. (1991). The role of structure of personal narratives. *Journal of Cognitive Psychotherapy, 5,* 257–274.

White, M., & Epston, D. (1990). *Narrative means to therapeutic ends.* New York: Norton.

7

OPERATIONALIZED PSYCHODYNAMIC DIAGNOSTICS: A NEW DIAGNOSTIC APPROACH IN PSYCHODYNAMIC PSYCHOTHERAPY

WOLFGANG SCHNEIDER, PETER BUCHHEIM, MANFRED CIERPKA, RAINER W. DAHLBENDER, HARALD J. FREYBERGER, TILMANN GRANDE, SVEN O. HOFFMANN, GEREON HEUFT, PAUL L. JANSSEN, JOACHIM KÜCHENHOFF, ARIBERT MUHS, GERD RUDOLF, ULRICH RÜGER, AND GERHARD SCHÜSSLER

Since the end of the 1960s, clinical psychiatrists have favored operationalized approaches, such as the American Psychiatric Association's *Diagnostic and Statistical Manual of Mental Disorders* (DSM; various editions) system in the United States and the *International Classification of Diseases* (10th ed.; *ICD–10*; World Health Organization, 1990) system in Europe. Many psychodynamically oriented psychotherapists and psychoanalysts have reacted to these models with skepticism and have rejected them for several reasons. The primary reason is that the syndromatic systems of classification represented by the various editions of the *DSM* (e.g., the 3rd revised edition [*DSM–III–R*], American Psychiatric Association, 1987; the 4th edition [*DSM–IV*], American Psychiatric Association, 1994) and *ICD–10*, especially with respect to treatment planning (Beutler & Clarkin

1990), have very low validity. In other words, the use of these instruments in the clinical practice of psychotherapy is often unsatisfactory. These models abandon the term *neurosis* and cling to phenomenological and biological concepts that emphasize reliability much more than the validity of a construct (Schneider & Freyberger, 1990; Schneider & Hoffmann, 1992). Psychodynamically inclined psychotherapists deplore the lack of terms and constructs, which are important for psychodynamic conceptualization of personality development and an understanding of mental disorders (e.g., intrapsychic and interpersonal conflicts, egofunction; Blanck & Blanck, 1974). These constructs are also helpful in establishing links between symptoms, triggering conflicts, the dysfunctional relations of patients, and their life history in a broad sense. Furthermore, many psychotherapists evaluate the subjective experience of illness and processes of coping with the disorder when they plan therapy, areas that are not considered in these classification systems (Schneider, Freyberger, Muhs, & Schüssler, 1993).

Another reason for rejecting contemporary models is that these models often define the nature and structure of the therapist–patient relationship and the process of treatment in a manner that is counterproductive to psychodynamic theory. For example, in these models the patient is defined as being a passive object of the diagnostic process. This role is not conducive to the psychotherapeutic process as defined in psychodynamic theory.

Systematic approaches to diagnosis and the diagnostic process have had a long tradition within psychodynamic psychotherapy (Balint, Ornstein, & Balint, 1972; Freud, 1977; Gill, Newman, & Redlich, 1954; Kernberg, 1981). From these perspectives, diagnostics are relational in nature. They define how individuals respond to others. An operationalization of relational diagnostics has been developed by various research groups, relying heavily on the work of Luborsky (e.g., Luborsky & Kächele, 1988). For example, Weinryb and Roessel (1991) have developed Karolinska Psychodynamic Profile (KAPP), a psychodynamic operational system with which several areas of diagnostic characteristics can be registered. The KAPP includes 18 subscales and is used to evaluate patients' psychic functioning in relation to self-perception and object relationships. The assorted areas (subscales) are conceptually described on various levels of abstraction allowing for interpretive aspects of evaluation. This approach allows the expansion of diagnostics beyond the level of behavior. Kernberg (1996) developed a psychodynamic classification of personality organization, which ranges from neurotic personality organization to borderline personality organization and psychotic personality organization. On the basis of this model, Kernberg's group developed and evaluated a psychodynamic treatment for patients with borderline personality organization (Clarkin, Yeomans, & Kernberg, 1999). Important problems and ways to operationalize psychodynamic issues are more extensively discussed in the publications of the OPD Working Group (1996, in German; English publication, 2000).

Based mainly on the work of German researchers and therapists, and at the initiation of M. Cierpka (Heidelberg) and W. Schneider (Rostock), our research team decided to develop an operationalized psychodynamic diagnostic (OPD) system in addition to the *ICD–10*, which we believed would be better suited to understanding psychotherapeutic processes. The first impetus of this approach, which was introduced in the early 1990s in Germany, benefitted from the experiences of the *ICD–10* field trials (the introduction of the research criteria; Schneider et al., 1993). As a first step, the aims, structure, and methods of the multicenter team were set down in a joint article. The aim of our effort was to further the prior efforts to objectify the diagnostic process and to ensure its scientific and material soundness. The group wanted to find a way to present our diagnostic model to the medical and psychotherapeutic communities at large and to coordinate its development and use with the work of the international *ICD–10* group as far as possible. At the first meeting the group defined the axes to be developed and determined the necessary organizational structure. S. O. Hoffmann (Mainz) was chosen as spokesman (1992–1999). Since 1999, M. Cierpka (Heidelberg) has been the spokesperson of the OPD Working Group. These spokespersons were commissioned to coordinate the acitivities of the group as a whole and to represent the group externally. Furthermore, the group chose a committee to approve publications and other research aims that pertained to the objectives of the OPD group.

Five subgroups of experts from the OPD Working Group were undertook the task of developing the axes of the diagnostic system. A group was formed for each axis and was commissioned to write a description of the theoretical foundations of the axis and to collect a compendium of relevant clinical examples. Each group had to take into account or adapt existing approaches when setting up a clinically relevant psychodynamic proposal. We reasoned that this should result in usable instruments while being moderately abstract and halfway between pure description of behavior and pure metapsychological concepts. Moreover, the aim was to develop a set of uniform and precise concepts that were clearly formulated within a usable terminology that was independent of any particular psychoanalytic and psychotherapeutic school, in order to be acceptable to different psychotherapeutic approaches.

We designed the OPD to do the following:

- provide clinical diagnostic guidelines, which are relatively open in their formulation and which allow users ample scope for their own assessment;
- be useful for training in psychodynamic psychotherapy by

providing practice both in psychodynamic and in phenomenological classification;

- improve communication within the scientific community regarding psychodynamic constructs; and
- be useful for scientific research (e.g., by setting stricter diagnostic critieria).

These purposes served as criteria for the adequacy of OPD. In turn,
these criteria should allow homogeneous samples in research to be built.
They also should provide clearer baselines about the course of illness, testing for indication of therapy and differential indication and for examining
the efficiency and effectiveness of treatments.

In the sections that follow, we present the conceptual structure of the
OPD. The diagnostic procedure is based on a semistructured clinical interview in which the interviewer or diagnostician rates patient behavior
that reflects the relational OPD categories.

STRUCTURE OF THE OPD

The OPD defines five diagnostic axes:

Axis I: Experience of Illness and Prerequisites of Treatment

Axis II: Relational Issues

Axis III: Conflict

Axis IV: Structure

Axis V: Syndrome diagnostics according to Chapter V (F) of the
ICD–10

Axis I: Experience of Illness and Prerequisites of Treatment

The patient's experience of illness and treatment motivation, cognitive and affective resources, and status on critical environmental variables
(e.g., the availiability of social support) play a central role in therapy indication. We think that this view is valid for both somatic and psychotherapeutic treatment. Whatever treatment is indicated, however, the patient must feel ready and informed enough to accept it and cooperate. To
undergo psychotherapy, it is important that the patient demonstrates some
signs of suffering, shows insight into important psychosocial variables (e.g.,
psychodynamic factors) that are influencing the illness, and has adequate
personal and social resources.

With this common understanding, we operationalized the axis Experience of Illness and Prerequisites of Treatment. We prefer our term *ex-*

perience of illness to the common term *illness behavior* because it better identifies the influence of affective processes in the critical context.

Individual items in the OPD rating system are evaluated on a 5-point scale with the following anchors: 0 = *absent*, 1 = *low*, 2 = *moderate*, 3 = *high*, and 4 = *unassessable*. Typical examples are given for each level of severity and are intended to further increase diagnostic dependability. The first axis contains 19 items, as shown in Table 7.1.

Axis II: Relational Issues

Most major schools of psychotherapy consider interpersonal behavior as being relevant in the genesis and maintenance of mental disorders. Psychodynamic psychotherapy especially focuses on the question of how an individual lives and experiences his or her relationships to others. Intrapsychic conflicts contribute much to the dysfunctional behavior in interpersonal relationships. We understand relational behavior as expressing the dynamics between more or less conscious desires for relationships, the patient's activated inner fears, and the patient's apprehension about how another might react to these desires. Habitual relational behavior can be regarded as a long-term psychosocial compromise between relational desires and apprehensions. The psychodynamic concepts about the development of the self and its relation to others differ greatly (e.g., Kernberg 1986, Mahler, 1975; Stern, 1985; see OPD Working Group, 2000).

Because our conceptualization of Axis II of the OPD is based mainly on empirical approaches to explore relational patterns, we do not discuss the psychodynamic theories about the origin of interperonal relationships in this chapter. We have worked out our conceptualization of this axis by drawing on empirical approaches that derive from psychoanalytic and interpersonal tradition. The following methods are particularly important and influential in the conceptualization of Axis II: structural analysis of social behavior (Benjamin, 1974, 1993), central relational conflict (Luborsky & Crits-Cristoph, 1990), and cyclically maladaptive patterns (Strupp & Binder, 1984), all of which examine personal interactions by means of observation. These methods and schemes are based on the assumption that there is at least one, and possibly several, central relational conflicts at the root of the patient's problem. These conflicts are explored in associated assessment methods and research studies. In the usual clinical assessment methods, the horizon of interpersonal patterns, as well as the necessary methods to examine them, are more complex. Therefore, the resulting inferences or judgments are more subjective. This could be problematic in the process of rating interpersonal patterns, and it could result in low interrater reliability. Therefore, it was important for us to define and formulate the different interpersonal modi clearly and precisely. We decided to define a *conflictual interpersonal pattern of relation* as a specific constella-

TABLE 7.1
Axis I–Experience of Illness

Dimensions	Grading		
	Low (1)	Moderate (2)	High (3)
1. Severity of physical symptoms			
2. Severity of mental symptoms			
3. Patient's subjective suffering	Overall, patient suffers little	Overall, patient suffers moderately	Patient suffers severely
4. Sense of self and self-image	Self-functions are preserved; aspects of illness are integrated into the personality	Self-functions are partly preserved; aspects of illness are only partly integrated	The self is highly endangered; aspects of illness are not integrated
5. Extent of physical disabilities	Physical functions are slightly impaired	Physical functions are moderately impaired	Physical functions are severely impaired
6. Secondary benefit from illness	Psychosocial advantages are hardly noticeable or desired	Psychosocial advantages are noticeable or desired	Psychosocial advantages are very noticeable or desired
7. Comprehending and accepting psychodynamic–psychosomatic associations	Patient cannot see links between mental stress and symptoms	Patient sees some links	Strong recognition of the links
8. Comprehending and accepting somatopsychic associations	Patient hardly sees links between somatic illness and mental state	Patient has moderate insight	Patient has strong insight

9. Patient's opinion regarding a suitable form of treatment (psychotherapy)	Patient sees psychotherapy as unsuitable for tackling his or her problems	Patient sees psychotherapy as possibly suitable	Patient sees psychotherapy as highly suitable
10. Patient's opinion regarding a suitable form of treatment (medical treatment)	Patient sees somatic treatment as unsuitable	Patient sees such treatment as possibly suitable	Patient sees such treatment as highly suitable
11. Motivation for psychotherapy	Little interest in taking part in it	Moderate interest	Strong interest
12. Motivation for medical treatment	Hardly any interest	Moderate interest	Strong interest
13. Compliance	Low	Moderate	High
14. Symptoms presented are physical symptoms	Low	Moderate	High
15. Symptoms presented are mental symptoms	Low	Moderate	High
16. Psychosocial integration	Patient poorly integrated in social and professional domain	Patient has moderate integration	Patient has good integration
17. Personal resources	Patient has low ability to develop skills useful for tackling his or her problems	Patient has moderate ability	Patient has a great deal of ability
18. Social support	Patient experiences little social support	Patient experiences moderate social support	Patient experiences a great deal of social support
19. Appropriateness of patient's subjective assessment of illness	Not very appropriate	Moderately appropriate	Quite appropriate

tion of habitual behavior in the patient and the typical ways others react to this.

The structure of the relational pattern consists of two interpersonal positions: the patient's habitual relational behavior ("the patient always experiences himself such that . . .") and typical reactions of others in terms of how the patient experiences them ("the patient experiences others always such that . . ."). Again, we have to describe the perspective of the patient, but the variable is also observed by the therapist–rater who is an interacting partner of the patient and so has insight into how others might feel in interaction with the patient.

Because therapists must assess the events perceived and described by the patient, their possibly different perceptions can alter their view and judgment of the patient. Therefore, we included the special rating of the therapist's view of the patient's relational style and the reactions induced by that style in the therapist. These perspectives include elements of the psychoanalytic concept of countertransference.

The two structural elements are categorized on the basis of the circumplex model of interpersonal behavior, which has been established in clinical psychology and psychotherapy for a long time (Wiggins, 1982). The model implies that partners interacting in social relations adapt their behavior to the definition of status and the proximity desired. *Interpersonal behavior* is defined by two orthogonal and bipolar dimensions: control (dominant vs. submissive) and affiliation (friendly vs. hostile). Different qualities of interpersonal behavior are seen as results of different mixtures of these basic dimensions and are indicated by different sites on the circle (see Figure 7.1).These models and their attending measuring instruments have been well tested and validated in personality, social, and clinical psychology.

The assessment of experiential perspectives is done with the help of two lists of items, which are formulated on the basis of the interpersonal patterns familiar from the circumplex model (e.g., the patient continually places himself or herself in the position in which he or she overidealizes others, or others find themselves repeatedly in the position of being particularly admired or idealized by the patient). The rater has to select no more than three of the most salient items for each of the four perspectives:

- the patient's interpersonal behavior from his or her perspective,
- the behavior of others from the patient's perspective,
- the patient's behavior from the therapist's perspective, and
- the reactions of the therapist in the interview from his or her own perspective.

The interviewer–rater can then draw on these items to formulate a

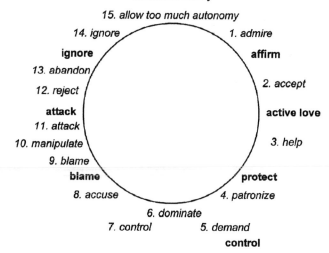

Active mode

allow autonomy

15. *allow too much autonomy*

14. *ignore*   1. *admire*

ignore   affirm

13. *abandon*

12. *reject*   2. *accept*

attack   active love

11. *attack*

10. *manipulate*   3. *help*

9. *blame*

blame   protect

8. *accuse*   4. *patronize*

6. *dominate*

7. *control*   5. *demand*

control

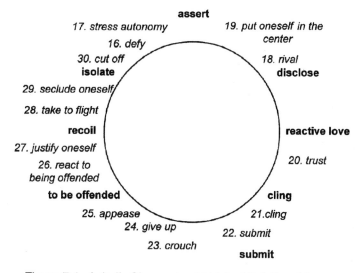

Reactive mode

assert

17. *stress autonomy*   19. *put oneself in the*
16. *defy*   *center*

30. *cut off*   18. *rival*
isolate   disclose

29. *seclude oneself*

28. *take to flight*

recoil   reactive love

27. *justify oneself*

26. *react to*   20. *trust*
being offended

to be offended   cling

25. *appease*   21.*cling*

24. *give up*   22. *submit*

23. *crouch*

submit

Figure 7.1. Axis II: Circumplex Model of Relational Issues

psychodynamic hypothesis about the maladaptive interpersonal behavior of the patient. In working with relational experiences and episodes, the interviewer should look for objects initially reported by the patient and then query the concrete relation. Alternatively, the interviewer can move from the account of complaints to the relational experiences by asking the patient how others react to the illness, if the patient does not mention it. The interviewer should always search for individual and concrete episodes of interactions. This latter step is very important when the patient only presents broad overviews of his or her experiences with other people. Often it is necessary to take a deeper look into situational details to get an impression about the typical interpersonal patterns. It is always important to analyze how the interpersonal patterns developed over time and whether these characteristics are representative of the patient's current behavior.

Axis III: Conflict

Life involves conflicting interests within and between individuals. Many individuals are unable to integrate these tensions to fit internal and external demands. The conflicts described below demonstrate mainly unconscious oppositions and problem areas. We must distinguish unconscious conflicts from conscious tensions. The conflict patterns that are described here recur time and again in the lives of those who have not yet been able to master them. The patterns may remain active and enduring, and they may determine the experience and actions of persons affected.

Furthermore, conflictual and stressful situations inevitably occur. Radical changes in lifestyle and attendant burdens (such as those that occur with the death of a loved one, illness, or injury), even when not repetitive, can evoke physical and mental diseases. Long-term unconscious conflicts show up in clinical accounts of observable modes of behavior and experience. Often they are linked with leading affects (e.g., anger at narcissistic injuries), or they occur directly in transference and countertransference.

Our definitions of conflict do not rest on assumptions from developmental psychology or explicitly on classical psychoanalysis (id, ego, and super-ego), although we deal with conflicts both within and between persons. Traditional psychoanalytic terminology is used differently in different schools of thought; therefore, we have largely avoided a close conceptual orientation to a specific psychoanalytic position about conflict (e.g., anal and oral conflict) when we conceptualized and defined this topic.

Working through special current conflicts does not trivialize the importance of past traumatic experiences. The consequences of extreme traumatic experiences during childhood can probably be found in mainly structural deficits. Conflict and structure are poles of a clinical series. Conflicts reveal themselves in the essential areas of a person's life. A. Dührssen (1981) described the following areas: choice of partnership, bonding behavior and family life, domain of the family into which one is born, the field of work and profession, behavior toward property, sociocultural surroundings, and experience of illness.

In the process of diagnosing conflicts, it is important to focus on the verbal material and the behavior and expression of affects that are observable. The interviewer must know precise definitions of the conflicts and the specific diagnostic categories and descriptions. Invalid and unreliable ratings can result if the diagnostician uses concepts that are based on specific training and education rather than the OPD criteria and definition.

Each conflict level has a passive and an active (antiphobic) mode. This differentiation reflects the experience of a basic polarity between the passive and the active, between the relation to self and relation to objects. The retreat to the self demonstrates the passive mode; the searching for the object demonstrates the active process. In ratings using the OPD, the most important conflicts are more likely to be associated with pathogenesis and pathodiagnostic significance. However, these conflicts do not need to be a focus of therapeutic treatment.

OPD distinguishes the fundamental conflicts that are shown in Exhibit 7.1.

On Axis III, the method of coping with conflicts is rated on a 5-point scale with the following anchors: 0 = *absent*, 1 = *present but insignificant*, 2 = *present and significant*, 3 = *present and very significant*, 4 = *nonassessable*. The respondent is asked to identify two or more conflict areas and then to rate their significance using the 5-point scale.

Axis IV: Structure of Disorder

Along with the classification of intrapsychic conflicts and the patient's typical relational style, the most important task of psychodynamic diagnostics is the evaluation of the structural disorder. Structural diagnostics must be based on a theoretical concept. We find different concepts of structure in personality psychology (Wiggins & Trapnell, 1997) as well as in psychoanalysis (Rudolf, 1993). We do not intend to discuss the many different psychoanalytic approaches to psychodynamic structure at this point (see OPD Working Group, 2000). Here we want to explain our specific view of structure and to present in a next step our description of this diagnostic dimension.

Mental structure is a typical disposition for experience and behavior in individuals. Its patterns become manifest and visible through interactions with others. In the process of diagnostics, the interviewer experiences aspects of patients' structure in direct encounters, gaining a picture from patients' stories about their daily routines and life histories. Furthermore, patients' interactions in the diagnostic process and their report about past interactions and experiences are cues for understanding their structure. The diagnostic assessment of structure should include patients' interactions of the preceding 2 years. These past behaviors provide hints about the important underlying structure of patients' interactions that are as useful as the actual behavior manifested during a period of mental disorder. Acute disorders are often characterized by regressive states and crises. These symptoms do not determine the diagnoses of structure but can be an indicator for structure, too.

EXHIBIT 7.1
Axis III–Conflict

1 Internal long-term conflicts	
1.1 Dependence vs. autonomy	Looking for relationship (but not caring for) with marked dependence (passive mode) or build-up of an emotional independence (active mode) with suppression of desire for bonds (family–partnership–profession). Illnesses produce welcome dependence or are existentially menacing.
1.2 Submission vs. control	Obedience–submission (passive mode) vs. control–resistance (active mode) determine interpersonal relationship and internal experience. Illnesses are "fought" or are a fate to be endured to which one must submit, as to the doctor.
1.3 Desire for care vs. autarchy	Wish for care and shelter lead to strong dependence (passive mode, dependent and demanding) or are warded off as self-sufficiency and unpretentiousness (basic attitude of altruism, positive mode). In the case of illness, such people cling passively or refuse help. However, dependence and independence are not in the foreground as primary needs (see 1.1).
1.4 Conflicts of self-value (self vs. objects)	Feelings of self-value are fragile or resigned, given up (passive mode), or compensating efforts to maintain by threatened feelings dominate (pseudo-self-assurance, active mode). Illness leads to crisis of self-value but may restore the self-image.
1.5 Guilt conflicts (egoistic vs. prosocial tendencies)	Guilt is readily admitted (to the point of masochistic submission) and self-reproach prevails (passive mode), or there are no guilt feelings at all; they are assigned to others and others are held responsible for illness (active mode).
1.6 Oedipal-sexual conflicts	Eros and sexuality lack perception, insight, and feeling (passive mode), or determine all spheres of life without achieving satisfaction (active mode). (General disorders of sexual function from other sources are excluded from this category.)
1.7 Identity conflicts (identity vs. dissonance)	There are sufficient ego functions (see Axis IV, structure, identity diffusion) but also conflictual self-domains (identity dissonance): sexual identity, role identity, parent/child identity, religious and cultural identity and the like. The assumption of lack of identity (passive mode) is countered by compensatory efforts to outplay insecurities and breaks (active mode).
2 Limited perception of conflicts and feelings	Feelings and needs of oneself and of others are not perceived and conflicts are overlooked (passive mode) or replaced by objective technical descriptions (active mode).
II Conflictual external stress	External stress is present, and coping is adequate to explain mental and bodily symptoms. The conflicts listed above will probably not be repeated. Typical examples are grief after loss, illness, crises, or posttraumatic fear. If need be, extra mention as stressful reaction and disordered adjustment in Axis V.
III Mode of processing	Life-determining conflicts, or current ones, are worked through either passively (retreat, adaptation, or resignation) or actively (defensively and against fear).

The OPD concept of structure primarily combines object-relational approaches with those from self or ego psychology. Structure characterizes and influences the way the self shapes itself and functions in relation to others. Structure can be broken down into several aspects: self-perception, self-regulation, mechanism of defense, object perception, communication, and attachment.

The basic development of these structural elements occurs in early childhood, during the first 5 to 6 years. Structural disorders in adults are seen as deficient growths or regressive merging. The relationship between conflict (Axis III) and structural disorder (Axis IV) is manifold. Obviously, the two constructs describe distinct aspects of a common reference system. The concept of conflict describes the genesis of disease in the form of triggering events. Structure is related more to how one adapts to the disease, one's vulnerability, and one's capacity to work things out.

The six structural dimensions of the axis can be described on four levels of integration, which are operationalized by diagnostic criteria and clinical description and examples (see Table 7.2).

Axis V: Syndrome Diagnostics According to Chapter V (F) of the ICD–10

Chapter V (F) of the *ICD–10* (World Health Organization, 1993; Dilling, Mombour, & Schmidt, 1993; Dilling, Mombour, Schmidt, & Schulte-Markwort, 1994) operationalizes mental disorders according to descriptive principles based on comparably defined diagnostic criteria. For these characteristics, the level of severity is clearly established on relatively easily observable or explorative data. Another favored descriptive parameter is the course of a disease (see, e.g., the affective disorders in *ICD–10*). More complex psychopathological phenomena or aspects of experience that require a higher level of theoretical or interpretive abstraction are largely neglected. Following rules of association (algorithms), specific combinations of these individually formulated criteria constitute particular diagnoses (diagnostic classes). Here, differentiation based on level of severity is of primary importance, particularly in the case of affective and anxiety disorders. Remaining diagnostic categories applied for patients without specifically definable diseases are based on a hierarchical system and represent a solid component of this classification approach.

In relation to its various areas of application, the *ICD–10* is found in a number of different manuals and is considered a member of the "family of instruments." Furthermore, a large number of structured and standardized interview approaches exist (Stieglitz, Dittmann, & Mombour, 1992). These interview approaches can be advantageous in research. However, because

TABLE 7.2
Axis IV–Structure

Level of integration	Good	Moderate	Low	Disintegrated
Self-perception: Ability for self-reflection to gain self-image and identity, and for introspection and differentiation of affects	Self-reflective ability and identity feeling basically present and sometimes limited by neurotic conflicts. Leading affects are joy, pride, fear, guilt, contempt, shame, grief	Gaining a self-image is difficult, as is differentiating affects; identity insecure. Leading affects are fear, anger, disappointment, self-devaluation, ambivalence	Self-reflective functions largely absent, identity is diffuse; leading affects are chronic fear, anger, depression, emptiness, alienation	Self-reflective ability absent; social and sexual identity largely missing (schizophrenia) or excessive identification with social roles (manic-depressive psychosis)
Self-regulation: Ability to regulate one's own needs, affects and self-esteem, tolerance for ambivalences and negative affects	Ability to regulate impulses, affects and self-esteem basically present, possibly with neurotic limitations	Overregulation or possible breakthroughs of impulses; emotional flexibility limited, self-devaluating, auto-aggressive tendencies; regulation of self-esteem (easily offended)	Impulsive behavior, self-punishing tendencies, intolerance for negative affects; fragile regulation of self-esteem (very easily offended, grandiosity)	Inadequate idea of causing his or her own actions, possibly strong disorders or self-regulation, (breakthroughs of drives to the point of psychotic excitement)
Defense: Ability to maintain or restore mental balance in internal or external conflicts by certain defense mechanisms	Defense stable, effective; directed against drives and affects; repression, rationalizing, displacing	Defense less flexible, excessive, or missing; denial, turning against oneself, reaction formation, isolation, projection	Defense by change in self-representation and object-representation; splitting, projective identification, idealization or devaluation	Defense unstable, inflexible; withdrawn from objects; psychotic denial, psychotic projection
Object-perception: Ability to differentiate clearly between internal and external reality, perceiving external reality, perceiving external objects wholly, coherently and with one's own rights and aims; ability to empathize	The image of the other is accurately perceived, though possibly tinged with neurotic conflict; ability for empathy present; object-related affects are possible (care, sympathy, guilt, grief, shame)	Little ability for empathy; conflict-tinged perception of the other. In conflicts, the other can be frightening or there is a threat that the other becomes lost through the conflict	No empathy; the other is not allowed his or her rights and aims; the other is an object that satisfies one's needs or that pursues one	Psychotic confusion of representations; selective perception of single parts of objects

Communication: Ability to adapt to others, to communicate with them and grasp their affective signals	Readiness to communicate basically present; need for communication possibly conflictually limited or increased	Ability to communicate can be disordered; readiness for it is limited by offended, aggressive, needy attitude	Ability to communicate impaired; difficulty in grasping the other's affective signals; breakdowns of communication; confusion, misunderstandings	Misinterpretation of affective signals; everything can acquire communicative significance
Attachment: Ability to set up internal images of the other and deal with them effectively over time (internalization, object constancy); variable attachment; alternation between attachment and separation; rules of interaction to protect the relationship	Good internal objects are present; different internal objects basically allow triadic relations; possible difficulty to integrate attachment with different people. Central fear: loss of the love of the object	Few good internal objects, images of objects reduced to few patterns; wishful and dyadic relations predominate. Central fear: losing the important object	Few good objects are internalized; internal objects punished and devaluated; dependence on external objects. Central fear: the bad object or the loss of the good one might destroy the self	To protect against feared merging, attachments are shunned, possibly to the point of autistic isolation; on a regressive level, stable attachments can be maintained
Global rating: Structure of self in relation to others; available internal and interpersonal regulating functions to maintain autonomy and ability to relate	Largely autonomous self; regulating functions available; internal mental space structured (internal conflict possible). Super-ego strict but integrated	Fewer available regulating functions. Inner conflicts more destructive and more archaic; super-ego strict and possibly externalized; exaggerated ego-ideal	Inner mental space and substructures underdeveloped; regulating functions clearly reduced; conflicts are interpersonal rather than internal	No cohesive self is developed hence risk of disintegration of fragmentation under stress; psychotic collapse may be followed by psychotic restitution

they are oriented to symptoms, they can lead to a devaluation of psycho-dynamic information and at least a partial elimination of the relational aspect together with the associated results for the therapeutic process and professional training. Nevertheless, this level of symptomology clearly ex-emplifies a relevant diagnostic dimension. It allows clinicians to formulate hypotheses concerning the type of disorder and provides an important var-iable to be considered within the context of psychotherapy. Although psy-choanalytical approaches to psychotherapy are not primarily symptom ori-ented, symptom reduction remains a pertinent goal of our treatment.

A series of suggestions for diagnostics and documentation, as well as for the differentiation of problematical diagnostic categories, are included in Axis V to adapt the current version of chapter V in the *ICD–10* to the features of psychotherapy and psychosomatics.

Because many disorders are comorbid, clinicians generally code no more than three secondary diagnoses in addition to the main diagnosis. Principally, the main diagnosis should be the diagnosis with the highest clinical and psychopathological relevance. Additional diagnoses should only be coded when they contribute to the understanding of the overall situation or represent modifying aspects related to the progression of the condition.

In contrast to *DSM–III–R* (American Psychiatric Association, 1987) and *DSM–IV* (American Psychiatric Association, 1994), *ICD–10* codes psychiatric and somatic diagnoses on the same axis. In the *DSM* system, somatic conditions and personality disorders are represented on individual axes. To allow for comparison with the *DSM* approach, particularly in the area of research, we suggest that *ICD–10* syndrome-related diagnoses in OPD be categorized on Axis Va, the personality disorders according to *ICD–10* on Axis Vb, and the somatic disorders on Axis Vc. With respect to relational issues, no more than two personality disorders in the categories F60 and F61 should be diagnosed, with a differentiation between the pri-mary and secondary diagnosis. However, in relation to the OPD, the di-agnoses for personality disorders found in *ICD–10* should be used only for descriptive purposes so that all diagnoses, parallel to the structural diag-noses, can be registered on Axis V.

To work with *ICD–10*, we propose two modifications of diagnostic categories for use in psychosomatics and psychotherapy.

1. Because of its theoretical and clinical significance, narcissistic personality disorder has been added to the existing person-ality disorders under the code number F60.81.
2. Central changes are related to the category F54 (psychic fac-tors and behavioral influences in diseases classified else-where).

We propose to classify a more differentiated mode of somatopsychosocial interactions as done in the *ICD–10*. Psychosocial dimensions in psychosomatic diseases can have an etiological relevance, they can join and influence the course of the disease, or they can be a consequence of a serious chronic disease. We know that the critical interactions are often much more complex than described here, but our intent is to motivate the examiner to reflect on specific conditions in individual cases (for more detailed principles of classification, see OPD Working Group, 2000).

EXPERIENCES WITH OPD: RESEARCH, TRAINING, AND CLINICAL WORK

In 1996 the OPD manual was published in Germany. The first reliability studies on OPD were done by the working group during the development phase. We evaluated the interrater reliability for the single axis and found acceptable interrater coefficients for the different axes (Freyberger et al., 1996). The study had a simple design. A number of untrained raters had to judge three video-documented interviews with OPD. This first empirical step has had the primary task of determining whether the system would be applicable by the clinician, whether it would be accepted, and whether it could be used with an acceptable level of reliability. We anticipated that the system would have a satisfactory validity, too, because it was a result of an extensive discussion among experts.

Since 1996, many working groups have done research involving OPD at multiple sites. The topics included different approaches to reliability (e.g., multisite studies of interrater reliability and retest reliability; Grande, Rudolf, & Oberbracht, 2000), which could demonstrate a satisfying interrater reliability for raters well-trained in OPD diagnostics.

To prove the reliability of OPD, several studies were done under clinical and research conditions. The reliability coefficients under clinical conditions have shown satisfactory but not excellent results (weighted kappa ranges = 0.35 to 0.50) for Axes I to IV. In two clinical studies, the OPD ratings were done by several clinicians directly after the interviews were held under normal clinical conditions with inpatients of psychotherapeutic hospitals. Another group of studies to test the reliability of the OPD was done under research conditions. These studies were based on videotaped OPD interviews and were led by trained interviewers. The results of these analyses were better and have shown the following mean reliability coefficients (weighted kappa; Cohen, 1968): Axis II "relational issues" (0.62); Axis III "conflict" (0.61 over all different conflicts); Axis IV "structure" (0.71). No studies have yet been conducted for Axis I. The practicability and feasibility of OPD in clinical contexts were examined in several studies and have shown acceptable to good results (Freyberger et al., 1996).

Another important kind of research focused on questions of validity;

some of these studies were done at multiple sites. A strong argument for the content validity is the process of developing OPD. About 50 experts were involved in the process of formulating diagnostic classes and criteria that describe the important dimensions in a practicable and observable manner.

Validity studies were done to examine a variety of questions. Here we give some examples to demonstrate selected findings for special topics.

Clinical validity: Interesting questions were raised: Can the OPD dimensions describe different groups of patients? Do different groups of patients show different OPD profiles? Axis I was tested in different clinical contexts (inpatients vs. outpatients, liaison service) and was applied to different groups of patients (e.g., with neurotic disorders, personality disorders, and somatization) and patients of different ages and sex. As we expected, Axis I discriminated between these different kinds of clinical groups and between patients of different ages. Older patients and patients of the consultation and liaison service comprehended and accepted significantly fewer psychodynamic and psychosomatic perspectives to explain and change their disorders–problems and had a lower motivation for psychotherapy than younger patients and patients who were examined in psychotherapeutic institutions. A comparison of patients with neurotic disorders and personality disorders (classified by *ICD–10* on Axis IV, Structure) showed that the neurotic patients had a better structural level $(1, 97)$ than patients with personality disorders $(2,37; p > .01)$.

Construct validity: Does the OPD, or single axis, correlate sufficiently with instruments that assess similar constructs? The OPD is a new and specific instrument, and so we do not have comparable tests for every axis (e.g., for Axis III, Conflict). Axis I showed satisfactory correlations between items that focus on the patients' comprehension and acceptance of psychodynamic and psychosomatic factors and their motivation for treatment and the questionnaire for measuring psychotherapy motivation, a self-rating instrument to measure the motivation for psychotherapy (Schneider, Basler, & Beisenherz, 1989; Schneider & Klauer, 2001). A correlation coefficient of .41 to .43 ($ps > .001$) is acceptable if we compare two tests that are based on different types of assessment (self-rating vs. expert rating). Stasch et al. (2000) examined the correspondence between selected aspects of Axis II (Relational Patterns) and the Inventory of Interpersonal Problems (Horowitz et al., 1988), which is also based on the circumplex model. Their results showed acceptable correlations between the clusters of both diagnostic models (correlation coefficients from .34 to .25, $ps > .001$, for expert vs. self-ratings). Rudolf and Grande (1999) showed acceptable correlations between the OPD Axis IV (Structure) and Wallerstein's (1988) Scales of Psychological Capacities, an instrument that allows the assessment of structural characteristics as well.

Predictive or treatment validity: Of interest is whether OPD or a single axis allows a prognosis about the effects of psychotherapeutic treatment. To explore this question, several studies have been done in different centers.

1. To prove the predictive validity of Axis I, psychotherapy inpatients were divided into two groups with either a high level or a low level of important Axis I characteristics (ns = 70 and 41, respectively). The effects of the psychotherapeutic interventions were measured by the Inventory of Interpersonal Problems (Horowitz et al., 1988) and the SCL–90 (Derogatis). We could show main effects and selected interactions (analysis of variance) for the SCL–90 and the inventory total scores and for single subscales of both tests. The best predictive estimation was given by the OPD items Comprehending and Accepting Psychodynamic/Psychosomatic Association (7) and Mental Symptoms Presented (15).

2. Stasch et al. (2000) have shown that Axis II characteristics (Interpersonal Relations) could distinguish among different clinical groups concerning symptomatic outcome during inpatient psychotherapy.

3. The predictive validity of Axis IV was examined in various studies. Rudolf, Grande, Oberbracht, and Jakobsen (1996) showed that structural ratings were good predictors of the therapeutic effects as they were judged by the therapists and by the patients. Of special interest in this context was the dimension Attachment, which allowed the prediction of the therapeutic effects on the best level (correlation with the patients' judgment, .42; with the therapists' judgment, .46; ps > .01). These findings were confirmed in a study by Strauss, Hütteman, and Schulz (1997), who found that patients with a better structural level could profit more from group psychotherapy than patients with a lower level of structure. Once again, the dimensions Attachment, Object Perception, and Defense allowed predictive estimations in the sense that patients with higher values in these characteristics were more successful under the intervention than patients with lower values.

Our primary intent here is to present the concept of OPD and the process of developing it rather than to discuss the empirical findings associated with the model. However, research on the sorts of questions listed above has led to many interesting results, which allow a deeper view into the dynamics of patients and change processes. Evidence from contemporary studies indicates that the axes differentiate between important clinical groups (e.g., neurotics vs. personality disorders, patients with somatic diseases vs. patients with mental diseases), that the different axes are useful in planning therapy, and that therapeutic foci can be developed on the basis of the diagnostic results. A good overview of the most important empirical studies and these findings can be found in Schneider and Freyberger (2000). They discuss eventual modifications of the OPD based on empirical data. The aim of the OPD Working Group was to orient the future development of the instrument using the empirical findings. The group is also discussing the question of how rapidly important changes in OPD should be made. This question implies a potential conflict between the needs of clinicians for consistency and continuity in learning and practicing the OPD and the implications of research for change and development. John Clarkin (2000) proposed two different forms of OPD for this reason: a clinical approach and a research approach. These developments are also being intensively discussed in the OPD Working Group.

In research as in clinical practice, the application of OPD must be competent in order to achieve the good results possible with OPD diagnostics. This means that diagnosticians must accept the principles of OPD. As a psychodynamically oriented diagnostic model, OPD requires a basic acceptance of fundamental psychodynamic positions among users as well as a particular level of theoretical and practical experience, which may include self-analysis. Future developments along these lines will certainly be revealed with further experience in the training and application of OPD. Furthermore, the closer conceptual references and operationalization of the theoretical constructs of OPD must become known and applied. In our work with OPD, it is necessary for us to distance ourselves from the specific connotations of previously familiar idioms and to replace or at least to modify them with others. This situation is particularly pertinent to the axes conflict and structure, which represent thematic areas multifariously determined in psychoanalysis.

For these reasons, we offered OPD training sessions after publishing the OPD manual in 1996. To ensure the quality of these training seminars, the OPD Working Group established a committee for "educational planning" in addition to authorizing a series of training centers.

The goals of OPD training include acquiring a knowledge of the theoretical areas of reference of the OPD as well as conceptualizing diagnostic classes, the important criteria and algorithms, and the standards and method of the OPD interview. Of central importance in OPD interviewing is the determination of specific problem constellations, such as the identification of maladaptive relational patterns or typical configurations of conflict. To achieve this goal, clinicians must engage in active and repetitive questioning in order to clarify specific permutations and expressions of particular problems. On the other hand, scenic material, including the relationship between the patient and investigator, represents relevant diagnostic parameters that can be particularly important for the evaluation of the critical diagnostic features.

We think that the OPD interview is compatible with the psychodynamic or psychoanalytic interview as it is used in everyday clinical practice and as it is taught during specialized training. This conclusion is based on our experience training clinicians in OPD for more than 5 years. At first, we were astonished by the large number of psychodynamic oriented psychotherapists or candidates who were motivated to receive OPD training. To date, we have had between 1,500 to 2,000 such clinicians participate in our training seminars. These clinicians come from Germany, Austria, and Switzerland and are interested in working with OPD in the field of clinical practice or research.

The acceptance of OPD in German-speaking countries is very high and represents a qualitative development in psychodynamic psychotherapy. This fact reflects, on the one hand, the need in the field of psychotherapy to control and evaluate the clinical work. On the other hand, it might be an expression of the dissatisfaction of many of psychodynamic or psychoanalytic psychotherapists with the widely noncommittal or unscientific status of psychoanalytic–psychodynamic theory and practice. We cannot judge how systematically and carefully OPD is integrated in the clinical work of psychotherapists who have been trained in OPD. This is a result of our own inexperience in dealing with and controlling such a big project. However, we do have a sophisticated documentation of our trainings and their members, so it will be possible to control the effects of the trainings in a future study.

Over the past 6 years, we have had three international OPD congresses in Germany (Göttingen in 1996, Rostock in 1998, and Ulm in 2000). These meetings were attended by psychotherapists and researchers from different European countries (e.g., Sweden, Italy, Hungary, Portugal, and France) and by researchers from the United States and Canada. OPD has been presented several times at various congresses of the Society of Psychotherapy Research since 1996 and received wide interest there. The OPD manual has been translated into several languages, including Hungarian, Italian, French, and English. We are currently preparing Spanish and Portuguese translations.

For us, the development of the OPD has been a real challenge. We were familiar with constructing such a system and controlling it in the field of research, but we had no prior experience in organizing such a project in the sociopolitical and organizational dimensions. This will be the future challenge of working with OPD. We cannot predict the extent to which OPD will influence future psychotherapeutic research and practice on a national and international level. We are prepared to deal with this task, but we believe that we need help and support to meet this challenge successfully.

REFERENCES

American Psychiatric Association. (1987). *Diagnostic and statistical manual of mental disorders* (3rd ed., rev.). Washington, DC: Author.

American Psychiatric Association. (1994). *Diagnostic and statistical manual of mental disorders* (4th ed.). Washington, DC: Author.

Balint, M., Ornstein, P. H., & Balint, E. (1972). *Focal psychotherapy: An example of applied psychoanalysis.* London: Tavistock.

Benjamin, L. (1974). Structural analysis of social behavior. *Psychological Review, 81,* 392–425.

Benjamin, L. (1993). *Interpersonal diagnosis and treatment of personality disorders.* New York: Guilford Press.

Beutler, L., & Clarkin, J. F. (1990). *Systematic treatment selection: Toward targeted therapeutic intervention.* New York: Brunner/Mazel.

Blanck, G., & Blanck, R. (1974). *Angewandte Ich-Psychologie.* Stuttgart: Klett-Cotta.

Clarkin, J. (2000). Die OPD aus der Sicht eines Aussenstehenden. In W. Schneider & H. J. Freyberger (Eds.), *Was leistet die OPD?* (pp. 17–24). Bern: Huber.

Clarkin, J., Yeomans, F., & Kernberg, O. (1999). *Psychotherapy for borderline personality.* New York: Wiley.

Cohen, J. (1968). Weighted Kappa: Nominal scale agreement with provision for scaled disagreement or partial credit. *Psychological Bulletin, 70,* 213–220.

Dilling, H., Mombour, W., & Schmidt, M. H. (Hrsg.). (1993). *Internationale Klassifikation psychischer Störungen. ICD–10, Kapitel V (F). Klinisch–diagnostische Leitlinien. 2. Aufl.* Bern, Göttingen, Toronto, Seattle: Huber.

Dilling, H., Mombour, W., Schmidt, M. H., & Schulte-Markwort, E. (Hrsg.). (1994). *Internationale Klassifikation psychischer Störungen. ICD–10, Kapitel V (F). Forschungskriterien.* Bern, Göttingen, Toronto, Seattle: Huber.

Dührssen, A. (1981). *Die biographische Anamnese unter tiefenpsychologischen Aspekten.* Gottingen: Vendenhoeck & Ruprecht.

Freud, A. (1977). Assessment of childhood disturbances. In A. Freud (Ed.), *Psychoanalytic assessment: The diagnostic profile* (pp. 1–10). New Haven, CT: Yale University Press.

Freyberger, H. J., Dierse, B., Schneider, W., Strauss, B., Heuft, G., Schauenburg, H., Pouget-Schors, D., Seidler, G., Küchenhoff, J., & Hoffmann, S. O. (1996). Operationalisierte Psychodynamische Diagnostik (OPD) in der Erprobung Ergebnisse einer multizentrischen Anwendungs- und Praktikabilitätsstudie. Psychotherapie. *Psychosomatik, Medizinische Psychologie, 46,* 356–365.

Gill, M. M., Newman, R., & Redlich, F. C. (1954). *The initial interviews in psychiatrie practice.* New York: International Universities Press.

Grande, T., Rudolf, G., & Oberbracht, C. (2000). Veränderungsmessung auf OPD-Basis: Schwierigkeiten und ein neues Konzept. In W. Schneider & H. J. Freyberger (Eds.), *Was leistet die OPD?* (pp. 148–161). Bern: Huber.

Horowitz, L. M., Rosenberg, S. E., Baer, B. A., Ureno, G., & Villasenor, V. S. (1988). The Inventory of Interpersonal Problems: Psychometric properties and clinical applications. *Journal of Consulting and Clinical Psychology, 56,* 885–895.

Kernberg, O. (1981). Structural interviewing. *Psychiatric Clinics of North America, 56,* 169–195.

Kernberg, O. (1986). *Severe personality disorders: Psychotherapeutic strategies.* New Haven, CT: Yale University Press.

Kernberg, O. (1996). A psychoanalytic theory of personality disorders. In J. F. Clarkin & M. Lenzenweger (Eds.), *Major theories of personality disorders* (pp. 106–137). New York: Guilford Press.

Luborsky, L., & Crits-Cristoph, P. (1990). *Understanding transference.* New York: Basic Books.

Luborsky, L., & Kächele, H. (Hrsg.). (1988). *Der zentrale Beziehungskonflikt ein Arbeitsbuch.* Ulm: PSZ-Verlag.

Mahler, M., Pine, F., & Bergmann, A. (1975). *The psychological birth of the human infant.* New York: Basic Books.

OPD Working Group. (Ed.). (1996). *Operationalisierte Psychodynamische Diagnostik: Grundlagen und Manual.* Bern: Huber.

OPD Working Group. (Ed.). (2000). *Operationalized psychodynamic diagnostics foundations and manual.* Seattle, WA: Hogrefe & Huber.

Rudolf, G. (1993). Die Struktur der Persönlichkeit. In G. Rudolf (Ed.), *Psychotherapeutische Medizin.* Stuttgart: Enke.

Rudolf, G., & Grande, T. (1999). *Vergleich und Validierung zweier Instrumente zur Einschätzung von Struktur und struktureller veränderung. The Scales of Psychological Capacities (RS Wallerstein) und Operationalized Psychodynamic Diagnostisis (Arbeitsgruppe OPD).* Unveröffentlichter Abschlussbericht eines von der IPV finanzierten Forschungsprojektes.

Rudolf, G., Grande, T., Oberbracht, C., & Jakobsen, T. (1996). Erste empirische Untersuchungen zu einem neuen diagnostischen System: Die Operationalisierte Psychodynamische Diagnostik (OPD). *Z psychosomat Med Psychother 42,* 343–357.

Schneider, W., Basler, H.-D., & Beisenherz, B. (1989). *Fragebogen zur Psychotherapiemotivation (FMP).* Weinheim: Beltz Test GmbH.

Schneider, W., & Freyberger, H. J. (1990). Diagnostik in der psychoanalytischen Psychotherapie unter besonderer Bercüksichtigung deskriptiver Klassifikationsmodelle. *Forum der Psychoanalyse, 6,* 316–330.

Schneider, W., Freyberger, H. J., Muhs, A., & Schüssler, G. (Hrsg.). (1993). *Diagnostik und Klassifikation nach ICD–10, Kap. V (F). Eine kritische Auseinandersetzung. Ergebnisse der ICD–10 Forschungskriterienstudie aus dem Bereich Psychosomatik/Psychotherapie.* Vandenhoeck & Ruprecht.

Schneider, W., Heuft, G., Freyberger, H. J., & Janssen, P. L. (2000). Diagnostic concepts, multimodal and multiaxial approaches in psychotherapy and psychosomatics. *Psychotherapy and Psychosomatics, 63,* 63–70.

Schneider, W., & Hoffmann, S. O. (1992). Diagnostik und Klassifikation neurotischer und psychosomatischer Störungen. *Fundament Psychiatrica, 6,* 137–142.

Schneider, W., & Klauer, T. (2001). Symptom level, treatment motivation, and the effects of inpatient psychotherapy. *Psychotherapy Research, 11,* 153–167.

Schneider, W., Klauer, T., Freyberger, H. J., Hake, K., & Wietersheim, J. (2000). Die Achse I "Krankheitserleben und Behandlungsvoraussetzungen" der Operationalisierten Psychodynamischen Diagnostik. *Psychother Psychosom Med Psychol, 50,* 454–463.

Stasch, M., Kraul, A., Schmal, H., Benninghoven, D., Cierpka, H., & Hillenbarand E. (2000). Die empirische überprüfung der reinszenierungshypothese in der stationären Psychotherapie. In W. Schneider & H. J. Freyberger (Hrsg.), *Was leistet die OPD? Empirische Befunde und klinische Erfahrungen mit der Operationalisierten Psychodynamischen Diagnostik* (pp. 179–195). Göttingen: Huber.

Stern, D. (1985). *The interpersonal world of the infant: A view from psychoanalysis and developmental psychology.* New York: Basic Books.

Stieglitz, R. D., Dittmann, V., & Mombour, W. (1992). Erfassungsmethoden und Instrumente zur ICD-10. *Fundamenta Psychiatrica, 6,* 128–136.

Strauss, B., Hüttemann, B., & Schulz, N. (1997). Kategorienhäufigkeit und prognostische Bedeutung einer operationalisierten psychodynamischen Diagnostik. Erste Erfahrungen mit der "OPD-1" im stationären Rahmen. *Psychother Psychosom Med Psychol, 47,* 58–63.

Strupp, H., & Binder, J. J. (1984). *Psychotherapy in a new key. A guide to time-limited dynamic psychotherapy.* New York: Basic Books.

Wallerstein, R. S. (1988). Assessment of structural change in psychoanalytical therapy and research. *Journal of the American Psychoanalytic Association, 36,* 241–261.

Weinryb, P., & Roessel, R. J. (1991). Karolinska Psychodynamic Profile KAPP. *Acta Psychiatrica Scandinavica, 83,* 1–23.

Wiggins, J. S. (1982). Circumplex models of interpersonal behavior in clinical psychology. In P. C. Kendall & J. N. Butcher (Eds.), *Handbook of research methods in clinical psychology.* New York: Wiley.

Wiggins, J. S., & Trapnell, P. D. (1997). Personality structure: The return of the big five. In R. Hogan, J. Johnson, & S. Briggs (Eds.), *Handbook of personality psychology* (pp. 737–758). New York: Wiley.

World Health Organization. (1993). *International classification of diseases* (10th ed.). Geneva, Switzerland: Author.

8

CHILD AND ADOLESCENT DIAGNOSIS: THE NEED FOR A MODEL-BASED APPROACH

ANN DOUCETTE

The imperfections and shortcomings of diagnostic approaches for children and adolescents are well noted in the literature (Evans, 1991; Scotti, Morris, McNeil, & Hawkins, 1996). Despite the inadequacy of diagnostic approaches, there is a recognized need to identify and categorize children and adolescents in terms of their mental health challenges and their related service needs. Although imprecise, diagnostic frameworks have been used and continue to be used for multiple purposes (Adams & Cassidy, 1993). For the most part, diagnosis is used for clinical and research purposes and as the primary criterion for service eligibility and reimbursement for services.

Diagnostic frameworks allow practitioners across many disciplines (psychology, psychiatry, medicine, social work, education, etc.) to communicate with one another, to share information and reach judgments regarding how to characterize the presenting problems of children and adolescents. Profiling the characteristics of specific diagnostic groups has utility in defining more effective treatment approaches, and it helps to inform decisions regarding which interventions are warranted for particular diagnostic categories. Diagnostic frameworks also permit the classification of individuals for the purposes of estimating the prevalence of particular mental health disorders and articulating disorder-specific prognoses. The recent movement toward manualized treatment approaches builds on such information.

The clinical use of diagnostic frameworks, however, is secondary to their function in service and reimbursement arenas. The most prevalent use of diagnostic classification is to support and justify service eligibility and financial reimbursement for mental health services. Diagnostic classifications and their associated numerical codes, such as those found in the *Diagnostic and Statistical Manual of Mental Disorders* (4th ed.; DSM–IV; American Psychiatric Association, 1994) have become a hallmark for both service eligibility and payer reimbursements. Despite scrutiny and speculation regarding the function of diagnostic categorizations in selective reimbursement schedules, and the potential for gaming the system by diagnostic categories and codes that are more likely to result in higher levels of service and reimbursement authorizations, diagnostic frameworks for children and adolescents are likely to stay.

The wide-ranging discussion regarding the use of diagnostic classification for children and adolescents is also not likely to dissipate. The most recent revision of the DSM (DSM–IV) is premised on the assumption that classification taxonomies are valuable in establishing a more rigorous scientific approach to understanding child and adolescent mental health disorders and the treatments expected to produce favorable outcomes. The DSM–IV revisions reflect an emphasis on empirical integrity supported by strong recommendations to base modifications on comprehensive and exhaustive literature reviews and sound statistical meta-analytic techniques (Widiger, Frances, Pincus, Davis, & First, 1991).

The emphasis on empirical foundations is somewhat inconsistent with the atheoretical approach that permeates the initial development of the DSM system (Faust & Miner, 1986). The DSM system originally espoused an atheoretical position in an attempt to increase its utility across multiple disciplines. The DSM purports to build on social consensus rather than on theoretical constructs. However, it is clear that as development and refinement continued, DSM classification has moved toward theoretical constructs. The changing organization and fine-tuning of the DSM is illustrative of a Lakatosian (Lakatos, 1978) perspective where modifications take place in a protective belt surrounding the core beliefs which remain intact, in this case the diagnostic nomenclature of the DSM system. The revisions of the DSM are grounded in an attempt to provide more adequate construct validity and reliable judgment; this is fundamentally distinct from cursory observation of seeming similarities (Medin & Shoben, 1988). The emphasis on science without a theoretical underpinning appears somehow contradictory. A classification system simply cannot sustain itself by proliferating categories in the absence of a theoretical framework. It also begs the question of whether the various review committees can simply dismiss their theoretical bias in articulating the criteria for diagnostic categories.

Furthermore, one can view the criteria under each disorder as a coherent organization of descriptors that support or falsify a specific diagnosis. Falsification is a central tenet of scientific theory (Popper, 1968). In addition, the shift from the medical disease model of earlier versions, where emotional disorders were considered to be a function of individual dynamics, to a biopsychosocial framework, where emotional problems are considered in part the consequence of environmental reinforcing and eliciting stimuli, appears to be driven by the theoretical advances of behavioral psychology.

Although the current *DSM–IV* does not address or identify a theoretical basis, it does not openly endorse an atheoretical stance as it initially did. Understanding the foundational underpinning of *DSM–IV* or any classification system is crucial, given the high stakes associated with diagnosis (eligibility for services and treatment and reimbursement).

THE NEED FOR CLASSIFICATION:
THE NOMOTHETIC–IDIOGRAPHIC DICHOTOMY

Despite the *DSM–IV* emphasis on objective and empirically based diagnostic classification, the diagnostic process is not likely to be informed solely by science-based evidence. Casual observations, clinical intuition, and experience are also likely to shape diagnostic practice. The primacy of science over practice has been a focal point of much debate. Much of the earlier literature argued on behalf of science over clinical judgment (Meehl, 1954). The current dialogue emphasizes the need for balance between science and practice—in other words, idiographic and nomothetic distinctions (Beutler, Williams, Wakefield, & Entwistle, 1995; Seligman, 1996; Stricker & Trierweiler, 1995).

The *nomothetic* approach can be defined as an objective process of accumulating information and grouping it into similar and dissimilar categories. Essentially it is an inductive process. Additional information is collected to test and refine these categories. Theories are constructed and classification taxonomies are developed. This approach focuses on aggregate actuarial, objective data and its quantitative and predictive properties. This process allows us to build on what is already known about mental health disorders as opposed to starting from scratch each time a child or adolescent is seen in the clinic.

The movement toward more objective diagnostic processes is not without its critics. The reliance on manual-driven treatment approaches that are most often linked with categorically defined diagnostic classes overshadows the inclusion of idiographic analysis of individual children and adolescents. A singular focus on objective data and information has been criticized as ignoring more subjective, qualitative information about the child or adolescent and his or her family that may contribute to diagnostic precision. Manualized treatments and categorical diagnostic strategies have been characterized as an impediment to more comprehensive clinician attention to the case complexities of an individual child or adolescent (Davidson, 1998). When classification taxonomies are applied to individual children and adolescents in the clinic setting, they are likely to include more subjective qualitative aspects and clinical judgments—*idiographic* appraisals about the individual (Mischel, 1968). Used alone, idiographic classification lacks a systematic approach and is less likely to be precisely applied across all children and adolescents seen by specific clinicians. Coupled with nomothetic approaches, idiographic appraisals provide additional data on which to make diagnostic judgments. Empirically based approaches that focus on function and how psychosocial and environmental resources, strengths, and deficits exacerbate or reduce dysfunction include a synthesis of nomothetic and idiographic approaches (Achenbach, McConaughy, & Howell, 1987; Hayes & Follette, 1992; Scotti et al., 1996).

AN OVERVIEW OF CHILD AND ADOLESCENT DIAGNOSTIC CLASSIFICATION SYSTEMS

Two major classification systems address the needs of children and adolescents challenged with emotional disorders: the *DSM* system and the system based on special education law (Individuals with Disabilities Education Act—IDEA).

The DSM System

The *DSM* is a psychiatrically based system developed initially in 1952. There have been several revisions to this system, the latest being the 4th edition published by the American Psychiatric Association in 1994. The *DSM–IV* uses a multiaxial model in its classification of emotional disorders. Axis I and Axis II focus on clinical and personality disorders, respectively. Axis I defines clinical disorders along 16 general categories, and Axis II focuses on personality disorders along 11 dimensions. The remaining three axes delineate psychosocial, environmental, and general medical conditions as well as the level of adaptive function (Axis III: General Medical; Axis IV: Psychosocial and Environmental Problems; Axis V: Global Assessment of Functioning).

Although *DSM–IV* provides some subcategorical classifications, for the most part, single diagnostic categories are likely to identify a hetero-geneous group of individuals assumed to have the same disorder. The *DSM's* inability to identify disorder subtypes and overlapping symptomatology may lead to less than effective and nonspecific treatment. Children and ado-lescents identified with the same diagnosis may be assumed to need the same treatment approach. Because disorders are constellations of symptoms, history, and biological markers, it is possible for two children to meet cri-teria but not have identical profiles in terms of which diagnostic criteria are met. In this instance, children with differing profiles (disorder subtypes) would likely need treatment approaches that specifically address the uniqueness of their disorder subtype. Figure 8.1 provides an illustration of the complexities and the assumptions made regarding diagnosis. The illus-tration depicts a 7-year-old child and a 17-year-old youth, both with a diagnosis of conduct disorder. This diagnosis is arrived at through the man-ifestation of different symptoms and behaviors; both, however, receive the same 3-digit, 1–2 decimal *DSM–IV* diagnostic code.

The use of a single standard can be problematic in diagnosing chil-dren, adolescents, and adults. Whereas both children in the above illus-tration are given the same diagnosis, they are likely to need different treat-ment interventions given their respective developmental status. This characteristic of the *DSM–IV* system is pervasive across the child–adolescent–adult developmental span, and it is underscored in *DSM–IV* in the following statement, "The provision of a separate section for dis-orders that are usually first diagnosed in infancy, childhood, or adolescence is for convenience only and is not meant to suggest that there is any clear

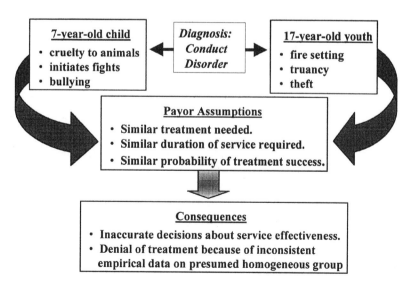

Figure 8.1. Meeting Diagnostic Criteria: Differing Profiles and Developmental Complexity

distinction between childhood and adult disorders" (American Psychiatric Association, 1994, p. 37). Disorder subtypes and symptom overlap not addressed by the *DSM–IV* classification system may go unnoticed in this one size fits all categorical approach.

The inattention to symptom overlap and symptom variations attributable to age, etiology, and environmental context is also problematic in using *DSM–IV* for child and adolescent diagnosis. The specification of symptoms broadly assigned to specific disorders does not differ across the developmental life span or discretely indicate specific disorders. For example, the diagnostic criteria for major depression are the same for children, adolescents, and adults, although the *DSM–IV* system does note that somatization and social withdrawal are common for children (p. 324); and *poor concentration* is included as a diagnostic criterion under dysthymic, depressive, generalized anxiety, and attention deficit disorders. Symptom overlap underscores the weakness in the *DSM* assertion of a classification system purporting to present distinct categories. As noted above, diagnostic criteria are not unique to specific disorders.

Assessment and the DSM System

Another difficulty in using the *DSM* system is the absence of psychometric distinction (Krueger & Finger, 2001; Mineka, Watson, & Clark, 1998) among *DSM* disorders, as well as the absence of specific assessment strategies that are linked to distinct *DSM* diagnostic categories. With regard to psychometric support for the *DSM* classification system, several research studies provide evidence of a set of common characteristics that are present for a broad group of disorders but provide little in the way of accurate diagnosis of distinct disorders (Krueger, Caspi, Moffitt, & Silva, 1998; Krueger & Finger, 2001; Weiss, Süsser, & Catron, 1998). For example, Krueger and Finger found evidence that unipolar and mood disorders (depressive, dysthymic, panic, generalized anxiety, and phobic disorders) are more accurately thought of as aspects of an internalizing factor, as opposed to specific and separate disorders. Furthermore, differentiating these aspects in terms of their contribution to the variance in this internalizing factor is more likely to appear in those individuals presenting more severe levels of impairment than in those individuals with moderate or mild symptoms. Similar findings attesting to the absence of specific disorder criteria or a shared set of common characteristics for childhood disorders were reported by Lambert, Wahler, Andrade, and Bickman (2001); Krueger et al. (1998); Weiss et al. (1998); and Ingram (1990). Similarly, Achenbach's (1978, 1986, 1995) factor analytic work on child psychopathology reveals dimensions (narrow band syndromes) that cluster into two overarching disorders: internalizing and externalizing disorder groups (broad band).

The wide range of assessment instrumentation for child and adolescent diagnosis presents additional difficulties. These instruments include general symptom lists (Achenbach, 1986; Quay & Peterson, 1996), specific symptom lists (Kovacs, 1991; Piers & Harris, 1969; Reynolds & Richmond, 1985), functional status (American Psychiatric Association, 1994 [Global Assessment of Functioning]; Hodges, 1990; Reynolds & Kamphaus, 1992), and behavioral strengths (Epstein & Sharma, 1998). Moreover, these instruments include a variety of respondent formats, youth self-reports, parent–caregiver reports, teacher reports, and clinician ratings, as well as a variety of temporal recall periods.

The variation in assessment instrumentation results in considerable variance in terms of the precision of assessment in confirming diagnostic classifications. A clinical diagnosis may be associated with assessment scores that do not meet empirical thresholds or cutoff scores, and assessment scores within clinical ranges may not result in a diagnosis for a specific disorder. This may in part be due to the inability of standardized assessment tools to capture all elements needed to make a diagnosis as specified by the DSM–IV system. For example, some depression instruments may include items tapping suicidal ideation, whereas others do not. Weight loss and psychomotor agitation are seldom included in standardized assessments of depression for children and adolescents, although these criteria are included in DSM–IV diagnosis of depressive disorders.

Assessment and Diagnostic Accuracy

Variation in assessment methods also contributes to variance in diagnostic accuracy, as do characteristics of the diagnostician, the training in and the fidelity to the methods used, and the response of the parent and child (Cone, 1980). Interview methods may yield decidedly different findings than do self-report survey methods. Moreover, information is collected from multiple informants (parent, teacher, child), but there is often little correspondence between these reports, other than to say they differ. The salience of discrepant information from various informants is often left to the discretion of the diagnostician as to whose information is more heavily weighted in making a diagnostic decision.

As noted previously, the degree of symptom overlap in DSM–IV disorder classifications adds to the complexity of using assessment instruments to make diagnoses. In a secondary analysis of the Ft. Bragg Evaluation Project (Bickman et al., 1995) sample data, Bickman and Lambert (1998) found that the internal consistency of conduct disorder symptoms (α = .68) was only slightly higher than the internal consistency of symptoms chosen at random (α = .63). This analysis used a compilation of symptom items across two mental health assessment instruments, the Parent-reported Child Assessment Schedule (Hodges, Kline, Stern, Cytryn, & McKnew, 1982) and the Child Behavior Checklist (Achenbach, 1986).

A second analysis using the Ft. Bragg Evaluation Project sample was conducted for inclusion in this edited volume. The Symptom Severity Inventory (SSI; Bickman & Doucette, 2001), adapted from the Vanderbilt Functioning Index (Bickman, Lambert, Karver, & Andrade, 1998) was used in this analysis. The SSI items tap symptom severity for attention deficit hyperactivity disorder (ADHD), oppositional conduct, generalized anxiety, and depressive disorders, and it reflects DSM–IV criteria. The SSI is intended to monitor symptom change concurrent with treatment and to indicate the need for more comprehensive and thorough assessment in specific diagnostic areas. Children selected for this analysis were diagnosed with a single primary diagnosis of conduct disorder, ADHD, depression, and anxiety with no secondary or tertiary comorbid diagnoses. Table 8.1 indicates that children were more likely to have higher mean scores on subscales in accordance with their specific diagnosis. For example, children diagnosed with ADHD had a higher mean score for the ADHD subscale. This was true for all four diagnostic groups, as is indicated by the boldface type. However, children with ADHD were also likely to have highly correlated scores on other scales, such as depression, anxiety, and so forth as is indicated by the boldface type in Table 8.1. Children diagnosed with depression and anxiety show considerable symptom overlap as well.

Psychometric analyses of various scales assessing anxiety and depression indicate that these disorders have distinct characteristics but overlapping symptoms (Hewitt & Norton, 1993; Hinden, Compas, Howell, & Achenbach, 1997; Watson et al., 1995). For example, social withdrawal is indicative of both depression and anxiety on many scales assessing these disorders. Furthermore, in the case of depression and anxiety, it may be that the presence of negative affect can be attributed to both depression

TABLE 8.1
Mean Scores for Children With Single Diagnosis
(no comorbid condition)

DSM–III–R diagnosis	Symptom Severity Index (mean scale score)			
	Conduct (6 items)	ADHD (6 items)	Depression (7 items)	Anxiety (4 items)
Conduct	**3.39**	3.39*	3.77	1.66
ADHD	1.88	**4.35***	2.99	1.36
Depression	1.94	3.32*	**4.43***	1.89*
Anxiety	1.64	3.49*	4.11*	**2.05***

Note. DSM–III–R = Diagnostic and Statistical Manual of Mental Disorders (3rd ed., rev.). Reported Symptom Severity Index items assess severity for attention deficit hyperactive, conduct, anxiety, and depressive disorders (α = .89–.93). Children were more likely to have higher mean scores on the subscale related to their specific diagnosis (scores denoted by boldface type). In many instances there was a significant correlation (denoted by an asterisk [*]) indicating an overlap of symptoms across many of the diagnoses for the children in this sample. Additional information on the Symptom Severity Index can be found at http://www.vanderbilt.edu/VIPPS/CMHP/cmhphome.html.

and anxiety, but the absence of positive affect may be more strongly associated with and distinctive of depression. Many assessment instruments do not address the differential effects of both positive and negative responses indicating the presence or absence of symptoms and behaviors and how they might function in distinguishing between diagnostic categories.

The overlap of symptomatology is not only a characteristic of assessment instrumentation; it is also a reflection of the reality of co-occurring disorders. Lambert et al. (2001) noted that children diagnosed with conduct disorder were more likely to have an average of 2.2 diagnoses as compared to 1.3 diagnoses for children without a diagnosis of conduct disorder. Caron and Rutter (1991) reported that depressive mood is a common nonspecific indication of several other diagnoses. Weiss and colleagues (1998) found that the presence of low self-esteem is common for several syndromes but that it is seldom indicative of a specific disorder. Cole and Carpentieri (1990) reported a correlation of .73 between depressive symptoms and aggression or conduct disorder after accounting for sources of shared method variance. Studies like these and others (Angold & Costello, 1993; Garber, Quiggle, Panak, & Dodge, 1991) highlight the difficulty in distinguishing between disorders; they call into question the need for more research to further understand the dynamics of co-occurring disorders and questioning whether they reflect distinct and separate disorders or are part of a more global condition.

The DSM system also delineates time intervals—periods of time when the child or adolescent would have to experience the symptom in order to be eligible for a particular diagnosis. For example, the diagnosis of oppositional defiant disorder specifies that the symptoms should have persisted for at least 6 months. However, the element of time in the DSM–IV system is not always specified for individual criteria. Symptoms and behaviors are often characterized in terms of subjective frequencies ("often loses temper," "often angry or resentful," and so forth). Furthermore, many standardized assessment instruments specify time frames that are inconsistent across instruments, and more important, inconsistent with the symptom or behavior time frame specified in the DSM–IV system (i.e., a disturbance of at least 6 months in duration). Whereas the Child Behaviors Checklist (Achenbach, 1986) and the Behavioral Assessment System for Children (Reynolds & Kamphaus, 1992) specify that the respondent report on symptoms and behavior over the last 6 months, the Children's Depression Inventory (Kovacs, 1991) asks for respondent reports for the past 2 weeks. There is a range in asking respondents to retrospectively reflect on past experience. There is little definitive data regarding the correspondence of the time frame and the accuracy of retrospective reflection.

As previously mentioned, variation in the length of temporal recall associated with various assessment instruments may not adhere to the DSM–IV criteria. Some disorders require the persistence of a symptom for

2 weeks, whereas other disorders are defined by symptom duration of 6 months to a year or more. For example, the Child Behavior Checklist (Achenbach, 1986) asks respondents to recall the past 3 months, a time period sufficient for depressive disorder but too short for attention deficit disorder, generalized anxiety (requiring distress of 6 months), and dysthymia (requiring symptom persistence of a year or more for children and adolescents).

Diagnostic Classification and Special Education Law (IDEA)

DSM–IV is the most widely used diagnostic classification system within mental health professions. Children and adolescents interface with many service systems. For this group, schooling and education represent the largest block of time spent in any one activity. As a result, much attention has been given to optimizing educational achievement. In doing so, there is a general recognition that emotional disorders, as well as other conditions, often compromise school performance. For some children, these conditions result in exclusion from public school systems.

In response to the exclusion of children from school systems resulting from emotional, mental retardation, neurological, and medical conditions, the U.S. Congress passed the Education for All Handicapped Children Act of 1975 (P.L. 94–142). After more than 25 years, this law under its current legislative authorization as the Individuals with Disabilities Education Act (IDEA) has great influence in terms of diagnostic classification and related assessment practices. This section focuses on emotional disorders that are covered under IDEA. The 1997 reauthorization of IDEA has dropped the descriptor *serious* in references to emotional disorders. It is important to note that the definition of *emotional disturbance* is essentially the same as the definition of *serious emotional disturbance* that was used in the past, prior to the reauthorization of IDEA.

Assessment and IDEA Guidelines

Special education services are tied to assessment procedures and requirements. The school or the parent–caregiver can request an assessment for eligibility for special education services. The use of standardized assessment instruments is required under IDEA, as is the use of a multidisciplinary team that is driven by the suspected disorder and need of the child or adolescent (education, psychology, occupational and physical therapists, and so forth). An Individualized Education Plan is the outcome of such an assessment and classification approach. No assessment inventory can be used as a single criterion for diagnostic classification or school service eligibility, and no single clinician is able to make a unilateral decision regarding the child or adolescent's status. Clinicians in community mental health centers are sometimes unaware that a diagnosis within their respective mental health service systems is not automatically accepted in school systems.

Differences Between DSM–IV and IDEA

The diagnosis of severe emotional disturbance under IDEA is similar to that of DSM–IV, with one exception. Special education diagnostic classifications do not include social maladjustment disorders unless the child or adolescent is also diagnosed with other serious emotional disturbances. The diagnoses of conduct disorder and antisocial behavior are not typically covered by school-based services. Children with these DSM–IV diagnoses are more often than not denied school-based services under IDEA. IDEA provides strict criteria that protect children and adolescents with these diagnoses from school expulsion but deny them the much-needed services that could promote more favorable educational outcomes. Many individuals characterize this situation as a legal loophole that sanctions the denial of services for these children and adolescents. Although some states choose to ignore the social maladjustment and conduct disorder service exclusion clause, the majority of the states endorse some form of exclusion (Skiba, Grizzle, & Minke, 1994). The IDEA guidelines offer no criteria for identifying social maladjustment, but legalistic interpretation of the DSM–IV by educational professionals strongly suggests that social maladjustment is equivalent to DSM–IV diagnosis of conduct disorder (Slenkovitch, 1992a, 1992b).

Despite compelling arguments in favor of dropping the social maladjustment exclusionary language from the IDEA, this is unlikely to happen in the near future (Nelson, Rutherford, Center, & Walker, 1991; Skiba, 1992). Children and adolescents with social maladjustment who are diagnosed with other disorders meeting IDEA and DSM–IV criteria are eligible for school-based mental health services. On the surface, this may appear as a workable solution, but many professionals have found the interpretation of this IDEA addendum to be incomprehensible. As a result, many children and adolescents with diagnoses of conduct disorder are unable to access the services they need.

The National Association of School Psychologists is currently lobbying for the adoption of new legislative language that will effectively eliminate the loophole for excluding children and adolescents identified as socially maladjusted (Dwyer & Stanhope, 1997). The new language would provide more precise operational definitions of *emotional* and *behavioral disturbances* and also provides more specific definitions of how *emotional* and *behavioral disturbances* can co-occur with social maladjustment/conduct disorder.

Moving Beyond Classification Topologies

Although the revisions of *DSM–IV* have led to increased reliability in diagnostic practice, further refinement of diagnostic categories, and an implied emphasis on empirical evidence, the *DSM–IV* continues to be criticized for neglecting the idiosyncrasies of child and adolescent emotional disorders as distinct from those of their adult counterparts. IDEA, a child-specific system, follows much the same pattern, but as noted in the above discussion, it provides additional barriers in terms of service access. Decades of developmental research provide compelling evidence that the developmental process (childhood, adolescence, adulthood) is not simply incremental or additive—children are not just small adults. The mental health service experience of children and adolescents differs from adults in other ways as well. For example, children and adolescents are not likely to come to the mental health clinic on their own. Parents, caregivers, teachers, and juvenile justice officials make up the referral system for many of the children and youth seen in community mental health clinics. The lack of correspondence between youth, parent–caregiver, and teacher reports is an indication that children and adolescents and the individuals responsible for their care do not always see the world in the same way or share the same perspective regarding the problematic nature of their behavior (Achenbach et al., 1987; Doucette-Gates, 1996).

Although the *DSM–IV* and IDEA offer a foundation for more precise diagnostic practice, they ignore the importance of family, social, and other environmental circumstances. Family history, family function in eliciting and reinforcing behavioral manifestations of emotional disorders, child–adolescent skills and competency levels, and the consequences of emotional and behavioral disorders for children and adolescents are also largely ignored by the *DSM–IV* and IDEA systems. There is also little or no consideration of endogenous versus exogenous disorders and the differential treatment durations for each (e.g., pervasive, endogenous depression is likely more difficult to treat than depression resulting from specific situations). The assumption is that similar treatment approaches and durations are needed, a one size fits all approach. The presence of comorbid conditions is also a factor. Neither the *DSM–IV* nor IDEA precludes multiple diagnoses, but no attention is given to how multiple disorders affect one another or how these comorbidities may affect symptom and behavior manifestations.

For example, as Table 8.1 indicates, the children in the Ft. Bragg study with a single primary diagnosis of ADHD, as a group, exhibited symptoms of anxiety and depression. Given the difficulties many children with ADHD have in the classroom, this finding is not surprising. It begs the question of how anxiety and depression might affect manifestations of ADHD and how informative a diagnosis of ADHD is if it ignores indications of other symptomatic and behavioral problems that do not meet diagnostic criteria. It is important to note that these children were not diagnosed with any disorder other than ADHD.

Perhaps the most significant shortcoming of these diagnostic systems is the lack of emphasis on the idiographic behavioral function and how it contributes to the explanation of child and adolescent emotional and behavioral impairment. How does the behavior function in terms of the context in which the child or adolescent lives? Several researchers are advocating such an approach (Achenbach, 1991; Hayes & Follette, 1992; Scotti, Evans, Meyer, & DiBenedetto, 1991; Scotti et al., 1996; Scotti, Evans, Meyer, & Walker, 1991) that incorporates information on the functional relationships that affect the behavior of interest—the covariation of various behaviors associated with the target diagnostic behavior. Research evidence indicates that blending a functional approach that focuses on the idiographic assessment of individuals with the aggregate structural information and criteria provided in the DSM–IV has favorable outcomes. For example, when functional information was used to modify treatment for individuals with self-harmful behavior, the outcomes were significantly more favorable than for their counterparts who received standard treatment approaches (Iwata et al., 1994). The current emphasis on strength-based approaches for children and adolescents builds on such a functional approach (Epstein, 1999).

CONCLUSION AND RECOMMENDATIONS

Although diagnostic classification systems have advanced and become more reliable, several shortcomings remain. There is little evidence of treatment validity as a result of using these classification systems, yet treatment plans continue to be based on diagnostic classifications, and payers continue to structure reimbursement on the basis of those diagnostic categories. The refinement of the DSM system and IDEA have not led to a proliferation of effective treatments specific to diagnostic categories. This is in part due to the wide variation found within these diagnostic categories and the lack of sensitivity to contexts in which these disorders occur.

As these classification systems are refined in future revisions or in new models, diagnostic classifications must translate into treatment and intervention plans. A DSM diagnosis of 313.81 (oppositional defiant disorder) or 312.8 (conduct disorder) provides little in the way of a foundation for treatment planning if variations in the child or adolescent's behavior in the home, school, and community go unnoticed. Assessment systems must be developed to gather information across multiple contexts and from multiple informants in order to better our understanding of the child and adolescent's experience of emotional and behavior disorders.

The present *DSM–IV* framework could be expanded to incorporate such considerations. Axis IV could house such an approach. As noted earlier, Axis IV focuses on psychosocial and environmental difficulties that may affect treatment—educational and relational problems (peer, family, teachers, authority figures, etc.) and living conditions. It is commonly believed that individuals with psychosocial and relational problems experience less impairment than those individuals with Axis I or Axis II diagnoses, and therefore merit lower clinical and funding priorities. However, little or no data support this claim. In a small study conducted by Simola, Parker, and Froese (1999), relational problems (V-codes) were associated with clinical severity in much the same way as were Axis I and II diagnoses. More investigation on the associations between relational problems and psychosocial and environmental difficulties, and Axis I and II diagnoses is needed, as is a broader definition of Axis IV and acknowledgement that relational V-codes warrant treatment (Silverman, 2000). A focus on Axis IV and relational problems also speaks to a much-needed focus on prevention and enhancing the mental health outcomes for children and adolescents. The approach addresses two of the significant developmental milestones of childhood and adolescence: a movement toward independence and the growth of friendship, peer, and authority (e.g., teachers, employers) relationships. Attention to psychosocial, environmental, and relational issues would not only identify problems, but would also recognize areas of strength on which to build more effective treatment and intervention plans.

The above recommendations focus on working within the existing structure. A more far-reaching proposal, in light of the prominence of symptom overlap and comorbidity patterns, calls for a change in how we see diagnostic category structures. From an empirical perspective, we must ask ourselves whether there is sufficient evidence to support a diagnostic system comprising separate disorder classifications; or whether these disorders are actually aspects of overriding larger latent traits, such as internalizing and externalizing disorders or other more global patterns. A cursory review of the literature reveals empirical support for such a position (Achenbach & Edelbrock, 1978; Andrews, 1996; Krueger et al., 1998; Lambert et al., 2001; Mineka et al., 1998) for both internal and external symptomatology.

The recommendation to adopt a classification scheme that identifies broad disorder groupings rests on a psychometric approach that includes confirmatory factor analysis (CFA) and item response theory (IRT). A comprehensive explanation of CFA and IRT is beyond the scope of this chapter. A brief description of the advantages of each and how CFA and IRT can be used in the development of a potentially more precise empirically based diagnostic classification system is described below.

CFA provides advantages in modeling data such as the ability to specify a priori theoretically meaningful models, to estimate parameters adjusting for measurement error, to estimate correlated measurement error, to compare different models, and to estimate the overall model fit including the ability to identify parameters that if excluded would increase model precision (Bollen, 1989). A CFA approach would provide stronger evidence on the construct validity or lack of it in the present *DSM–IV* structure and allow the crafting of a more precise structure if indicated.

IRT is a model-based measurement approach (Lord & Novick, 1968) that provides both assessment scale (item-level) and individual (person-level) information. IRT allows us to examine the contributions of symptom-specific sets of items (such as depression, anxiety, panic, and phobia items) on a continuum of severity ranging from low to high on a broader, more global classification category (in this case internalization disorder). Individuals are assumed to differ along a continuum from high to low (e.g., little or no impairment to severe impairment, depressed versus nondepressed). Individuals with serious impairment endorse items indicating higher levels of severity, whereas those with minimal or no functional impairment would not endorse those items. Other advantages include the ability to identify error at the item level, as opposed to the scale level; shorter measures can be more reliable than longer measures; and comparable scores can be obtained across multiple measures (Embretson, 1996). IRT essentially locates the item and the individual along the same dimension—a continuum ranging from minimal or no severity to marked or profound severity.

Using CFA, one would be able to examine symptomatology across the present diagnostic categories to determine a more adequate diagnostic model structure, one that might provide a more parsimonious structure than the present array of diagnoses. IRT would allow the examination of the contributions of symptom specific sets of items, such as depression, anxiety, panic, phobia items, and so forth, to estimate their contribution in a continuous estimate of severity ranging from low to high on a broader more global classification category (in this case, internalization).

Krueger and Finger (2001) provided an example using an IRT approach in the examination of adult internalizing symptomatology. They found that depressive symptoms reflected a lower severity than did anxiety disorder symptoms on an internalizing continuum and that a diagnosis of depression required less overall internalizing symptomatology than did anxiety. This finding also indicates that an individual endorsing anxiety-related symptom items would likely have endorsed depression-related symptom items, but not vice versa. The duration of symptoms for depression is not consistent with anxiety and may contribute to the IRT ordering of internalizing symptoms. Depression requires symptom persistence of 2 weeks, whereas anxiety requires a duration period of 6 months.

The CFA-IRT modeling approach also addresses the concern regarding the lack of criterion weights for *DSM* diagnostic criteria. IRT models provide estimates at the item level. For example, *DSM* criteria for ADHD–Inattentive requires meeting six out of nine symptoms, assuming all nine criteria are equal in importance. Conduct disorder requires the presence of one criterion ranging from bullying, intimidation of others, to car theft and physical cruelty to others, again assuming these criteria to be equal. IRT item estimates would indicate a more precise calibration of criterion contribution of each specific item.

In addition to more precise item information, IRT also provides an opportunity to examine differential item function such as age, gender, and race–ethnicity across groups of individuals (Hambleton, Swaminathan, & Rogers, 1991). Differential item function provides much-needed information regarding item bias across groups of interest, a provision that the current *DSM* system all but ignores. Furthermore, as was noted previously, much of the psychological assessment of children includes reports across a number of informants, such as parents–caregivers, teachers, and child or adolescent self-reports. Although the focus is on the child or adolescent, there is likely to be variance in terms of how the target individual and others see the extent of the symptoms and behavior problems. IRT also offers a modeling approach to capture the "rater effect" called a multifaceted model (Linacre, 1994). In essence, this multifaceted model provides an estimate of the harshness or leniency of the individuals providing information on the child or adolescent. On an individual basis, this is particularly useful in interpreting teacher reports from multiple teachers associated with the child; on an aggregate basis, estimates would be provided in terms of the harshness or leniency of parent–caregiver reports compared to child or adolescent's self-reports.

In summary, the recommendation of moving toward a model-based measurement approach is in line with the *DSM* movement toward a stronger empirical base. The proposed restructuring of the diagnostic system toward more global groupings is in accordance with the empirical evidence identifying symptom overlap and the (more likely than not) comorbid diagnostic patterns. In an environment where clinicians are struggling with evidence-based treatment, outcome monitoring systems, and reimbursement practices based on diagnostic codes and researchers are under pressure to identify more effective treatment and predict outcome trajectories with more precision, the structural taxonomy of a system such as *DSM–IV* is inadequate in its representation of child and adolescent mental health disorders.

REFERENCES

Achenbach, T. M. (1978). The child behavior profile: Boys aged 6–11. *Journal of Consulting and Clinical Psychology, 46,* 478–488.

Achenbach, T. M. (1986). *Child Behavior Checklist—direct observation form* (rev. ed.). Burlington, VT: University Associates in Psychiatry.

Achenbach, T. M. (1991). *Manual for the Child Behavior Checklist and 1991 profile.* Burlington, VT: University of Vermont.

Achenbach, T. M. (1995). Empirically based assessment and taxonomy: Applications to clinical research. *Psychological Assessment, 7,* 261–274.

Achenbach, T. M., & Edelbrock, C. S. (1978). The classification of child psychopathology: A review and analysis of empirical efforts. *Psychological Bulletin, 85,* 1275–1301.

Achenbach, T. M., McConaughy, S. H., & Howell, C. T. (1987). Child/adolescent behavioral and emotional problems: Implications of cross-informant correlations for situational specificity. *Psychological Bulletin, 101,* 213–232.

Adams, H. E., & Cassidy, J. F. (1993). The classification of abnormal behavior: An overview. In P. B. Sutker & H. E. Adams (Eds.), *Comprehensive handbook of psychopathology* (2nd ed., pp. 3–25). New York: Plenum.

American Psychiatric Association. (1994). *Diagnostic and statistical manual of mental disorders* (4th ed.). Washington, DC: Author.

Andrews, G. (1996). Comorbidity in neurotic disorders: The similarities are more important than the differences. In R. M. Rapee (Ed.), *Current controversies in anxiety disorders* (pp. 3–20). New York: Plenum.

Angold, A., & Costello, E. J. (1993). Depressive comorbidity in children and adolescents: Empirical, theoretical, and methodological issues. *American Journal of Psychiatry, 150,* 1779–1791.

Beutler, L. E., Williams, R. E., Wakefield, P. J., & Entwistle, S. R. (1995). Bridging scientist and practitioner perspectives in clinical psychology. *American Psychologist, 50,* 984–994.

Bickman, L., & Doucette, A. (2001). *Child Adolescent Measurement System (CAMS) manual.* Manuscript in preparation.

Bickman, L., Guthrie, P. R., Foster, E. M., Lambert, E. W., Summerfelt, W. T., Breda, C., & Heflinger, C. A. (1995). *Evaluating managed mental health services: The Fort Bragg Experiment.* New York: Plenum.

Bickman, L., & Lambert, E. W. (1998, March). *Psychiatric diagnosis: Valid for services research?* Paper presented at the 11th annual research conference on Children's Mental Health, Tampa, FL.

Bickman, L., Lambert, E. W., Karver, M. S., & Andrade, A. R. (1998). Two low-cost measures of child and adolescent functioning for services research. *Evaluation and Program Planning, 21,* 263–275.

Bollen, K. A. (1989). *Structural equations with latent variables.* New York: Wiley.

Caron, C., & Rutter, M. (1991). Comorbidity in child psychopathology: Concepts, issues and research strategies. *Journal of Child Psychology and Psychiatry, 32,* 1063–1080.

Cole, D. A., & Carpentieri, S. (1990). Social status and the comorbidity of child depression and conduct disorder. *Journal of Consulting and Clinical Psychology, 58,* 748–757.

Cone, J. C. (1980). Psychometric considerations. In M. Hersen & A. S. Bellack (Eds.), *Behavioral assessment* (pp. 36–68). New York: Pergamon Press.

Davidson, G. C. (1998). Being bolder with the Boulder model: The challenge of education and training in empirically supported treatments. *Journal of Consulting and Clinical Psychology, 66,* 163–167.

Doucette-Gates, A. (1996). *Annual Report to Congress: Comprehensive community mental health services for children and families with serious emotional disturbances program* (Contract No. 280–94–0012). Rockville, MD: Substance Abuse and Mental Health Services Administration.

Dwyer, K. P., & Stanhope, V. (1997). *IDEA '97: Synopsis and recommendations* (Rev. ed.). Washington, DC: National Association of School Psychologists.

Education for All Handicapped Children Act (Public Law 94–142), 89 Stat. 773 (1975).

Embretson, S. (1996). The new rules of measurement. *Psychological Assessment, 8,* 314–349.

Epstein, M. (1999). The development and validation of a scale to assess the emotional and behavioral strengths of children and adolescents. *Remedial & Special Education, 20,* 258–263.

Epstein, M. H., & Sharma, J. M. (1998). *Behavioral and Emotional Rating Scale: A strength-based approach to assessment.* Austin, TX: PRO-ED.

Evans, I. M. (1991). Testing and diagnosis: A review and evaluation. In L. H. Meyer, C. A. Peck, & L. Brown (Eds.), *Critical issues in the lives of people with severe disabilities* (pp. 25–44). Baltimore: Paul H. Brookes.

Faust, D., & Miner, R. A. (1986). The empiricist and his new clothes: DSM–III in perspective. *American Journal of Psychiatry, 143,* 962–967.

Garber, J., Quiggle, N. L., Panak, W., & Dodge, K. A. (1991). Aggression and depression in children: Comorbidity, specificity, and social cognitive processing. In D. Cicchetti & S. Toth (Eds.), *Rochester Symposium on Developmental Psychopathology: Internalizing and externalizing expression of dysfunction* (Vol. 2, pp. 225–264). Hillsdale, NJ: Erlbaum.

Hambleton, R. K., Swaminathan, H., & Rogers, H. J. (1991). *Fundamentals of item response theory.* Newbury Park, CA: Sage.

Hayes, S. C., & Follette, W. C. (1992). Can functional analysis provide a substitute for syndromal classification. *Behavioral Assessment, 14,* 345–365.

Hewitt, P. L., & Norton, G. R. (1993). The Beck Anxiety Inventory: A psychometric analysis. *Psychological Assessment, 5,* 408–412.

Hinden, B. R., Compas, B. E., Howell, D. C., & Achenbach, T. M. (1997). Covariation of the anxious-depressed syndrome during adolescence: Separating fact from artifact. *Journal of Consulting and Clinical Psychology, 65,* 6–14.

Hodges, K. (1990). *The Child Adolescent Functional Assessment Scale.* Unpublished manuscript.

Hodges, K., Kline, J., Stern, L., Cytryn, L., & McKnew, D. (1982). The development of a child assessment interview for research and clinical use. *Journal of Abnormal Child Psychology, 10,* 173–189.

Individuals with Disabilities Education Act–IDEA (Public Law 105–17), 20 U.S.C. 1400 (1997).

Ingram, R. E. (1990). *Contemporary psychological approaches to depression: Theory, research, and treatment.* New York: Plenum.

Iwata, B. A., Pace, G. M., Dorsey, M. F., Zarcone, J. R., Vollmer, T. R., Smith, R. G., Rodgers, T. A., Lerman, D. C., Shore, B. A., Mazaleski, J. L., Goh, H. L., Cowdry, G. E., Kalsher, M. J., McCosh, K. C., & Willis, K. D. (1994). The functions of self-injurious behavior: An experimental epidemiological analysis. *Journal of Applied Behavioral Analysis, 27,* 215–240.

Kovacs, M. (1991). *The Children's Depression Inventory* (CDI). North Tonawanda, NY: Multi-Health Systems.

Krueger, R. F., Caspi, A., Moffitt, T. E., & Silva, P. A. (1998). The structure and stability of common mental disorders (DSM–III–R): A longitudinal–epidemiological study. *Journal of Abnormal Psychology, 107,* 216–227.

Krueger, R. F., & Finger, M. S. (2001). Using item response theory to understand comorbidity among anxiety and unipolar mood disorders. *Psychological Assessment, 13,* 140–151.

Lakatos, I. (1978). The methodology of scientific research programmes (Philosophical Papers Vol. 1). Cambridge, England: Cambridge University Press.

Lambert, E. W., Wahler, R. G, Andrade, A. R., & Bickman, L. (2001). Looking for the disorder in conduct disorder. *Journal of Abnormal Psychology, 110,* 110–123.

Linacre, J. M. (1994). *Many-facet Rasch measurement.* Chicago: MESA Press.

Lord, F., & Novick, M. (1968). *Statistical theories of mental tests.* New York: Addison-Wesley.

Medin, D. L., & Shoben, E. J. (1988). Context and structure in conceptual combination. *Cognitive Psychology, 20,* 158–190.

Meehl, P. E. (1954). *Clinical vs. statistical prediction: A theoretical analysis.* Minneapolis: University of Minnesota Press.

Mineka, S., Watson, D., & Clark, L. A. (1998). Comorbidity of anxiety and unipolar mood disorders. *American Review of Psychology, 100,* 245–261.

Mischel, W. (1968). *Personality and assessment.* New York: Wiley.

Nelson, C. M., Rutherford, R. B., Center, D. B., & Walker, H. M. (1991). Do public schools have an obligation to serve troubled children and youth? *Exceptional Children, 57,* 406–415.

Piers, E., & Harris, D. (1969). *The Piers-Harris Self-Concept Scale.* Nashville, TN: Counselor Recordings and Tests.

Popper, K. (1968). The logic of scientific discovery. New York: Harper & Row.

Quay, H. C., & Peterson, D. R. (1996). *Manual for the Revised Behavior Problem Checklist—PAR version.* Odessa, FL: Psychological Assessment Resources.

Reynolds, C. R., & Kamphaus, R. W. (1992). *Behavior Assessment System for Children (BASC).* Circle Pines, MN: American Guidance.

Reynolds, C. R., & Richmond, B. O. (1985). *Revised Children's Manifest Anxiety Scale*. Los Angeles: Western Psychological Services.

Scotti, J. R., Evans, I. M., Meyer, L. H., & DiBenedetto, A. (1991). Individual repertories as behavioral systems: Implications for program design and evaluation. In B. Remington (Ed.), *The challenge of severe mental handicaps: A behaviour analytic approach* (pp. 139–163). London: Wiley.

Scotti, J. R., Evans, I. M., Meyer, L. H., & Walker, P. (1991). A meta-analysis of intervention research with problem behavior: Treatment validity and standards of practice. *American Journal on Mental Retardation, 3*, 233–256.

Scotti, J. R., Morris, T. L., McNeil, C. B., & Hawkins, R. P. (1996). DSM–IV and disorders of childhood and adolescence: Can structural criteria be functional? *Journal of Consulting and Clinical Psychology, 64*, 1177–1191.

Seligman, M. E. (1996). Science as an ally of practice. *American Psychologist, 51*, 1072–1079.

Silverman, W. H. (2000, August). *V-codes, additional conditions, or primary presenting problems: The trivialization of social psychological problems*. Paper presented at the 108th annual Convention of the American Psychological Association, Washington, DC.

Simola, S. K., Parker, K. C. H., & Froese, A. P. (1999). Relational V-code conditions in a child and adolescent population do warrant treatment. *Journal of Marriage & Family Counseling, 25*, 225–236.

Skiba, R. (1992). Qualifications v. logic and data: Excluding conduct disorders from the SED definition. *School Psychology Review, 21*, 23–28.

Skiba, R., Grizzle, K., & Minke, K. M. (1994). Opening the floodgates? The social maladjustment exclusion and state SED definition. *Journal of School Psychology, 32*, 267–282.

Slenkovitch, J. (1992a). Can the language "social maladjustment" in the SED definition be ignored? *School Psychology Review, 21*, 21–22.

Slenkovitch, J. (1992b). Can the language "social maladjustment" in the SED definition be ignored? The final words. *School Psychology Review, 21*, 43–44.

Stricker, G., & Trierweiler, S. J. (1995). The local clinical scientist: A bridge between science and practice. *American Psychologist, 50*, 995–1002.

Watson, D., Weber, K., Assenheimer, J. S., Clark, L. A., Strauss, M. E., & McCormick, R. A. (1995). Testing the tripartite model: I. Evaluating the convergent and discriminant validity of anxiety and depression scales. *Journal of Abnormal Psychology, 104*, 3–14.

Weiss, B., Süsser, K., & Catron, T. (1998). Common and specific features of childhood psychopathology. *Journal of Abnormal Psychology, 107*, 118–127.

Widiger, T. A., Frances, A. J., Pincus, H. A., Davis, W. W., & First, M. B. (1991). Toward an empirical classification for the DSM–IV. *Journal of Abnormal Psychology, 100*, 280–288.

9

SIMPLIFYING DIAGNOSIS USING A PROTOTYPE-MATCHING APPROACH: IMPLICATIONS FOR THE NEXT EDITION OF THE *DSM*

DREW WESTEN, AMY KEGLEY HEIM, KATE MORRISON,
MARCUS PATTERSON, AND LAURA CAMPBELL

Accurate diagnosis is crucial for both clinical work and research. In the last three decades, major strides forward have been made in the development of diagnostic categories and criteria that can improve research into etiology, prognosis, and treatment response. Yet problems persist, as evidenced in debates about the validity of various diagnoses (e.g., atypical depression), the criteria for diagnoses (e.g., the number of weeks of continuous depression required for a diagnosis of major depression, or the number of binges per week required for a diagnosis of bulimia nervosa), and the separation of clinical syndromes from personality syndromes known to predispose individuals to certain disorders (e.g., major depression and borderline personality disorder). Equally important are concerns by clinicians that the 4th edition of the *Diagnostic and Statistical Manual of Mental Disorders* (*DSM–IV*; American Psychiatric Association, 1994) is cumbersome to apply and not tied closely enough to clinical decision-making.

In this chapter we address some of these problems and suggest a strategy for generating diagnostic groupings empirically and diagnosing patients clinically. Throughout, our focus is twofold: how to use empirical strategies to develop a valid classification system and how to keep that classification system close to clinical reality and readily usable by clinicians. Classification systems always exist for a purpose. The aim of classification in psychopathology is not only to "carve nature at its joints" but also to guide clinical observation and treatment. Thus, an optimal classification system is one that is not only nature friendly but also user friendly.

HOW WELL DO THE CURRENT DIAGNOSTIC CATEGORIES WORK?

In this first section we address the question of how well the current diagnostic categories in *DSM–IV* fulfill the functions of carving nature at its joints and facilitating practice and research. We begin by briefly describing a series of problems that recur across diagnoses, and then we illustrate these problems by considering the evolution of three major classes of Axis I syndromes: mood, anxiety, and psychotic disorders.

Common Problems Across Diagnoses

Every decision made in creating a diagnostic classification system has its costs and benefits. The *DSM–IV*, like any evolved "organism," represents not only adaptations of the recent past but also older adaptations that constrain future ones. Categorical diagnosis, for example, was an "adaptation" of a disease model of illness made by the pioneering psychiatric taxonomists of a century ago that remains a part of the nucleus of the current diagnostic system.

DSM–IV represents the best of psychiatric diagnostic thinking as of the early 1990s. Since that time, several problems have come to the fore that suggest the need for rethinking some old and newer adaptations. Here we focus on six central issues.

First is the question of whether psychopathology should be classified categorically, as discrete syndromes; dimensionally, as continua; or both. For example, major depression could be on a continuum with less severe depression, but it could also represent a biologically distinct syndrome, characterized, for example, by a disturbance of the hypothalamic–pituitary axis, which only emerges when the severity of depression crosses a threshold. Alternatively, depression could be represented as a continuous dimension, with a relatively arbitrary cutoff defined as major depression, much as physicians diagnose and treat high blood pressure when a dimensional measure of blood pressure exceeds an arbitrary threshold.

The most persuasive arguments for dimensional diagnosis have come from the literature on personality disorders (e.g., Frances & Widiger, 1986; Livesley, Schroeder, Jackson, & Jang, 1994; Widiger, 1993), largely because of the rich tradition of dimensional trait measurement in personality psychology. However, as we will see, research on the range of Axis I disorders has begun to raise many of the same questions, even in disorders such as schizophrenia, which are clearly discontinuous from normal functioning and hence seemingly most amenable to categorical diagnosis.

A second and related problem is the existence of "subclinical" phenomena. A growing body of research suggests that subclinical cases are at least as prevalent as clinical cases of many if not most disorders. For example, roughly 60% of patients treated for enduring, maladaptive personality patterns cannot be diagnosed on Axis II (Westen & Arkowitz-Westen, 1998). Nevertheless, these patients suffer from clinically significant problems recognized and treated by clinicians of all theoretical orientations, ranging from difficulties regulating self-esteem and problems with assertiveness or aggression to repetitive interpersonal patterns that interfere with relational functioning and satisfaction.

Third is the problem of comorbidity. The virtual explosion of research on comorbidity has been, at least in part, a byproduct of the more careful and systematic delineation of diagnostic categories and criteria in the last three editions of the DSM. Whether this represents incremental knowledge about psychopathology or simply the amassing of data documenting the problems of distinguishing disorders best conceptualized as fuzzy sets is unclear. A classic case is the literature on comorbidity of personality disorders and virtually every Axis I syndrome, such as depression, eating disorders, or panic. As suggested by theoretical traditions as disparate as psychoanalysis (e.g., Kernberg, 1984), trait psychology (e.g., Eysenck, 1994), and Millon's (1990) evolutionary social learning approach, the roughly 50% comorbidity of virtually every Axis I disorder with Axis II pathology of some sort likely reflects the fact that most forms of psychopathology (e.g., anxiety disorders) emerge from personality vulnerabilities (e.g., high neuroticism, trait anxiety, or borderline personality disorder) that can often be observed long before the development of the first Axis I episode. (On the longitudinal prediction of Axis I symptoms in early adulthood from Axis II symptoms in adolescence, see Johnson et al., 1999). Of particular importance in this regard are numerous studies showing that the presence of multiple Axis I syndromes in a patient is essentially a proxy measure for the presence of Axis II pathology, with an exponential rise in likelihood of Axis II diagnosis with each additional Axis I diagnosis (e.g., Lewinsohn, Rohde, Seeley, & Klein, 1997; Newman, Moffitt, Caspi, & Silva, 1998).

Fourth is the proliferation of mixed, atypical, and not otherwise specified categories with each successive revision of the DSM. Careful delimitation of virtually every Axis I category has brought with it the recognition of border cases that require a new categorical diagnosis, because strict adherence to a set of specific, and often quasi-arbitrary, diagnostic criteria necessarily leads to nondiagnosis of subclinical or atypical syndromes.

A fifth problem is the difficulty researchers have had in reproducing many current diagnostic categories and criterion sets using statistical aggregation procedures such as factor analysis, cluster analysis, latent class analysis, and structural equation modeling (e.g., Brown, Chorpita, & Barlow, 1998). This could, of course, reflect problems in the items, samples, or algorithms used to develop classifications (algorithms that sometimes have difficulty reproducing known structures in Monte Carlo simulations; see, e.g., Waller & Meehl, 1998). Alternatively (or, more likely, additionally), the problem may lie in the way diagnostic groupings have evolved, namely, through gradual clinical and empirical refinements of distinctions first made more with less precise tools by pioneering taxonomists such as Kraepelin, Bleuler, and Schneider.

A final problem is the difficulty in implementing the fine distinctions made in *DSM–IV* in clinical practice. As we discuss later, the current method of combining criteria to diagnose a patient—namely, counting criteria and subcriteria—often reflects arbitrary cutoffs and algorithms and is too cumbersome to be used by clinicians in everyday practice. With several hundred criteria for several dozen disorders, actually following the decision rules outlined in *DSM–IV* would be incredibly time-consuming. Not surprisingly, clinicians usually do not make diagnoses this way (e.g., Jampala, Sierles, & Taylor, 1988).

More important, perhaps, is the question of whether the procedure specified in the *DSM–IV* for making diagnoses has any advantage in terms of predictive validity (e.g., accurately predicting prognosis or treatment response) over the intuitive prototype-matching process clinicians are more likely to use if left to their own devices. The *DSM–IV* procedure often seems to clinicians (the primary consumers of the diagnostic manual) artificial or irrelevant to treatment decisions. In clinical practice, we suspect most clinicians get the "gist" of the patient's pathology (e.g., is the patient depressed, having trouble sleeping, losing weight, and thinking about suicide) and diagnose accordingly (the patient has major depression), whether or not the patient has three, four, or five of the criteria required for the diagnosis. The real question, then, pertains to the incremental validity of counting symptoms over prototype matching—particularly if clinicians were to learn criterion sets as prototypes rather than as sets of isolated symptoms to be counted.

The symptom-counting algorithm for arriving at a diagnosis was developed in an effort to increase reliability of diagnosis in the move from the 2nd to the 3rd editions of the *Diagnostic and Statistical Manual of Mental Disorders* (*DSM–II*; American Psychiatric Association, 1968; *DSM–III*; American Psychiatric Association, 1980). An unintended consequence, however, was an increasing disconnect between clinical and research diagnoses and a growing antagonism between researchers and clinicians. Researchers tend to view clinicians as sloppy diagnosticians who do not use structured interviews (which, in fact, now provide the only way to make reliable diagnoses if accurate diagnosis requires knowing exactly how many criteria out of four, five, six, or more per disorder the patient meets). Clinicians, in contrast, often view researchers as symptomatic bean counters who require precise answers to questions (such as exactly how long and how often a patient has had symptoms of major depression) that patients often cannot answer accurately and that may not even be relevant to treatment planning. Indeed, another unintended consequence of greater precision in diagnosis has been the loss of information about the large percentage of patients who fall just short of one diagnosis or another, because they are routinely excluded from studies of psychopathology and treatment. We know very little, for example, about the treatment of garden-variety depression, because most outcome studies focus on major depression (see Morrison & Westen, 2000).

Having counted the symptoms of *DSM–IV*, we now examine the way they manifest in three kinds of disorder: mood, anxiety, and psychotic disorders. We conclude our "case formulation" with recommendations for treatment of the *DSM*.

Classifying and Diagnosing Depression

Mood disorders are the most commonly diagnosed of the Axis I disorders, yet their specific nature continues to be an object of considerable debate (Chen, Eaton, Gallo, Nestadt, & Crum, 2000). The 1st edition of the *Diagnostic and Statistical Manual of Mental Disorders* (*DSM–I*; American Psychiatric Association, 1952) proposed three broad categories of mental illness: psychoses, personality disorders, and psychoneuroses. Each of these categories included depressive phenomena (e.g., the psychoses included manic–depressive reactions and psychotic depressive reactions). A central feature of both *DSM–I* and *DSM–II* (1968) was a reliance on etiological theories as a basis for taxonomic organization, including organization of the mood disorders. For example, depression resulting from early childhood experiences constituted a subcategory of mood disorder. Debate later ensued over the appropriateness of basing the definition of psychological disorders on etiological theories that often had little basis in research (see Skinner, 1986).

DSM–III marked a shift toward a Schneiderian taxonomic approach based exclusively on directly observable phenomena. This shift occurred in response to increasing demands for a classification system capable of yielding more reliable and empirically valid diagnoses. On the road to *DSM–III*, researchers developed specific criteria and interviews to assess those criteria with the aim of providing an empirical basis for distinctions among subtypes of depression (Feighner, Robins, Guze, Woodruff, & Winokur, 1972; Spitzer, Endicott, & Robins, 1978). The resulting criteria included symptom, duration, and exclusion specifications that added precision to diagnoses and dramatically increased their reliability across treatment and research sites. The *DSM–III* also deleted all personality disorder diagnoses characterized primarily by depression, thereby confining depressive symptomatology to Axis I. One result of this has been continuing debate about the existence of a depressive personality style that meets all the general criteria for a personality disorder outlined in the introductory material to Axis II in *DSM–IV* (e.g., Klein, 1999; Phillips & Gunderson, 1999; Westen & Shedler, 1999b).

Attempts to clarify the classification of mood disorders empirically also led to application of a variety of statistical aggregation procedures, including factor analysis, cluster analysis, and, more recently, structural equation modeling. Early studies utilizing factor analysis (e.g., Mendels & Cochrane, 1968) corroborated the inclusion of some version of the endogenous–reactive distinction that appeared in the first two editions of the *DSM*. Many researchers then turned to cluster analysis as a way of producing categorical diagnoses (see, e.g., Everitt, 1979; Fleiss, Lawlor, Platman, & Fieve, 1971; Grove & Andreasen, 1986). Whereas factor analysis groups symptoms together on the basis of their co-occurrence in the population of interest, cluster analysis groups patients together on the basis of similarity of their profiles on the criteria of interest. Thus, cluster analysis appeared potentially more appropriate for uncovering symptoms that may covary in different ways in different groups (if such true taxa, or discrete groups, exist). In a number of studies, researchers used cluster analysis to try to group patients with depression to see if they could uncover syndromes (e.g., Andreasen & Grove, 1982; Everitt, 1979).

Despite the initial promise of this method, it eventually fell into disuse. One reason had to do with the varied success of efforts to validate empirically derived clusters on the basis of treatment response (Paykel, 1971; Raskin & Crook, 1976). Perhaps the main reason for the decline of cluster analysis, however, was the lack of replicability of cluster solutions. In their review of 11 cluster-analytic studies of depression, Blashfield and Morey (1979) found that all studies isolated an endogenous subtype but that little agreement emerged on any other subtypes (although several yielded an anxious subtype as well).

Related to the problem of replicability were a number of other issues that led to dampened enthusiasm for cluster analysis. Cluster analysis always yields cluster solutions, even if no orderly or coherent classification scheme is inherent in the data, and different cluster algorithms frequently yield disparate groupings for the data set (Blashfield & Morey, 1979; Everitt, 1979). Furthermore, most researchers using cluster analysis tended to assume that the data were best understood categorically rather than dimensionally, leading to the problem of subclinical and atypical diagnoses encountered currently in *DSM–IV* (Grove & Andreasen, 1986).

DSM–IV introduced several changes to the classification of mood disorders, such as the inclusion of an atypical subtype, characterized by increase in appetite, weight gain, hypersomnia, and psychomotor agitation (and preferential response to MAO inhibitors, although this is not a diagnostic criterion). As was the case with previous cluster-analytic studies, investigations of this new category using statistical aggregation techniques such as latent class analysis have yielded some support, although different analyses have suggested different criteria (Kendler et al., 1996; Sullivan, Kessler, & Kendler, 1998).

Two major problems with the diagnostic system for mood disorders are subthreshold cases and comorbidity. The extent to which the current categories provide a way to diagnose most patients who present clinically with depression is a matter of some debate, with some data suggesting that most cases can be encompassed using current criteria and other data suggesting that subthreshold cases may be common (Barrett, Barrett, Oxman, & Gerber, 1988; Keller et al., 1995). Depression is also highly comorbid with a variety of disorders (see, e.g., Kessler et al., 1994), raising the question of whether it is a discrete syndrome. In an attempt to deal with the high comorbidity of mild forms of anxiety and depression, a category of mixed anxiety-depression (MAD) was proposed during the development of *DSM–IV*. The common co-occurrence of major depressive disorder and dysthymic disorder also raises the issue of whether two discrete mood disorders are present, whether "double depression" is actually a category unto itself, whether depression really falls on a continuum, or whether the vulnerability for major depression seen in double depression is more readily understood in terms of personality and temperament (e.g., Keller & Lavori, 1984). Figure 9.1 is a prototype approach to diagnosing depression.

Classifying and Diagnosing Anxiety

The systematic classification of anxiety disorders has a relatively short history when compared with depression and schizophrenia. Freud's descrip-

5	very strong match (patient has a prototypical case of the disorder)	Major depressive disorder
4	strong match (patient has the diagnosis; categorical diagnosis applies)	
3	moderate match (patients has significant features of this disorder)	Clinically significant depression
2	slight match (patient has minor features of this disorder)	
1	no match	

Figure 9.1. A Prototype Approach to Diagnosing Depression

tion of "anxiety-neurosis" paved the way for the syndromal classification of anxiety disorders used today. As noted above, *DSM–I* and *DSM–II* used the term *neurosis* as a superordinate diagnostic term. In addition to deleting the ties to psychodynamic etiological theories and turning to a more descriptive diagnostic system, *DSM–III* assigned greater importance and specificity to the anxiety disorders by creating a separate category. The *anxiety neuroses* became *panic disorder* and *generalized anxiety disorder* (GAD), whereas the *phobic neuroses* became *agoraphobia*, *social phobia*, and *simple phobia*.

A key change in the 3rd revised edition of the *Diagnostic and Statistical Manual of Mental Disorders* (*DSM–III–R*; American Psychiatric Association, 1987) involved a shift in emphasis from agoraphobic behavior to panic, with the designation of panic disorder with agoraphobia replacing the previous diagnosis of agoraphobia with panic attacks. *DSM–III–R* also eliminated much of the hierarchical ordering of diagnoses, which had, for example, relegated GAD to a residual status not to be diagnosed in the presence of other diagnosable disorders. In *DSM–III–R*, GAD became a nonresidual diagnostic category with its own defining feature of excessive worry that was more diffuse than worry associated with other Axis I anxiety disorders. In *DSM–IV*, GAD was retained as a diagnosis after some debate. Changes to the GAD diagnosis in the most recent edition of the *DSM* included an emphasis on the uncontrollability of the worry process and removal of associated symptoms that reflected autonomic hyperactivity rather than motor tension or vigilance.

The current classification system for anxiety disorders suffers from many of the same problems as the classification of depression, notably subclinical cases and comorbidity. Numerous studies have documented the prevalence of cases of subthreshold anxiety disorders (e.g., Zinbarg, Barlow, Liebowitz, & Street, 1994). Olfson et al. (1996) surveyed 1,001 primary care patients in a large health maintenance organization and found that 30% of them met their criteria for subthreshold symptoms of a variety of Axis I disorders; the most prevalent diagnoses were panic (11%), depression (9%), and anxiety (7%).

Comorbidity of anxiety and other disorders is also extremely high, particularly anxiety and depression (see Clark, 1989; Kessler et al., 1996). Clark and Watson (1991) found that many items on measures of anxiety and depression symptoms do not discriminate between individuals with anxious and depressive symptoms. Indeed, instruments such as the Beck Depression Inventory (Beck, Ward, Mendelson, Mock, & Erbaugh, 1961), Spielberger State–Trait Anxiety Inventory (Spielberger, Gorsuch, & Lushene, 1970), and Neuroticism factor of the NEO–PI–R (McCrae & Costa, 1990) tend to intercorrelate upwards of .60 in both clinical and nonclinical populations.

As noted below, one way of resolving this problem is to look for a combination of general and specific factors that both unite and distinguish anxiety and depression, much as researchers in the field of intelligence have distinguished g factors (general intelligence) and s factors (specific intellectual factors). Another proposal is to create a mixed anxiety and depression category (MAD), which is included in *DSM–IV* as a diagnosis needing further study. Indeed, many patients with subclinical levels of co-occurring anxious and depressive symptoms do not meet criteria for any *DSM–IV* anxiety or mood disorder (Katon & Roy-Byrne, 1991). Far from being an anomalous group, patients fitting the MAD profile frequently present for treatment and overuse primary care services (Barrett et al., 1988). In a field trial designed to investigate the MAD diagnosis, Zinbarg et al. (1994) found that patients presenting with subthreshold anxious or depressed symptoms were "at least as common as patients with several of the already established anxiety and mood disorders in each of the seven sites."

Research using factor analysis and structural equation modeling has provided both support for and challenges to the current classification of anxiety disorders. Clark and Watson (1991) found that although anxiety and depression share a common negative affect factor, depression is uniquely associated with low positive affect, and anxiety is specifically associated with autonomic arousal. Zinbarg and Barlow (1996) found that a single, higher order factor of negative affect distinguished those diagnosed with an anxiety or mood disorder from those who received no diagnosis, but they also found a number of lower order factors that differentiated between patients meeting criteria for the distinct categories in the anxiety disorders section of the *DSM–IV*. Using structural equation modeling, Brown et al. (1998) similarly found a shared negative affect factor as well as a latent factor of autonomic arousal that was differentially related to panic disorder (sympathetic hyperarousal) and GAD (sympathetic inhibition).

Recent data suggest, however, that the current classification system may create distinctions that are so fine-grained that they miss broader, underlying characteristics that may be as or more important to understanding and treating anxiety disorders (Brown et al., 1998; Zinbarg & Barlow, 1996). Studies by Barlow, Clark, and others suggest that personality dispositions, notably negative affect, may put individuals at risk for a variety of conditions. Indeed, the current taxonomy of anxiety disorders focuses only minimally on the relationship between anxiety and personality. Although personality constellations were implicit in the early conceptualization of anxiety as anxiety neurosis, *DSM–IV* focuses on anxiety states rather than traits that may predispose to these states. It is interesting that although *DSM–IV* includes depressive personality disorder as a diagnosis worthy of further study, no analogous category has been proposed for anxious personality (although the avoidant diagnosis has evolved in that direction over multiple editions of the *DSM*). A much more complex but likely possibility is that a mapping of trait anxiety onto state anxiety as a diathesis may be too simple, given data suggesting that patients with co-morbid anxiety and depressive symptoms are likely to have a variety of personality disorders (e.g., Newman et al., 1998). Genetic factors as well as environmental factors such as sexual abuse can create diatheses for multiple negative affect states, including major depression, minor depression, panic, generalized anxiety, and posttraumatic phenomena (see., e.g., Barlow, 2002).

Classifying and Diagnosing Schizophrenia

Although a syndrome akin to schizophrenia was identified early in the 19th century (see Morel, 1852; Pinel, 1801/1962), the first systematic conceptualizations of the disorder emerged around a century ago, in the work of Emil Kraepelin (1898) and Eugene Bleuler (1911/1950). Kraepelin distinguished *dementia praecox* (later renamed *schizophrenia* by Bleuler) and manic-depressive illness and linked phenotypically diverse forms of schizophrenia (i.e., hebephrenic, catatonic, and paranoid) on the basis of what he regarded as their shared underlying features: early onset, a deteriorating course, and poor prognosis.

Bleuler viewed the deficit shared by these diverse phenotypic expressions as a disconnection among emotions, thoughts, and behaviors and introduced the term *schizophrenia* (literally "split brain") to represent this view. Unlike Kraepelin, Bleuler emphasized signs and symptoms over outcome and course (Andreasen & Carpenter, 1993). Bleuler viewed the hallucinations and delusions essential to the Kraepelinian concept of the disorder as secondary to four key symptoms: affective disturbance, autism, ambivalence, and associational looseness. Bleuler's definition cast a wider net than Kraepelin's and resulted in a substantial increase in the number of patients diagnosed with schizophrenia (especially in the United States, where Bleuler's views held sway, as opposed to the Kraepelinian view, which was favored in Europe).

Bleuler's view was reflected in both *DSM–I* and *DSM–II*, which contained brief, relatively vague definitions of schizophrenia with no operational criteria (Tsuang, Stone, & Faraone, 2000). A "neo-Kraepelinian revolution" began in the 1960s and early 1970s (Lenzenweger, 1999), as Kraepelin's narrower, tighter approach to defining schizophrenia lent itself well to improving diagnostic reliability and validity. The narrower definition of schizophrenia resulted in a significant reduction in diagnoses of schizophrenia, so much so that within 5 years of the publication of *DSM–III*, diagnoses of schizophrenia in a large university hospital decreased by 50% (Loranger, 1990). The move to a more Kraepelinian definition also resulted in a greater emphasis on blatantly psychotic symptoms (e.g., hallucinations) and a commensurate de-emphasis of negative symptoms (e.g., affective flattening, alogia; Andreasen & Carpenter, 1993; Lenzenweger, 1999).

DSM–III also saw the inclusion of Kraepelin's subtypes (catatonic; hebephrenic, renamed *disorganized*; and paranoid), although the heterogeneity of symptoms seen in schizophrenia has led to other classification schemes, notably the distinction among positive, negative, and disorganized symptoms (Strauss, Carpenter, & Bartko, 1974). Researchers have also attempted to subtype schizophrenia on the basis of prognosis, adaptive functioning, and biological measures, such as electrodermal response (Lencz, Raine, & Sheard, 1996) and EEG (John et al., 1994), and will no doubt do so in the future using functional neuroimaging.

The move from DSM–III to DSM–III–R resulted in relatively minor changes to the schizophrenia category, such as elimination of the age limit for diagnosis (age 45) and changes in the criteria for paranoid schizophrenia (see Kendler, Spitzer, & Williams, 1989). DSM–IV saw more extensive changes, perhaps the most important being the placement of schizophrenia within the broader category of psychotic disorders, with the aim of facilitating differential diagnosis. Other significant changes to the schizophrenia diagnosis made it both broader (increased emphasis on negative and disorganized symptoms) and narrower (increase in threshold for duration of active symptoms from 1 week to 1 month; American Psychiatric Association, 1998).

Despite these efforts to revise the DSM nomenclature, critics continue to voice concern over several aspects of the schizophrenia diagnosis. Two prominent concerns include problems with the categorical approach and the absence of biological factors among the diagnostic criteria. A major problem with categorical diagnosis has been the difficulty in distinguishing a clear schizophrenic syndrome from other psychotic syndromes (such as schizoaffective disorder) and the correlative problem of reproducing the subtypes in the diagnostic manual using statistical aggregation procedures such as cluster and latent class analyses (e.g., Dollfus et al., 1996; John et al., 1994; Kendler, Karkowski-Shuman, et al., 1997; Kendler, Karkowski, & Walsh, 1998; Lencz et al., 1996; Sham, Castle, Wessely, Farmer, & Murray, 1996; Van der Does, Dingemans, Linszen, Nugter, & Scholte, 1995). As with anxiety and mood disorders, reviewed above, many researchers have argued that a categorical classification system creates artificial boundaries and does not describe significant numbers of patients with schizophrenia (e.g., Van der Does, Dingemans, Linszen, Nugter, & Scholte, 1993). In response, several researchers have proposed dimensional diagnostic systems, one of which is included in Appendix B of DSM–IV for further study (American Psychiatric Association, 1994). This system, which is particularly promising, has clinicians rate the extent to which the patient has positive symptoms, disorganized symptoms, and negative symptoms, using a 4-point severity scale (from *absent* to *severe*). Lenzenweger (1999) suggested adding a fourth dimension, premorbid social functioning.

A second concern with the diagnosis of schizophrenia as defined in *DSM–IV* involves the absence of biological and neuropsychological abnormalities among the diagnostic criteria (e.g., Lenzenweger, 1999; Tsuang et al., 2000). Tsuang et al. argued that the exclusive focus on phenomenological criteria may have been appropriate in a prior era in which data on pathophysiology were lacking, however, amassing data support a diagnosis first suggested by Meehl (1962), *schizotaxia*, that can be assessed using markers such as eye tracking and structural brain abnormalities. They suggested a diagnosis of schizotaxia (characterized in large measure by negative symptoms) with and without psychosis, much as we currently distinguish psychotic and nonpsychotic depression. According to Tsuang and colleagues (2000), psychosis may be the fever of severe mental disorders—a relatively nonspecific symptom seen in a range of neuropsychiatric conditions such as schizophrenia, bipolar disorder, dementia, and Huntington's disease.

Andreasen (1999) has offered an alternative, neo-Bleulerian approach, a unified theory of schizophrenia that links the multiple phenotypic expressions of the disorder to an underlying "misconnection" of neural circuits. This misconnection produces generalized cognitive dysfunction or "dysmetria" (Andreasen, Paradiso, & O'Leary, 1998). On the basis of functional neuroimaging studies, Andreasen argued that schizophrenia is a neurodevelopmental disorder involving faulty wiring in a circuit running from the frontal lobes through the thalamus and cerebellum.

CLASSIFYING PSYCHOPATHOLOGY AND IDENTIFYING CASES: HOW SHOULD WE CREATE AND IMPLEMENT A CLASSIFICATION SYSTEM?

In the preceding sections, we reviewed evolving efforts to classify the forms of psychopathology for which we have the best data. The review suggests both the enormous progress made in the 20th century and the enormous task that remains ahead in the current century in resolving basic taxonomic issues. In this section we take a step back from specific diagnoses to ask two questions: How should we create a classification system, and how should we diagnose patients after we have settled on an appropriate set of categories or dimensions?

It is important to note that the questions of *how to create a classification system* and *how to identify cases once such a system is in place* are in fact distinct. An important way these processes differ is in the number of criteria used (Sokol, 1974). Developing a classification system means using all available data to select the variables (criteria) that best distinguish patients with different forms of psychopathology. Whether this is done impressionistically, as when Kraepelin (1898) listed all the patients he had observed on note cards and sorted them into piles based on similarity of their symptoms, or statistically, using procedures such as factor and cluster analyses, the process of creating a diagnostic system requires inclusion of many more variables than the process of diagnosing a patient after the most discriminating variables have been identified. The reason for this difference is apparent if one considers the process of constructing a psychological test. In test construction, a researcher always does well initially to maximize content validity, by including items that comprehensively cover the domain in question, using all available clinical, theoretical, and empirical knowledge to develop items that sample the domain as exhaustively as possible. After applying this item set to multiple samples, the researcher is then in a position to examine the factor structure of the item set and the intercorrelations of the items and eliminate items, many of which will be redundant or minimally predictive of criterion measures theoretically related to the construct.

After a researcher has developed an instrument, or a committee has developed a diagnostic system, the next question is how to use that "instrument" to diagnose individual cases. (On the analogy between diagnostic systems and psychological tests, see Livesley & Jackson, 1992.) The method specified for making diagnoses in the shift from *DSM–II* to *DSM–III* and *DSM–III–R* was for the clinician or interviewer to make a dichotomous forced-choice decision about each criterion as present or absent and then to count the number present, sometimes following algorithms specifying a certain number of subcriteria from Criteria A, B, and so forth). As we show, this is only one of a range of options for combining criteria to make a diagnosis, and one that may have been a useful first step toward a simpler and psychometrically more useful algorithm.

Central Questions in Developing a Classification System

In creating a diagnostic system, its framers have to make a number of key decisions, each of which should be explicitly considered. Here we briefly outline some of the most important (see Westen, 1999).

The first issue concerns the content of the variable list or item set to be used to distinguish disorders or dimensions. The variables used in defining syndromes historically have been derived from two leading contenders, phenomenology (symptomatology) and etiology. At different times, different authors have called for greater attention to one or the other. *DSM–II* was filled with etiological statements, few of which had a firm empirical basis. In large part as a response to the growing theoretical pluralism in the field by the 1970s (with psychoanalysis no longer dominant), *DSM–III* eliminated all such statements in the criterion sets and moved to a focus on symptomatology. Researchers such as Tsuang and colleagues (2000) have suggested that, for disorders in which etiological data are accumulating, we begin to reconsider etiological criteria.

This situation in many ways parallels developments in both medicine and biological taxonomy. In medicine, disorders often begin with descriptive, phenomenological classification until etiological agents are better understood (e.g., in the evolution of the diagnosis of AIDS). In biology, Linne developed a classification of species based on overt features, which was later challenged by, and ultimately integrated with, evolutionary theories (comparable to etiology in psychiatry; Skinner, 1981).

Although factor- and cluster-analytic studies in psychiatric nosology have typically used exclusively phenomenological item sets, nothing about these statistical techniques requires one form of data or another. Indeed, some recent studies of schizophrenia have applied cluster-analytic techniques to psychophysiological data (e.g., Tsai et al., 1998). Note that etiological agents need not be genetic; environmental factors ranging from exposure to viruses and malnutrition, to sexual abuse and emotional criticism, have been linked to various disorders. To date, it may well be worth assembling a list of genetic and environmental variables linked to one or more psychiatric conditions and include them in studies aimed at classifying psychological disorders. In our own cluster- and factor-analytic work on personality disorders (Westen & Chang, 2000; Westen & Shedler, 1999a, 1999b), we are experimenting with mixed models, in which the units of analysis include both personality variables and etiological variables.

A second key question concerns the level of inference required in rating the variables used for aggregation. An assumption made by most researchers is that the lower the level of inference, the more valid, reliable, and useful the data are likely to be. This has inspired the architects of successive editions of the DSM to become progressively more specific in their diagnostic criteria. For example, the diagnostic criteria for paranoid personality disorder are now all behavioral examples of ways of being distrustful, which could be collapsed into a single, higher order statement such as "is distrustful of people and preoccupied with fears of betrayal, maltreatment, and so on."

As we discuss below, the preference for minimal inference may not be well founded. In our own research, we are finding substantially higher correlations between interview and clinician diagnoses of personality disorders (median correlations around .80) than previously reported in the literature, using the least structured, most highly inferential rating procedure currently available for assessing personality disorders. (We use a Q-sort based on either the clinician's knowledge of the patient over the course of multiple sessions, or an interviewer's inferences regarding the 200 items that constitute the Q-sort after completing an interview focused primarily on narratives rather than questions about diagnostic criteria; Westen &

Muderrisoglu, 2001). Some of the most reliable and valid personality questionnaires, such as the NEO–PI–R (McCrae & Costa, 1990), require individuals to make a number of generalizations about themselves that go well beyond a descriptive behavioral level, such as whether they tend to be anxious, which is a highly subjective and inferential question, given that the metric can mean different things to different people (how much anxiety is "moderate"?).

A third question related to the development of a classification system concerns the observer or rater: Whose observations are the most reliable and valid for rating the variables to be entered into a factor analysis, cluster analysis, or other structural model? The implicit assumption of the early taxonomists such as Kraepelin and Bleuler was that skilled clinicians with many years of experience were in the best position to try to discriminate types of patients, although they lacked the kinds of statistical procedures for doing so that we have today. The implicit assumption of most personality psychologists and psychopathologists is that self-observation, perhaps filtered through the eyes of a research assistant administering a structured interview, is sufficient or even optimal. This assumption should be carefully considered, given the problems with self-reports, including lack of expert knowledge, the problems of using explicit (self-report) measures to report an implicit processes, and self-deception (see, e.g., Shedler, Mayman, & Manis, 1993; Westen, 1995, 1997). An alternative procedure that we have been pursuing is to use the observations of experienced clinicians, not to offer their best guesses about how patients should be categorized, but simply to describe patients using a psychometrically sound measure, which then provides data for statistical aggregation.

A fourth question related to a classification system is whether diagnoses should be categorical, dimensional, some combination of the two, or functional. As described earlier, the issue of categorical versus dimensional diagnosis has received considerable attention over the past two decades, particularly in relation to personality disorders. The basic issues are similar for many Axis I syndromes, for which subclinical presentations are common. Categorical classification is familiar in everyday life (e.g., an object in the office is classified as a chair, not .85 chairlike and .32 sofalike, even though it may bear some resemblance to a sofa) and feels equally "natural" in clinical practice. Categorical diagnosis is efficient and parsimonious, and it renders communication among professionals relatively easy (e.g., "the patient suffers from major depression," vs. "the patient has a Hamilton depression score of 22"). Furthermore, some psychiatric disorders, like some medical disorders, appear to be taxonic—that is, to represent discrete categories—or at the very least to be something other than located along a continuum with healthy functioning, as suggested by data on the genetic epidemiology of syndromes such as schizophrenia and bipolar disorder, for which a genetic diathesis is virtually a *sine qua non*.

By contrast, dimensional systems tend to be complex and cumbersome. Their advantages, however, are twofold. First, they tend to fit the data better for most disorders and prevent many of the problems of comorbidity and creation of atypical, mixed, and not otherwise specified categories that dog the current diagnostic system. This advantage is amplified when the dimensions are selected empirically through procedures such as factor analysis. Second, and related, dimensional systems do not arbitrarily cut continuous variables into dichotomous variables (present–absent) and hence tend to be much more reliable and valid.

It is worth noting an alternative (or perhaps more accurately, a complement) to both categorical and dimensional diagnosis, one that is particularly useful clinically: functional diagnosis (Westen, 1998; Westen & Arkowitz-Westen, 1998). A functional diagnosis is an assessment of how the patient is functioning in each of several central psychological domains. A functional diagnosis is fundamental to case formulation. Rather than asking whether the patient has major depressive disorder (categorical diagnosis) or whether the patient is high on neuroticism (dimensional diagnosis), a functional assessment asks questions such as these: What is the patient's affective functioning like (e.g., is he depressed, anxious)? How effectively can he regulate his emotions (e.g., when he is angry, can he contain it, or does he express it through physical assault or passive aggression)? How is the patient's interpersonal functioning (e.g., do current or long-standing problems interfere with his ability to maintain a job or relationships)?

In all likelihood, our classification systems ultimately have to integrate functional with diagnostic (categorical and dimensional) assessment, particularly for personality. The closest to a functional component of the DSM–IV is the Global Assessment of Functioning (GAF) scale. However, GAF scores provide little insight into which aspects of the patient's functioning are problematic and what psychological processes underlie aspects of both pathological and healthy functioning. As argued elsewhere (Westen, 1998; Westen & Shedler, 2000), a functional assessment of personality is not only quantifiable (e.g., assessing the extent to which the patient has various characteristics that interfere with the capacity to maintain relationships) but also translatable into a personality diagnosis.

A fifth question is whether we should use exploratory or confirmatory procedures in developing a classification system. At the heart of this question are two corollary issues, regarding the role of theory and the extent to which we should begin with familiar classification systems. According to one point of view, a diagnostic system is essentially a theory (Livesley & Jackson, 1992; Skinner, 1981, 1986), which includes propositions about how the criteria that constitute a diagnosis should relate to one another (internal consistency) and how the diagnosis should relate to external criteria (criterion or construct validity). In this view, the crucial question is how the current classification system compares to another theoretically-derived system. A somewhat different, yet related, approach is to use theory and observation not to construct diagnoses a priori but to select the *item set* to which statistical aggregation procedures can be applied. Theory and clinical judgment again enter into the equation in deciding which factor or cluster solutions to retain.

A final question is how to validate a diagnostic system. In general, there are three broad classes of validating criteria: *internal criteria, external criteria,* and *clinical criteria* (see, e.g., Skinner, 1981, 1986). *Internal criteria* refer to characteristics such as the coherence, nonredundancy (discriminant validity), replicability, and comprehensiveness of a diagnostic system, irrespective of its ability to predict external variables. These internal characteristics are necessary but not sufficient to validate a classification system. The current diagnostic system fails on a number of internal criteria: Although most of its categories are coherent (i.e., they "hang together" as syndromes), many diagnoses are redundant (highly comorbid or lacking in discriminant validity), have proven only variably reproducible through empirical procedures such as cluster and factor analysis, and leave too many patients undiagnosed (borderline and subclinical cases).

With respect to external criteria, the central question is whether the diagnostic categories or dimensions predict theoretically relevant criterion variables (such as prognosis, treatment response, level of adaptation, and etiology; see Livesley & Jackson, 1992; Robins & Guze, 1970). With respect to clinical criteria, the validity of a diagnostic system depends on the extent to which its diagnoses appear faithful to clinical reality, provide clinically useful information, and are practical and user friendly. Although taxonomists may disagree on the relative weight to place on these three types of validating criteria, all three are clearly important in evaluating alternative diagnostic systems.

A Prototype-Matching Approach to Diagnosis

Creating versus applying a diagnostic system are two different enterprises and require very different methods. A central thesis of this chapter is that a painstaking, symptom-counting approach, even more systematic than the current procedure required by *DSM–IV*, is essential for creating a more valid diagnostic system, but that a much more inferential, intuitive, less obsessional approach is optimal for applying that system.

Diagnosing a patient using the symptom-counting approach of *DSM–IV* requires a lengthy, systematic, structured interview that inquires about each of several hundred criteria outlined in Axis I and Axis II. We would argue that this is not optimal for either refinement of the current diagnostic system or for clinical diagnosis. To refine the current system, factor- or cluster-analyzing the current criteria would be of only limited utility because the criteria have been selected over the last three editions of the DSM precisely to maximize internal consistency and minimize comorbidity. We can learn much about where these efforts have succeeded or failed but very little about how to improve them unless we include alternative criteria. If we are to apply statistical aggregation procedures to any item set, it should include current diagnostic criteria for all *DSM–IV* disorders as well as at least as many other potential criteria for the constructs included in the *DSM–IV* and their subclinical variants (e.g., subclinical eating disorder symptoms, such as preoccupation with food preparation or irrational restriction of food intake that produces weight loss not severe enough to warrant a *DSM–IV* diagnosis of anorexia nervosa). Variables included in efforts to develop diagnoses empirically should also be coded dimensionally unless we have good reason to believe that they are dichotomously distributed in nature, given the loss of validity, reliability, and statistical power that generally occurs when continuous variables are dichotomized.

With respect to diagnosing cases using a refined diagnostic system, the current rules for diagnostic decision making, which require assessing and counting hundreds of criteria, are neither clinically practical nor, one may argue, optimal for making valid and reliable clinical or research diagnoses. We propose, instead, a simple, intuitive approach based on prototype theory.

Prototype Theory and the Current Polythetic Diagnostic Criteria

The most recent editions of the DSM have shifted away from a defining features approach to categorization toward a prototype approach, based in large part on changing views of classification in cognitive psychology (see Cantor & Genero, 1986; Cantor, Smith, French, & Mezzich, 1980; Horowitz et al., 1981; Smith, 1995). Defining features views of categorization suggest that people categorize an object by comparing its features with a list of qualities that are essential (that is, necessarily present). Most concepts used in daily life, however, are fuzzy concepts, whose members bear a family resemblance to one another but do not share a set of necessary and sufficient features (Malt, 1993; Rosch, 1978). Thus, people usually classify objects by matching the similarity of the object to a prototype in memory—that is, to a mental representation of members of the category that has been abstracted across multiple instances, or to a prominent or prototypical exemplar of the category, such as the best example of a patient with borderline personality disorder one has seen previously (or, we suspect, although no one has tested the roles of affect or primacy in prototype matching, a borderline patient seen while one was in training who was the source of particular anxiety, anger, or rescue fantasies).

The shift from monothetic criterion sets (classification based on the presence of a set of singly necessary and sufficient attributes) to polythetic criterion sets (classification based on the presence of multiple attributes, no one of which is sufficient, and most of which are not necessary for diagnosis) was in fact an attempt to operationalize a prototype view of diagnosis (Frances, 1982; Widiger & Frances, 1985). The architects of the DSM since DSM–II were concerned with several problematic aspects of DSM–II, including two of particular importance here: its lack of reliability and its assumption of categories defined by necessary and sufficient features. The solution to both problems was to develop specific criteria that could be evaluated one at a time as present or absent and to develop a simple procedure for diagnosing a given patient: counting the number of symptoms present from each criterion set and determining whether the patient meets a cutoff for diagnosis. The explicit assumption was that clinical judgment is inherently unreliable and that more specific, operational criteria would increase reliability of diagnosis. As Widiger and Frances (1985) put it, "If interrater reliability is to be achieved, the amount of inference required by the diagnostic criteria must be decreased . . ." (p. 617).

An Alternative Operationalization of a Prototype-Matching Approach

An alternative hypothesis (which we are currently testing with respect to Axis II diagnosis) is that clinical inference can in fact be reliable if clinicians are not forced to make dichotomous (present–absent) decisions about either diagnoses treated as a whole (DSM–II) or individual diagnostic criteria treated individually (DSM–III through DSM–IV). Thus, for clinical purposes, diagnoses could be made rapidly and efficiently by having clinicians make simple Likert-type ratings of the extent to which the patient's symptoms taken as a whole match each of several diagnostic prototypes, with the prototypes developed empirically through application of statistical aggregation techniques to large data sets. The result would be a series of prototypicality ratings that would provide a symptom profile, much like that provided by the Minnesota Multiphase Personality Inventory–2nd edition profile.

Westen and Shedler (1999b, 2000) have attempted to develop such a procedure for the classification and diagnosis of personality disorders. Over the course of several studies, they presented large, randomly selected samples of clinicians with a 200-item personality pathology Q-sort procedure that included not only versions of the 80-plus criteria currently included on Axis II but also a broad range of items assessing aspects of personality functioning and pathology not currently included on Axis II. The task of the clinician was simply to describe a randomly selected patient's personality in two studies of a patient currently diagnosed on Axis II: in one study, a patient with subclinical personality pathology, and in another, an adolescent patient being treated for enduring, maladaptive patterns of thought, feeling, motivation, or behavior (whether or not severe enough to warrant an adult Axis II diagnosis). The investigators aggregated these descriptions using Q-analysis (inverted factor analysis), a clustering procedure that groups cases together on the basis of their similarity across the 200-variable item set.

The results, in both adult and adolescent samples (see Westen & Chang, 2000; Westen, Shedler, Glass, Zimmerman, & Martens, 2001), were a series of clinically and empirically coherent prototypes, some of which (e.g., narcissistic, paranoid) resemble current Axis II categories, whereas others (e.g., dysphoric personality disorder) do not. Patients' scores on each diagnosis are calculated by correlating their 200-item profile with the 200-item empirically derived prototype (Q-factor) for each diagnosis, and converting these to T scores (with a mean of 50 and standard deviation of 10). Using this approach, patients can receive both dimensional diagnoses (which index the extent to which their personality profile matches —that is, correlates with—each prototype) and categorical diagnoses (e.g., T-score elevation of 1.5 standard deviations). In several samples, these T scores have yielded theoretically predicted correlations with relevant external criterion variables, such as measures of adaptive functioning and etiology (see Westen & Shedler, 2000).

We are currently testing whether diagnosis by Q-sort with 200 variables is as or more reliable and valid than current diagnostic procedures for research purposes. For clinical purposes, we are proposing for the next edition of the *DSM* a simplified prototype-matching procedure that may prove a useful alternative to the current symptom-counting algorithm.[1] In this model, Axis II would consist of a set of prototype personality descriptions, each including 15–20 statements about the patient's characteristic patterns of thought, feeling, motivation, interpersonal functioning, and so forth. Rather than consider symptoms one at a time, dichotomize them as present or absent, and count the number of symptoms present, the clinician's task is much simpler: Examine each criterion set as a gestalt and decide to what extent the patient's personality matches the prototype.

Figure 9.2 presents the narcissistic prototype, empirically derived through Q-analysis of a sample of 496 patients, and converted to paragraph form (by grouping together items with related content). After reading through the items that constitute this prototype, the clinician makes a simple prototype rating, using the scale reproduced in the figure. The patient's dimensional score represents the extent to which he or she resembles the prototype. From a categorical point of view, patients who receive a score of 4 or 5 would be considered to have the disorder.

A similar procedure could be used to diagnose disorders such as those currently coded on Axis I. For example, the Axis I description of depression might include 8–10 symptoms that constitute the syndrome of major de-

---

[1]The current version of this prototype matching approach was developed in consultation with Robert Spitzer and Michael First.

pression, and the clinician's task is to rate the extent to which the patient's condition matches the prototype taken as a whole (see Figure 9.2). A score of 4 or 5 would mean that the patient's symptoms approximate the complete prototype and would warrant a categorical diagnosis of major depression. A score of 3 would mean that the patient's symptom picture resembles the prototype in many respects but not enough to warrant a categorized diagnosis of major depression. The patient would thus receive a subclinical diagnosis. There is little need, using this method, for the not otherwise specified categories. The same patient may or may not receive a high prototype rating on depression, panic, generalized anxiety, social phobia, and so on.

What is important in this example, as in the example of narcissistic personality disorder, is that the clinician is not asked to dichotomize symptoms that are probably continuously distributed in nature or to count the number of symptoms rated as present. This simplifies the clinicians' task immensely—and is probably much closer to the prototype-matching process clinicians intuitively use in everyday practice. Using the current diagnostic algorithms, clinicians who engage in intuitive prototype matching of this sort, which we suspect most do, invariably make invalid and unreliable diagnoses, precisely because of the diagnostic decision rules built into *DSM–IV*. Using a more straightforward prototype-matching process such as the one described here, a clinician familiar with a patient could rate the entire range of syndromes in the diagnostic manual in 3 to 5 minutes.

Four points deserve brief mention here. First, the method of diagnosis we are proposing represents in some respects a hybrid between *DSM–II*

5 very strong match (patient's personality *exemplifies* this disorder; prototypical case)		
4 strong match (patient *has* this disorder; diagnosis applies)		**Diagnosis**
3 moderate match (patient has *significant features* of this disorder)		**Features**
2 slight match (patient has minor features of this disorder)		
1 no match (description does not apply to the patient)		

Figure 9.2. A prototype-matching approach to diagnosis of narcissistic personality disorder. Individuals who match this prototype have fantasies of unlimited success, power, beauty, talent, brilliance, and so on. They appear to feel privileged and entitled, and they expect preferential treatment. They have an exaggerated sense of self-importance and believe they can only be appreciated by, or should only associate with, people who are high-status, superior, or otherwise "special." Individuals who match this prototype seek to be the center of attention and seem to treat others primarily as an audience to witness their own importance, brilliance, beauty, etc. They tend to be arrogant, haughty, or dismissive; to be competitive with others (whether consciously or unconsciously); to feel envious; and to think others are envious of them. They expect themselves to be "perfect" (e.g., in appearance, achievements, performance) and are likely to fantasize about finding ideal, perfect love. They tend to lack close friendships and relationships; to feel life has no meaning; and to feel like they are not their true selves with others, so that they may feel false or fraudulent. Adapted from Westen and Shedler, 2000.

and more recent editions of the diagnostic manual and would lead to similar hybrid forms of clinical and research interviewing. *DSM–II* had two virtues: brevity and prototypic descriptions of disorders whose "gist" clinicians could readily capture. However, it had several problems, including lack of empirically derived or empirically testable criteria (because diagnostic criteria were not separated), lack of empirically derived diagnostic groupings, built-in but untested etiological assumptions, assumptions about the categorical nature of disorders that rendered reliability of diagnosis impossible (a patient either had or did not have a given diagnosis, depending on whether the patient fit the description), and an implicit if not explicit assumption of a defining-features approach to categorization.

We are essentially suggesting a return to a manual consisting of prototype descriptions of disorders, with the brevity of *DSM–II* but the systematic empirical selection of criteria—and hence the minimization of comorbidity that may be an artifact of redundant and mixed diagnoses—and the prototype model of categorization characteristic of later editions of the *DSM*. The implication for assessment would be that interviewers can use clinical skill in determining how much to ask about each disorder, as in the *DSM–II* era, but follow a more explicit structure that guarantees comprehensiveness of diagnosis, which makes use of some of the semistructured interview techniques that emerged in the late 1970s. In our research on Axis II, we are using an interview that resembles a 3-session exploratory psychiatric-psychotherapy intake assessment (see Westen & Muderrisoglu, 2001; Westen, Muderrisoglu, Fowler, Shedler, & Koren, 1997). The interviewer begins by asking patients to describe themselves, what brought them in for treatment, the history of their symptoms, and their family and developmental history. The interviewer then elicits a series of narrative descriptions of patients' significant family, friend, work, and love relationships over the course of their lives.

To assess current states and Axis I syndromes, the clinician is guided by some general rules (e.g., always ask about mood, substance use, eating patterns, antisocial behavior, and clinical and subclinical thinking disturbance, whether or not the patient notes problems along these lines) but only asks about most criteria of most disorders if the clinical material indicates a reason to do so. Thus, an interviewer does not typically ask a patient who is in a stable relationship and functioning well at work whether he hears voices, and the interviewer does not ask a patient who shows no signs of depression in a 150-minute interview whether his or her eating patterns have changed in the last 2 weeks. Although this procedure may produce a small number of false negatives, it is more parsimonious, less cumbersome, and provides, we believe, a better balance between data collection and alliance maintenance. It differs little from decision-tree approaches to structured diagnosis in which the patient's answers to certain questions lead the interviewer either to inquire or not inquire further about symptoms of particular syndromes. The difference is that our method is less dependent on a scripted list of questions and is more interactive and sensitive to the alliance, which we believe is likely to offset any losses associated with less standardization of wording.

Second, and implicit in the first point, if a prototype-matching algorithm for diagnosis were built into the next edition of DSM, the prototypes should, to the extent possible, be developed empirically, just as researchers have distinguished positive, negative, and disorganized symptoms of schizophrenia; distinct aspects of panic, generalized anxiety and depression, and so forth. We have been able to eliminate comorbidity from personality diagnosis in our studies of adult and adolescent patients with personality pathology, and these data are cross-replicating in new samples. Numerical taxonomic efforts are no panacea, and expert committees with large pools of clinical consultants will always be required to choose among alternative solutions. Nevertheless, a committee with access to the results of four or five studies applying statistical aggregation techniques to large samples using large item sets, each including data against which to validate the various potential solutions, would likely make better decisions than a committee attempting to refashion the categories and criteria that evolved from Bleuler and Kraepelin's extraordinary but intuitive taxonomic methods from a century ago, as modified by data and committee compromises over the last half century.

Third, using a simple prototype-matching system such as the one outlined here, the diagnostic manual could avoid arbitrary temporal cutoffs (e.g., the episode must have lasted at least 2 weeks), just as it could avoid arbitrary cutoffs for number of criteria present to constitute the diagnosis. For all diagnoses on which the patient receives a score of 3 or more (indicating at least moderate match to the prototype), the clinician would simply rate duration of the current episode other potentially useful variables such as severity of current symptoms and age of onset of first episode. This approach would render a diagnosis much closer to a case formulation: The clinician would describe the symptom and then the duration and one or two other variables relevant to the treatment decision, rather than only describe the symptom if it meets arbitrary duration criteria.

Finally, in the next edition of DSM, we will need to rethink the multiaxial system, so that the system has three characteristics that it currently approximates only imperfectly. First, the axes should be defined more clearly. Axis I, for example, includes both states and enduring personality conditions, and it arbitrarily includes some enduring conditions (such as dysthymic disorder) while excluding others (such as personality disorders). We suspect that the only consistent way to create a first axis that codes symptoms is to limit it to states, assessed prototypically, so that patients would receive a series of 1–5 ratings for panic, generalized anxiety, depression, mania, positive symptoms of psychosis, negative symptoms, and so forth. A clinician could make this kind of Axis I diagnosis very quickly, by only listing diagnoses on which the patient receives a score greater than 1, with 1 (i.e., no match to the prototype) being the default score. Second, the axes should yield a case formulation, each providing nonredundant information about the major things a clinician needs to know and communicate about a patient, including current condition (state), duration of the condition, history of psychiatric conditions, personality context, etiological context, and recent stressors. Third, the axes should be statistically nonredundant: We should consider using a multiple regression model in deciding whether to add any potential axes, asking whether it provides data that predict incremental variance in clinically relevant variables.

CONCLUSION

Any proposals for refinement of the current diagnostic system should acknowledge the considerable divergence between the aims and observations of clinicians and researchers and the importance of incorporating both perspectives. A diagnostic manual should not be moored in unsystematic clinical observation and clinical hypotheses, as were *DSM–I* and *DSM–II*; these early editions of *DSM* were first approximations of a classification system developed without the tools we now have at our disposal. On the other hand, if a diagnostic system diverges so far from clinical experience that clinicians begin to disregard major aspects of it, such as the algorithms it provides for making diagnoses, we should be careful before we pathologize clinicians for not using the manual appropriately (or set up training programs for their remediation) and consider the equally plausible explanation that the manual requires reconfiguration.

We believe this is what has happened with aspects of *DSM–IV*. If assessing hundreds of diagnostic criteria by asking a series of questions about each one; making forced-choice, present–absent decisions about each criterion; and then counting them yielded information that helped clinicians treat their patients, we suspect that, 20 years after the introduction of *DSM–III*, clinicians would have caught on to the benefit of doing so. Clinical practice is an imperfect mechanism for assessing clinical utility, but it is certainly a useful bellwether.

In our own research, we have enlisted the help of hundreds of experienced clinicians, not by pooling their intuitive theories or biases about the nature of psychopathology, but by enlisting their expertise by asking them to describe a patient using a psychometrically sound instrument, and then pooling their knowledge through statistical aggregation procedures. There are many ways to approach the classification of psychiatric disorders, and this is just one of them. The prototype-matching approach we have proposed here requires much more research on implementation to see whether clinicians can use it reliably and whether doing so leads to increases or decreases in reliability and predictive validity. We suspect, however, that the approaches that will ultimately prove most successful are ones that will engage clinicians and researchers in an ongoing, collaborative effort that acknowledges the strengths and limitations of each of their vantage points.

REFERENCES

American Psychiatric Association. (1952). *Diagnostic and statistical manual of mental disorders*. Washington, DC: Author.

American Psychiatric Association. (1968). *Diagnostic and statistical manual of mental disorders* (2nd ed.). Washington, DC: Author.

American Psychiatric Association. (1980). *Diagnostic and statistical manual of mental disorders* (3rd ed.). Washington, DC: Author.

American Psychiatric Association. (1987). *Diagnostic and statistical manual of mental disorders* (3rd ed., rev.). Washington, DC: Author.

American Psychiatric Association. (1994). *Diagnostic and statistical manual of mental disorders* (4th ed.). Washington, DC: Author.

American Psychiatric Association. (1998). *DSM–IV sourcebook (Vol. 4)*. Washington, DC: Author.

Andreasen, N. (1999). A unitary model of schizophrenia: Bleuler's "fragmented phrene" as schizencephaly. *Archives of General Psychiatry, 56*(9), 781–787.

Andreasen, N. C., & Carpenter, W. T., Jr. (1993). Diagnosis and classification of schizophrenia. *Schizophrenia Bulletin, 19*(2), 199–214.

Andreasen, N. C., & Grove, W. M. (1982). The classification of depression: Traditional versus mathematical approaches. *American Journal of Psychiatry, 139*, 45–52.

Andreasen, N. C., Paradiso, S., & O'Leary, D. S. (1998). "Cognitive dysmetria" as an integrative theory of schizophrenia: A dysfunction in cortical–subcortical–cerebellar circuitry? *Schizophrenia Bulletin, 24*(2), 203–218.

Barlow, D. (2002). *Anxiety and its disorders* (2nd ed.). New York: Guilford Press.

Barrett, J. E., Barrett, J. A., Oxman, T. E., & Gerber, P. D. (1988). The prevalence of psychiatric disorders in a primary care practice. *Archives of General Psychiatry, 45*, 1100–1106.

Beck, A. T., Ward, C. H., Mendelson, M., Mock, J., & Erbaugh, J. (1961). An inventory for measuring depression. *Archives of General Psychiatry, 4*, 561–571.

Blashfield, R. K., & Morey, L. C. (1979). The classification of depression through cluster analysis. *Comprehensive Psychiatry, 20*, 516–527.

Bleuler, E. (1950). *Dementia praecox or the group of schizophrenias* (J. Zinkin, Trans.). New York: International Universities Press. (Original work published 1911)

Brown, T. A., Chorpita, B. F., & Barlow, D. H. (1998). Structural relationships among dimensions of the *DSM–IV* anxiety and mood disorders and dimensions of negative affect, positive affect, and autonomic arousal. *Journal of Abnormal Psychology, 107,* 179–192.

Cantor, N., & Genero, N. (1986). Psychiatric diagnosis and natural categorization: A close analogy. In T. Millon & G. Klerman (Eds.), *Contemporary directions in psychopathology: Toward the DSM–IV* (pp. 233–256). New York: Guilford Press.

Cantor, N., Smith, E., French, R., & Mezzich, J. (1980). Psychiatric diagnosis as prototype categorization. *Journal of Abnormal Psychology, 89,* 181–193.

Chen, L., Eaton, W. W., Gallo, J. J., Nestadt, G., & Crum, R. M. (2000). Empirical examination of current depression categories in a population-based study: Symptoms, course, and risk factors. *American Journal of Psychiatry, 157,* 573–580.

Clark, L. A. (1989). The anxiety and depressive disorders: Descriptive psychopathology and differential diagnosis. In P. C. Kendall & D. Watson (Eds.), *Anxiety and depression: Distinctive and overlapping features* (pp. 83–129). San Diego, CA: Academic Press.

Clark, L. A., & Watson, D. (1991). Tripartite model of anxiety and depression: Psychometric evidence and taxonomic implications. *Journal of Abnormal Psychology, 100,* 316–336.

Dollfus, S., Everitt, B., Ribeyre, J. M., Assouly-Besse, F., Sharp, C., & Petit, M. (1996). Identifying subtypes of schizophrenia by cluster analyses. *Schizophrenia Bulletin, 22,* 545–555.

Everitt, B. S. (1979). Unresolved problems in cluster analysis. *Biometrics, 35,* 169–181.

Eysenck, H. J. (1994). Personality and temperament. In D. Tantam & M. J. Birchwood et al. (Eds.), *Seminars in psychology and the social sciences* (College Seminars Series, pp. 187–202). London: Gaskell Royal College of Psychiatrists.

Feighner, J. P., Robins, E., Guze, S. B., Woodruff, R. A., & Winokur, G. (1972). Diagnostic criteria for use in psychiatric research. *Archives of General Psychiatry, 26,* 56–73.

Fleiss, J. L., Lawlor, W., Platman, S. R., & Fieve, R. (1971). On the use of inverted factor analysis for generating typologies. *Journal of Abnormal Psychology, 77,* 126–133.

Frances, A. (1982). Categorical and dimensional systems of personality diagnosis: A comparison. *Comprehensive Psychiatry, 23,* 516–527.

Frances, A., & Widiger, T. A. (1986). Methodological issues in personality disorder diagnosis. In T. Millon, G. Klerman (Eds.), *Contemporary directions in psychopathology: Towards the DSM–IV* (pp. 381–400). New York: Guilford Press.

Grove, W. M., & Andreasen, N. C. (1986). Multivariate statistical analysis in psychopathology. In T. Millon & G. L. Klerman (Eds.), *Contemporary directions in psychopathology: Towards the DSM–IV* (pp. 347–362). New York: Guilford Press.

Horowitz, L. M., Post, D. L., de Sales French, R., Wallis, K. D., & Siegelman, E. Y. (1981). The prototype as a construct in abnormal psychology: 2. Clarifying disagreement in psychiatric judgments. *Journal of Abnormal Psychology, 90,* 575–585.

Jampala, V. L., Sierles, F. S., & Taylor, M. A. (1988). The use of *DSM–III* in the

United States: A case of not going by the book. *Comprehensive Psychiatry, 29,* 39–47.

John, E. R., Prichep, L. S., Alper, K. R., Mas, F. G., Cancro, R., Easton, P., & Sverdlov, L. (1994). Quantitative electrophysiological characteristics and subtyping of schizophrenia. *Biological Psychiatry, 36,* 801–826.

Johnson, J. G., Cohen, P., Skodol, A., Oldham, J., Kasen, S., & Brook, J. S. (1999). Personality disorders in adolescence and risk of major mental disorders and suicidality during adulthood. *Archives of General Psychiatry, 56,* 805–811.

Katon, W., & Roy-Byrne, P. (1991). Mixed anxiety and depression. *Journal of Abnormal Psychology, 100,* 337–345.

Keller, M. B., Klein, D. N., Hirschfeld, R. M. A., Kocsis, J. H., McCullough, J. P., Miller, I., First, M. B., Holtzer, C. P., Keitner, G. I., Marin, D. B., & Shea, T. (1995). Results of the *DSM–IV* mood disorders field trial. *American Journal of Psychiatry, 152,* 843–849.

Keller, M. B., & Lavori, P. W. (1984). Double depression, major depression, and dysthymia: Distinct entities or different phases of a single disorder? *Psychopharmacology Bulletin, 20,* 399–402.

Kendler, K. S., Karkowski, L. M., & Walsh, D. (1998). The structure of psychosis. *Archives of General Psychiatry, 55,* 492–499.

Kendler, K. S., Karkowski-Shuman, L., O'Neill, A., Straub, R. E., MacLean, C. J., & Walsh, D. (1997). Resemblance of psychotic symptoms and syndromes in affected sibling pairs from the Irish study of high-density schizophrenia families: Evidence for possible etiologic heterogeneity. *American Journal of Psychiatry, 154,* 191–198.

Kendler, K. S., Neale, M. C., Prescott, C. A., Kessler, R. C., Heath, A. C., Corey, L. A., & Eaves, L. J. (1996). Childhood parental loss and alcoholism in women: A causal analysis using a twin family design. *Psychological Medicine, 26,* 79–95.

Kendler, K. S., Spitzer, R. L., & Williams, J. B. W. (1989). Psychotic disorders in *DSM–III–R. The American Journal of Psychiatry, 146,* 953–962.

Kernberg, O. (1984). *Severe personality disorders.* New Haven, CT: Yale University Press.

Kessler, R. C., McGonagle, K. A., Zhao, S., Nelson, C. B., Hughes, M., Eshleman, S., Wittchen, H.-U., & Kendler, K. S. (1994). Lifetime and 12-month prevalence of *DSM–III–R* psychiatric disorders in the United States. *Archives of General Psychiatry, 51,* 8–19.

Kessler, R., Nelson, C., McGonagle, K., Liu, M., Swartz, M., & Blazer, D. (1996). Comorbidity of *DSM–III–R* major depressive disorder in the general population: Results from the US National Comorbidity Survey. *British Journal of Psychiatry, 168,* 17–30.

Klein, D. N. (1999). Depressive personality in the relatives of outpatients with dysthymic disorder and episodic major depressive disorder and normal controls. *Journal of Affective Disorders, 55*(1), 19–27.

Kraepelin, E. (1898). *The diagnosis and prognosis of dementia praecox.* Paper presented at the 29th Congress of Southwestern German Psychiatry, Heidelberg.

Lencz, T., Raine, A., & Sheard, C. (1996). Neuroanatomical bases of electrodermal hyporesponding: A cluster analytic study. *International Journal of Psychophysiology, 22,* 141–153.

Lenzenweger, M. F. (1999). Schizophrenia: Refining the phenotype, resolving the endophenotypes. *Behaviour Research and Therapy, 37,* 281–295.

Lewinsohn, P., Rohde, P., Seeley, J. R., & Klein, D. N. (1997). Axis II psychopathology as a function of Axis I disorders in childhood and adolescence. *Journal of the American Academy of Child and Adolescent Psychiatry, 36,* 1752–1759.

Livesley, W., & Jackson, D. (1992). Guidelines for developing, evaluating, and revising the classification of personality disorder. *Archives of General Psychiatry, 55,* 941–948.

Livesley, W. J., Schroeder, M., Jackson, D. N., & Jang, K. (1994). Categorical distinctions in the study of personality disorder: Implications for classification. *Journal of Abnormal Psychology, 103,* 6–17.

Loranger, A. W. (1990). The impact of *DSM–III* on diagnostic practice in a university hospital: A comparison of *DSM–II* and *DSM–III* in 10,914 patients. *Archives of General Psychiatry, 47,* 329–344.

Malt, B. (1993). Concept structure and category boundaries. In G. V. Nakamura, D. L. Medin, & R. Taraban (Eds.), *Categorization by humans and machines. The psychology of learning and motivation: Advances in research and theory* (Vol. 29, pp. 363–390). San Diego, CA: Academic Press.

McCrae, R. R., & Costa, P. T. (1990). Personality disorders and the five-factor model. *Journal of Personality Disorders, 4*(4), 362–371.

McCrae, R. R., & Costa, P. T. (1997). Personality trait structure as a human universal. *American Psychologist, 52*(5), 509–516.

Meehl, P. (1962). Schizotaxia, schizotypy, schizophrenia. *American Psychologist, 17,* 827–838.

Mendels, J., & Cochrane, C. (1968). The nosology of depression: The endogenous-reactive concept. *American Journal of Psychiatry, 11,* Supplement.

Millon, T. (1990). *Toward a new personology: An evolutionary model.* New York: Wiley.

Morel, B. A. (1852). *Traité de maladies mentales* [Treatise on mental disorders]. Paris: Masson.

Morrison, K., & Westen, D. (2000). *The external validity of psychotherapy trials: An empirical investigation.* Unpublished manuscript, Boston University.

Newman, D. L., Moffitt, T., Caspi, A., & Silva, P. A. (1998). Comorbid mental disorders: Implications for treatment and sample selection. *Journal of Abnormal Psychology, 107,* 305–311.

Olfson, M., Broadhead, W. E., Weissman, M. M., Leon, A. C., Farber, L., Hoven, C., & Kathol, R. (1996). Subthreshold psychiatric symptoms in a primary care group practice. *Archives of General Psychiatry, 53,* 880–886.

Paykel, E. S. (1971). Classification of depressed patients: A cluster analysis derived grouping. *British Journal of Psychiatry, 137,* 275–288.

Phillips, K. A., & Gunderson, J. G. (1999). Depressive personality: Fact or fiction? *Journal of Personality Disorders, 13*(2), 128–134.

Pinel, P. (1962). *A treatise on insanity*. New York: Hafner. (Reprinted from article published in 1801 in *Psychology, 100*, 337–345).

Raskin, A., & Crook, T. H. (1976). The endogenous–neurotic distinction as a predictor of response to antidepressant drugs. *Psychological Medicine, 6*, 59–70.

Robins, E., & Guze, S. B. (1970). Establishment of diagnostic validity in psychiatric illness: Its application to schizophrenia. *American Journal of Psychiatry, 126*, 983–986.

Rosch, E. (1978). Principles of categorization. In E. Rosch & B. Lloyd (Eds.), *Cognition and categorization*. New York: Wiley.

Sham, P. C., Castle, D. J., Wessely, S., Farmer, A. E., & Murray, R. M. (1996). Further exploration of a latent class typology of schizophrenia. *Schizophrenia Research, 20*(1–2), 105–115.

Shedler, J., Mayman, M., & Manis, M. (1993). The illusion of mental health. *American Psychologist, 48*, 1117–1131.

Skinner, H. A. (1981). Toward the integration of classification theory and methods. *Journal of Abnormal Psychology, 90*, 68–87.

Skinner, H. A. (1986). Construct validation approach to psychiatric classification. In T. Millon & G. L. Klerman (Eds.), *Contemporary directions in psychopathology: Towards the DSM–IV* (pp. 307–329). New York: Guilford Press.

Smith, E. E. (1995). Concepts and categorization. In E. Smith & D. Osherson (Eds.), *Thinking: An invitation to cognitive science* (Vol. 3, 2nd ed., pp. 3–33). Cambridge, MA: MIT Press.

Sokol, R. R. (1974). Classification: Purposes, principles, progress, prospects. *Science, 185*, 1115–1123.

Spielberger, C. D., Gorsuch, R. I., & Lushene, R. E. (1970). *Manual for the State–Trait Anxiety Inventory (Self-Evaluation Questionnaire)*. Palo Alto, CA: Consulting Psychologists Press.

Spitzer, R. L., Endicott, J., & Robins, E. (1978). Research diagnostic criteria: Rationale and reliability. *Archives of General Psychiatry, 35*, 773–782.

Strauss, J. S., Carpenter, W. T., Jr., & Bartko, J. J. (1974). The diagnosis and understanding of schizophrenia: Part III. Speculations on the processes that underlie schizophrenia signs and symptoms. *Schizophrenia Bulletin, 1*(11), 61–69.

Sullivan, P. F., Kessler, R. C., & Kendler, K. S. (1998). Latent class analysis of lifetime depressive symptoms in the National Comorbidity Survey. *American Journal of Psychiatry, 155*, 1398–1406.

Tsai, G., van Kammen, D. P., Chen, S., Kelley, M. E., Grier, A., & Coyle, J. T. (1998). Glutamatergic neurotransmission involves structural and clinical deficits of schizophrenia. *Biological Psychiatry, 44*, 667–674.

Tsuang, M. T., Stone, W. S., & Faraone, S. V. (in press). Towards reformulating the diagnosis of schizophrenia. *American Journal of Psychiatry*.

Van der Does, A. J. W., Dingemans, P. M., Linszen, D. H., Nugter, M. A., & Scholte, W. F. (1993). Symptom dimensions and cognitive and social functioning in recent-onset schizophrenia. *Psychological Medicine, 23*, 745–753.

Van der Does, A. J. W., Dingemans, P. M. A. J., LinSzen, D. H., Nugter, M. A., &

Scholte, W. F. (1995). Dimensions and subtypes of recent-onset schizophrenia: A longitudinal analysis. *Journal of Nervous and Mental Disease, 183*, 681–687.

Waller, N., & Meehl, P. (1998). *Multivariate taxometric analysis.* New York: Sage.

Westen, D. (1995). A clinical–empirical model of personality: Life after the Mischelian ice age and the NEO-lithic era. *Journal of Personality, 63*, 495–524.

Westen, D. (1997). Divergences between clinical and research methods for assessing personality disorders: Implications for research and the evolution of Axis II. *American Journal of Psychiatry, 154*, 895–903.

Westen, D. (1998). Case formulation and personality diagnosis: Two processes or one? In James Barron (Ed.), *Making diagnosis meaningful* (pp. 111–138). Washington, DC: American Psychological Association.

Westen, D. (1999). *Personality disorders in DSM–IV: A critical appraisal.* Unpublished manuscript, Boston University.

Westen, D., & Arkowitz-Westen, L. (1998). Limitations of Axis II in diagnosing personality pathology in clinical practice. *American Journal of Psychiatry, 155*, 1767–1771.

Westen, D., & Chang, C. M. (2000). Adolescent personality pathology: A review. *Adolescent Psychiatry, 25*, 61–100.

Westen, D., & Muderrisoglu, S. (2001). *Reliability and validity of personality disorder assessment using a systematic clinical interview.* Unpublished manuscript, Boston University.

Westen, D., Muderrisoglu, S., Fowler, C., Shedler, J., & Koren, D. (1997). Affect regulation and affective experience: Individual differences, group differences, and measurement using a Q-sort procedure. *Journal of Consulting and Clinical Psychology, 65*, 429–439.

Westen, D., & Shedler, J. (1999a). Revising and assessing Axis II: Part I. Developing a clinically and empirically valid assessment method. *American Journal of Psychiatry, 156*, 258–272.

Westen, D., & Shedler, J. (1999b). Revising and assessing Axis II: Part II. Toward an empirically based and clinically useful classification of personality disorders. *American Journal of Psychiatry, 156*, 273–285.

Westen, D., & Shedler, J. (2000). A prototype matching approach to personality disorders: Toward DSM–V. *Journal of Personality Disorders, 14*, 109–126.

Westen, D., Shedler, J., Glass, S., Zimmerman, C., & Martens, A. (2001). *Personality disorders in adolescence, II: An empirically derived classification.* Unpublished manuscript, Boston University.

Widiger, T. (1993). Validation strategies for the personality disorders. *Journal of Personality Disorders*, Supplement, 34–43.

Widiger, T., & Frances, A. (1985). The *DSM–III* personality disorders: Perspectives from psychology. *Archives of General Psychiatry, 42*, 615–623.

Zinbarg, R. E., & Barlow, D. H. (1996). Structure of anxiety and the anxiety disorders: A hierarchical model. *Journal of Abnormal Psychology, 105*, 181–193.

Zinbarg, R. E., Barlow, D. H., Liebowitz, M., & Street, L. (1994). The *DSM–IV* field trial for mixed anxiety–depression. *American Journal of Psychiatry, 151*, 1153–1162.

10

DIAGNOSIS AND TREATMENT GUIDELINES: THE EXAMPLE OF DEPRESSION

LARRY E. BEUTLER AND MARY L. MALIK

Depression is perhaps the most frequently studied and discussed behavioral disorder of the 365 disorders identified by the American Psychiatric Association (1994, 2000). Numerous books and manuals have been written on how to treat it, special interest and professional groups have published numerous educational pamphlets and videotapes that urge those affected by it to seek treatment, and some of these groups even collaborate with federal agencies (e.g., National Institute of Mental Health) to sponsor a national depression screening day in order to identify those in the population who have this "disease." When identified, these individuals are encouraged to seek treatment and typically are provided with a list of referrals. The federal government, pharmaceutical companies, and private organizations collectively have invested billions of dollars in developing and advertising new medications to treat depression. Radio, television, and newsprint advertisements promote the view that depression is a disease and attempt to persuade potential patients that a particular medication can cure their ills. Because of the high profile of this disorder and of the assumptions that permeate its description and treatment, major depression is an ideal prototype by which to view some of the strengths and weaknesses of the current *Diagnostic and Statistical Manual of Mental Disorders* (DSM) system.

Consistent with the *DSM* perspective, depression is viewed in most public information campaigns as a disease. The disease model is accepted implicitly, to be analogous to a variety of physical diseases and medical conditions with which the public may be familiar, seeking both to demystify it and to convey an attitude of acceptance regarding this "illness." For example, Coyne (in press) compared the costs of depression to heart disease and arthritis, implying that the estimated $41 billion per year in lost production could be recouped if people received appropriate treatment. Indeed, one is hard put to find any mass-produced literature from any large, national organization that touts depression as anything other than an illness.

The pervasive tendency to invoke a particular theory of change in discussing deviant behavior was not lost on those who developed the diagnostic nomenclature. However, despite an explicit effort to avoid theoretical constructs, both the 4th edition of the *DSM* (*DSM–IV*; American Psychiatric Association, 1994) and the *DSM–IV Text Revision* (*DSM–IV–TR*; American Psychiatric Association, 2000) are constructed around a medical analogy of depression, using it to derive statistics on prevalence and incidence and figures on public health costs. Putting the efforts to remain atheoretical aside, the theory that depression is a medical condition is central to contemporary approaches to the development of treatment guidelines by the Agency for Health Care Policy and Research (Depression Guideline Panel, 1993) and the American Psychiatric Association (1993; American Psychiatric Association Steering Committee on Practice Guidelines, 2000).

All of these figures and activities rest on the implicit premise that depression has an underlying cause or common set of causes that can be recognized, diagnosed, and treated. In accordance with the illness analogy, the implied cause links depression to biochemical and neurological conditions. Usually, for example, depression is described as a "chemical imbalance" that can be treated with a specific intervention, usually an antidepressant medication, a perspective that many believe is inconsistent with the current state of scientific knowledge (see Barlow, 1994; Carson, 1997; Valenstein, 1998).

Accurate or not, publicity campaigns that present depression as a "treatable disease" that is associated with a "chemical imbalance" are working. An editorial in the *Psychiatric News* ("Medicare proposal could be dangerous," November 19, 1999) reported that in October 1999, the designated Medicare carrier for the state of Connecticut drafted regulations that, among other things, proposed to deny coverage for the treatment of depression unless antidepressant medication was used. This recommendation follows logically from the view that depression is a chemical imbalance or dysfunction and that it is a condition that represents a break or "break down" from normal experience. Such recommendations, as well as the rationale of the reigning diagnostic system, the associated prevalence figures, the nature of guidelines for its treatments, and the resultant public health campaigns, make two cardinal assumptions about depression that bear closer inspection.

First, all of these activities assume that depression is a reliably identifiable "thing," an entity or condition that can be recognized through careful diagnostic procedures by an expert, analogous to those used to diagnose arthritis, heart disease, or cancer. After all, only if one assumes that it can be reliably identified and recognized does it make sense to count it, to compute its costs, or to make comparisons of work production, incidence, and prevalence rates among those who are and are not depressed.

Second, the emphasis on counting costs of depression and numbers of people who have it implies that some consequence of importance follow from an accurate identification of who has it. Specifically, it is tacitly and often explicitly assumed that obtaining effective treatment depends on accurately determining who has this insidious syndrome. An effective treatment is assumed to be one that is uniquely suited, or at least reasonably specific, for that condition. The value placed on deriving an accurate diagnosis conveys the assumption that this label allows a skilled professional to select an appropriate treatment from among a variety of possibilities, some of which are inappropriate, ineffective, or even damaging. If it was not assumed that there are specific treatments for a syndrome of depression, there would be no value in either identifying the condition or in educating the public to recognize when they are depressed in the first place.

In this chapter, we briefly review the evidence for these two assumptions that are cardinal to the DSM construction of diagnoses, and then we consider an alternative procedure that is based on diagnostic dimensions that are specific to the development of treatments.

ASSUMPTION NO. 1: DEPRESSION IS A RECOGNIZABLE AND DISCRETE DISORDER

It is widely held that among the 397 major mental health conditions, depression is both the most prevalent and the most costly. Employee Assistance Program managers report that depression ranks with family crisis and stress as the most frequent and costly problem to affect the workplace, even surpassing the more widely recognized workplace problem of alcohol abuse as a detriment to productivity ("Study finds adequacy of care," October 7, 1996). Yet, and surprisingly, it has been difficult to derive a clear estimate of prevalence. Two major stratified probability samples have provided the most ecologically valid survey information on incidence and lifetime prevalence rates for depressive disorders. The National Institute of Mental Health Epidemiological Catchment Area (ECA) studies (Regier et al., 1984) gathered structured diagnostic and treatment information from over 20,000 adults at five sites between 1980 and 1985. It estimated the current prevalence of depression to be under 10%. On the other hand, the National Comorbidity Survey (Kessler et al., 1994) was drawn from a sample of more than 8,000 adults, from 5 to 7 years after the ECA study. It estimated current prevalence of major depression to be nearly 20%, twice that suggested by the ECA study.

What is to be made of the wide disparity between these estimates? An inspection of the methods used suggests that we can rule out differences in sampling strategies, dramatic changes in prevalence during the inter-survey interval, and variable distribution of depression in different geo-graphic regions. Most authorities attribute the differences to how depression was defined in the two surveys (e.g., Howard et al., 1996). The National Comorbidity Survey study, for example, used the criteria of depression as defined in the *DSM–IV*, whereas the earlier, ECA study used criteria from an earlier edition of the *DSM*. Given both the variability of criteria and the reliance of these versions of the diagnostic manual on extant opinion of experts, supplemented and confirmed by vote of members of the American Psychiatric Association, one may have cause to wonder how a disease of the magnitude and importance as that attributed to depression can logically double in prevalence as a simple function of a vote. Such reactivity to opinions that clearly change with societal values suggests a high level of fickleness in the definition of this important syndrome. Moreover, its variability as a function of a political process (i.e., a vote) certainly raises the possibility that the condition could follow the lot of previously defined diseases, including self-defeating personality, homosex-uality, and neurosis, all of which have come and gone (and sometimes, come again), depending more on views of what is politically acceptable than on deviations of organic states. Such diseases are both created and cured by a culturally sensitive (or overly sensitive) vote by a politically reactive body of experts.

When the door is opened to create and cure diseases on the basis of their political acceptability, it is a short step to using the power of the vote to increase the severity and prevalence of depressive disorders whenever economic conditions make it expedient to do so. There is something in-sidious in the possibility that the individuals who financially benefit from treating "ill" people are the same ones who were empowered to define the "treatable disorders" in the first place (Carson, 1997).

The differences in the descriptions that underwrote these two surveys may be attributable to a substantial increase in knowledge in the 5 years that separated them. However, if our understanding of depression is increasing, it is not reflected in the ability of professionals to recognize it. Nor is it reflected in the criteria that are usually characteristic of discrete illnesses: (a) a reliably observed set of symptoms, (b) a predictable course, and (c) a pattern of interrelating symptoms that distinguishes the disorder from other syndromes.

Symptom Reliability

Ample testimony of the instability and ambiguous nature of depressive syndromes is provided by the dramatic failure of clinicians to consistently recognize criteria cases of those who present with depressive syndromes. As few as 10% of syndromally depressed patients may be detected by primary care providers (Ormel, Koeter, van den Brink, & van de Willige, 1991; Quill, 1985), and as few as 30% of such patients are detected by psychiatrists (Wells & Sturm, 1996), even after they are systematically trained to recognize it. One of the reasons for this lack of diagnostic specificity is that the various symptoms that comprise the syndromes of depression may occur in very different patterns of interrelationship. The *DSM–IV* and *DSM–IV–TR* identify and distinguish among various depressive conditions by the spacing and severity of discrete depressive "episodes." Recognizing that there is little constancy among the symptoms that comprise these episodes, however, the diagnostic criteria place no priority on various symptoms. The constant criterion is one based on time. The symptoms, whatever they happen to be, must be present for an arbitrarily defined 2-week period. Beyond this criterion, the index of a depressive episode is the presence of any of five symptoms extracted from a list of nine. These "vegetative signs" include such things as depressed mood, change of weight, change in sleeping pattern, alteration of motor activity, and diminished interest in social and sexual activities. However, the symptoms are given equal weight, and so no single symptom, not even the experience of depression, is considered to be a defining or essential element in the diagnosis. Thus, there are several hundred statistically possible variations and combinations of symptom patterns that could, conceivably, meet diagnostic criteria.

One might think that dysphoria, depression, or sadness would occupy a central position in the diagnosis of a depressive syndrome, but given the nature of the definition, these symptoms may be absent without jeopardizing or invalidating the diagnosis. A layperson may well ask, "how can one be depressed without feeling depressed?" In professional circles, we have learned to explain this point by asserting that not only are the various symptoms of depression functionally equivalent, but entirely different symptom patterns may be "depressive equivalents." For example, alcohol dependence is often described as being a disease that is the functional equivalent of depression (Winokur & Clayton, 1967), meaning that its presence marks an undisclosed depression. In fact, the strength of such functionally equivalent conditions is such that depression is often said to exist without a single *DSM* symptom of depression being manifest. No wonder, then, that it is hard to identify.

Course and Prognosis of Depression

Not only is there variability in how symptoms are clustered and manifest, but also the various symptom clusters that are said to indicate a depressive syndrome undergo idiosyncratic changes over time. These variations only loosely are associated with different depressive syndromes, and they introduce even more variability into the diagnostic system. Thus, some depressions within each separate syndrome are alleviated without treatment, and others require extensive treatment; some are recurrent and others are not. The variable course and prognosis that exist within any and all of the depressive syndromes are not conducive to concluding that there is a common underlying pathogen among the various disorders. If depression is a medical condition, it is certainly not a single one, but an extremely broad collection of different conditions.

To expand, it is notable that descriptions of depression often suggest a greater degree of consistency in the course and nature than actually is present. For example, major depression is often described as having a cyclical course, being self-limiting, and equally likely to pass whether treated or untreated (Klerman, Weissman, Rounsaville, & Chevron, 1984). The high response rate among waiting list control or placebo groups certainly confirms that the symptoms are changeable and often diminish with little intervention. Indeed, the high response rates to little or no treatment is one of the major obstacles to research on the treatment of depression (Hollon, 1996). However, Widiger (1997) pointed out that on close inspection, there is more variability in the course and symptom pattern, both within and among depressive disorders, than would be expected if the several patterns were, indeed, simply manifestations of a disorder that has a single etiology or pathogen. Because of the lack of a stable pattern, the developers of the *DSM* were forced to include several subtypes of depressive syndromes (and other disorders, as well) and several qualifiers (recurrent, single episode, etc.) to fill the gaps between the expected and the observed patterns. Thus, atypical depression, mixed affective disorder, double depression, and depression not otherwise specified—which constitute fully half of the syndromes—were all inserted to account for those whose depression did not follow the "expected" course. Less overtly, these terms ensure that the diagnosis of depression as an independent illness could survive the variability that existed in symptom patterns, course, and etiology.

Distinctiveness of Depressive Symptoms

One way of determining whether depression is an independent, discrete condition is to inspect its overlap with other conditions and diseases. If depression is a true, independent syndrome, it would be expected to be relatively independent of other discrete disorders. Whereas one may have two discrete illnesses simultaneously, these illnesses would not be expected to co-occur at higher than a chance rate. Thus, much can be learned about the nature of depression by looking at its pattern of co-occurrence with other disorders. Consider these contrasting examples:

1. Syndrome A is almost always present when Disease B is present, but it does not co-occur with Diseases C, D, or E.
2. Syndrome A co-exists with many different diseases, including B, C, D, and E, but these latter diseases do not occur with one another at a rate higher than chance.

In the first case, one would have to conclude that Syndrome A is one of the manifestations of Disease B—both are manifestations of the same disease. If they were separate disorders, they would not be expected to co-occur at a high rate. Contrast this pattern with the second example in which Syndrome A co-exists with many different discrete and independent diseases. In this latter instance, one must conclude that Syndrome A constitutes a set of symptoms that are common (although not uniform) to all of several different disease processes. A fever is an example of Syndrome A, in this case. It is a common symptom in many different, unrelated diseases, but it is not a disease in its own right. Like a fever, Syndrome A, in this instance, could be used as a general marker of disease, but not as a specific marker of any single disease. Nor would it be an independent disease state.

The latter scenario parallels the way that depression is related to established syndromes. Depression in all of its forms overlaps greatly with a variety of other psychiatric disorders. Indeed, few psychiatric conditions do not co-occur with depression a high percentage of the time. Depression is a co-morbid condition among 60% of general psychiatric patients and among more than 40% of those with anxiety disorders (Regier et al., 1988; Regier et al., 1993). Major depression is even present in from 30% to 70% of patients who have a personality disorder (Farmer & Nelson-Gray, 1990), figures that rival the interrater reliability of the diagnostic interview.

Depression (and its diagnostic representations) also overlaps with many medical illnesses (Maser, Weise, & Gwirtsman, 1995; Schulberg & McClelland, 1987), and it is one of the most frequently occurring problems in medical practice (Schulberg & McClelland, 1987). One or another depression-related diagnosis has been observed to be present among 80%

of medical patients (Rodin & Voshart, 1986; Stevens, Merikangas, & Merikangas, 1995).

Viewing the high degree of overlap between depression and a wide array of other psychiatric and medical conditions, it is difficult to justify the conclusion that depression is an independent disorder. Instead, it seems to serve as a signal or "marker" of disease, much like a fever is a marker for infection. The high level of co-variation of depression with many other conditions suggests that it is a general index of dysfunction or disturbance rather than a separate disorder or disease. However, depression is not a perfectly specific disease marker, because independent diseases and psychiatric syndromes can occur in its absence.

The implications of the latter conclusions can be seen by exploring the pattern of interdependence that exists between depression and anxiety. In conventional diagnostic logic, these two phenomena are assumed to represent very different disorders. Disturbances of mood (depression) and anxiety are the basis for two major subcategories in the DSM, affective disorders and anxiety disorders, respectively. However, they may be so codependent that it is virtually impossible for clinicians to distinguish between them. Dobson (1985) concluded that the correlation between almost any test of depression and almost any test of anxiety was as high as or higher than the test–retest correlations of either of the separate measures. A considerable amount of research (e.g., Downing & Rickels, 1974; Gersh & Fowles, 1979) suggests that depression and anxiety virtually completely overlap in patient reports of subjective experience.

However, some authors (e.g., Coyne, 1994) have argued that one must consider specific signs, rather than just subjective states, in defining the condition of depression. They pointed out that anxiety disorders are characterized by such specific symptoms as compulsions, phobias, panic attacks, and the like, whereas major depression is characterized by the presence of vegetative signs that are best judged by a clinical observer. One might think that this specificity would allow clinicians to discriminate cleanly between syndromes of anxiety and syndromes of depression. However, after an extensive review of literature, Dobson (1985) concluded that clinicians cannot distinguish between anxiety and depressive syndromes any better than they can distinguish between the subjective states of anxiety and depression. He found that clinicians performed at levels only slightly better than chance when attempting to distinguish between individuals with formal anxiety disorders and major depression.

Dobson observed that at no specific point could a clinician reliably differentiate between the two conditions, using either "objective" or "subjective" symptoms. He concluded that the severity of dysphoria and distress, the primary qualities shared by both anxious and depressed patients, is distributed normally both in the general population and similarly within each diagnostic group. He argued that anxiety and depression should be regarded as different manifestations of the same condition. Obviously, the distinction between anxiety disorders and depressive disorders is clearer conceptually than it is empirically.

Conclusions

In summary, the ability to identify accurately the presence of depression, the ability to distinguish reliably among subcategories of depression, and the ability to differentiate between depression and other forms of psychopathology are all critical to concluding that depression is a distinguishable biochemical or disease entity. Even if one can conclude that depression is identifiable, making such distinctions is a cardinal criterion for determining whether it is a single disorder, a multitude of related conditions, or a normative, nonspecific response to stress that potentiates or reflects the presence of other conditions. Theoreticians have been equivocal in their support for either a discontinuous or continuous view of the relationship between pathological and nonpathological behavior. However, a good deal of the literature suggests that depression is better seen as a marker of stress, thus co-occurring with a variety of normal and unusual events (and illnesses), than as a discrete disorder or syndrome that is discontinuous with normal experience and independent from other behavioral disturbances.

The best evidence available indicates that (a) depression does not fit the pattern of interrelationships with other disorders that would justify its identification as an independent psychiatric syndrome, and (b) depression reflects a common negative emotional state that marks the presence of most stressors and diseases. That is, what the *DSM* developers have identified as major depression appears to be a generalized response to situational stressors as well as a marker for other symptom patterns that are more easily defined as independent syndromes.

Taken together, these findings suggest that subjective dysphoria is a nonspecific or general index of disturbance rather than a single specific disorder. Even those who assert the discontinuity of depression as a diagnostic entity accept the observation that most symptoms of depression are continuously and normally distributed in the population. Only a few symptoms, some of the vegetative signs, are demonstrably and qualitatively different from phenomena that exist in the experiences of most people. To scholars who assert the continuity of depression and its lack of diagnostic specificity, depressive conditions are thought to be best defined, not by the few qualitative characteristics that appear in the profiles of some depressed individuals, but by the pattern of their performance along two or more continua. What we think of as depressive disorders can perhaps better be represented by the intersection of continua reflecting severity of social impairment and intensity of dysphoria. As continua, these dimensions are not the exclusive property of disordered groups, and certainly are not unique to "major depression," but are present both in normal populations and among individuals presenting with many different psychological and medical problems. Any major life change or particular crisis might result in both elevated dysphoria and higher levels of social impairment. Extreme scores on these and perhaps related, co-existing dimensions could, thus, account for the appearance of both as an independent response to normal stress and as a co-morbid condition with other symptoms that rise to diagnosable levels.

Flett, Vredenburg, and Krames (1997) agreed with the foregoing formulation and concluded that the best description of depression is embodied in a continuity, multidimensional view that extends to social and interpersonal patterns of behavior, to immune system functioning, and to biological correlates of depressed mood. They concluded that there is "mounting evidence of continuity" (p. 411) in the experience and expression of depression. They generally agreed with Dobson (1985) in suggesting that two or more intersecting but continuously distributed dimensions, including dysphoria and severity of impairment, capture most of the variation of depressive presentations.

ASSUMPTION NO. 2: THERE ARE SPECIFIC TREATMENTS FOR DEPRESSION

Although being able to provide a discrete and specific treatment is a clear objective of diagnosis, the issues of whether depression is a discrete illness and whether there is a specific treatment for it are not inextricably linked. As long as depression or dysphoria can be reliably recognized or measured, a specific treatment may be developed. Thus, the effort to identify empirically supported treatments (e.g., Chambless et al., 1998) need not hinge on the assumption that depression is a discrete syndrome that is manifest in a common etiology, even though this is an explicit assumption underlying the way the list of treatments is constructed. If a given symptom quality, such as dysphoria or severity, can be measured, it is possible that a treatment can be created to ameliorate it. Fortunately, reliable measures of dysphoria are available, despite the lack of reliable syndromal categories.

Evidence of the specificity of a depression treatment could come from positive indications in two related kinds of comparisons: (a) A significant difference in effectiveness is noted when one compares a depression-focused treatment to a no-treatment or placebo treatment control; and (b) depression-focused treatments are more effective among depressed patients than treatments that are designed to alter anxiety or other nondepressive disorder. Both types of evidence must be present to support the presence of condition specific treatments.

An example of the first type of evidence might be a demonstration that a given treatment was more effective than no treatment at all in changing a behavior or feeling associated with depression. Taken alone, this type of evidence would not be persuasive of treatment specificity, however. An indication that one depression-focused treatment surpassed another in efficacy would be a stronger indication of treatment specificity, but it would still be a weak indication of treatment specificity. After all, some treatments may be generally more powerful than others, and evidence of this would not ensure that the effective treatment is specific for depression.

To confirm the presence of a depression-specific treatment, one must add another layer of evidence, one that reveals a differential effect. That is, the depression-specific treatment must work better than an anxiety-specific treatment among depressed patients, but the reverse should be in evidence among patients with anxiety disorders. In other words, if Treatment A works for depression but not for Anxiety, it would be a convincing demonstration of depression specificity. However, to make this case, it must be demonstrated (a) that Treatment A, a treatment that is designed to ameliorate depression, is more effective than Treatment B, a treatment that is designed to treat anxiety, a supposedly unrelated disorder, and (b) that the relative value of the two treatments is reversed when applied to patients who meet anxiety disorder criteria but not depressive disorder criteria. This cross-over effect would indicate specificity, in which each of the two treatments is more effective than the other when a problem is treated with the treatment designed for use with that condition (Snow, 1991).

Successful Treatments for Depression

A variety of different treatments are effective at reducing or ameliorating depressive symptoms. The evidence for initial benefits of treatment is quite consistent regardless of whether it derives from controlled (i.e., randomized) or naturalistic designs. Researchers who have conducted meta-analytic reviews of controlled studies (e.g., Nietzel, Russell, Hemmings, & Gretter, 1987; Robinson, Berman, & Neimeyer, 1990; Steinbrueck, Maxwell, & Howard, 1983; Wampold, 2001) and specific naturalistic investigations (e.g., Howard et al., 1996; Howard, Kopta, Krause, & Orlinsky, 1986; Kopta, Howard, Lowry, & Beutler, 1994; Seligman, 1995) have concluded that both a general and a depression-designed treatment reduces one's symptoms to subclinical levels during a relatively brief treatment course in about 70% of the cases.

The durability of effects of these treatments is more uncertain. For example, the evidence suggests few major differences in initial efficacies of pharmacotherapy and psychosocial approaches to treatment, but the effects of medication are somewhat faster and the effects of psychosocial treatments are more durable (e.g., Hollon et al., 1992; Hollon, Shelton, & Loosen, 1991).

Differential Effects of Treatments Across Different Disorders

Whereas depressive symptoms can be effectively treated in many ways, the evidence that these treatments are specific for depression is not strong. Consequently, the evidence that depression is a specific and independent disorder is difficult to produce. These conclusions are seen in two lines of research: (a) comparisons of two or more treatments on a homogeneous group of depressed patients and (b) comparisons of one or more extant treatments on two or more disorders.

When different treatments are compared within homogeneously defined groups of depressed patients, research convincingly indicates that all treatments produce similar results (e.g., Kirsch & Sapirstein, 1998; Linde et al., 1996; Smith, Glass, & Miller, 1980; Wampold, 2001). Within the domain of psychotherapeutic interventions, roughly similar magnitudes of effects are observed across a wide range of treatments and patient factors (e.g., Nietzel et al., 1987; Robinson et al., 1990; Steinbrueck et al., 1983; Wampold, 2001; Wampold et al., 1997). These studies have found very few differences that favor one type of psychotherapy over another, leading to the so-called *do-do bird verdict* (Luborsky, Singer, & Luborsky, 1975). These findings are all the more significant because they do not hold among samples of other disorders. Chambless and Ollendick (2001), for example, have concluded that whereas all treatments produce virtually identical results among depressed patients, treatments for the anxiety disorders produce consistent and clinically significant results.

The similarity of treatments also holds when we shift from a consideration of psychosocial to biological treatments. Thus, Greenberg, Bornstein, Greenberg, and Fisher (1992) have found that the effect size attributable to medication in treating depression is more dependent on how recently the medication was released for study than on its chemical structure. In one of the few direct meta-analytic comparisons of different antidepressant medications, Kirsch and Sapirstein (1998) inspected 19 studies that compared the effects of tricyclic, tetracyclic, and selective suppression reuptake inhibitors (SSRI) antidepressants. They concluded that all treatments produce moderate and comparable effect sizes. In a related finding, Linde et al. (1996) determined that the magnitude of effect attributable to St. John's wort, an herbal treatment that has been most frequently studied as a nonspecific or active placebo intervention for mild depressive symptoms, was similar to the more specific and ostensibly specific antidepressants.

Whether one looks at specific studies or at the results of meta-analyses, it is clear that the effects of all treatments for depression are variable, with some patients improving, some getting worse, and some staying the same (Howard, Krause, Saunders, & Kopta, 1997). All treatments are associated with substantial and positive effects among some patients and poor effects among others. One way of trying to understand such variability is to inspect the outcomes of treatments that combine interventions. If treatments for depression are specific, they should have effects that are unique or independent of one another. Thus, one might expect that combining treatments would have an additive effect, and early findings (e.g., Luborsky et al., 1975) suggested that this might be the case for treatments that combine psychotherapy and antidepressant medication.

However, careful analyses of the rigorous methods developed and applied in recent years have found little evidence for the advantages of combining pharmacotherapy and psychotherapy (Antonuccio, Thomas, & Danton, 1997; Nezu, Nezu, Trunzo, & McClure, 1998; Reynolds, Frank, Perel, Mazumdar, & Kupfer, 1994). Antonuccio, Danton, and DeNelsky (1995) have suggested that the major studies on which this popular conclusion is based are all relatively old and predated the use of structured and specific psychotherapies, and Wexler and Cicchetti (1992) found no advantage in combining treatment when outcomes were categorized into classes reflecting success, failure, and dropout rates. In a hypothetical cohort of 100 patients with major depression, Wexler and Cicchetti concluded that 29 would recover with pharmacotherapy alone, 47 would improve with psychotherapy alone, and 47 would improve if given both pharmacotherapy and psychotherapy. Adding treatments would not increase either the likelihood or the magnitude of benefits, strongly suggesting that both pharmacotherapy and psychotherapy are treating the same aspects of the condition.

As noted earlier, the most persuasive evidence of treatment specificity would come from a comparison of the effects of a depression-specific treatment with a specific treatment for another condition, using a sample that included both types of patients. One would expect, if there are specific effects, an advantage of the depression treatment among depressed patients and an advantage for the other treatment among the nondepressed patients. Unfortunately, no studies have directly studied the same treatment among two or more diagnostic groups. The closest approximation to methods that could address this issue was offered by Kirsch and Sapirstein (1998). They initiated a novel comparison of the effects of antidepressant and anxiolytic medication in the treatment of depression, following the logic that a depression-specific treatment would yield better effects for depression than for an anxiety disorder. From their meta-analysis, they concluded that antidepressants and anxiolytics produced effects that were virtually identical in magnitude among depressed patients. Stimulated by these findings, Beutler (1998) reinspected the results of other studies that included anxiety medications and confirmed this conclusion.

There are no parallel studies on the psychotherapeutic front, but it is noteworthy that the cognitive and interpersonal treatments that have been developed specifically for treating depression have been widely transferred to work with many other conditions, including anxiety disorders, eating disorders, and chemical abuse and dependence. To check the comparability of these treatments across disorders, we (Malik, Alimohamed, Holaway, & Beutler, 2000) profiled four different models and formats of cognitive therapy that had been applied to different patient groups (e.g., depression, alcohol dependence), comparing these with other treatments for these disorders. The results confirmed that the profiles of various cognitive therapies were similar in structure and form, regardless of either their format (group, individual, couple) or the population to which they were applied (depressed, anxious, chemical abuse). However, they were not identical. Cognitive therapy was variable in practice, but it was uncertain if this was a function of setting, patient sample, or the format of treatment. If there was a specific psychotherapeutic treatment for depression, we would expect that all effective treatments for depression, regardless of the guiding theoretical model, would be similar and that all would be different from those that are effective with patients with different disorders. However, this was not the case in our analysis. The process profiles of effective, noncognitive, treatments for depression did not resemble the profiles of the four cognitive therapies. These findings suggest that there was more similarity across disorders than between disorders in the application of a given treatment model—in this case, cognitive therapy.

Conclusions

Although there is evidence that different treatments are effective in altering depressive symptoms, there is little evidence that specific treatments exist for a syndrome of major depression. The preponderance of evidence suggests that most psychological treatments yield similar effects among depressed patients, but not among those with other diagnostic conditions, and that pharmacological and psychological interventions are equally effective across diagnostic groups of similar severity. Still a third finding indicates that treatments for depression work about as well for anxiety disorders as for depression and vice versa. Thus, we must conclude that the evidence does not support the proposition that currently available treatments are specific to depression.

That is not to say that differential effects do not occur. Ample documentation indicates that patient variables do moderate the effects of different treatment models and different classes of intervention (see Beutler, Clarkin, & Bongar, 2000; Beutler, Goodrich, Fisher, & Williams, 1999; Beutler, Moleiro, & Malik, 2000). Our research group has found more than 300 studies in which some patient variable was significantly and successfully used as a predictor of the differential effects of one or another treatment type (Beutler, Clarkin, & Bongar, 2000). However, similar patterns of interaction seem to occur among depressed patients as among those with addictive disorders and anxiety. Moreover, when differences do occur within depressed samples, the predictive variables are seldom diagnostic in nature. Diagnostic criteria are not among the most useful patient indicators of differential response. Instead, the variables that predict differential response best are those that cut across diagnostic conditions (Beutler, Clarkin, & Bongar, 2000).

CROSS-CUTTING GUIDELINES TO TREATING THE DEPRESSED PATIENT

Medical diagnoses have traditionally been used to provide information about the etiology, the course or prognosis, and the specific treatment of the condition (Beutler, 1989). Accordingly, if the differential diagnosis of granular nephritis and ulcers did not lead to different predictions of course, different assumptions about cause, or different treatment decisions, the diagnoses would be of limited or questionable use. The research reviewed here casts strong doubt on the specificity of the diagnosis of major depression, suggesting that it has a nonspecific etiology, an irregular course, and no specific treatment. If this is true of the most frequently diagnosed and most problematic of the mental health disorders, by extension one must be concerned about the very nature of the assumptions underlying the DSM itself.

In 1973, Beutler argued that the absence of diagnostic specificity in predicting course, identifying etiology, or suggesting treatments called for a new or supplemental diagnostic system on the basis of treatment selection. This issue is worthy of additional consideration, and contemporary research points both to some historical rationale and some preliminary dimensions on which a treatment-based diagnostic system could be built.

Historical Foundations to Treatment-Relevant Diagnosis

Until the mid-1970s, the usual practice in psychotherapy research was to study consecutively admitted patients, randomly assigning them to treatments that were defined by therapist-selected preferences. The Treatment of Depression Collaborative Research Program (Elkin, 1994) initiated the application of randomized trials, borrowed by psychotherapy from psychopharmacological research. This method relied on identifying individuals on the basis of their compliance with diagnostic criteria (usually major depression) and randomly assigning them to treatments that were structured and run by manuals. The selection of diagnostically homogeneous groups for research studies is based on two premises: (a) that this reduces important, patient contributors to the wide variability of outcomes that characterize response to treatments and (b) that standardized (manualized) treatments enhance the probability of treatment success.

On its face, the decision to study homogenous groups of patients and clearly identified treatments has clear advantages from a methodological standpoint, and it seemed like a reasonable way to overcome the problems of extreme variability of response. However, the approach is defensible only if the dimensions on which patients are homogenized are relevant to the treatments that are prescribed in a manual.

In terms of method used, in order to reduce outcome variance related to patient factors, a grouping (i.e., diagnostic) variable must be one that is associated with a treatment that is specific to the selected group and that allows one to test a given treatment against those that have a different effect on this group or on a contrasting group. That is, the grouping variable must be one that meaningfully contributes to the non–treatment-related patient variance among outcomes, and it must also be selectively responsive to treatments. However, we have absolutely no evidence that depression meets any of these qualifications.

More specifically, the decision to use the *DSM* criteria was implemented as one way of addressing Kiesler's (1966) concern about the patient uniformity myth. Kiesler, reflecting on the practice of studying in sequence all patients who were admitted to treatment, argued that this introduced very wide variability among patients and argued against the assumption implicit in such methods, that patients–participants in psychotherapy research were interchangeable. He asserted that the level of variability of patient factors served as noise that prevented treatment effects from emerging. The myth of patient uniformity was founded on the belief that all patients would respond in similar ways to a given treatment. This myth is a concern only if the variability among patients is correlated with outcomes, but once again, observation confirms that this is not the case. Outcome is not highly correlated with the specific *DSM* diagnosis when chronicity and demographic factors are controlled.

As we have argued, there is little evidence that the variability among outcomes has been affected by the decision to group patients by their *DSM* diagnosis. The distribution of improvement, deterioration, and failure to change rates continues to be about the same in one treatment as it is in another, accounting for why the dodo bird verdict continues to be so prevalent (Howard, Krause, & Lyons, 1993; Wampold, 2001). Indeed, we have no evidence that treatment effects would be any less variable among patients with major depression than they would be if we included those with generalized anxiety, situational disturbances, or chemical abuse disorders, nor is there evidence that they are less variable than they were prior to Kiesler's call to reduce patient variability.

A dispassionate observer may accuse contemporary researchers of having substituted the patient uniformity myth for a diagnostic homogeneity myth, believing that patients with the same diagnosis are interchangeable. That observer may wonder why we had not originally selected a more useful variable on which to select homogenous samples for study. Certainly, it seems plausible that a more rational and meaningful variable than diagnosis could have been defined and selected from among the many patient factors that do correlate with outcome (e.g., severity, distress, interpersonal style; Beutler, 1991).

Similar concerns exist for the assumption that grouping patients facilitates the study of homogeneous and specific treatments, allowing us to more clearly observe the effects of treatments that are designed to influence patients in the targeted group. As we have observed in previous sections of this chapter, there is little evidence that treatments designed for depression, either pharmacological or psychological, have effects that are unique to depressed groups. Treatments for depression, such as cognitive therapy and interpersonal psychotherapy, have been applied with little modification to work with many conditions, including eating disorders, anxiety disorders, and chemical abuse (Beutler, Clarkin, & Bongar, 2000).

Furthermore, some researchers (see Strupp & Anderson, 1997; Beutler, 1998; Caspar, in press) have cogently argued that the efforts to develop uniform treatments for depression, based on patient diagnostic status, have resulted in overly rigid, stilted treatments that do not adapt well to the relevant ways in which patients differ from one another.

If depression cannot be reliably identified as a syndrome, and if its identification does not meaningfully reduce variability of patient response to treatment, and if the treatments that are designed to treat it work equally well for anxiety and other conditions, why not select a different basis for diagnosis and, thereby, for defining and stratifying research groups? Imagine what would happen if diagnostic decisions actually did direct us to qualities of treatment that improved outcomes. Although one might have to forgo the reliance on diagnosis to tell us something about etiology or prognosis, a treatment focused diagnosis might at least encourage and advance treatment research. By bifurcating research samples on a treatment-related variable and crossing the identified patient variable with a treatment factor, studies would yield much more information than is currently possible with a diagnostic system that is so poorly related to treatment effects. Moreover, we would be positioned to develop a set of markers that would direct the selection of a specific treatment.

We (Beutler, Clarkin, & Bongar, 2000) have taken these points seriously and have embarked on an endeavor to find dimensions that have more relevance than categorical definitions of either depression or treatment. We wanted to look beyond conventional diagnostic groupings of patients and treatments (e.g., cognitive, interpersonal, pharmacological), favoring instead a classification system that identified common families of interventions and dimensional perspectives of people and their problems.

Using depressive symptoms as a dependent variable, we searched the literature on depression, chemical abuse, anxiety disorders, and the like for variables that (a) predicted outcome across treatment types, (b) could be reliably identified from traitlike measures, and (c) may serve as moderators of different classes or families of interventions. Several extensive literature reviews resulted in the reliable identification of eight dimensions that meet these criteria and that could form the initial basis for a treatment-relevant diagnostic system: Functional Impairment, Complexity, Chronicity, Distress, Social Support, Coping Style, Readiness for Change, and Resistance Level (Beutler et al., 1999).

An impressive number of studies have addressed one or another of these variables as differential predictors of improvement or of differential treatment indicators. Beutler, Clarkin, and Bongar (2000) identified over 300 studies that provided evidence of differential treatment effects. Beutler, Harwood, Alimohamed, and Malik (in press) found that available studies strongly supported the hypotheses that patient impairment level and coping styles could be used to differentially select various classes of interventions. Beutler, Moleiro, and Talebi (in press) found similarly strong evidence in extant research that patient resistance traits were strongly related to the effectiveness of directive, nondirective, and self-directed interventions. Several comparisons of different treatment models (e.g., Beutler, Engle, et al., 1991; Beutler, Mohr, et al., 1991; Karno, Beutler, & Harwood, in press) have confirmed these conclusions, and a prospective test of therapist–patient matching factors has suggested that as much as 90% of the outcome variance may be predicted by these differential indicators of treatment (Beutler, Moleiro, & Malik, 2000).

Direct tests of the relative validity of these patient dimensions for identifying and predicting the contributions of patient, treatment, relationship, and Patient × Therapy Fit factors resulted in the identification of an initial list of 18 treatment principles by Beutler, Clarkin, and Bongar (2000). For clarity, they divided these principles into two classes: basic principles that guided treatment but did not require a direct inspection of the inner workings of the treatment itself, and optimal principles that required a direct understanding of the inner processes of the treatment.

The final list of principles are examples of how these patient dimensions can be integrated with the qualities of treatment to predict outcome. Outcome predictions, in turn, are derived from understanding the principles that guide different treatment to be more or less effective. Models of behavior that are based on principles and dimensions, and that include qualities of both patients and treatments, clearly depart from the categorical thinking that is usually applied to defining patient qualities (i.e., diagnoses) and to treatments (e.g., cognitive therapy, interpersonal psychotherapy) that fit them. That is, our list of working principles form the basis of treatment guidelines that cut across specific symptoms and specific models of treatment. The guiding principles from which a treatment-based diagnosis could follow are described in the section that follows.

Basic Guidelines

1. The likelihood of improvement (prognosis) is a positive function of social support level and a negative function of functional impairment.
2. Prognosis is attenuated by patient complexity–chronicity and by an absence of patient distress.
3. Psychoactive medication has its best effects on those patients with high functional impairment and high complexity–chronicity.

The first two principles relate to the estimation of a patient's likelihood of change (prognosis) and the identification of social support, functional impairment, and chronicity as factors that one should consider when evaluating the probable benefit of treatment. The third principle relates to the conditions under which psychoactive medication should be considered. Note, however, that none of these principles are differential in that they do not predict the effects of alternative treatments.

4. The likelihood and magnitude of improvement is increased among patients with complexity–chronic problems by the application of multiperson therapy.
5. Benefit corresponds with treatment intensity among functionally impaired patients.

These two principles are truly principles of differential treatment. They define conditions that should lead one to consider some form of multiperson therapy, such as group or marital–family treatment. Principle No. 5 identifies an indicator for differentially assigning different levels of care. Treatment intensity may be adjusted by increasing the frequency, reducing the spacing, changing the setting, or adding modalities.

6. Risk is reduced by a careful assessment of risk situations in the course of reviewing the patient's symptoms and history.
7. Risk is reduced and patient compliance is increased when the treatment includes family intervention.
8. Risk is reduced and retention is increased if the patient is realistically informed about the probable length and effectiveness of the treatment and has a clear understanding of the roles and activities that are expected of him or her during the course of treatment.

9. Risk is reduced if the clinician routinely questions patients about suicidal feelings, intent, and plans.
10. Ethical and legal principles suggest that documentation and consultation are advisable.

These principles were not defined by empirical test in our analyses. They were added as cautionary statements to guide clinicians in working with very dangerous and unstable patients. Unlike the other principles defined here, the data supporting these five principles were not obtained through a direct assessment of patient benefit. They reflect the results of an assessment of clinician consensus about the nature of good practices to use when treating individuals who pose significant risks of harm to themselves or others.

Optimal Guidelines

1. Therapeutic change is greatest when the therapist is skillful and inspires trust, acceptance, acknowledgment, and collaboration and conveys respect for the patient, within an environment that supports risk and provides maximal safety.

This principle defines what aspects of the beneficial therapeutic relationship depends on therapist activity. Central to this relationship is the provision of a safe environment.

2. Therapeutic change is most likely when the patient is exposed to the objects or targets of behavioral and emotional avoidance.

This principle reflects the overarching significance of exposing patients to the objects of their irrational fears in the course of treatment. It emerged in our analysis as a fundamental principle that seemed to underlie a wide variety of different therapeutic approaches and techniques.

3. Therapeutic change is greatest when the relative balance of interventions either favors the use of skill building and symptom removal procedures among externalizing patients or favors the use of insight and relationship-focused procedures among internalizing patients.

This principle guides the use of insight and relationship oriented interventions relative to symptom removal and skill building procedures. This principle is not designed to indicate whether a behavioral or psychodynamic therapy should be attempted, but to suggest a balancing of procedures. We observed that all models of intervention include the use of some techniques that are applied to facilitate self-understanding and insight and others that are designed or applied in order to alter symptoms, skills, and behaviors. This principle guides the clinician to use these techniques with a different level of balance, depending on the relative level of internalizing and externalizing coping style traits.

4. Therapeutic change is most likely if the initial focus of change efforts is to alter disruptive symptoms.

This principle guides the initial focus in all treatments. Our findings indicated that early behavioral change was important to facilitating all treatments. Different models of treatment and different therapists, however, may have different ways of focusing on these symptoms and facilitating change. The principle leaves the means and techniques to be used, to the therapist.

5. Therapeutic change is most likely when the therapeutic procedures do not evoke therapeutic resistance.
6. Therapeutic change is greatest when the directiveness of the intervention is either inversely correspondent with the patient's current level of resistance or authoritatively prescribes a continuation of the symptomatic behavior.

These two principles guide the clinician in the use of directed versus evocative interventions. It makes the relative use of these procedures dependent on the patient's level of traitlike resistance. Again, the principle is designed to suggest not one or another form of therapy, but rather the use of clinician discretion to set up a balance of interventions that corresponds with and is responsive to the patient's style of coping with stress.

7. The likelihood of therapeutic change is greatest when the patient's level of emotional stress is moderate, neither excessively high nor excessively low.
8. Therapeutic change is greatest when a patient is stimulated to emotional arousal in a safe environment until problematic responses diminish or disappear.

The final two principles guide the clinician in the relative use of procedures that confront, thereby raising distress levels, and those that support or reduce arousal and distress. These principles suggest that the effective clinician manages patient distress by variously applying support and confrontation.

SUMMARY

For a treatment-based diagnostic system, such as the one we propose, to work, it would be imperative to ensure that the principles guiding the fit of treatment and patient do not favor one treatment model over another.

The principles guiding this system must be truly cross-cutting and empirically derived.

What are the implications of abandoning the viewpoint that conditions like major depression are independent and discrete syndromes? One implication is that we would be less inclined to rely on a participant's fit with nomothetic, diagnostic criteria in treatment research trials, at least as applied to depression. Would we lose anything by doing this? We think not, and we may have a great deal to gain, especially as applied to the development of treatment guidelines. Such a model could supplement or supplant the contemporary diagnostic system that so inaccurately predicts treatment course, patient etiology, or prognosis.

Another implication of the type of diagnostic system that we have sketched here is that it would require the field to adopt a new perspective of diagnosis, seeing the diagnosis as something that occurs within a system rather than as something that exists within an individual. As such, problems would be clearly linked to the requirement that the system and treatment environments be inspected to find qualities that effectively fit patient qualities. Happily, we think, attention would be drawn to a representation of environments and resources rather than to pathologies alone.

REFERENCES

American Psychiatric Association. (1993). Practice guidelines for major depressive disorder in adults. *American Journal of Psychiatry, 150*(Suppl. 4), 1–26.

American Psychiatric Association. (1994). *Diagnostic and statistical manual of mental disorders* (4th ed.). Washington, DC: Author.

American Psychiatric Association. (2000). *Diagnostic and statistical manual of mental disorders* (4th ed., Text Revision). Washington, DC: Author

American Psychiatric Association Steering Committee on Practice Guidelines. (2000). *Practice guidelines for the treatment of psychiatric disorders*. Washington, DC: American Psychiatric Association.

Antonuccio, D. O., Danton, W. G., & DeNelsky, G. Y. (1995). Psychotherapy versus medication for depression: Challenging the conventional wisdom with data. *Professional Psychology: Research and Practice, 26*, 574–585.

Antonuccio, D. O., Thomas, M., & Danton, W. G. (1997). A cost-effectiveness analysis of cognitive behavior therapy and fluoxetine (Prozac) in the treatment of depression. *Behavior Therapy, 28*, 187–210.

Barlow, D. H. (1994). Psychological interventions in the era of managed competition. *Clinical Psychology: Science and Practice, 1*, 109–122.

Beutler, L. E. (1973). The therapy dyad: Yet another look at diagnostic assessment. *Journal of Personality Assessment, 37*, 393–398.

Beutler, L. E. (1989). Differential treatment selection: The role of diagnosis in psychotherapy. *Psychotherapy, 26*, 271–281.

Beutler, L. E. (1991). Have all won and must all have prizes? Revisiting Luborsky et. al.'s verdict. *Journal of Consulting and Clinical Psychology, 59,* 226–232.

Beutler, L. E. (1998). Prozac and placebo: There's a pony in there somewhere. *Treatment and Prevention, 1*(1). Available at http://journals.apa.org/prevention/volume 1/pre 0010001c.html. (Article 0004c)

Beutler, L. E., Clarkin, J. F., & Bongar, B. (2000). *Guidelines for the systematic treatment of the depressed patient.* New York: Oxford University Press.

Beutler, L. E., Engle, D., Mohr, D., Daldrup, R. J., Bergan, J., Meredith, K., & Merry, W. (1991). Predictors of differential and self-directed psychotherapeutic procedures. *Journal of Consulting and Clinical Psychology, 59,* 333–340.

Beutler, L. E., Goodrich, G., Fisher, D., & Williams, O. B. (1999). Use of psychological tests/instruments for treatment planning. In M. E. Maruish (Ed.), *The use of psychological tests for treatment planning and outcome assessment* (2nd ed., pp. 81–113). Hillsdale, NJ: Erlbaum.

Beutler, L. E., Harwood, T. M., Alimohamed, S., & Malik, M. (in press). Functional impairment and coping style: Patient moderators of therapeutic relationships. In J. Norcross (Ed.), *Psychotherapy relationships that work: Therapists' relational contributors to effective psychotherapy.* New York: Oxford University Press.

Beutler, L. E., Mohr, D. C., Grawe, K., Engle, D., & MacDonald, R. (1991). Looking for differential effects: Cross-cultural predictors of differential psychotherapy efficacy. *Journal of Psychotherapy Integration, 1,* 121–142.

Beutler, L. E., Moleiro, C., & Malik, M. (2000, June). *The UC Santa Barbara Study of fitting therapy to patients: First results.* Paper presented at the annual meeting of the Society for Psychotherapy Research (international), Chicago, IL.

Beutler, L. E., Moleiro, C., & Talebi, H. (in press). Customizing psychotherapy to patient resistance. In J. Norcross (Ed.), *Psychotherapy relationships that work: Therapists' relational contributors to effective psychotherapy.* New York: Oxford University Press.

Carson, R. C. (1997). Costly compromises: A critique of the diagnostic and statistical manual of mental disorders. In S. Fisher & R. P. Greenberg (Eds.), *From placebo to panacea: Putting psychiatric drugs to the test* (pp. 98–112). New York: Wiley.

Caspar, F. (in press). Introduction to the issue of therapist inner processes and their training. In F. Caspar (Ed.), *The inner processes of psychotherapists: Innovations in clinical training.* New York: Oxford University Press.

Chambless, D. L., Baker, M. J., Baucom, D. H., Beutler, L. E., Calhoun, K. S., Crits-Christoph, P., Daiuto, A., DeRubeis, R., Detweiler, J., Haaga, D. A. F., Johnson, S. B., McCurry, S., Mueser, K. T., Pope, K. S., Sanderson, W. C., Shoham, V., Stickle, T., Williams, D. A., & Woody, S. R. (1998). Update on empirically validated therapies, II. *The Clinical Psychologist, 51,* 3–16.

Chambless, D. L., & Ollendick, T. H. (2001). Empirically supported psychological interventions: Controversies and evidence. *Annual Review of Psychology, 52,* 685–716.

Coyne, J. C. (1994). Self-reported distress: Analog or ersatz depression? *Psychological Bulletin, 116*, 29–45.

Coyne, J. C. (in press). Mood disorders. In Kazdin (Ed.), *Encyclopedia of psychology.* Washington, DC: Oxford University/American Psychological Association.

Depression Guideline Panel. (1993). *Depression in primary care: Vol. 2. Treatment of major depression* (Clinical Practice Guideline, No. 5, Agency for Health Care Policy and Research Publication No. 93–0551). Rockville, MD: U.S. Department of Health and Human Services, Public Health Service, Agency for Health Care Policy and Research.

Dobson, K. S. (1985). The relationship between anxiety and depression. *Clinical Psychology Review, 5*, 307–324.

Downing, R. W., & Rickels, K. (1974). Mixed anxiety depression: Fact or myth? *Archives of General Psychiatry, 30*, 312–317.

Elkin, I. (1994). The NIMH treatment of depression collaborative research program: Where we began and where we are. In A. E. Bergin & S. Garfield (Eds.), *Handbook of psychotherapy and behavior change* (4th ed., pp. 114–139). New York: Wiley.

Farmer, R., & Nelson-Gray, R. O. (1990). Personality disorders and depression: Hypothetical relations, empirical findings, and methodological considerations. *Clinical Psychology Review, 10*, 453–476.

Flett, G. L., Vredenburg, K., & Krames, L. (1997). The continuity of depression in clinical and nonclinical samples. *Psychological Bulletin, 121*, 395–416.

Gersh, F. S., & Fowles, D. C. (1979). Neurotic depression: The concept of anxious depression. In R. A. Depue (Ed.), *The psychobiology of the depressive disorders* (pp. 81–104). New York: Academic Press.

Greenberg, R. P., Bornstein, R. F., Greenberg, M. D., & Fisher, S. (1992). A meta-analysis of antidepressant outcome under "blinder" conditions. *Journal of Consulting and Clinical Psychology, 60*, 664–669.

Hollon, S. D. (1996). The efficacy and effectiveness of psychotherapy relative to medications. *American Psychologist, 51*, 1025–1030.

Hollon, S. D., DeRubeis, R. J., Evans, M. D., Wiemer, M. J., Garvey, M. J., Grove, W. M., & Tuason, V. B. (1992). Cognitive therapy and pharmacotherapy for depression: Singly and in combination. *Archives of General Psychiatry, 49*, 774–781.

Hollon, S. D., Shelton, R. C., & Loosen, P. T. (1991). Cognitive therapy and pharmacotherapy for depression. *Journal of Consulting and Clinical Psychology, 59*, 88–99.

Howard, K. I., Cornille, T. A., Lyons, J. S., Vessey, J. T., Lueger, R. J., & Saunders, S. M. (1996). Patterns of mental health service utilization. *Archives of General Psychiatry, 53*, 696–703.

Howard, K. I., Kopta, S. M., Krause, M. S., & Orlinsky, D. E. (1986). The dose–effect relationship in psychotherapy. *American Psychologist, 41*, 159–164.

Howard, K. I., Krause, M. S., & Lyons, J. (1993). When clinical trials fail: A guide for disaggregation. In L. S. Onken & J. D. Blaine (Eds.), *Behavioral treatments* for *drug abuse and dependence* (National Institute of Drug Abuse Research Monograph No. 137, pp. 291–302). Washington, DC: National Institute of Drug Abuse.

Howard, K. I., Krause, M. S., Saunders, S. M., & Kopta, S. M. (1997). Trials and tribulations in the meta-analysis of treatment differences: Comment on Wampold et al. (1997). *Psychological Bulletin, 122,* 221–225.

Karno, M., Beutler, L. E., & Harwood, T. M. (in press). Interactions between psychotherapy process and patient attributes that predict alcohol treatment effectiveness: A preliminary report. *Addictive Behaviors.*

Kessler, R. C., McGonagle, K. A., Zhao, S., Nelson, C. B., Hughes, M., Eshleman, S., Wittchen, H., & Kendler, K. S. (1994). Lifetime and 12-month prevalence of *DSM–III–R* psychiatric disorders in the US: Results from the National Comorbidity Survey. *Archives of General Psychiatry, 51,* 8–19.

Kiesler, D. J. (1966). Some myths of psychotherapy research and the search for a paradigm. *Psychological Bulletin, 65,* 110–136.

Kirsch, I., & Sapirstein, G. (1998). Listening to Prozac by hearing placebo: A meta-analysis of antidepressant medications. *Treatment and Prevention, 1*(1). Available at http://journals.apa.org/prevention/volume 1/pre 0010001c.html. (Article 0001c)

Klerman, G. L., Weissman, M. M., Rounsaville, B. J., & Chevron, E. S. (1984). *Interpersonal psychotherapy of depression.* New York: Basic Books.

Kopta, S. M., Howard, K. I., Lowry, J. L., & Beutler, L. E. (1994). Patterns of symptomatic recovery in time-unlimited psychotherapy. *Journal of Consulting and Clinical Psychology, 62,* 1009–1016.

Linde, K., Ramirez, G., Mulrow, C. D., Pauls, A., Weidenhammer, W., & Melchart, D. (1996). St. John's wort for depression: An overview and meta-analysis of randomised clinical trials. *British Medical Journal, 313,* 253–258.

Luborsky, L., Singer, B., & Luborsky, L. (1975). Comparative studies of psychotherapies. *Archives of General Psychiatry, 32,* 995–1008.

Malik, M., Alimohamed, S., Holaway, R., & Beutler, L. E. (2000, June). *Are all cognitive therapies alike? Validation of the TPRS.* Paper presented at the annual meeting of the Society for Psychotherapy Research, Chicago.

Maser, J. D., Weise, R., & Gwirtsman, H. (1995). Depression and its boundaries with selected Axis I disorders. In E. E. Beckham & W. R. Leber (Eds.), *Handbook of depression* (2nd ed., pp. 86–106). New York: Guilford Press.

Medicare proposal could be dangerous. (1999, November 19). *Psychiatric News,* p. 4.

Nezu, A. M., Nezu, C. M., Trunzo, J. J., & McClure, K. S. (1998). Treatment maintenance for unipolar depression: Relevant issues, literature review, and recommendations for research and clinical practice. *Clinical Psychology; Science and Practice, 5,* 496–512.

Nietzel, M. T., Russell, R. L., Hemmings, K. A., & Gretter, M. L. (1987). Clinical significance of psychotherapy for unipolar depression: A meta-analytic approach to social comparison. *Journal of Consulting and Clinical Psychology, 55,* 156–161.

Ormel, J., Koeter, M. W., van den Brink, W., & van de Willige, G. (1991). Recognition, management and course of anxiety and depression in general practice. *Archives of General Psychiatry, 48,* 700–706.

Quill, T. E. (1985). Somatization disorder: One of medicine's blind spots. *Journal of the American Medical Association, 254,* 3075–3079.

Regier, D. A., Boyd, J. H., Burke, J. D., Jr., Rae, D. S., Myers, J. K., Kramer, M., Robins, L. N., George, L. K., Karno, M., & Locke, B. Z. (1988). One-month prevalence of mental disorders in the United States based on five Epidemiologic Catchment Area sites. *Archives of General Psychiatry, 45,* 977–986.

Regier, D. A., Myers, J. K., Kramer, M., Robins, L. N., Blazer, D. G., Hough, R. L., Eaton, W. W., & Locke, B. Z. (1984). The NIMH Epidemiologic Catchment Area program. *Archives of General Psychiatry, 41,* 934–941.

Regier, D. A., Narrow, W. E., Rae, D. S., Manderscheid, R. W., Locke, B. Z., & Goodwin, F. (1993). The de facto US mental and addictive disorders service system: Epidemiologic Catchment Area prospective 1-year prevalence rates of disorders and services. *Archives of General Psychiatry, 50,* 85–94.

Reynolds, C. F., Frank, E., Perel, J. M., Mazumdar, S., & Kupfer, D. J. (1994). Maintenance therapies for late-life recurrent depression. *International Psychogeriatrics, 7* supp., 27–39.

Robinson, L. A., Berman, J. S., & Neimeyer, R. A. (1990). Psychotherapy for the treatment of depression: A comprehensive review of controlled outcome research. *Psychological Bulletin, 108,* 30–49.

Rodin, G., & Voshart, K. (1986). Depression in the medically ill: An overview. *American Journal of Psychiatry, 143,* 696–705.

Schulberg, H. C., & McClelland, M. (1987). Depression and physical illness: The prevalence, causation, and diagnosis of comorbidity. *Clinical Psychology Review, 7,* 145–167.

Seligman, M. E. P. (1995). The effectiveness of psychotherapy: The Consumer Reports study. *American Psychologist, 50,* 965–974.

Smith, M. L., Glass, G. V., & Miller, T. I. (1980). *The benefits of psychotherapy.* Baltimore: Johns Hopkins University Press.

Snow, R. E. (1991). Aptitude–treatment interaction as a framework for research on individual differences in psychotherapy. *Journal of Consulting and Clinical Psychology, 59,* 205–216.

Steinbrueck, S. M., Maxwell, S. E., & Howard, G. S. (1983). A meta-analysis of psychotherapy and drug therapy in the treatment of unipolar depression with adults. *Journal of Consulting and Clinical Psychology, 51,* 856–862.

Stevens, D. E., Merikangas, K. R., & Merikangas, J. R. (1995). Comorbidity of depression and other medical conditions. In E. E. Beckham & W. R. Leber (Eds.), *Handbook of depression* (2nd ed., pp. 147–199). New York: Guilford Press.

Strupp, H. H., & Anderson, T. (1997). On the limitations of therapy manuals. *Clinical Psychology: Science and Practice, 4,* 76–82.

Study finds adequacy of care for mental illness perceived as low. (1996, October 7). *Psychiatric News,* p. 1, 6.

Valenstein, E. S. (1998). *Blaming the brain.* New York: Free Press.

Wampold, B. E. (2001). *The great psychotherapy debate: Models, methods, and findings.* Hillsdale, NJ: Erlbaum.

Wampold, B. E., Mondin, G. W., Moody, M., Stich, F., Benson, K., & Ahn, H. (1997). A meta-analysis of outcome studies comparing bona fide psychotherapies: Empirically, "All must have prizes." *Psychological Bulletin, 122,* 203–215.

Wells, K. B., & Sturm, R. (1996). Informing the policy process: From efficacy to effectiveness data on pharmacotherapy. *Journal of Consulting and Clinical Psychology, 64,* 638–645.

Wexler, B. E., & Cicchetti, D. V. (1992). The outpatient treatment of depression: Implications of outcome research for clinical practice. *The Journal of Nervous and Mental Disease, 180,* 279–286.

Widiger, T. A. (1997). Mental disorders as discrete clinical conditions: Dimensional versus categorical classification. In S. M. Turner & M. Hersen (Eds.), *Adult psychopathology and diagnosis* (3rd ed., pp. 3–23). New York: Wiley.

Winokur, G., & Clayton, P. J. (1967). Family history studies: II. Sex differences and alcoholism in primary affective illness. *British Journal of Psychiatry, 113,* 973–979.

11

TO HONOR KRAEPELIN ... : FROM SYMPTOMS TO PATHOLOGY IN THE DIAGNOSIS OF MENTAL ILLNESS

JOHN F. KIHLSTROM

I consider hospitals only as the entrance to scientific medicine: they are the first field of observation which a physician enters; but the true sanctuary of medical science is a laboratory; only there can he see explanations of life in the normal and pathological states by means of experimental analysis.

Claude Bernard (1865/1957, p. 146)

Less than two years after the publication of the 4th edition of the *Diagnostic and Statistical Manual of Mental Disorders* (*DSM–IV*; American Psychiatric Association, 1994), we were already gearing up for the 5th edition (e.g., Blashfield & Fuller, 1996). In trying to predict what *DSM–V* will look like, perhaps the only sure bet is that it will be longer, as the categories of mental illness proliferate beyond schizophrenia and manic–depressive illness, phobia, and obsessive–compulsive disorder to sibling relational problem (*DSM–IV* code V61.8) and nicotine-related disorder not otherwise specified (code 292.9). Those who enjoyed past controversies over the status of homosexuality, masochistic personality disorder, post-traumatic stress disorder, and periluteal phase dysphoric disorder can look forward to many similar debates in the not-too-distant future (Caplan, 1995; Kutchins & Kirk, 1997).

The point of view presented in this chapter is based in part on research supported by National Institute of Mental Health Grant #MH-35856. I thank Lucy Canter Kihlstrom and subscribers to the Society for a Science of Clinical Psychology listserv for the helpful discussions and challenges they provided during the writing of this chapter.

279

However, the really interesting debate will be not whether one or another illness should be included or excluded from the nomenclature. Rather, it will be over how the nosology itself might change—that is, over the way we construe diagnosis and indeed mental illness as a whole. For psychologists, much of this more interesting debate is stimulated by the belief that the current diagnostic system is based on the medical model of psychopathology, which is viewed as a bad thing. Although it is true that the current diagnostic practice is based on the medical model, it is not necessarily true that this is a bad thing. Attitudes to the contrary are predicated on a misconception of the medical model—a misconception that is widely shared by psychologists and psychiatrists alike.

MEDICAL MODEL OF PSYCHOPATHOLOGY

The first thing that has to be understood is that, like it or not, the medical model pervades our discourse about mental illness. Consider the following:

- We speak of *symptoms* of mental illness, publicly observable manifestations of psychological abnormality; *syndromes* of mental illness, clusters of symptoms that tend to occur together; and mental *diseases*, syndromes with a known pathology.
- We speak of the *etiology*, *course*, and *prognosis* of mental disease.
- There is *diagnosis*, an activity in which a clinician assigns a classificatory label to a patient on the basis of his or her presenting symptoms.
- *Mental illness* is included in the *International Classification of Diseases* published by the World Health Organization (e.g., the 10th edition, published in 1990) of the United Nations.
- We refer to people as *mental patients* if they have mental illness, we establish *mental hospitals* to treat such illnesses (with techniques that include *therapy* and *rehabilitation*), and we teach *mental hygiene* in the hope of preventing it.

These kinds of analogies between physical and mental illness form the backbone of the medical model of psychopathology. However, there are considerable misunderstandings abroad about the nature of the medical model—including misunderstandings perpetrated by many writers of introductory textbooks in psychology. For example, the 4th edition of Gleitman's *Psychology* (1995), the book that I have used most often in teaching introductory psychology, described the medical model as follows:

Some authors endorse the medical model, a particular version of the pathology model [which assumes that symptoms are produced by an underlying pathology, and that the main goal of treatment is to discover and remove this pathology], that assumes . . . that the underlying pathology is organic. Its practitioners therefore employ various forms of somatic therapy such as drugs. In addition, it takes for granted that would-be healers should be members of the medical profession. (p. 722)

Many other introductory textbooks (as well as texts in abnormal and clinical psychology) have similar passages. For the most part, these passages are intended to distinguish an ostensibly somatogenic medical model from the psychogenic models associated with cognitive and behavioral therapy, or to distinguish the profession of psychiatry, with its emphasis on drugs and other physical treatments, from clinical psychology, with its emphasis on behavioral interventions. This common association of the medical model with somatogenic theories and biological treatments reflects a deep misunderstanding, and what follows is an attempt to give an alternative perspective on this issue, based on Siegler and Osmond's (1974) sociological analysis of the medical model, *Models of Madness, Models of Medicine* (see also Shagass, 1975).[1]

According to Siegler and Osmond, the history of psychology can be traced in terms of three major models of psychopathology. The *supernatural model* prevailed before the 18th century Enlightenment. It assumes that psychology reflects the possession of the individual by demons; by implication, the proper response to psychopathology is exorcism. The *moral model*, which prevailed in the late 18th and early 19th centuries, assumes that psychopathology—or, more precisely, abnormal behavior—is deliberately adopted by the individual, much in the manner of criminal behavior; by implication, the proper response to psychopathology is confinement and other forms of punishment. The *medical model*, which began to emerge in the 19th century, assumes only that psychopathology is the product of natural causes that can be identified by the techniques of empirical science. By implication, the proper response to psychopathology is diagnosis according to a scientifically validated system and attempts at cure or rehabilitation by means of scientifically proven methods. Contrary to the popular view, the medical model does not assert that psychopathology is the product of an abnormal biological condition or that it should be treated only with drugs or surgery. Rather, the medical model is centered on particular rules regulating two primary social roles: the doctor and the patient.

The doctor (who does not have to be a physician or even hold a doctoral degree) possesses a special kind of authority called *Aesculapian* (after Aesculapius, the Greek god of medicine). Aesculapian authority is

---

[1]Siegler and Osmond have also promoted their perspective on the medical model in a number of journal articles on mental illness (Siegler & Osmond, 1969, 1971, 1974a; Siegler, Osmond, & Mann, 1969), alcoholism (Siegler, Osmond, & Newell, 1968), and drug addiction (Siegler & Osmond, 1968).

a combination of three other kinds of authority recognized by sociologists: *sapiential* authority, by virtue of the doctor's special knowledge and expertise; *moral* authority, by virtue of the doctor's concern for the afflicted individual; and *charismatic* authority, by virtue of the afflicted person's faith that the doctor can help. Note that doctors lack *structural* authority: They cannot enforce their prescriptions, resulting in a markedly low rate of compliance. The doctor's role is to investigate the disorder at hand, by means of procedures that might be unpleasant, intrusive, or even frightening. On the basis of this investigation the doctor makes a diagnosis, informs the afflicted person about the nature of his or her problem, absolves the patient of blame (it is critical to medical ethics that people are not blamed, and thus punished, for their illnesses), and finally creates the conditions for the afflicted person to return to health and his or her proper role in society.

The patient enacts his or her part by taking on the *sick role*: he or she must seek help from the doctor and cooperate with treatment; in return, the patient is exempt from some or all responsibilities during treatment. Note that a doctor's order has supreme authority in society—it can exempt the person from jury duty, military service, and final examinations. It has this power by virtue of our society's implicit adoption of the medical model and the sick role. However, patients cannot remain in the sick role forever; they must leave it eventually, either by recovering or dying.

A special case is when the illness is chronic and nothing more can be done to achieve a cure. Under these circumstances the role relationships change. It is the responsibility of the doctor to remove the sick role and confer the impaired role on the afflicted patient. At this point the patient must leave the hospital and active treatment. What once was an illness is transformed into a handicap, and the doctor is replaced by a rehabilitation specialist. Patients are no longer absolved from their responsibilities: They must return to some socially productive activity, do things for themselves, and cope with their handicaps as well as possible.

What has just been described is what Siegler and Osmond (1974b) referred to as the *clinical medical model*, which is one of many different versions. All versions of the medical model posit that disease is the product of natural causes and that the proper response is scientifically based treatment. However, they differ in terms of their role relationships. In the clinical medical model, the goal is to cure disease in an individual, and the role relationships are doctor and patient. In the public health medical model, the goal is to control illnesses that cannot be cured on an individual basis. Its focus is on prevention of disease in a population, rather than an individual, and in fact its prescriptions for public health may damage some individuals; moreover, the public health official may decide to permit some diseases to occur, perhaps for economic reasons. Note that the role relationships differ in the public health medical model. The doctor is replaced by the public health official, who has structural as well as sapiential authority—he or she has the power of the law and the courts to enforce "doctor's orders" and to force us to fluoridate our water or be immunized against smallpox and polio. The patient is replaced by the citizen, who by his or her vote can place limits on the public health official's authority to act.

In the *scientific medical model*, there is no direct interest in intervention (prevention or cure), but there is interest in the acquisition of scientific knowledge about the nature of disease. Again, the role relationships change. The doctor is replaced by the investigator who has only sapiential authority. The investigator has no obligation to cure and prevent disease and in certain circumstances may even inflict disease (or allow it to occur) as part of a controlled experiment. The patient is replaced by the research participant who volunteers his or her services. These individuals are under no obligation to participate in research, and usually they do so only when they are compensated in some way for their services. They have rights that patients and citizens do not have: They must be protected from harm, and they must be assured that the procedures to which they are subjected are worthwhile; their only responsibility is to honor their commitment to the study.[2]

I explore the medical model in detail because it has been subject to so much misunderstanding—and also because it gives me the opportunity to unite two social sciences, psychology and sociology, at least for a moment. However, the interested reader should reflect on the implications of the medical model or models for understanding the nature, causes, treatment, and prevention of psychopathology and on the proposition that many of the abuses frequently attributed to mental health professionals— such as the confinement of mental patients in the back wards of mental hospitals, without any active treatment—actually represent violations, not expressions, of the medical model.

THE KRAEPELINIAN LEGACY

Diagnosis lies at the heart of the medical model of psychopathology: The doctor's first task is to decide whether the person has a disease and what that disease is. Everything else flows from that. A diagnostic system is, first and foremost, a classification of disease—a description of the kinds

---

[2]This is a good point to register my objection to the American Psychological Association's decision to substitute the term *participants* for the traditional *subjects*. In fact, there are several different participants in the social interaction known as the psychological experiment (Orne, 1962, 1973), including (but not limited to) the experimenter, the subject, and any confederates of the experimenter. The distinction is one of role, not of power: The experimenter conducts the experiment, whereas the subject provides the data (subjects might also be observers, respondents, or even informants). For more on the experimenter–subject relationship, see Danziger (1990) and Bayer and Shotter (1997).

of illnesses one is likely to find in a particular domain. However, advanced diagnostic systems go beyond description. They carry implications for underlying pathology, etiology, course, and prognosis; they tell us how likely a disease is to be cured and which cures are most likely to work; failing a cure, they tell us how successful rehabilitation is likely to be; and they tell us how we might go about preventing the disease in the first place. Thus, diagnostic systems are not only descriptive; they are also predictive and prescriptive. Diagnosis is also critical for scientific research on psychopathology—as Cattell (1940) put it, nosology precedes etiology. Uncovering the psychological deficits associated with schizophrenia requires that we be able to identify people who have the illness in the first place.

Diagnosis Before Kraepelin

Before Kraepelin, the nosology of mental illness was a mess. Isaac Ray (1838/1962) followed Esquirol and Pinel in distinguishing between insanity (including mania and dementia) and mental deficiency (including idiocy and imbecility), but otherwise denied the validity of any more specific groupings (Grob, 1991; Kendell, 1990; Shorter, 1997). It fell to Kraepelin to systematically apply the medical model to the diagnosis of psychopathology, attempting a classification of mental illnesses that went beyond presenting symptoms (Havens, 1965; Shorter, 1997). In this respect, however, Kraepelin's program largely failed. Beginning in the 5th edition (1896) of his *Textbook*, and culminating in the 7th and penultimate edition (the second edition to be translated into English), Kraepelin acknowledged that classification in terms of pathological anatomy was impossible, given the present state of medical knowledge. His second choice, classification by etiology, also was unsuccessful: Kraepelin freely admitted that most of the etiologies given in his text were speculative and tentative. In an attempt to avoid classification by symptoms, Kraepelin fell back on classification by course and prognosis: What made the manic-depressive psychoses similar, and different from the dementias, was not so much the difference between affective and cognitive symptoms, but rather that manic-depressive patients tended to improve whereas demented patients tended to deteriorate.

By focusing on the course of illness, in the absence of definitive knowledge of pathology or etiology, Kraepelin hoped to put the psychiatric nosology on a firmer scientific basis. In the final analysis, however, information about course is not particularly useful in diagnosing a patient who is in the acute stage of mental illness. Put bluntly, it is not much help to be able to say, after the disease has run its course, "Oh, so *that's* what he had!". Kraepelin appears to have anticipated this objection when he noted that there is a fair assumption that similar disease processes will produce identical symptom pictures, identical pathological anatomy, and an identical etiology. If, therefore, we possessed a comprehensive knowledge of any one of these three fields,—pathological anatomy, symptomatology, or etiology,—we would at once have a uniform and standard classification of mental diseases. A similar comprehensive knowledge of either of the other two fields would give not only just as uniform and standard classifications, but all of these classifications would exactly coincide. Cases of mental disease originating in the same causes must also present the same symptoms, and the same pathological findings. (Kraepelin & Diefendorf, 1904/1907, p. 117)

Accordingly, Kraepelin and Diefendorf (1904/1907) divided the mental illnesses into 15 categories, most of which remain familiar today, including dementia praecox (renamed schizophrenia), manic–depressive insanity (bipolar and unipolar affective disorder), paranoia, psychogenic neuroses, psychopathic personality, and syndromes of defective mental development (mental retardation). What Kraepelin did for the psychoses, Pierre Janet later did for the neuroses (Havens, 1966), distinguishing between hysteria (dissociative and conversion disorders) and psychasthenia (anxiety disorder, obsessive–compulsive disorder, and hypochondriasis).

The Evolution of DSM

Paradoxically, Kraepelin's assertion effectively justified diagnosis on the basis of symptoms—exactly the practice that he was trying to avoid. For more than a century now, that is just what the mental health professions have continued to do. True, the predecessors of the DSM, such as the *Statistical Manual for the Use of Institutions for the Insane* (see Grob, 1991) or the War Department Technical Bulletin, Medical 203 (see Houts, 2000) spent a great deal of time listing mental disorders with presumed or demonstrated biological foundations. For the most part, however, actual diagnoses were made on the basis of symptoms, not on the basis of pathological anatomy—not least because, as Kraepelin himself had understood, evidence about organic pathology was usually impossible to obtain, and evidence about etiology was usually hard to obtain. In distinguishing between psychosis and neurosis, between schizophrenia and manic–depressive disorder, or between phobia and obsessive–compulsive disorder, the clinician based the diagnosis exclusively on symptoms.

Similarly, while the 1st edition of the *Diagnostic and Statistical Manual of Mental Disorders* (DSM–I; American Psychological Association, 1952) may have been grounded in psychoanalytic and psychosocial concepts, diagnosis was still based on lists of symptoms and signs. So too, for the 2nd edition (DSM–II; American Psychiatric Association, 1968). For example, the classical distinctions among simple, hebephrenic, catatonic (excited or withdrawn), and paranoid schizophrenia were based on presenting symptoms, not on the basis of pathological anatomy; they were "functional," of unknown etiology or even course (all chronic and deteriorating).

In point of fact, the first two editions of the *DSM* gave mental health professionals precious little guidance about how diagnoses were actually to be made—which is one reason why diagnoses proved to be so unreliable (e.g., Spitzer & Fleiss, 1974; Zubin, 1967). Correcting this omission was one of the genuine contributions of what has come to be known as the *neo-Kraepelinian movement* in psychiatric diagnosis (Blashfield, 1985; Klerman, 1977), as exemplified by the work of the "St. Louis Group" centered at Washington University School of Medicine (Feighner et al., 1972; Woodruff, Goodwin, & Guze, 1974), and the Research Diagnostic Criteria (RDC) promoted by a group at the New York State Psychiatric Institute (Spitzer, Endicott, & Robins, 1975). The 3rd, 3rd revised, and 4th editions of the *Diagnostic and Statistical Manual of Mental Disorders* (*DSM–III*, *DSM–III–R*, and *DSM–IV*; American Psychiatric Association, 1980, 1987, 1994, respectively) were largely the product of these groups' efforts.

Diagnosis by symptoms was codified in the Schedule for Affective Disorders and Schizophrenia (Endicott & Spitzer, 1978), geared to the RDC, and in analogous instruments geared to the *DSM*: the Structured Clinical Interview for *DSM–III–R* (SCID; Spitzer, Williams, Gibbon, & First, 1990) and Structured Clinical Interview for *DSM–IV* Axis I Disorders (SCID-I; First, Spitzer, Gibbon, & Williams, 1997). The neo-Kraepelinian approach exemplified by *DSM–IV* and SCID-I has arguably made diagnosis more reliable, if not more valid. For example, clinicians can show a high rate of agreement in diagnosing multiple personality disorder (in *DSM–III*; in *DSM–IV*, renamed dissociative identity disorder), but it is difficult to believe that the "epidemic" of this diagnosis observed in the 1980s and 1990s represented a genuine increase in properly classified cases (Kihlstrom, 2001).

A more important feature of *DSM–III* and *DSM–IV*, one not often remarked on (for an exception, see Blashfield & Flanagan, 1999), was a shift in the structure of the psychiatric nosology. Before *DSM–III*, psychiatric diagnoses were, at least tacitly, construed as proper sets: summaries of instances (syndromes) that shared a set of defining features (symptoms), which in turn were singly necessary and jointly sufficient to identify an entity as an example of the category. Thus, in *DSM-II*, all the psychoses were characterized by disorders of reality testing, whereas all the neuroses were characterized by anxiety. In Bleuler's classic work (1911/1950), the "group of schizophrenias" was united by the presence of the "four As" (associative disturbance, affective disturbance, ambivalence, and autism). Similarly, Janet (1907) discussed the defining "stigmata" of hysteria. The construal of the diagnostic categories as proper sets, to the extent that anyone thought about it at all, almost certainly reflected the classical view of categories handed down from the time of Aristotle. Indeed, much of the dissatisfaction with psychiatric diagnosis, at least among those inclined toward diagnosis in the first place, stemmed from the problems of partial and combined expression (e.g., Eysenck, 1961). Many patients did not fit into the traditional diagnostic categories, either because they did not display all the defining features of a particular syndrome, or because they displayed features characteristic of two or more contrasting syndromes. It was to handle cases such as these that such labels as *schizotypal personality disorder* and *schizoaffective disorder* were proposed.

In the 1970s, however, psychologists and other cognitive scientists began to discuss problems with the classical view of categories as proper sets and to propose other models, including the *probabilistic* or *prototype* model (for a review of these problems, and an explication of the prototype model, see Smith & Medin, 1981). According to the prototype view, categories are *fuzzy sets*, lacking sharp boundaries between them. The members of categories are united by *family resemblance* rather than a package of defining features. Just as a child may have her mother's nose and her father's eyes, so the instances of a category share a set of *characteristic features* that are only probabilistically associated with category membership. No feature is singly necessary, and no set of features is jointly sufficient, to define the category. Categories are represented by prototypes, which possess many features characteristic of the target category and few features characteristic of contrasting categories.

The prototype view solves the problems of partial and combined expression, and in fact a seminal series of studies by Cantor and her colleagues showed that mental health professionals tended to follow it, rather than the classical view, when actually assigning diagnostic labels (Cantor & Genero, 1986; Cantor, Smith, French, & Mezzich, 1980; Genero & Cantor, 1987). In a striking instance of art imitating life, *DSM–III* tacitly adopted the prototype view in proposing rules for psychiatric diagnosis. For example, *DSM–III* permits the diagnosis of schizophrenia if the patient presents any one of six symptoms during the acute phase of the illness and any two of eight symptoms during the chronic phase. Thus, to simplify somewhat (but only somewhat), two patients—one with bizarre delusions, social isolation, and markedly peculiar behavior, and the other with auditory hallucinations, marked impairment in role functioning, and blunted, flat, *or* (emphasis added) inappropriate affect—could both be diagnosed with schizophrenia. No symptom is singly necessary, and no package of symptoms is jointly sufficient, for a diagnosis of schizophrenia as opposed to something else. Although the packaging of symptoms changed somewhat, *DSM–IV* followed suit.

Other views of categorization have emerged since the prototype view, including an exemplar view and a theory-based view. Moreover, there are several versions of the prototype view, including one based on discrete features and another based on continuous dimensions (Medin, 1989; Medin, Goldstone, & Gentner, 1993; Smith & Medin, 1981). Space does not permit elaboration of these alternatives here; it is enough to say that, except for work by Cantor and Genero on expertise in diagnosis, these models have not been applied to psychiatric diagnosis. I think we can safely predict that *DSM–V* will also be organized along probabilistic, prototypical lines—suggesting that the diagnostic categories themselves, and not just the categorization process, are organized as fuzzy sets. However, this is not enough for many psychologists, who (as exemplified by many contributors to this volume) seek to embrace another basis for diagnosis entirely.

Critiques of Categorization

This is more than a debate over whether one diagnosis or another should be included in the new nomenclature. Some colleagues, heirs of the psychodynamically and psychosocially oriented clinicians who dominated American psychiatry before the neo-Kraepelinian revolution, wish to abandon diagnosis entirely. So do contemporary anti-psychiatrists, although for quite different reasons. Classical behavior therapists also abjure diagnosis, seeking to modify individual symptoms without paying much attention to syndromes and diseases. For these groups, the best *DSM* is no *DSM* at all. Beyond these essentially ideological critiques, there appear to be essentially two (not unrelated) points of view: one that seeks only to put diagnosis on a firmer empirical basis, and another that seeks to substitute a dimensional for a categorical structure for the diagnostic nosology. Both seek to abandon the medical model of psychopathology represented by the neo-Kraepelinians who formulated *DSM–III* and *DSM–IV*.

The empirical critique is exemplified by Blashfield (1985), who has been critical of the "intuitive" (p. 116) way in which the neo-Kraepelinians did their work and who wants the diagnostic system to be placed on firmer empirical grounds. For Blashfield and others like him, a more valid set of diagnostic categories will be produced by the application of multivariate techniques, such as factor analysis and cluster analysis, which will really "carve nature at its joints," showing what really goes with what. The result may very well be a nosology organized along fuzzy-set lines, as *DSM–III* was and *DSM–IV* is. However, at least diagnosis will not depend on the intuitions of a group of professionals imbued with the traditional nomenclature. If schizophrenia or some other traditional syndrome fails to appear in one of the factors or clusters, that's the way the cookie crumbles: Schizophrenia will have to be dropped from the nomenclature. Less radically, the analysis may yield a syndrome resembling schizophrenia in important respects, but the empirically observed pattern of correlations or co-occurrences may require revision in specific diagnostic criteria.

Whereas Blashfield (1985) appears to be agnostic about whether a new diagnostic system should be categorical or dimensional in nature, so long as it is adequately grounded in empirical data, other psychologists, viewing diagnosis from the standpoint of personality assessment, want to opt for a dimensional alternative. Exemplifying this perspective are Clark, Watson, and their colleagues (Clark, Watson, & Reynolds, 1995; Watson, Clark, & Harkness, 1994).[3] They have argued that categorical models of psychopathology are challenged by such problems as comorbidity (e.g., the possibility that a single person might satisfy criteria for both schizophrenia and affective disorder) and heterogeneity (e.g., the fact that the present system allows two people with the same diagnosis to present entirely different patterns of symptoms). Clark et al. are also bothered by the frequent provision in *DSM–IV* of a subcategory of "not otherwise specified," which really does seem to be a mechanism for assigning diagnoses that do not really fit, and by a forced separation between some Axis I diagnoses (e.g., schizophrenia) and their cognate personality disorders on Axis II (e.g., schizotypal personality disorder).

Clark and Watson's points (some of which are essentially reformulations of the problems of partial and combined expression) are well taken, and it is clear—and has been clear at least since the time of Eysenck (1961)—that a shift to a dimensional structure would go a long way toward addressing them. At the same time, such a shift is not the only possible fix. After all, heterogeneity is precisely the problem which probabilistic models of categorization are designed to address (the exemplar and theory-based models also address them), although it seems possible that such categories as schizophrenia, as defined in *DSM–III* and *DSM–IV*, may be a little too heterogeneous. Comorbidity is a problem only if diagnoses label people rather than diseases.[4] After all, dual diagnosis has been a fixture in work on alcohol and drug abuse, mental retardation, and other disorders at least since the 1980s (e.g., Penick, Nickel, Cantrell, & Powell, 1990; Woody, McClellan, & Bedrick, 1995; Zimberg, 1993). There is no a priori reason why a person cannot suffer from both schizophrenia and affective disorder, just as a person can suffer from both cancer and heart disease.[5]

---

[3]Watson and Clark edited a collection of articles exploring the connection between diagnostic categories and personality dimensions, published as a special issue of the *Journal of Abnormal Psychology* (1994, Vol. 101, No. 1).

[4]Perhaps not even then. Although it may be true that adjectival nouns such as *schizophrenic* encourage stereotyping and prejudice, they are awfully convenient for linguistic expression, and I for one am sorry to see them eliminated by the forces of political correctness. There is no reason why people cannot be referred to as *schizophrenics* when discussing their schizophrenia (assuming that this is a valid disease entity), just as they might be referred to as *Irish* when discussing their ethnicity, or *males* when discussing their gender. (Is "Irish male" a case of comorbidity?)

[5]Time for a personal anecdote: When I was a clinical psychology intern in 1974, my first patient was an adolescent who was both suicidally depressed and mentally retarded (during the intake interview, he fished two bullets out of his pocket and began clicking the tip of one against the firing pin of the other). This combination of conditions created problems for disposition, because local inpatient services for mentally ill children did not want to take

There is no doubt that the diagnostic nosology should be put on a firmer empirical basis, and it may well be that a shift from a categorical to a dimensional structure will improve the reliability and validity of the enterprise. It should be noted, however, that both proposals essentially represent alternative ways of handling information about *symptoms*—subjectively experienced or publicly observable manifestations of underlying disease processes. So long as they remain focused on symptoms, proposals for revision of the psychiatric nomenclature, nosology, and diagnosis amount to rearranging the deck chairs on the *Titanic*. Instead of debating alternative ways of handling information about symptoms, we should be moving beyond symptoms to diagnosis on the basis of underlying pathology. In doing so, we would be honoring Kraepelin rather than repealing his principles, and following in the best tradition of the medical model of psychopathology, rather than abandoning it.

THE LABORATORY REVOLUTION IN MEDICINE—OR, WHATEVER HAPPENED TO FEVER?

In his reliance on symptoms, Kraepelin and other early psychiatrists (there were no clinical psychologists yet) were simply following the practice of their colleagues in other medical specialties. The categories of medical disease changed little from the time of Hippocrates and Galen to that of Pasteur and Koch (Magner, 1992; Rosenberg, 1987; Starr, 1982). Well into the 19th century, prevailing theories still ascribed disease to imbalances in the four bodily humors, and treatment emphasized palliatives that made the patient as comfortable as possible while the disease ran its course. In fact, diagnosis was not a major enterprise for physicians, who, until well into the 19th century, emphasized the individuality of the patient. All that changed, however, with what has been called the *laboratory revolution in medicine* (Cunningham & Williams, 1992; see also Berger, 1999a, 1999b, 1999c, 1999d).

Historians of medicine (e.g., Ackerknecht, 1967) commonly distinguish between three epochs in medical history. The transition from *bedside medicine*, which prevailed from the Middle Ages well into the 18th century, to *hospital medicine*, which encompassed the late 18th and early 19th centuries, has been much discussed, most famously by Foucault (1973). It was marked not just by a shift in the site where medicine was practiced, but also by the introduction of the postmortem autopsy to discover the correlations between symptoms and anatomical lesions. The findings of hos-

---

someone who was retarded, and the residential centers for mentally retarded children did not want to take someone who was mentally ill. However, nobody on our staff had any problem recognizing that this young man had two problems, not just one, and working to address them both.

pital medicine forced physicians to shift their theory of disease, from the prevailing humor theory to an emphasis on pathological anatomy, but pathological anatomy could only be determined after the patient had died. In hospital medicine, as in bedside medicine, diagnosis of living patients was essentially subjective, based on symptoms and signs—the patient's complaints and whatever physicians and others could observe with their unaided senses (Ogilvie & Evans, 1997). Physicians rarely even touched their patients during examination, and it was remarkably common for them to diagnose and treat illnesses at a distance, by letter, without an office or home visit.

The further transition to laboratory medicine began in the middle of the 19th century and gained momentum with advances in microbiology, biochemistry, and radiation physics (Cunningham & Williams, 1992; Magner, 1992). Measurements of body temperature, pulse rate, and blood pressure were introduced in the 18th and 19th centuries; use of the stethoscope, ophthalmoscope, and laryngoscope became common only in the 1850s. The experimental physiology of Bernard (1865/1957) and the discovery by Pasteur and Koch of the microscopic organisms responsible for cholera and anthrax paved the way for the introduction of laboratory tests to detect such diseases as tuberculosis, typhoid, and diphtheria. Physicians no longer had to wait for autopsies to determine what made their patients ill: They could rely on laboratory tests—microscopic examination of specimens, blood chemistry, and, soon, X-rays—to determine the nature of disease in living patients. By the end of the 19th century, hospital pathology laboratories were well established in France, Germany, England, and the United States.

Perhaps the signal event of the laboratory revolution in medicine was the discovery, in 1905, of the syphilis spirochete. In terms of the clinical presentation of symptoms and signs, syphilis is positively protean (Magner, 1992). It mimics a great number of other diseases, including leprosy, tuberculosis, scabies, fungal infections, and skin cancers, to such an extent that diagnosis cannot be based on symptoms alone and must be confirmed by the Wasserman test for the presence of the syphilis spirochete in the affected individual's blood. Syphilis is diagnosed by a positive Wasserman test, regardless of the patient's symptoms and signs. Similarly, the diagnosis of HIV/AIDS is not based on symptoms such as pneumonia, diarrhea, seborrhoeic dermatitis, or even Kaposi's sarcoma, but rather by laboratory tests revealing the presence of specific antibodies in the blood. We have prostate-specific antigen tests and mammograms to detect cancers of the prostate and breast long before symptoms or signs appear. Accordingly, patients can be treated before they ever present symptoms, and treatments can be focused on what the patient's problem really is.

The increasingly prominent role of the laboratory in medical diagnosis has changed the organization of medical practice. Doctors must still learn about symptoms and signs, but increasingly the final authority over diagnosis rests with clinical pathologists and other specialists (who may not even be medical doctors) working in laboratories often far removed from the patient's bed and the practitioner's office. Symptoms and signs enable the practitioner to generate hypotheses about what ails the patient. Increasingly, however, this hypothesis is tested, treatment decisions made, and outcomes evaluated on the basis of laboratory tests. Although managed care has reduced indiscriminate testing (including tests performed by laboratories in which doctors themselves have a financial stake), the laboratory has played an increasing role in the practice of "evidence-based" medicine.

The condition of "fever" provides a case in point. Around the turn of the last century, physicians recognized dozens of different kinds of fever, running virtually from A (blackwater fever) to Z (yellow fever), depending on whatever other symptoms the patient presented besides fever and chills.[6] Physicians may still diagnose Rocky Mountain spotted fever, in a way that they no longer diagnose yellow fever, but they no longer do so solely on the basis of symptoms of fever and rash (e.g., Ogilvie & Evans, 1997). Nor do they treat fever, except as a palliative, or attempt to prevent it. Rather, observation of fever and rash often leads a physician to order one or more blood tests. Positive results (*Rickettsia rickettsii* serology and Weil-Felix reaction) confirm the diagnosis (Zaret, 1997). Public-health efforts to prevent Rocky Mountain spotted fever focus on eliminating the ticks that spread the disease. Scarlet fever, yellow fever, and paratyphoid fever (which, in the DSM, probably would be labeled *typhoid fever not otherwise specified*) are diagnosed, treated, and prevented similarly.

Diagnosis, treatment, and prevention based on an understanding of underlying pathology, in turn based on an understanding of normal anatomy and physiology, are the surest signs of advanced medical practice. The medical profession has evolved a rich armamentarium of diagnostic tests, including the biochemical analysis of body fluids (chiefly blood and cerebrospinal fluid), imaging techniques (including X-rays, ultrasound, and magnetic resonance imaging), endoscopy, biopsy, and genetic analysis. Clinical pathology is a recognized medical specialty, backed by specially trained laboratory technicians and specialized laboratory facilities. Testing not only informs diagnosis but is also used in the evaluation of treatment; in fact, testing is used more frequently to monitor the progress of treatment than it is to establish a diagnosis in the first place (Zaret, 1997).

---

[6]For the record, a computer search of *Webster's New Collegiate Dictionary* turned up the following subtypes, in addition to those already named (and ignoring such entries as *buck fever*, *cabin fever*, and *spring fever*): breakbone fever, canicola fever, cat-scratch fever, childbed fever, dengue fever, fever blister, glandular fever, hay fever, hemorrhagic fever, Lassa fever, milk fever, paratyphoid fever, parrot fever, phlebotomous fever, puerperal fever, Q fever, rabbit fever, ratbite fever, relapsing fever, snail fever, (Rocky Mountain) spotted fever, trench fever, typhoid fever, undulant fever, and valley fever.

TAKING PSYCHOPATHOLOGY SERIOUSLY
(PARDON THE DUALISM)

In medicine, the laboratory has radically altered our understanding of disease itself. Diseases are no longer categorized and diagnosed by their prominent symptoms; instead, they are categorized in terms of etiology and underlying pathology. It is the underlying pathology, not the palpable signs and symptoms, that brings unity to the symptoms associated with syphilis. Likewise, differences in pathology, not differences in skin color, distinguish between scarlet, spotted, and yellow fever. This is the direction we should be heading in formulating a new diagnostic system for mental illness.

I want to make it clear, however, that I am not suggesting that the diagnosis of mental illness be based on underlying pathologies of anatomy and physiology. Diagnosing brain lesions is a neurologist's job, and psychology is not just something to do until the biologist comes along. Rather, I am suggesting that we base diagnosis on underlying mental abnormalities —disorders of cognitive, emotional, and motivational function that underlie the abnormalities of experience, thought, and action that present themselves as palpable signs and symptoms of mental illness. As in the case of clinical medicine, diagnosing mental illness might well begin with the practitioner's evaluation of symptoms and signs, but it would end in the psychopathology laboratory with the application of objective psychological tests—not paper and pencil questionnaires, but actual laboratory procedures—interpreted in light of a comprehensive understanding of normal mental function.[7]

Of course, this is an old story. The study of psychological deficits has a long history, including early studies by C. G. Jung on word associations, David Shakow on attention, and Kurt Goldstein on concept formation (for overviews, see Hunt & Cofer, 1944; Kihlstrom & McGlynn, 1991). Historically, most attention has been devoted to psychological deficits in schizophrenia (e.g., Chapman & Chapman, 1973; Magaro, 1980; Matthysse, Spring, & Sugarman, 1979; Oltmanns & Neale, 1982), although there has also been interest in anxiety and depression (e.g., Ingram & Kendall, 1987; Ingram & Reed, 1986; Mineka & Gilboa, 1998; Mineka & Zinbarg, 1998), psychopathy (e.g., Wallace, Schmit, Vitale, & Newman, 2000), and other disorders.

Kraepelin himself contributed to this tradition. Trained at Leipzig under Wundt, in the world's first psychology laboratory, Kraepelin performed seminal studies on the timing of various mental processes (in Wundt's terms, sensation, apperception, motor reaction) using Donders's

---

[7]Along the same lines, Nasby and I proposed that laboratory-based assessments of personality replace traditional test methods, such as questionnaires and projective tests (Kihlstrom & Nasby, 1981; Nasby & Kihlstrom, 1986).

method of mental chronometry (Boring, 1950). Later, as a psychiatrist, he conducted research on continuous performance in dementia praecox (Hunt & Cofer, 1944). Had he not been distracted from experimental psychopathology by clinical psychiatry, we might well have expected him to report experiments on the timing of various mental processes in schizophrenia.[8]

As noted earlier, Kraepelin preferred diagnosis based on pathological anatomy or etiology to diagnosis based on symptoms. However, there are reasons for thinking that, had psychological knowledge and theory been as advanced as biological knowledge of anatomy and physiology, Kraepelin might well have promoted diagnosis based on psychopathology. After all, in both the 6th and 7th editions of his *Textbook*, Kraepelin and Diefendorf (1904/1907) preceded the description of the "Forms of Mental Diseases" (pp. 113ff) with the following chapters: "Disturbances of the Process of Perception" (pp. 3–22), "Disturbances of Mental Elaboration" (pp. 23–61), "Disturbances of the Emotions" (pp. 62–76), and "Disturbances of Volition and Action" (pp. 77–112). In this respect, Kraepelin appears to have been following Immanuel Kant's classic proposal that cognition, emotion, and motivation constitute the fundamental and irreducible faculties of mind (Hilgard, 1980). The implications are that, whatever their biological substrates might be, the psychopathology underlying the various mental illnesses reflects deficits in certain basic psychological operations. Abnormalities in these basic mental functions, not observable signs and symptoms, should form the basis of the diagnosis of psychopathology.

Cognitive neuropsychology provides a model for this sort of diagnostic testing. Neuropsychological findings are often presented as dissociations in task performance interpreted within a theoretical framework known as the *modularity of mind* (e.g., Fodor, 1983; Pinker, 1997). Suppose, for example, that one brain-injured patient has severe difficulty reading words but exhibits intact writing abilities, and another patient shows precisely the reverse pattern of deficits. This contrast, known as a *double dissociation*, may lead to the conclusion that reading and writing words are tasks that are performed by two separate cognitive modules. The modularity framework conceives the mind as a system of mental modules, or psychological faculties, analogous to the various organs of the body. In the same way that the function of the stomach is to digest food and the function of the heart is to circulate blood, each of these mental modules is specially geared to perform a particular cognitive, emotional, motivational, or behavioral task. Indeed, as Pinker (1997) noted, the linguist Noam Chomsky has often referred to these modules as *mental organs*.

The general idea in neuropsychology is that these modules, or the

---

[8]In fact, almost a century later Wishner and his colleagues (Wishner, Stein, & Peastrel, 1978) performed just such a study, using Sternberg's (1969) adaptation of Donders' technique.

connections among them, can be selectively damaged, resulting in particular patterns of psychological deficits. Damage to modules involved in attention or reasoning may be implicated in what we now know as schizophrenia; damage to particular modules involved in the perception, experience, or expression of emotion may be implicated in the various affective disorders. Psychopathy may involve damage to motivational modules associated with behavioral inhibition as opposed to behavioral activation. Attention deficit disorder may involve damage to a module that focuses attention, leaving modules that disengage or shift attention intact. At present, experimental psychopathologists compare the performance of various diagnostic groups, diagnosed by symptoms and signs, in an attempt to reveal underlying psychological deficits. The present proposal is, essentially, to reverse the process: to test for differential psychological deficits, in the same way that clinical pathologists now test blood for the presence of antigens and antibodies or image the body to detect lesions in various tissues and organs, and create a new nosology based on psychopathological findings. It may well be that such a testing program, systematically applied, will reveal the psychological deficit(s) uniting "the group of schizophrenias." Alternatively, it may well be that laboratory tests will revise the diagnostic system entirely, consigning the term *schizophrenia* to the dustbin of history, replacing it with a new nomenclature more closely tied to underlying psychopathology.

Laboratory testing may also unite syndromes that heretofore have been considered to be separate. Consider, for example, the vicissitudes of the diagnosis of hysteria (Kihlstrom, 1994). In the time of Pierre Janet and Morton Prince, what we now call the dissociative and conversion disorders were joined together under the rubric of *hysteria*. By contrast, *DSM–IV* lists the conversion disorders under the rubric of *somatoform disorder*, separate from the dissociative disorders. The ostensible reason for this is that the symptoms of the conversion disorders resemble those of medical illnesses (Martin, 1992, 1994). However, the underlying psychopathology in the conversion disorders is clearly dissociative (Kihlstrom, 1992; Kihlstrom, Barnhardt, & Tataryn, 1992). Just as psychogenic amnesia, fugue, and multiple personality disorder involve an impairment of conscious memory, so "hysterical" blindness and deafness involve impairments of conscious sensation and perception, and "hysterical" paralysis involves an impairment of conscious motor control. Dissociations between explicit and implicit perception, analogous to familiar dissociations between explicit and implicit memory (Schacter, 1987), are easily revealed by appropriate laboratory tests (Kihlstrom, 1992; Kihlstrom et al., 1992). In this way, evidence of shared underlying psychopathology, derived from formal laboratory tests, warrants rearrangement of the psychiatric nosology to rejoin the conversion and dissociative disorders.[9]

Most research in experimental psychopathology has not been explicitly guided by the notion of modularity, but the pervasive developmental deficit known as *autism* provides an example of how diagnosis might be based on psychological testing, rather than on observation of symptoms and signs. In *DSM–IV*, autistic disorder is diagnosed on the basis of impairments in social interaction and communication and repetitive and stereotyped patterns of behavior, interests, and activities. These symptoms are subjectively assessed by the clinician. However, according to one prominent theory (Baron-Cohen, 1995), autism results from a specific deficit in a particular mental module, called the *theory-of-mind mechanism*. This module, one of four deemed by Baron-Cohen to be critical to social cognition (the others are an intentionality detector, an eye-direction detector, and a shared-attention mechanism), permits one to infer other people's mental states from their behavior. Each of these social-cognitive modules can be assessed by specially designed laboratory tests; for example, the theory-of-mind mechanism is assessed by a "false beliefs" task (e.g., Peterson & Siegal, 1999).

Indeed, research by Baron-Cohen and others has revealed that autistic children perform normally on assessments of intentionality and eye-direction detection; however, one subgroup of autistic children performs normally on the shared-attention mechanism but poorly on the theory-of-mind mechanism, whereas another performs poorly on both. Children with mental retardation, by contrast, show intact performance in all four domains. In other words, we appear to have two quite different forms of autism, which deserve different labels in the nomenclature. Differential diagnosis of these conditions should not be based on symptoms (both groups met the *DSM–IV* criterion for autistic disorder), but rather on the results of laboratory tests. Application of rigorous, laboratory-based diagnostic tests may indicate whether we are really experiencing an epidemic of autism (in California the number of children enrolled in autism programs more than doubled from 1987 to 1998), or whether large numbers of children are being misdiagnosed on the basis of the subjective assessment of symptoms and signs. Similar benefits might accrue from the use of laboratory tests to diagnose attention deficit disorder.

---

[9]Actually, it must be said that such a rearrangement would be justified solely on symptomatic grounds, even in the absence of laboratory evidence of shared underlying psychopathology. After all, the symptoms of conversion disorder do not merely resemble those of medical disorders; they specifically resemble those of neurological disorders, just as the dissociative disorders do. However, in *DSM–IV* the conversion disorders remained where they had been in *DSM–III*, classified as somatoform. A source involved in this decision told me, not for attribution, that conversion was "the jewel in the crown" of the somatoform disorders and that the committee in charge of drafting the somatoform portion of *DSM–IV* "would never give it up."

SYMPTOMS ARE NOT THE DISEASE

In modern medicine, the laboratory has supplanted symptomatic complaints, medical histories, and physical examinations as the chief way of knowing (Warner, 1992). In addition to advancing biomedical knowledge, however, the laboratory is the basis of modern medical power—the ultimate source of the practitioner's sapiential, as opposed to moral or charismatic, authority. The laboratory performs diagnostic tests, identifies diseases, and evaluates the progress of treatment. Individual practitioners disregard laboratory findings at their peril. Patients (and, for that matter, third-party payers) have more faith if doctors' diagnoses and prescriptions are based on laboratory tests. It can be this way in psychopathology, as well. In an era of evidence-based medicine, including evidence-based psychotherapy, the use of laboratory tests to diagnose mental illness and evaluate the progress of treatment will help unify (or re-unify; see Kihlstrom & Canter Kihlstrom, 1998) science and practice. By placing diagnostic concepts and practices on a firmer scientific base, a shift from symptoms to laboratory tests will also reinforce the status and autonomy of clinical psychology, as well as the profession's claim to third-party payments for services. Connecting the laboratory more closely to the living material of the clinic will make basic research and theory more interesting.

S. S. Stevens (1961) sought to honor Fechner by repealing his law. In considering Kraepelin's legacy for psychopathology, we should remember that Kraepelin himself was a psychologist as well as a psychiatrist. When it comes to the diagnosis of mental illness, we can honor Kraepelin not by repealing his principles, but by reaffirming them—by moving beyond symptoms and diagnosing mental illness in terms of underlying pathology. For Kraepelin, diagnosis by symptoms was a temporary fallback, to be used only because diagnosis by pathology and etiology was not possible. This "fallback" has dominated our thinking for more than a century, and it is time to press forward, with all deliberate speed.

REFERENCES

Ackerknecht, E. H. (1967). *Medicine at the Paris Hospital, 1794–1848*. Baltimore: Johns Hopkins University Press.

American Psychiatric Association. (1952). *Diagnostic and statistical manual of mental disorders*. Washington, DC: Author.

American Psychiatric Association. (1968). *Diagnostic and statistical manual of mental disorders* (2nd ed.). Washington, DC: Author.

American Psychiatric Association. (1980). *Diagnostic and statistical manual of mental disorders* (3rd ed.). Washington, DC: Author.

American Psychiatric Association. (1987). *Diagnostic and statistical manual for mental disorders* (3rd ed., rev.). Washington, DC: Author.

American Psychiatric Association. (1994). *Diagnostic and statistical manual of mental disorders* (4th ed.). Washington, DC: Author.

Baron-Cohen, S. (1995). *Mindblindness: An essay on autism and theory of mind.* Cambridge, MA: MIT Press.

Bayer, B. M., & Shotter, J. (Eds.). (1997). *Reconstructing the psychological subject: Bodies, practices and technologies.* Thousand Oaks, CA: Sage.

Berger, D. (1999a, July). A brief history of medical diagnosis and the birth of the clinical laboratory: Part 1. Ancient times through the 19th century. *Medical Laboratory Observer*, pp. 28–40.

Berger, D. (1999b, August). A brief history of medical diagnosis and the birth of the clinical laboratory: Part 2. Laboratory science and professional certification in the 20th century. *Medical Laboratory Observer*, pp. 32–38.

Berger, D. (1999c, October). A brief history of medical diagnosis and the birth of the clinical laboratory: Part 3. Medicare, government regulation, and competency certification. *Medical Laboratory Observer*, pp. 40–44.

Berger, D. (1999d, December). A brief history of medical diagnosis and the birth of the clinical laboratory: Part 4. Fraud and abuse, managed care, and lab consolidation. *Medical Laboratory Observer*, pp. 38–42.

Bernard, C. (1957). *Introduction to the study of experimental medicine.* New York: Dover. (Original work published 1865)

Blashfield, R. K. (1985). *The classification of psychopathology: Neo-Kraepelinian and quantitative approaches.* New York: Plenum.

Blashfield, R. K., & Flanagan, E. (1999). *The DSM as a folk taxonomy.* Unpublished manuscript, Auburn University.

Blashfield, R. K., & Fuller, A. K. (1996). Predicting the *DSM–V. Journal of Nervous & Mental Disease, 184*, 4–7.

Bleuler, E. (1950). *Dementia praecox or the group of schizophrenias.* New York: International Universities Press. (Original work published 1911)

Boring, E. G. (1950). *A history of experimental psychology.* New York: Appleton-Century-Crofts.

Cantor, N., & Genero, N. (1986). Psychiatric diagnosis and natural categorization: A close analogy. In T. Millon & G. L. Klerman (Eds.), *Contemporary directions in psychopathology: Toward the DSM–IV* (pp. 233–256). New York: Guilford Press.

Cantor, N., Smith, E. E., French, R., & Mezzich, J. (1980). Psychiatric diagnosis as prototype categorization. *Journal of Abnormal Psychology, 89*, 181–193.

Caplan, P. J. (1995). *They say you're crazy: How the world's most powerful psychiatrists decide who's normal.* Reading, MA: Addison-Wesley.

Cattell, R. B. (1940). The description of personality: I. Foundations of trait measurement. *Psychological Review, 50*, 559–594.

Chapman, L. J., & Chapman, J. P. (1973). *Disordered thought in schizophrenia*. Englewood Cliffs, NJ: Prentice-Hall.

Clark, L. A., Watson, D., & Reynolds, S. (1995). Diagnosis and classification of psychopathology: Challenges to the current system and future directions. *Annual Review of Psychology, 46*, 121–153.

Cunningham, A., & Williams, P. (Eds.). (1992). *The laboratory revolution in medicine*. Cambridge, England: Cambridge University Press.

Danziger, K. (1990). *Constructing the subject: Historical origins of psychological research*. New York: Cambridge University Press.

Endicott, J., & Spitzer, R. L. (1978). A diagnostic interview: The Schedule for Affective Disorders and Schizophrenia. *American Journal of Psychiatry, 25*, 131–139.

Eysenck, H. J. (Ed.). (1961). *Handbook of abnormal psychology*. New York: Basic Books.

Feighner, J. P., Robins, E., Guze, S. B., Woodruff, R. A., Winokur, G., & Munoz, R. (1972). Diagnostic criteria for use in psychiatric research. *Archives of General Psychiatry, 26*, 57–63.

First, M. B., Spitzer, R. L., Gibbon, M., & Williams, J. B. W. (1997). *Structured Clinical Interview for DSM–IV Axis I disorders: Clinician version: Administration booklet*. Washington, DC: American Psychiatric Press.

Fodor, J. A. (1983). *The modularity of the mind*. Cambridge, MA: MIT Press.

Foucault, M. (1973). *The birth of the clinic: An archaeology of medical perception*. New York: Pantheon

Genero, N., & Cantor, N. (1987). Exemplar prototypes and clinical diagnosis: Toward a cognitive economy. *Journal of Social & Clinical Psychology, 5*(1), 59–78.

Gleitman, H. (1995). *Psychology* (4th ed.) New York: Norton.

Grob, G. N. (1991). Origins of SDM–I: A study in appearance and reality. *American Journal of Psychiatry, 148*, 421–431.

Havens, L. L. (1965). Emil Kraepelin. *Journal of Nervous & Mental Disease, 141*, 16–28.

Havens, L. L. (1966). Pierre Janet. *Journal of Nervous & Mental Disease, 143*, 383–398.

Hilgard, E. R. (1980). The trilogy of mind: Cognition, affection, and conation. *Journal for the History of the Behavioral Sciences, 16*, 107–117.

Houts, A. C. (2000). Fifty years of psychiatric nomenclature: Reflections on the 1943 War Department Technical Bulletin, Medical 203. *Journal of Clinical Psychology, 56*, 935–967.

Hunt, J. M., & Cofer, C. N. (1944). Psychological deficit. In J. M. Hunt (Ed.), *Personality and the behavior disorders* (Vol. 2, pp. 971–1032). New York: Ronald.

Ingram, R. E., & Kendall, P. C. (1987). The cognitive side of anxiety. *Cognitive Research and Therapy, 11*, 523–536.

Ingram, R. E., & Reed, M. R. (1986). Information encoding and retrieval processes in depression: Findings, issues, and future directions. In R. E. Ingam (Ed.), *Information processing approaches to clinical psychology* (pp. 131–150). Orlando, FL: Academic Press.

Janet, P. (1907). *The major symptoms of hysteria.* New York: Macmillan.

Kendell, R. E. (1990). A brief history of psychiatric classification in Britain. In N. Sartorius, A. Jablensky, D. A. Regier, J. D. Burke, & R. M. A. Hirschfeld (Eds.), *Sources and traditions of classification in psychiatry* (pp. 139–152). Toronto: Hogrefe.

Kihlstrom, J. F. (1992). Dissociative and conversion disorders. In D. J. Stein & J. Young (Eds.), *Cognitive science and clinical disorders* (pp. 247–270). San Diego, CA: Academic Press.

Kihlstrom, J. F. (1994). One hundred years of hysteria. In S. J. Lynn & J. W. Rhue (Eds.), *Dissociation: Clinical and theoretical perspectives* (pp. 365–394). New York: Guilford Press.

Kihlstrom, J. F. (2001). Dissociative disorders. In P. B. Sutker & H. E. Adams (Eds.), *Comprehensive handbook of psychopathology* (3rd ed. pp. 259–276). New York: Plenum.

Kihlstrom, J. F., Barnhardt, T. M., & Tataryn, D. J. (1992). Implicit perception. In R. F. Bornstein & T. S. Pittman (Eds.), *Perception without awareness: Cognitive, clinical, and social perspectives* (pp. 17–54). New York: Guilford Press.

Kihlstrom, J. F., & Canter Kihlstrom, L. (1998). Integrating science and practice in an environment of managed care. In D. K. Routh & R. J. De Rubeis (Eds.), *The science of clinical psychology: Accomplishments and future directions* (pp. 281–293). Washington, DC: American Psychological Association.

Kihlstrom, J. F., & McGlynn, S. M. (1991). Experimental research in clinical psychology. In M. Hersen, A. E. Kazdin, & A. S. Bellack (Eds.), *Clinical psychology handbook* (2nd ed., pp. 239–257). New York: Pergamon.

Kihlstrom, J. F., & Nasby, W. (1981). Cognitive tasks in clinical assessment: An exercise in applied psychology. In P. C. Kendall & S. D. Hollon (Eds.), *Cognitive–behavioral interventions: Assessment methods* (pp. 287–317). New York: Academic Press.

Klerman, G. L. (1977). Mental illness, the medical model and psychiatry. *Journal of Medicine & Philosophy, 2,* 220–243.

Kraepelin, E., & Diefendorf, A. R. (1907). *Clinical psychiatry; a text-book for students and physicians* (7th ed.). New York: Macmillan. (Original work published 1904)

Kutchins, H., & Kirk, S. A. (1997). *Making us crazy: DSM: The psychiatric Bible and the creation of mental disorders.* New York: Free Press.

Magaro, P. A. (1980). *Cognition in schizophrenia and paranoia: The integration of cognitive processes.* Hillsdale, NJ: Erlbaum.

Magner, L. N. (1992). *A history of medicine.* New York: Dekker.

Martin, R. L. (1992). Diagnostic issues for conversion disorder. *Hospital & Community Psychiatry, 43,* 771–773.

Martin, R. L. (1994). Conversion disorder, proposed autonomic arousal disorder, and pseudocyesis. In T. A. Widiger, A. J. Frances, H. A. Pincus, R. Ross, M. B. First, & W. W. Davis (Eds.), DSM–IV sourcebook (Vol. 2, pp. 893–914). Washington, DC: American Psychiatric Press.

Matthysse, S., Spring, B. J., & Sugarman, J. (Eds.). (1979). Attention and information processing in schizophrenia. Oxford, England: Oxford University Press.

Medin, D. L. (1989). Concepts and conceptual structure. American Psychologist, 44, 1469–1481.

Medin, D. L., Goldstone, R. L., & Gentner, D. (1993). Respects for similarity. Psychological Review, 100, 254–278.

Mineka, S., & Gilboa, E. (1998). Cognitive biases in anxiety and depression. In W. F. Flack & J. D. Laird (Eds.), Emotions in psychopathology: Theory and research (pp. 216–228). New York: Oxford University Press.

Mineka, S., & Zinbarg, R. (1998). Experimental approaches to the anxiety and mood disorders. In J. G. Adair, D. Belanger, & K. L. Dion (Eds.), Advances in psychological science: Vol. 1. Social, personal, and cultural aspects (pp. 429–454). Hove, England: Psychology Press/Erlbaum.

Nasby, W., & Kihlstrom, J. F. (1986). Cognitive assessment in personality and psychopathology. In R. E. Ingram (Ed.), Information processing approaches to psychopathology and clinical psychology (pp. 217–239). Orlando, FL: Academic Press.

Ogilvie, C., & Evans, C. C. (Eds.). (1997). Chamberlain's symptoms and signs in clinical medicine: An introduction to medical diagnosis (12th ed.). Oxford, England: Butterworth-Heinemann.

Oltmanns, T. F., & Neale, J. M. (1982). Psychological deficits in schizophrenia: Information processing and communication problems. In M. Shepard (Ed.), Handbook of psychiatry (pp. 55–61). Cambridge, England: Cambridge University Press.

Orne, M. T. (1962). On the social psychology of the psychological experiment: With particular reference to demand characteristics and their implications. American Psychologist, 17, 776–783.

Orne, M. T. (1973). Communication by the total experimental situation: Why it is important, how it is evaluated, and its significance for the ecological validity of findings. In P. Pliner, L. Krames, & T. Alloway (Eds.), Communication and affect (pp. 157–191). New York: Academic Press.

Penick, E. C., Nickel, E. J., Cantrell, P. F., & Powell, B. J. (1990). The emerging concept of dual diagnosis: An overview and implications. Journal of Chemical Dependency Treatment, 3(2), 1–54.

Peterson, C. C., & Siegal, M. (1999). Representing inner worlds: Theory of mind in autistic, deaf, and normal hearing children. Psychological Science, 10(2), 126–129.

Pinker, S. (1997). How the mind works. New York: Norton.

Ray, I. (1962). A treatise on the medical jurisprudence of insanity. Cambridge, MA: Harvard University Press. (Original work published 1838)

Rosenberg, C. E. (1987). *The care of strangers: The rise of America's hospital system.* Baltimore: Johns Hopkins University Press.

Schacter, D. L. (1987). Implicit memory: History and current status. *Journal of Experimental Psychology: Learning, Memory, and Cognition, 13,* 501–518.

Shagass, C. (1975). The medical model in psychiatry. *Comprehensive Psychiatry, 16,* 405–413.

Shorter, E. (1997). *A history of psychiatry: From the era of the asylum to the age of Prozac.* New York: Wiley.

Siegler, M., & Osmond, H. (1968). Models of drug addiction. *International Journal of the Addictions, 3,* 3–24.

Siegler, M., & Osmond, H. (1969). The impaired model of schizophrenia. *Schizophrenia, 1,* 192–202.

Siegler, M., & Osmond, H. (1971). Goffman's model of mental illness. *British Journal of Psychiatry, 119,* 419–424.

Siegler, M., & Osmond, H. (1974a, November). Models of madness: Mental illness is not romantic. *Psychology Today,* pp. 70–78.

Siegler, M., & Osmond, H. (1974b). *Models of madness, models of medicine.* New York: Harper & Row.

Sigler, M., Osmond, H., & Mann, H. (1969). Laing's model of madness. *British Journal of Psychiatry, 115,* 947–958.

Siegler, M., Osmond, H., & Newell, S. (1968). Models of alcoholism. *Quarterly Journal of Studies on Alcohol, 29,* 571–591.

Smith, E. E., & Medin, D. L. (1981). *Categories and concepts.* Cambridge, MA: MIT Press.

Spitzer, R. L., Endicott, J., & Robins, E. (1975). *Research diagnostic criteria (RDC) for a selected group of functional disorders.* New York: New York State Psychiatric Institute.

Spitzer, R. L., & Fleiss, J. L. (1974). A re-analysis of the reliability of psychiatric diagnosis. *British Journal of Psychiatry, 125,* 341–347.

Spitzer, R. L., Williams, J. B. W., Gibbon, M., & First, M. B. (1990). *Structured Clinical Interview for* DSM–III–R. Washington, DC: American Psychiatric Press.

Starr, P. (1982). *The social transformation of American medicine: The rise of a sovereign profession and the making of a vast industry.* New York: Basic Books.

Sternberg, S. (1969). The discovery of processing stages: Extensions of Donders' method. In W. G. Koster (Ed.), *Attention and performance II* (Vol. 30, pp. 276–315). Amsterdam: North-Holland.

Stevens, S. S. (1961). To honor Fechner and repeal his law. *Science, 133,* 80–86.

Wallace, J. F., Schmitt, W. A., Vitale, J. E., & Newman, J. P. (2000). Experimental investigations of information-processing deficiencies in psychopaths: Implications for diagnosis and treatment. In C. B. Gacono (Ed.), *The clinical and forensic assessment of psychopathy: A practitioner's guide* (pp. 87–109). Mahwah, NJ: Erlbaum.

Warner, J. H. (1992). The fall and rise of professional mystery: Epistemology, authority and the emergence of laboratory medicine in nineteenth-century America. In A. Cunningham & P. Williams (Eds.), *The laboratory revolution in medicine* (pp. 140–141). Cambridge, England: Cambridge University Press.

Watson, D., Clark, L. A., & Harkness, A. R. (1994). Structures of personality and their relevance to psychopathology. *Journal of Abnormal Psychology, 101,* 18–31.

Wishner, J., Stein, M. K., & Peastrel, A. L. (1978). Information processing stages in schizophrenia. *Journal of Psychiatric Research, 14*(1, Suppl. 4), 35–45.

Woodruff, R. A., Goodwin, D. W., & Guze, S. B. (1974). *Psychiatric diagnosis.* New York: Oxford University Press.

Woody, G. E., McLellan, A. T., & Bedrick, J. (1995). Dual diagnosis. *American Psychiatric Press Review of Psychiatry, 14,* 83–104.

World Health Organization. (1990). *International classification of diseases* (10th ed.). Geneva, Switzerland: Author.

Zaret, B. L. (Ed.). (1997). *Patient's guide to medical tests.* Boston: Houghton-Mifflin.

Zimberg, S. (1993). Introduction and general concepts of dual diagnosis. In J. Solomon, S. Zimbarg, E. Shollar, & M. M. O'Neill (Eds.), *Dual diagnosis: Evaluation, treatment, training, and program development* (pp. 3–21). New York: Plenum.

Zubin, J. (1967). Classification of behavior disorders. *Annual Review of Psychology, 18,* 373–406.

AUTHOR INDEX

Carson, R. C., 8, *14*, 56, 60, 252, 254, *273*
Caspar, R., 267, *273*
Caspi, A., 206, *219*, *223*, *248*
Cassidy, J. F., 201, *217*
Castle, D. J., 231, *249*
Catron, T., 206, *220*
Cattell, R. B., 111, *119*, 284, 298
Center, D. B., 211, *219*
Chahal, R., *98*
Chambless, D. L., 260, 262, *273*
Chang, C. M., 234, 240, *250*
Chang, L. Y., 82, *100*
Channabasavanna, S. M., *101*
Chapman, J. P., 293, *298*
Chapman, L. J., 293, *298*
Charmz, K., 168, *173*
Chatterji, S., *103*
Cheek, J. M., 75, 92, *99*
Chen, L., 225, *246*
Chen, L.- S., *99*
Chen, S., *249*
Chevron, E. S., 256, *275*
Chorpita, B. F., 224, *245*
Cicchetti, D. V., 73, *105*, 263, *277*
Cierpka, H., *200*
Clark, L. A., 5, 7, 8, *14*, 92, *105*, 125, *145*, 206, *219*, *220*, 228, 229, *246*, 288, 288n3, *298*, *302*
Clarkin, J. F., 177, 178, 196, 198, 264, 265, 267, 268, *273*
Clayton, P. J., 255, *277*
Cliche, D., *102*
Cochrane, C., 226, *248*
Cofer, C. N., 293, *299*
Cohen, H., 133, *142*
Cohen, H. J., *101*
Cohen, J., 92, *103*
Cohen, P., 92, *103*, *247*
Coid, B., *101*
Cole, D. A., 209, *217*
Coley, J. D., 122, 123, 136, *142*, *144*
Colvin, C. R., 92, *99*, *101*
Compas, B. E., 208, *218*
Compton, W. M., 82, *99*
Cone, J. C., 207, *218*
Connell, M. M., 96, *98*
Conrad, P., 48, 60
Cook, P. E., 171, *173*
Cook, T. D., 71, 90, *99*
Cooper, L., 82, *99*
Corbin, J. A., 168, *176*

Corey, L. A., *247*
Cornille, T. A., *274*
Cororve, M., 119, *119*
Costa, P. T., 121, *142*
Costas, H., *99*
Costello, E. J., 209, *217*
Cottler, L. B., 82, 83, 99, *101*, *103*
Cowdry, G. E., *219*
Coyle, J. T., *249*
Coyne, J. C., 108, *119*, 252, 258, *274*
Craig, T. J., 93, *100*
Craik, K. H., 92, *100*
Crites, S., 162, *173*
Crits-Cristoph, P., 181, *199*, *273*
Cronbach, L. J., 27, 60
Crook, T. H., 226, *249*
Croughan, J., 74, *104*
Crum, R. M., 225, *246*
Cunningham, A., 290, 291, *298*
Cuquerella, M., *100*
Curtis, R., 22, 60
Cytryn, L., 207, *218*

Dahl, A., *101*
Daiuto, A., *273*
Daldrup, R. J., *273*
Danton, W. G., 263, *272*
Danziger, K., 283n2, *298*
Davidson, G. C., 204, *218*
Davies, M., *100*, *101*, *105*
Davis, W. W., 202, *220*
de la Osa, N., 92, *99*
de Sales French, R., *246*
Deborah, D., *102*
DelVecchio, W. F., 97, *103*
DeNelsky, G. Y., 263, *272*
Depression Guideline Panel, 252, *274*
DeRubeis, R., *273*, *274*
Detweiler, J., *273*
Dew, M. A., 96, *98*
Diamond, J., 123, *142*
DiBenedetto, A., 213, *220*
Diefendorf, A. R., 285, 294, *300*
Diekstra, R. F. W., *101*
Dierse, B., *198*
Dies, R. R., 77, *102*
Dilling, H., 189, *198*
Dingemans, P. M. A. J., 231, *249*, *250*
Dion, C., *102*
Dittmann, V., 189, *200*
Dobson, K. S., 258, 260, *274*

Kendall, P. C., 299

Kendell, R. E., 25, 27, 51, 62, 121, 133, 144, 284, 299

Kendler, K. S., 227, 231, 247, 249, 275

Kernberg, O., 178, 181, 198, 199, 223, 247

Kessler, R. C., 83, 102, 105, 227, 228, 247, 249, 275

Kiesler, D. J., 266, 275

Kihlstrom, J. F., 286, 293, 293n7, 295, 297, 299, 300, 301

Kim, J., 26, 62

Kintsh, W., 160, 161, 174

Kinyon, T., 165, 172

Kirchner, J. E., 82, 98

Kirk, S. A., 4, 6, 14, 25, 51, 62, 279, 300

Kirsch, I., 262, 263, 275

Klar, H., 98

Klauer, T., 194, 200

Klein, D. N., 93, 94, 95, 96, 97, 100, 101, 223, 226, 247, 248

Klein, M. H., 99

Klerman, G. L., 22, 55, 62, 121, 144, 256, 275, 286, 300

Kline, J., 207, 218

Knorr-Cetina, K. D., 46, 62

Kocsis, J. H., 101, 247

Koenig, H. G., 82, 100

Koeter, M. W., 255, 276

Kolakowski, L., 23, 62

Kolar, D. W., 92, 101

Kopta, S. M., 261, 263, 274, 275

Koren, D., 242, 250

Korfine, L., 119, 120

Korman, Y., 155, 162, 173, 174

Korten, A. E., 104

Kovacs, M., 207, 209, 219

Kovess, V., 83, 101

Kozak, M. J., 7, 14

Kraepelin, E., 3, 14, 230, 233, 248, 284, 285, 294, 300

Kramer, M., 98, 276

Krames, L., 108, 120, 260, 274

Krasner, L., 28, 61, 62

Kraul, A., 200

Kraus, A., 75, 103

Krause, M. S., 261, 263, 266, 274, 275

Kringlen, E., 73, 104

Krueger, R. F., 206, 214, 215, 219

Kubiszyn, T. W., 77, 102

Küchenhoff, J., 198

Kupfer, D. J., 263, 276

Kutchins, H., 4, 6, 14, 25, 51, 62, 279, 300

Lahey, B. B., 101, 104

Laing, R. D., 21, 62

Laird, N. M., 102

Lakatos, I., 202, 219

Lambert, E. W., 206, 207, 208, 209, 214, 217, 219

Larkin, E. J., 82, 104

Latour, B., 23, 46, 62

Lavallée, J.-C., 102

Lavori, P. W., 96, 103, 227, 247

Lawlor, W., 226, 246

Leader, J. B., 94, 100

Leahy, R. L., 168, 174

Leal, C., 100

Leckman, J. F., 93, 101

Leighton, A. H., 102

Lencz, T., 231, 248

Lenzenweger, M., 119, 120

Lenzenweger, M. F., 230, 231, 232, 248

Leon, A. C., 248

Lerman, D. C., 219

Levings, C. T., 104

Levitt, H., 156, 164, 172

Levitt, N., 45, 61

Levy, K. N., 95, 102

Lewinsohn, P., 223, 248

Li, H., 90, 101

Licht, M. H., 19, 63

Lichtman, J. H., 104

Liebowitz, M., 228, 250

Lilienfeld, S. O., 125, 132, 133, 135, 144

Linacre, J. M., 216, 219

Linde, K., 262, 275

Linszen, D. H., 231, 249, 250

Lipman, E. L., 103

Lira, L. R., 82, 98

Liu, M., 247

Livesley, W. J., 121, 142, 223, 233, 236, 237, 248

Locke, B. Z., 276

Loosen, P. T., 262, 274

Loranger, A. W., 73, 95, 101, 230, 248

Lord, F. 215, 219

Losilla, J. M., 92, 99

Lowe, M., 119, 119

Lowry, J. L., 261, 275

Luborsky, L., 178, 181, *199*, 262, 263, *275*
Lueger, R. J., *274*
Lushene, R. E., 228, *249*
Lynch, E. B., 122, 123, *142, 144*
Lyons, J., 266, *274*
Lyons, J. S., *274*
Lyotard, J. F., 23, *62*

MacDonald, R., *273*
Machado, P. P., 156, 167, 171, *174*
Machtinger, P. E., 99
MacLean, C. J., *247*
Maffei, C., 73, *102*
Magaro, P. A., 293, *300*
Mager, D., *103*
Mager, D. E., 82, 99
Magner, L. N., 290, 291, *300*
Mahler, M., 181, *199*
Mahoney, M. J., 165, *174*
Main, M., 161, *174*
Malgady, R. G., 74, *102, 104*
Malik, M., 264, 268, *273, 275*
Malt, B., 238, *248*
Mancuso, J. C., 158, *174*
Manderscheid, R. W., *276*
Mandler, J., 125, *144*
Mandler, J. M., 160, 161, 168, *174, 175*
Manis, M., 235, *249*
Margolis, J., 27, *62*
Marin, D. B., *101, 247*
Marino, L., 125, 132, 133, 135, *144*
Mariotto, M. J., 19, *63*
Márquez, G. G., 110, *120*
Martin, R. L., 295, *300*
Martinez, R., 99
Mas, F. G., *247*
Maser, J. D., 257, *275*
Mathisen, K. S., 82, *102*
Mattanah, J. J. F., 95, *102*
Matthysse, S., 293, *300*
Mavreas, V., 99, *103*
Maxwell, S. E., 261, *276*
Mayman, M., 235, *249*
Mayr, E., 27, *62*
Mazaide, M., 93, *102*
Mazaleski, J. L., *219*
Mazumdar, R. A., *276*
McAdams, D. P., 161, *172*
McClellan, A. T., 289, *302*
McClelland, M., 257, *276*

McClure, K. S., 263, *275*
McConaughy, S. H., 71, 97, 204, *217*
McCormick, R. A., *220*
McCosh, K. C., *219*
McCrae, R., 121, *142*
McCullough, J. P., *101, 247*
McCurry, S., *273*
McDonald-Scott, P., 98
McDonough, L., 125, *144*
McEvoy, L. T., *100*
McGlashan, T. H., 95, *102*
McGlynn, S. M., 293, *300*
McGonagle, K. A., *275*
McGuffin, P., 83, 99
McKay, J. R., 95, 98
McKnew, D., 207, *218*
McLeod, J., 156, *175*
McLeod, J. D., 82, *102*
McNeil, C. B., 201, *220*
McRae, R., 121, *142*
Meador, K. G., *101*
Medicare proposal could be dangerous, 252, *275*
Medin, D. L., 122, 123, 135, 136, *142, 144*, 202, *219*, 287, *300, 302*
Meehl, P. E., 27, 60, *62*, 108, 109, 110, 111, 112, 114, 117, 119, *120, 133, 144*, 203, *219*, 224, 232, *248, 250*
Megone, C., 134, *144*
Melchart, D., *275*
Meltzer, H., 98
Mendels, J., 110, *120*, 226, *248*
Merchant, A., 98
Meredith, K., *273*
Mérette, C., *102*
Merikangas, J. R., 258, *276*
Merikangas, K. R., 96, *103*, 258, *276*
Merry, W., *273*
Merton, R. K., 18, *62*
Mervis, C. B., 135, 136, *144*
Meyer, G. J., 74, 77, 90, 93, *102*
Meyer, L. H., 213, *220*
Meyer, R., 82, *100*
Mezzich, J., 6, *14*, 121, *142*, 238, 246, 287, 298
Micale, M. S., 23, *62*
Michell, J., 71, *102*
Miller, A. I., 45, *62*
Miller, C., 96, *103*
Miller, I., *101, 247*
Miller, M. W., 51, *62*

Miller, T. I., 262, 276
Millon, T., 48, 62, 121, 144, 223, 248
Mineka, S., 206, 214, 219, 293, 300
Miner, R. A., 202, 218
Minke, K. M., 211, 220
Mirkin, P., 82, 100
Mischel, W., 71, 102, 204, 219
Mitropoulou, V., 98
Moffitt, T., 223, 248
Moffitt, T. E., 206, 219
Mohr, D. C., 268, 273
Moleiro, C., 264, 268, 273
Mombour, W., 101, 189, 198, 200
Mondin, G. W., 277
Monson, R. R., 102
Montgrain, N., 102
Moody, M., 277
Morel, B. A., 230, 248
Moreland, K. L., 77, 102
Morey, L. C., 226, 227, 245
Morris, T. L., 201, 220
Morrison, K., 225, 248
Moskowitz, D. S., 92, 102
Muderrisoglu, S., 234, 242, 250
Muenz, L. R., 95, 105
Mueser, K. T., 273
Mufson, L., 96, 100
Muhs, A., 178, 199
Mulkay, M., 23, 61
Mulrow, C. D., 275
Mulvaney, F. D., 95, 98
Munoz, R., 14, 298
Murphy, J. M., 82, 102
Murphy-Eberenz, K. P., 119, 119
Murray, K. D., 155, 175
Murray, R. M., 231, 249
Myers, J. K., 276

Najavits, L. M., 95, 105
Namia, C., 102
Narrow, W. E., 276
Nasby, W., 293n7, 300, 301
Nathan, P. E., 4, 6, 7, 14 17, 27, 63
Navarro, J. B., 92, 99
Neale, J. M., 293, 301
Neale, M. C., 247
Nee, J., 72, 104
Neimeyer, R. A., 261, 276
Nelson, C., 247
Nelson, C. B., 247, 275
Nelson, C. M., 211, 219

Nelson-Gray, R. O., 257, 274
Nestadt, G., 225, 246
Nestadt, G. R., 98
Neufeld, K., 99
Newell, S., 281n1, 302
Newman, D. L., 223, 230, 248
Newman, J. P., 293, 302
Newman, L. S., 157, 172
Newman, R., 178, 198
Nezu, A. M., 263, 275
Nezu, C. M., 263, 275
Nickel, E. J., 289, 301
Nicole, L., 102
Nietzel, M. T., 261, 275
Nisbett, R. E., 71, 103
North, C. S., 82, 103
Norton, G. R., 208, 218
Novella, L., 102
Novick, M., 215, 219
Nugter, M. A., 231, 249, 250

Oberbracht, C., 193, 195, 198, 199
Ochs, E., 151, 171, 173
Offord, D. R., 92, 103
Ogilvie, C., 290, 292, 301
Oldham, J., 247
O'Leary, D. S., 232, 245
Olfson, M., 228, 248
Ollendick, T. H., 262, 273
Oltmanns, T. F., 293, 301
O'Neill, A., 231, 247
Ono, Y., 101
Onstad, S., 73, 104
OPD Working Group (1996), 179, 193, 199
OPD Working Group (2000), 179, 181, 187, 193, 199
Orlinsky, D. E., 261, 274
Ormel, J., 255, 276
Orne, M. T., 283n2, 301
Ornstein, P. H., 178, 198
Osmond, H., 281, 281n1, 282, 301, 302
Otto, R., 93, 98
Ouimette, P. C., 93, 101
Oxman, T. E., 227, 245

Pace, G. M., 219
Panak, W., 209, 218
Paradiso, S., 232, 245

World Health Organization (1990), 177,
     189, *200*, *280*, *302*
World Health Organization (1994), 6,
     15, 22, 25, 30, 31, 34, *67*
Wylie, M. S., 25, 51, 67

Yeh, E. K., 82, *100*
Yellen, A., 155, *175*
Yeomans, F., 178, *198*
Yonce, L., 109, 111, 114, 117, *120*

Zachar, P., 132, 135, *145*
Zarcone, J. R. *219*
Zaret, B. L., 292, *303*
Zhao, S., 83, *105*, *247*, *275*
Zimberg, S., 289, *303*
Zimmerman, M., 25, 51, *67*, 73, 73n1,
     95, *105*
Zinbarg, R. E., 228, 229, *250*, 293,
     300
Zubin, J., 285, *303*

SUBJECT INDEX

Brain disorders concept, 53
Bulimia nervosa, taxometric approach, 119

Canonical narrative structure, 160–161
Categorical approach
  criticism, 6, 8, 222–223, 235–236, 288–290
  depression weaknesses, 259–260
  dimensional approach comparison, 222–223, 235–236, 288–290
  DSM assumption, 108
  personality disorders, 235–236
  and prototype-matching, 241–243, 286–289
  psychiatrists' preference, 108
  schizophrenia weaknesses, 231–232
  symptoms basis of, 289–290
  taxometrics application, 107–119, 235–236
Charismatic authority, 282
Chemical imbalance concept, 48, 252–253
Child Behavior Checklist, 207, 209–210
Children, 201–216
  assessment issues, 206–210
  composite information validity, 92
  DSM system, 204–210
  model-based diagnosis need, 204–216
  multi-informant report correspondence, 75–76
  nomothetic-idiograhic approaches, 203–204, 213
  special education law implications, 210–211
  symptom duration, 209–210
  symptom overlap problem, 205–209
Children's Depression Inventory, 209
Chronicity
  diagnosis link, 268
  medical model implications, 282
  and treatment selection, 268–269
Circulatory disease diagnosis, 30–32
Circumplex model, 184–185
Clinical criteria, definition, 237
Clinical medical model, 282
Clinical practice
  DSM-IV implementation problems, 224–225
  prototype-matching approach link, 241–244

Clinical significance criterion, 52
Clinician report
  in classification system development, 235
  cross-informant report correspondence, 74–78
  reliability, 71–74
Cluster analysis
  depression classification, 226–227
  lack of replicability, 226–227
Cocaine addicts, narrative structure, 162
Cognitive abnormalities
  laboratory assessment, 293–296
  and psychopathology, 294
Cognitive neuropsychology, 294–296
Cognitive theory
  and folk taxonomies, 136–137
  and fuzzy set theory, 238–239
Cognitive therapies, non-specificity, 264
Committee method
  in controversy resolution, 54
  depression criteria, 254
  and "Roschian" concepts, 135
Comorbidity
  anxiety disorders, 222–229
  categorical approach problem, 257–260, 288–289
  children, 209
  depression, 227, 257–260
  as diagnostic problem, 223–224, 257–260
  prototype-matching advantage, 242
Composite International Diagnostic Interview
  reliability, 73
  validity determinants, 78–89
Computer-assisted diagnostic interviews, 73
Conduct disorder
  and special education classifications, 211
  symptom approach weakness, 205
  symptom overlap problem, 207
Confirmatory factor analysis, 214–216
  advantages, 214–215
  in child/adolescent diagnosis, 214–216
Conflict patterns, psychodynamics, 186–188
Confrontational interventions, 271
Consensual judgments. See Committee method

320   SUBJECT INDEX

Construct validation
  in *DSMs*, 27
  mono-method bias, 90
  in Operationalized Psychodynamic Diagnosis, 194
Continuity of symptoms, 259–260. *See also* Dimensional approach
Conversion disorders, underlying psychopathology, 295, 295n9
Coping style
  diagnosis link, 268
  and treatment selection, 268, 271
Countertransference, 184
Course of disease
  depression, 256
  Kraepelin's view, 284–285
Criterion contamination
  definition, 79
  reliability-validity continuum, 86
  and structured interview validity, 79–89
Criterion weighting, 216
Crohn's disease diagnosis, 34
Cultural factors. *See also* Social invention model/narrative
  and clinical significance criteria, 52–53
  in folk taxonomies, 135–137

Defense mechanisms, and *DSM* revisions, 55
Defensive Functioning Scale, 55
Delirium disorders, 72
Dementia praecox, 230
Depersonalization, 158–159
Depression, 251–272
  anxiety disorders comorbidity, 257–260
  children, 208–209
  cluster analysis limitations, 226–227
  comorbidity problem, 227, 257–260
  course and prognosis, 256
  diagnosis and treatment guidelines, 251–272
  disease model implications, 252–253
  DSM problems, 225–227, 253–272
  functionally equivalent conditions, 255–256
  multisource determination stability, 96
  prevalence estimate discrepancies, 253–254
  prototype matching approach, 227–228, 241

subclinical cases problem, 227
symptom distinctiveness problem, 257–260
symptom reliability, 255–256
taxometrics, 112–118
treatment-based diagnosis, 265–272
treatment non-specificity problem, 260–265
"Depressive equivalents," 255–256
Depressive personality, 226
Descriptive approach, 8
Developmental issues, *DSM* weakness, 205–206
Diagnostic category designs, 49
Diagnostic Interview Schedule, validity, 78–89
Diagnostic systems
  definition, 283–284
  Kraepelin's legacy, 283–290
Differential treatment response
  depression, 260–265, 269–272
  guidelines, 269–271
Digestive disease diagnosis, 30–32
Dimensional approach
  advantages, 236
  categorical approach comparison, 222–223, 235–236, 288–290
  depression, 259–260
  personality disorders, 235–236
  psychologists' preference, 108
  schizophrenia, 231–232
  symptom basis of, 289–290
  taxometrics application, 111, 117–118
Directive therapies, indications, 271
Discourse. *See* Narratives
Discovery model/narrative, 18
  criticism of, 22–44
  legitimizing effect of, 24
  logical empiricism perspective, 25–29
  medical analogy argument, 29–42
Discriminate validity, 237
  definition, 237
  DSM criteria, 57, 237
Disease model, 252. *See also* Medical model
"Disorder" concept, 135
Disorganized schizophrenia, 231–232
Dissociation
  and narrative incoherence, 158–159
  underlying psychopathology, 295
Dodo bird verdict, 262, 266
Donder's technique, 293, 293n8

Double dissociation, 294
"Double depression," 227
Drug industry marketing, 50–51
DSM-I
    development, 4
    etiological theory central feature, 225
    Kraepelin's influence, *xii*, 285
    number of diagnoses in, 19–20
    schizophrenia definition, 230
    symptoms and signs in, 285
DSM-II
    development, 4
    etiological theory central feature, 225
    expansion of diagnoses in, 19–20, 31, 33, 35
    prototype matching in, 242
    sleep disorders category, 33, 35, 37–38
    symptoms and signs in, 285
DSM-III
    development, 4–5
    expansion of diagnoses in, 19–20
    nosological structure shift, 286–287
    sleep disorders in, 36
DSM-III-R
    expansion of diagnoses in, 19–21
    sleep disorders in, 38
DSM-IV
    discovery model, 22–44
    expansion of diagnoses in, 19–59
    nosological structure shift, 286–287
    physical disease diagnosis comparison, 29–42
    publication profits, 51
    social invention model, 44–59
DSM-IV Guidebook, 52
DSM-IV Sourcebooks, 7, 55
DSM-IV Task Force
    criticism, 6–7
    new diagnostic label generation, 52–55
DSM-IV-TR, 19–44
DSM-V, 279
Dual diagnosis, 289. *See also* Comorbidity
Duration of symptoms
    children and adolescents, 209–210
    depression, 255
    in prototype-matching approach, 243
Dysfunction analysis. *See* Harmful dysfunction analysis
"Dysmetria," 232
Dysthymia, multisource determination, 96

Einstein, Albert, 45
Emotional abnormalities
    laboratory tests, 293–296
    and psychopathology, 294
Emotional disturbance, special education label, 210–211
Emotional processing
    in narratives, 163–167
    trauma survivors, 165
Empirical studies
    diagnostic system basis, 288
    in *DSM* revisions, weaknesses, 54–56
Environmental factors, children, 214
Epidemiological Catchment Area studies, 254
Epistemological problems
    folk taxonomy relevance, 135–137
    in harmful dysfunction analysis, 43
    psychopathology debate, 133–137
Essentialism, 133–137
Ethnic-racial factors, 216
Ethnobiological Classification (Berlin), 122–123
Ethnobiology, 121–141
Etiological explanation
    DSM-I and *DSM-II* central feature, 225
    in Scadding's taxonomic ladder, 40–41
    symptom approach comparison, 233–234
"Evidence-based" medicine, 291, 296
Evolutionary theory, 134
Exclusion rules, criticism, 5
Exemplar model, 287, 289
Experimenter-subject relationship, 283, 283n2
Expert opinion decisions
    multisource information synthesis, 93
    and number of diagnoses, 53
    social context, 54, 56
Exposure therapy, and therapeutic change, 270–271
External criteria, definition, 237
Externalizing disorders
    child psychopathology cluster, 206
    as overriding category, 214
    therapeutic change guidelines, 270–271

Factor analysis
    anxiety disorders, 229
    depression, 226

Falsification tenet, 203
Family therapists, political concessions to, 55
Family therapy, indications, 269
Feighner criteria, 4–5
Fever
    depression analogy, 258
    symptom diagnosis comparison, 292
Field trials, 7
Financial reimbursement, 202
Fisher, R.A., *xii, xiii*
Folk taxonomies, 121–141
    cognitive processes in, 136–137
    essentialism and nominalism, 135–137
    psychiatric classification similarities, 123–132
    structure of, 123–132
Ft. Bragg Evaluation Project, 207–208, 212
Function concept, 134
Functional impairment
    diagnosis link, 236, 268
    and treatment selection, 268–269
Functionally equivalent conditions, 255–256
Fuzzy sets, 287–288

Generalized anxiety disorder, 228–229
GENERIC categories
    in folk classification, 123–124, 127–128, 136–137
    in psychiatric classification, 128–129, 131–132, 138
Global Assessment of Functioning, 236
Global Assessment of Relational Functioning scale, 55
Grammatical structure, narratives, 160, 162
Grand narratives, 23, 44
Grounded theory analysis, 168–169
Group therapy, indications for, 269

Harmful dysfunction analysis, 42–44
    in essentialism-nominalism debate, 134–135
    problems with, 42–44
    in taxonomic hierarchical ladder, 42
Heart disease diagnosis, 32–34
Hempelian model, 26–27, 39–40
Heterogeneity problem, 289

Histrionic personality disorder, 95
Hitmax, 116–117
Hospital medicine, 290
Humor theory, 290
Hysteria, underlying psychopathology, 295

Idiographic approach
    children and adolescents, 203–204, 213
    definition, 204
    diagnostic system shortcoming, 213
Imaging techniques, 292
Impairment level. *See* Functional impairment
Individual with Disabilities Education Act, 210–212
Inductive reasoning, in folk taxonomies, 136–137
Infectious disease nomenclature, 39–40
Inference level, 234–235, 239
Informant report
    children and adolescents, 207, 216
    cross-source agreement, 74–78
    diagnostic information need, 72
    item response theory model, 216
Insight therapies, 270–271
Insurance benefits, diagnosis function, 48
Intellectualist view, 135–137
Internal criteria, definition, 237
Internalizing disorders
    child psychopathology cluster, 206
    item response theory application, 215
    as overriding category, 214
    therapeutic change guidelines, 270–271
International Classification of Diseases, 6, 29–42
Interpersonal psychotherapy, non-specificity, 264
Interpersonal relationships. *See* Relational issues
Interrater reliability
    clinical interviews, 73–74
    in Operationalized Psychodynamic Diagnosis, 193
Interview methods
    children and adolescents, 207
    cross-method convergent associations, 71–78
    reliability, 71–74

Intrapsychic conflicts, 186–188
Inventory of Interpersonal Problems, 194–195
Item response theory, 214–216
    advantages, 214
    in child diagnosis, 214–216
    and criterion weighting, 216
    internalizing symptoms application, 214–215

Janet, Pierre, 285

Kappa, multisource determinations, 94–95
Karolinska Psychodynamic Profile, 178
Kraepelin, Emil, 279–297
    influence of, *xii*, 3, 283–290
    psychological laboratory experience, 293
    psychopathology preference of, 293–294
    schizophrenia classification, 230–231
    symptom-based diagnosis, 285

Laboratory procedures
    and revolution in medicine, 290–292
    in psychology, 292–297
Language, 156–157. *See also* Narratives
Latent class analysis, 224
LEAD model, 81, 93
Level of inference, 234–235, 239
Life narratives. *See* Narratives
Literature reviews (*DSM-IV*), 8, 28
Logical empiricism, 25–29
Luvox, 50

Mach, Ernst, 45
Macronarratives, 157–158
Major depression. *See also* Depression
    children and adolescents, criteria, 206
    course and prognosis, 256
    distinctiveness of symptoms problem, 257–260
    multisource determinations, 96–97
    prototype-matching approach, 241
Manual-driven treatments, 203–204, 265–266

Marketing, diagnoses role, 50–51
Mathematical aggregation
    advantages and disadvantages, 91–92, 226–227
    in classification, 226–227
    multisource information synthesis, 90–92
MAXCOV-HITMAX procedure, 111, 113–114
Meaning making, narrative discourse role, 155–157
Meehl, Paul, 108–109
Mental disorders
    definitional controversy, 124–125
    essentialism versus nominalism debate 133–137
    folk taxonomy relevance, 132–141
    social context, 53
Mental health services. *See* Service eligibility
Medical model, 280–283. *See also* Physical medicine
    criticism, 6, 8
    depression implications, 252–253
    discovery narrative in, 23–24
    and *DSM* diagnoses expansion, 29–44
    history, 281–282
    mental disorders contrast, 39–42
    misconceptions of, 280–283
    and personal responsibility for disease, 48
    psychologists' attraction to, 152–154
    public health model comparison, 282–283
Micronarratives, 157–158
Mixed anxiety-depression, 227, 229
Mixed categories problem, 224
Mixed models, 234
Models of Madness, Models of Medicine (Siegler & Osmond), 281–283
Modularity theory, 294–296
Monothetic approach, 6
Monotypic classification categories, 127–129
Monte Carlo simulations, 224
Mood disorders, *DSM* problems, 225–230
Moral authority, 282
Moral model, 281
Motivation for psychotherapy, 194
Motivational abnormalities
    laboratory tests, 293–296
    and psychopathology, 294

Multiaxial system, rethinking of, 243–244

Multifaceted model, 216

Multi-method diagnosis, 69–97
    clinician integration of, 92–97
    mathematical aggregation, 90–92
    reliability, 93
    stability of, 94–96
    strategies, 89–97
    validity increase, 90–91

Myocardial infarction diagnosis, 32–34

Narcissistic personality disorder
    multisource determination, 95
    prototype-matching approach, 240–241

Narratives, 149–172. *See also* Discovery model/narrative; Social invention model/narrative
    authorship factor, 158, 162–163
    complexity of, 163–167
    in meaning construction process, 155–157
    core dimensions, 157
    "not knowing" stance of, 154
    prototype construction, 167–170
    in psychopathology assessment, 149–172
    structural coherence dimension, 157–163

National Comorbidity Survey, 254

Negative affect, as higher order factor, 229

Negative schizophrenic symptoms, 231–232

Neo-Kraepelinian movement, 286

Neuropsychological findings, 294–296

Neurosis term, 56–57

No-treatment condition, depression response, 260–261

Nominalism
    folk taxonomies view, 135–137
    psychopathology debate, 133–137

Nomothetic approach
    children and adolescents, 203–204
    definition, 203

Nosology
    Kraepelin's legacy, 283–290
    structural shifts in, 286–287

Not otherwise specified category
    criticism, 8, 289
    proliferation of, 224

Observed behavior, 75–77

Obsessive-compulsive personality
    and drug company marketing, 50–51
    multisource determination stability, 95
    narrative complexity restriction, 163
    narrative structure incoherence, 160

Ontological problems
    folk taxonomies relevance, 133–137
    harmful dysfunction analysis, 43–44
    mental disorders concept, 133–135

Operationalized Psychodynamic Diagnosis, 177–197
    axes, 180–193
    ICD-10 link, 179, 189, 192
    purposes of, 179–180
    reliability, 193
    structure, 180–193
    symptomatology considerations, 192
    validity, 193–195

Opiate addicts
    narrative structure, 162
    prototype narrative, 170

Osmond, H., 281–283

Outcome, and treatment selection, 268–272

Panic disorder
    DSM problems, 228–229
    narrative complexity restriction, 163
    prototype narrative, 171

Parent report
    cross-method convergence, 74–76
    and diagnostic accuracy, 207
    and item response theory, 216
    teacher report composite information, 92

Participants term, 283n2

Passive-aggressive personality, 95

Pathology
    and medical model history, 290–292
    and psychological laboratory tests, 292–297

Patient report. *See* Self-report

Patient uniformity myth, 266–267

Paul, Gordon, 19

Peer report, 75–77

Performance tasks, in diagnosis, 75–77

Personality Disorder Examination, 94

Personality disorders
    Axis I comorbidty problem, 223
    categorical versus dimensional classifi-
        cation, 235–236
    functional diagnosis, 235
    informant report need, 72
    multi-source determinations, 94–95
    Operationalized Psychodynamic Diag-
        nosis, 195
    prototype-matching approach, 239–241
Personality predisposition, anxiety disor-
    ders, 229–230
Pharmaceutical industry, marketing, 50–
    51
Phenomenology. *See* Symptoms approach
Phenylketonuria, as taxon, 110–111
Phobias
    DSM problems, 228
    multi-source determination stability, 96
    narrative structure incoherence, 159
Physical medicine
    diagnostic expansion in, *DSM* analogy,
        22, 29–44
    discovery narrative in, 23–24
    disease label reduction, 39–41
    etiological explanation in, 40–41
    mental disorders comparison, 39–42
    in Scadding's taxonomy ladder, 40–41
Placebo response, depression, 256
"Plausible dysfunction" concept, 43
Political process
    depression criteria, 254
    DSM-IV influence, 55
    and psychoanalytic theory influence,
        55
Polytypic classification categories, 125–
    127
Positive schizophrenic symptoms, 231
Positivism, 44–45
Postmodernism, 23, 44–45
Pragmatic truth
    in diagnosis, 47–51
    in social invention narrative, 45–51
Predictive validity, psychodynamic sys-
    tem, 194–195
Probabilistic model. *See* Prototype-match-
    ing approach
Professional identity, diagnostic system
    role, 48–50
Professional rivalries, 53, 55
Profit motive, *DSM* publications, 51–52
Prognosis

depression, 256
Kraepelin's view, 284–285
and treatment selection, 269–271
Projective tests, 293n8
Prototype-matching approach, 221–245,
    287–289
    and categorical approach, 241–243,
        286–289
    clinical practice link, 241–244
    cognitive psychology influence in, 238
    depression, 227–228
    DSM approach comparison, 224, 237–
        238, 287–289
    overview, 239–245
    personality disorders, 239–241
    versus symptom counting, 237–238,
        240
Prozac, 50
Psychiatric disorders concept, social con-
    text, 53
Psychiatrists, categorical approach prefer-
    ence, 108
Psychiatry profession, rivalries, 53
Psychoanalytic theory
    DSM-IV influence, professional rival-
        ries factor, 55
    explanatory influence of, 153
    and sleep disorders classification, 35
Psychodynamic diagnosis, 177–197
    ICD-10 link, 179, 189, 192
    operationalized system, 177–197
Psychological disorders concept, social
    context, 53
Psychological tests, laboratory-based,
    292–296
Psychologists, dimensional approach pref-
    erence, 108
Psychology profession, rivalries, 53
"Psychomedicalization," 154
Psychopathology
    epistemological problems, debate, 133–
        137
    Kraepelin's perspective, 293–294
    psychological laboratory tests, 292–297
Psychotherapy
    antidepressant combination, 263
    response non-specificity, depression,
        262–265
    therapeutic change guidelines, 270–
        271
Psychotropic drugs, marketing of, 50–51
Public health medical model, 282–283

Q-sort, 239–240
Questionnaires, 293n8

Racial-ethnic factors, 216
"Rater effect," 216
Ray, Isaac, 284
Reimbursement for services, 202
Relational issues
    circumplex model, 184–185
    operationalization, 178, 181, 184–186
    psychodynamic approach, 181, 184–186
    treatment link, DSM Axis IV, 214
Relationship-oriented interventions, 270–271
Relativism, and social invention model, 58
Reliability
    clinical interviews, 71–74
    definition, 86
    Operationalized Psychodynamic Diagnosis, 193
    in prototype-matching approach, 239
    structured interviews, 78–89
Research Diagnostic Criteria, 286
Research facilitation, diagnoses function, 49–50
Research studies, in DSM revisions, 54–56
Resistance level
    diagnosis link, 268–271
    and treatment selection, 268, 271
Roschian concepts, 135
Rosenhan pseudopatient study, 150, 154

Sapiential authority, 282–283
Schedule for Affective Disorders and Schizophrenia, 5, 286
Schizoaffective disorder, 287
Schizoid personality disorder
    multisource determination stability, 95
    narrative structure incoherence, 160
Schizophrenia
    as ambiguous generic category, 131–132
    biological factors, 232
    Bleulerian definition, 230
    categorical approach problems, 231–232

DSM problems, 230–232
    narrative structure incoherence, 159–160
    prototype view, 287
Schizotaxia, 232
Schizotypal personality disorder, 287
Science, social invention narrative in, 44–47
Scientific medical model, 283
Self-report
    children and adolescents, 207, 216
    clinical interview reliability, 71–74
    cross-method convergent associations, 74–78
    illusion of accuracy, 78–89
    and item response theory, 216
    multisource assessment improved validity, 89–97
    problems, 234
Semistructured interviews
    cross-method convergent associations, 74–78
    in prototype-matching approach, 242
    psychodynamic information devaluation, 189, 192
    reliability, 72–74
Serotonin re-uptake inhibitors
    marketing of, 50
    non-specificity problem, 262–264
Service eligibility
    diagnostic frameworks purpose, 202
    and special education diagnostic system, 211
Severity of symptoms. See Symptom severity
Short Textbook of Psychiatry (Kraepelin), 3
Sick role, 48, 282
Siegler, M., 281–283
Skill building procedures, 270–271
Sleep disorders
    classification trends, 33–39
    mental disorders relationship, 37–38
Social invention model/narrative, 18, 44–59
    diagnostic effects, 47–51
    philosophical assumptions, 45–46
    pragmatic truth in, 45–51
    problems with, 57–58
    relativism objection to, 58
Social Learning Program, 19
Social maladjustment disorders, 211

Therapist-patient matching, 268
Therapist-patient relationship, 178
Time frames. *See* Duration of symptoms
Trait anxiety, 230
Treatment-based diagnosis, 265–272
    guidelines, 269–271
    historical foundations, 265–269
Treatment response nonspecificity, depression, 260–265
Tricyclic antidepressants, 262
Tuberculosis, 41

Unconscious conflicts, 186
"Unique beginner" category, 124
Unstructured interviews
    cross-method convergent associations, 74–78
    reliability, 72–73
Utilitarian view, 135–137. *See also* Nominalism

V-codes, 214
Validity
    classification systems, 237
    and criterion contamination, 79

definition, 86
DSM-IV, 57
multi-method synthesis value, 89–97
Operationalized Psychodynamic Diagnosis, 193–195
reliability continuum, 78–89
and source overlap problem, 79
structured interviews, 78–89
Values
    and dysfunction, 134
    essentialism debate, 133–137
    in folk taxonomies, 137
    narrative model, 44–59
Vanderbilt Functioning Index, 208
"Vegetative signs," 255, 258–259
Vote method. *See* Committee method

Wakefield, J.C., 28–42, 134
Weighting of criteria, 216
Wright, Sewall, *xii, xiii*
Writing, therapeutic effects, 166

ABOUT THE EDITORS

Larry E. Beutler, PhD, is a Professor in the Counseling/Clinical/School Psychology Program at the University of California, Santa Barbara. He is the editor of the *Journal of Clinical Psychology* and a former editor of the *Journal of Consulting and Clinical Psychology*. He is a Fellow of the American Psychological Association (APA) and the American Psychological Society. He is the president of APA's Society for Clinical Psychology (Division 12), a past president of APA's Division of Psychotherapy (Division 290), and a two-term past president of the International Society for Psychotherapy Research. He is the author of approximately 350 scientific papers and chapters and is the author, editor, or coauthor of 15 books on psychotherapy and psychopathology. Dr. Beutler is currently coediting (with L. G. Castonguay) a book on empirically defined principles of therapeutic change that is cosponsored by the Society of Clinical Psychology and the North American Society for Psychotherapy Research. He is also finishing a second edition of his book on personality assessment.

Mary L. Malik has a doctorate in zoology and genetics from Duke University in Durham, North Carolina. She has published on a range of topics, including genetics, evolutionary biology, and psychotherapy process and outcome. She is currently a doctoral student in the Counseling/ Clinical/School Psychology Program at the University of California at Santa Barbara.